PASSAGES:

STUDIES *in* TRADITIONALISM *and* TRADITIONS

Volume I

Edited by
Jafe Arnold
Evgeny Nechkasov
Lucas Griffin
Luca Siniscalco

2023

PRAV Publishing
www.pravpublishing.com
prav@pravpublishing.com

Copyright © 2023 The Authors

All rights reserved. No part of this book may be reproduced or distributed in any form or by any means, electronic or mechanical, including photocopying, recording, or by any information storage and retrieval, without permission in writing from the publisher.

Cover image:
PROFONDITÀ ABITATA (2002), *Metafisica* series, by AimA (Luisa Papa)

ISBN 978-1-952671-15-9 (Paperback)
ISBN 978-1-952671-30-2 (Ebook)

PASSAGES:

STUDIES *in* TRADITIONALISM *and* TRADITIONS

Volume I

TABLE OF CONTENTS

From the Editors: Recollecting Traditionalism	9
René Guénon: Traditionalism as a Language *Alexander Dugin*	17
Regarding the Term "Traditional Authors" *Róbert Horváth*	57
Traditionalism as Understood by René Guénon and its Contemporary Understanding *Maxim Makovchik*	67
The Realisation of the Spirit of Tradition and the Culture of the Unrealised Spirit *Jonatán Gődény*	75
Guénon's Crisis, "Crisis Literature," and Negative Thought *Giovanni Sessa*	103
Anti-Tradition in the Age of Iron *Troy Southgate*	125
The Antitheses of Modernity *Gianfranco de Turris*	139

The Temporality of the Tiger: Some Notes
on the Evolian 'Riding the Tiger' 153
Giovanni Damiano

Traditionalism as the Tree and the Ark
of the Radical Selves for the Restoration
of the Erst Philosophy 167
Uligang Xanth Ansbrandt

Heart and Center in René Guénon:
On the Usage of Symbols 233
Jean-Pierre Laurant

Metaphysical Solipsism — A Fundamental Principle
of Tradition 257
Tamás Bencze

A Traditionalist Inquiry into Nature 271
Eduardo Zarelli

Heidegger Against the Traditionalists 285
Collin Cleary

Traditionalism and (Mis-)Understanding Heidegger 309
Askr Svarte

Yuri Mamleev's Fate of Being as a Response
to Guénon's Metaphysics 329
Charlie Smith

Tradition and Traditionalism in Contemporary
Slavic Native Faith: My Subjective View 343
Veleslav Cherkasov

The Political Dimension of Traditionalism
in René Guénon and Julius Evola:
Defining the Ideal Principles of Social Organization   353
   Dmitry Moiseev

Evola and Jung: For a Reactualisation of Tradition   371
   Roberto Cecchetti

About the Authors   389

FROM THE EDITORS: RECOLLECTING TRADITIONALISM

In 1951, in the special issue of *Études traditionnelles* published on the occasion of René Guénon's death, the German philosopher Leopold Ziegler noted emerging talk of "a group called traditionalists."[1] "Supposing that it is legitimate to speak of such a group," Ziegler wrote, "one might perhaps find in its existence a last, faint ray of hope for the West." According to Ziegler, this group promised to "bring forth something new that is at the same time something very ancient," and its trains of thought and networks heralded an international synergy between hitherto "secret" intellectual currents: "In the meanwhile, many clues suggest that to this secret France [of Guénon] corresponds a secret Austria, a secret Italy, as well as a secret Germany, which, as they mature, are silently converging with one another." In his concluding remarks, Ziegler put forth that this constellation of converging thinkers inspired by Guénon is united by a common struggle and cause: "*anamnesis*," that is "remembrance" or "recollection." Now, more than half a century later, Ziegler's remarks and the notion of "recollection" provide a fitting point of departure for thinking about what has indeed come to be called "Traditionalism."

In Platonic philosophy, which many Traditionalists consider to be part and parcel of the *Sophia Perennis*, "*anamnesis*" refers to the soul's capacity to "remember" or "recollect" the metaphysical knowledge that is originally innate to it, but which is lost in the course of the cycles of incarnation. *Anamnesis* involves an intellectual and spiritual activity aimed at regaining knowledge of the principles that are the dearest to the soul as such, yet the seemingly furthest away from the soul *hic et nunc*. The intellectual and spiritual

---

1 Leopold Ziegler, "René Guénon et le dépassement du monde moderne," *Études traditionnelles* 293-295 (1951), 212.

project advocated and articulated by René Guénon proposed *anamnesis* on a civilizational, cosmic scale: in the midst of globalizing Western Modernity, the Dark Age of the Kali-Yuga, in which traditions have been abandoned and traditional principles and knowledge have been lost, an intellectual elite must undertake the *anamnesis* of Tradition, to recollect the sacred, metaphysical knowledge that not only "explains" the "crisis of the modern world," but paves the way for "re-collecting" Tradition for another beginning. In the Traditionalist vein, this "new beginning" is not only a theoretical engagement, but an existential recognition, a response to the call emanating from the experience of what Mircea Eliade called the "nostalgia for origins" which motivates *Homo religiosus* just as much as it troubles the human being of Modernity.[2] In other words, Traditionalism raises the question of human existence and thinking in relation to Tradition and in relation to a world which is ostensibly the embodiment of anti-Tradition. For Guénon and his followers, collaborators, and like-minded correspondents, i.e., for the "group called traditionalists," this mission of recollecting Tradition did not mean merely "reconstructing" or "rejoining" one or another tradition; instead, the Traditional(ist) idea meant a dynamic, active, multidimensional way of interpreting and being, an *existentia hermeneutica*, a fully-fledged episteme for recollecting the sacred Tradition that has been manifest in various traditions, for rediscovering the metaphysical principles that have been at work in history and historical traditions, for reenacting the transformative spiritual realization of re-initiation into Tradition, and for re-sacralizing the lived world. The latter is an especially significant quality of Traditionalist thought: according to Antoine Faivre's famous definition, one of the fundamental pillars of Western esoteric thought in the situation of Modernity is represented by the so-called "practice of concordance,"[3] and the Traditionalists raised this concept

---

2   See Mircea Eliade, *Cosmos and History: The Myth of the Eternal Return*, trans. Willard R. Trask (New York: Harper & Brothers, 1959).

3   Antoine Faivre, "Introduction I" in Antoine Faivre, Jacob Needleman, and Karen Voss (eds.), *Modern Esoteric Spiritualities* (New York: Crossroad: 1992), xviii.

of perennial correspondence between traditions to a practical perception of the lived world, to a hermeneutical key. In other words, the (re)discovery of the paradigm of Tradition between traditions is translated into a unique interpretive and existential orientation that goes beyond individual attachment to a surviving tradition as well as stale conceptualizing of tradition. It is in this respect understandable why Guénon himself rejected the term "traditionalist," which for him rang with the connotation of "only a tendency that may be more or less vague and often wrongly applied, because it does not imply any effective knowledge of traditional truths."[4] By contrast, what has come to be known as the Traditional(ist) "school," "movement," or "method" after Guénon is distinguished by a sophisticated and multifaceted assemblage of philosophical and theological hermeneutics, a colorful range of aesthetic and academic applications, as well as a heritage of involvements in diverse religious and political currents. All of the latter and more has become amassed in a considerable body of literature and a rich history which have only begun to be (re)discovered. Today, still shy of a century since Ziegler's remarks, Traditionalist thought remains a lively engagement, as does the recollection of the Traditionalist past, present, and future. The questions and interpretations posed by Traditionalists remain actual and open-ended, as does the task of interpreting the very nature of Traditionalism's questioning and answering.

In another sense, thus, the "recollection" of Traditionalism pertains to how what was for Ziegler a "secret" landscape has since become an increasingly excavated archaeological site of academic scholarship.[5] The "mainstream" academic "discovery"

---

4   René Guénon, *The Reign of Quantity and the Signs of the Times*, trans. Lord Northbourne (Hillsdale: Sophia Perennis, 2004), 169, 211-213.

5   This development is to a considerable extent owed to Mark Sedgwick's influential (and controversial) *Against the Modern World: Traditionalism and the Secret Intellectual History of the Twentieth Century* (Oxford: Oxford University Press, 2004), which recently gained its sequel with *Traditionalism: The Radical Project for Restoring Sacred Order* (London: Pelican Books/Penguin Random House, 2023).

and "chronicling" of Traditionalism, at times crossing or spilling over into political journalism, has nevertheless lent credence to Ziegler's incipient intimation that Traditionalism names a much broader and deeper current of ideas which has only begun to come into view in the wake of its initial pioneers' legacies. On the other hand, it remains apparent that the "historical" or "historiographical" charting of various Traditionalists' lives and works runs the risk of distracting from seriously engaging their thinking, as well as losing sight of the Traditionalist activities and trains of thought which are still unfolding. Instead of historiographical "exorcism," the scholarly recollection of Traditionalism is in need of a reconnection with serious exegesis and critical reflection on the ideas, rather than individuals and authorships, in which Traditionalism consists.

Speaking of the "recollection" of Traditionalism is thus also a call to reconvene, to reassemble, rediscover, and rethink here and now — to re-raise the question of what Traditionalism means, has been, is, and could be. Authentically studying and discussing Traditionalism means treating not only a "topic" or "object," but engaging a method, a pathway of thought(s), which can be (and has been) put into dialogue with other relevant sources and fields. It is in this spirit that we bring forth and open up *Passages: Studies in Traditionalism and Traditions* as a journal not only "on," but "in" this current of history and thinking.

As things currently stand, *Passages* is emerging as the only English-language publication devoted explicitly to Traditionalism, and it is one among very few other publications across the world dealing with Traditionalist themes *sensu stricto* as well as *sensu lato*. In opening this new agora for the exploration of Traditionalism, the editors of *Passages* recognize ourselves to be part of a history — or better put, a *Wirkungsgeschichte* — of diverse attempts at establishing a textual forum for studies on and in Traditionalism. In the sphere of Guénon's native tongue, the original Traditionalist "organ," *Études traditionnelles*, concluded in 1992. The French academic journal *Politica Hermetica*, one of the foremost sites for specialist scholarship on Guénon and his associates, remains in publication and circulation, although its initial focus on Traditionalist themes has been considerably broadened and diluted in alignment with the academic field of Western Esotericism. In the English language, *Studies in Comparative Religion*, which prized itself as "The First English Journal on Traditional Studies," ceased publication in 2013. *The Initiate: Journal of Traditional Studies* lived to see only two issues between 2008 and 2010. Subsequently, 2011 saw the last issue of *Sophia: Journal of Traditional Studies*. Most recently, *Sacred Web: A Journal of Tradition and Modernity* was discontinued at the close of 2022. In the Russian-speaking world, where the wide-ranging development of Traditionalist literature and discourse has remained little accessible to other language spheres, the journal *Traditsiia* — two of whose volumes covered the international conference "Against the Post-Modern World: Actual Problems of Traditionalism" held in Moscow in 2011 — concluded with its fifth issue in 2013. The Russian Traditionalist almanac focused on pagan traditions, *Warha*, which ran two volumes in English as *Warha Europe*, was renamed *Alföðr* in 2021. The future of the pagan-focused American Traditionalist series *Tyr: Myth—Culture—Tradition*, whose last volume was published in 2018, remains unknown to us.

In Italy, several publications over the past few decades – most of them still active – have dealt with Traditionalist topics and sources, such as *Vie della Tradizione*, founded in 1971 by Gaspare Cannizzo, and *Arthos*, founded in 1972 by Renato Del Ponte. Many of them, however, have been characterized by an extreme specialization regarding the thematized doctrines and topics: for example, since 1961 *Rivista di Studi Tradizionali* has transmitted Guénon's approach, while *Studi evoliani* records research into Evola's thought, and *Politica romana* is devoted to studies on Roman tradition.

In view of this diverse array of previous publications hosting exhibitions of discourse on and in Traditionalism, many of which have since retired, *Passages* presents itself as an aspiring "new beginning" with an international scope. We seek to let the global rigor of Traditionalism, as a matrix of questions and answers to diverse philosophical, cultural, and social issues, contend itself. Let us recall Ziegler's remark on a "secret France, secret Austria, secret Italy, and secret Germany" — in the decades since Guénon's death, Traditionalist thought and scholarly retrievals of the Traditionalist heritage have expanded or been (re)discovered across even further horizons. Accordingly, *Passages* sets as one of its foremost tasks representing and acquainting Traditionalist currents and scholarship across continents, especially those less familiar in the domain of English-language literature. In this first volume, we are pleased to present readers with contributions from two of the homelands of Traditionalism, France and Italy, as well as from the United Kingdom, Hungary, Belarus, Russia, and the United States.

It is the conviction of the editorial board of *Passages* that authentic, meaningful exploration of and critical dialogue over Traditionalist ideas and histories can only unfold in the context of conversation. Like the ambassadorship between traditions that Guénon envisioned or the "polylogue of civilizations" proposed by Alexander Dugin, Traditionalism is a meta-discursive space for the meeting of traditions, for perspectives on and interpretations of traditions, and for critical dialogue on such perspectives and interpretations. Seeking to encourage such dialogue as a lively part of *Passages*, we welcome submissions of letters to the editors, responses to published articles, as well as book reviews.

The Call for Papers sent out for this first volume asked contributors to write in response to the open prompt of "thinking Traditionalism." In launching the series *Passages: Studies in Traditionalism and Traditions*, we extend the same invitation to readers and researchers to take the leap into "thinking Traditionalism" — that which, in words written nearly 50 years ago, was deemed "some of the most serious thinking of the twentieth century,"[6] yet by no means ended then.

Jafe Arnold,
Evgeny Nechkasov,
Lucas Griffin,
Luca Siniscalco

---

6   Jacob Needleman, "Foreword" in idem (ed.), *The Sword of Gnosis: Metaphysics, Cosmology, Tradition, Symbolism* (Baltimore: Penguin Books, 1974 / London: Arkana, 1986), 9.

RENÉ GUÉNON: TRADITIONALISM AS A LANGUAGE

Alexander Dugin

Structuralism: Language and Meta-Language

From the late 19th century onwards, so-called "structural linguistics" enjoyed significant development. One of its founders, Ferdinand de Saussure (1857-1913), discovered a number of this discipline's laws. This science turned out to be so popular and interesting (especially as a methodology), and so effective and operative for solving a whole series of problems, that it provided the foundations for a whole current in philosophy and scientific methodology in the 20th century, establishing so-called "structuralism" together with the "post-structuralism" that came from it.

Our century opened with a phrase by Nietzsche, astonishing in its precision (as are the rest of his aphorisms), that served as the title of his early work *We Philologists*. Having understood the extent to which we (as humans, as thinking beings) are "philologists", a whole group of philosophers turned their rapt attention to the problem of language.

In rather approximate terms, we can say that in structuralism, in structural linguistics, language is taken to be an autonomous category that presents us with a manifest world of predetermined themes, a world of structured and interconnected meanings. In other words, language is understood to be something that weds the intelligible, intellectual sphere, the sphere of thinking and noumena, to the sphere of the phenomenological, indirect ontic realities that are accessible to us in sensations – that to which we concretely relate. Thus, language lies between meaning (or let us say spirit) and concrete matters. As noted by the structural linguists, language possesses a certain "magical" autonomy — all corporeal things in this world harbor their own dissolution, their own entry into language. Wedded with the element of language, things are redeemed and recovered from the world of corporeality by taking on a name. At the same time, in the opposite direction, the sphere of the spirit affects the sphere of the flesh – matter – through language. Here we might recall Hoffman's tale (repeatedly cited by Evgeny Golovin), in which the protagonists used ordinary grammar to evoke spirits. In employing a developed conceptual apparatus, structural linguists have rationally expressed essentially the same magical idea: a thing dissolves into a word, and the word "solidifies" the thing.

According to the Sapir-Whorf hypothesis, "our surrounding reality is forged by our language." If a thing does not have a name, then it simply does not exist. In principle, the Sapir-Whorf hypothesis fully coincides with the notion, characteristic of the world of Tradition, that the present being of things is distilled within their names, and names are capable of creating, incarnating, and materializing concrete things. This is clear even on the level of everyday life: in a certain situation, one need only say "do" this or that, "be quiet", "die", "kill" or "don't kill" with the proper intonation, and the material world begins to change. At this point, it matters not which mechanisms start working and in what way; it is merely obvious that the word possesses colossal "theurgic" significance. "Theurgy" is what the ancient Greeks called the priestly art by means of which people used incantations and rituals to make a Deity manifest itself in a certain way.

Accordingly, the study of the word, language, and its models is its own kind of modern counterpart to "operative magic" whereby one can change and transform reality and simultaneously bring the concrete world of phenomena into a conceptual, abstract model, an eidetic reality in which present objects are dissolved into some kind of conceptual ensemble. A distorted notion of the magical arts of antiquity has been established today: it is as if these magical arts served only practical aims and used the spiritual world for influencing material situations and things. In fact, this was only one side of magic, namely operative, applied magic. There existed another – speculative – side of magic, intended not to change a present material situation, but to understand and clarify it, to restore it to its archetype, to divine the "sidereal meaning" laid up within it.

The central topic in today's lecture is Ferdinand de Saussure's (and, after him, structuralist philosophy's) division of the totality of language into two parts: the potential and the actual. This division might be expressed in different terminology across different languages. In French, *le language* ("all language") is divided into *la langue* (the potential part, "language proper") and *la parole* ("word") or *le discours* ("utterance"), the actual part. In Russian, one could speak of the distinction between *iazyk* ("language", "tongue" as the potential) and *rech'* ("speech" as the actual).

What is meant here? It is difficult to convey or translate these terms with any precision, because the discourse at hand is not about strict readymade definitions, but a complex spiritual operation, a subtle differentiation (*diakrisis*) that divides what is thought to represent a unified reality into two component parts. Language, in itself, is the ungraspable potential reality that withdraws from its natural state; it embodies and alienates itself in becoming "not itself" at the very moment when a person speaks, discourses, and utters. At precisely this moment, language actualizes. When a person says something, he is using some invisible "present" linguistic mass that is absent in actuality and is selectively withdrawn out of potentially present language in order to utter forth speech (whether simple or complex). There are two elements in language. The first is language proper: the totality of lexical, morphological patterns, the stock of vocabulary (thesaurus), and the laws governing the structure of propositions. This language, the structuralists insisted, constitutes a certain constant, synchronic value. It is always present, simultaneously and in its entirety. Perhaps the most interesting part of structural linguistics is its recognition of the autonomous reality of a certain synchronic complex array regarding language's being in potential space. Language exists in a certain permanent state of abstraction from concrete speech. Concrete speech (utterances, statements) withdraws fragments out of language and, in so doing, transmits the being of language from its synchronic state into a diachronic succession. All utterances or statements exist in succession, whereas language exists in simultaneity. Language is divided into two parts: that in which something is said, and that by means of which what is said, is said.

Language as the potential part inseparably merges with the sphere of meaning. When the structuralists discovered this circumstance, it turned out that language, coming about and showing through speech, is not identical to the totality of all existing utterances (and even all possible utterances); it is always broader than what is said within it, and it can figure as an autonomous object for research. Studying synchronic linguistic reality astoundingly allowed for highlighting the mechanisms of social behavior, the levels of the psychoanalytic cross-section of the personality, and the structure of norms and anomalies ranging all the way to radical somatic disorders. Hence arose the school of Lacan, the French psychoanalyst who synthesized structural linguistics and psychoanalysis, resulting in a rather capacious doctrine. It was in Freud's book on verbal slips that I first came across the idea of synthesizing psychoanalysis, structural linguistics – of linguistics as such. Lacan developed this topic, and poststructuralist authors like Deleuze and Guattari developed a methodology that traced the emergence of language, beginning from the first movement of the vegetative level of corporeality. This was a very interesting and extremely sharp-witted line of research. For example, in *The Logic of Sense*, Deleuze shows how a metastructure of language and logical thinking arises out of some first perturbations within the human being's bodily reality. Despite the modern, rationalistic context, here once again emerges the ancient, archaic idea of language's operational significance, which not only exposes and veils (the Latin verb *revelare* means "to uncover" and "to cover" at the same time) the state of affairs on the corporeal, unconscious-vegetative level of the human, but also, at the same time, affects a person, changes and controls his (and not only his) corporeality. Following upon this is the role of speech in psychiatric medical practice. Speech, conversation, narrating, and discourse are in some situations capable of curing severe mental illnesses.

Here we encounter an interesting moment: structural linguists and structuralists are in fact studying language with the help of language, by means of language. Here we come to the most important point: in methodologically studying language, the structuralists and structural linguists developed a certain special "super-language" or "meta-language."

A meta-language is the language by which a language is studied. This is an even greater degree of generalization.

The very fact of dissecting a language in separation from speech is already a deep immersion into a kind of "ontological revisionism," because ordinary consciousness (digital, binary, rational, proverbial "common sense") cannot grasp synchronic language. Ordinary consciousness understands language simply as speech, as a totality of discourses, or as a regularity manifesting itself in speech. Ordinary consciousness is discursive, but it is not linguistic consciousness, because it is attentive to speech but deaf to language.

The next step in understanding the ontology of language is to bring into relief the problem of the meta-language by means of which a certain language is to be studied. Here lies something of the utmost importance: the fact of the matter is that, in their study of language and models of language, the structuralists were not free from certain proto-influences, from certain paradigms prefiguring and predetermining the models by which they studied what lies at the basis of language.

Why are we now speaking about the crisis of structuralism and poststructuralism, about the exhaustion of these trends? Because the meta-linguistic paradigm upon which the structuralist school itself was based, which came either completely from positivistic-Kantian source (in Saussure) or from the Marxist paradigm (in the avant-garde version of the "new left"), is exhausted. In other words, language was studied in the structuralist model by means of some already given (and deeply entrenched) proto-ideological yet quite definite and limited models. The nature of language was studied from the standpoints of another language.

In the structuralists' case, the study of language was impure (whether the pure study of language is possible is still a question), deliberately set, limited, and predetermined by the models of an underlying meta-language. Hence structuralists' prioritized interest in the dynamics of speech change rather than in linguistic ontology.

It is from this that the crisis of contemporary "new left" philosophy ensues. I am not talking about the complete absence of its representatives in Russia. This philosophy has never been adequately understood in our country, and now there is nothing left to understand in it. Today the same Europeans who once (even 10 years ago) understood everything perfectly have ceased to understand what Deleuze or Lacan had in mind, because the basic meta-linguistic milestones have completely changed. The implicit Marxist understanding and the "new left" paradigm of contestation have been exhausted (though this, of course, does not mean "conclusively understood") and cannot serve as the common denominator of linguistic research. The sphere of linguistics, the sphere of the study of language, has reached a tragic line which demands a sort of radical overcoming. If we look closely at the optimism in the semiotic linguistic studies of the 1960s-70s (including in our country) and we compare how analogous problems are considered now, we will notice a sharp contrast. Nowadays this field is reigned by passivity and chaos. Scholars have lost the nerve for what they were doing, have suddenly forgotten the meaning and significance of what they were engaged in, and have lost the living content of their categorical apparatus.

But there is one person, one author (and the 20th-century philosophical current associated with his name), who remained outside of the sphere holding interest for structural linguistics. This author is very important for structuralism, even though he was never counted as a figure in the field. Now, when this sphere as a whole has lost its intellectual pulse (along with its implications), this author might enter (through his ideational heritage) into this sphere in full and unspent uniform like an "irresistible cuirass," like a new kind of weapon, for this sphere is empty while he is full. I am talking about René Guénon.

René Guénon

René Guénon was the most correct, the most intelligent, and the most important person of the 20th century. There was no one smarter, deeper, clearer, or more absolute than Guénon, and there probably could not have been. It is no coincidence that in one collected volume dedicated to René Guénon, the French Traditionalist René Alleau compared Guénon to Marx.[7] It would seem that these are two completely different, opposing figures. Guénon was a conservative hyper-traditionalist. Marx was a revolutionary innovator, a radical subverter of traditions. But, with the utmost accuracy, René Alleau discerned the revolutionary message behind every

---

7   René Alleau, "De Marx à Guénon: d'une critique 'radicale' à une critique 'principielle' des societés modernes" (Paris: Les dossiers H., 1984) [René Alleau, "De Marx à Guénon: d'une critique 'radicale' à une critique 'principielle' des sociétés modernes" in Pierre-Marie Sigaud (ed.), René Guénon (Lausanne: L'Âge d'Homme, 1984): 192-202].

one of Guénon's propositions, the extreme and most severe non-conformism of his position as it overturned everything, and the radical nature of his thought. The point is that René Guénon was the only author, the only thinker of the 20th century and perhaps many, many centuries before, who not only singled out and put secondary linguistic paradigms into confrontation, but also called into question the very essence of language (and meta-language). The language of Marxism was methodologically very interesting (especially at a certain historical stage), as it subtly reduced the historical existence of mankind to the evident and convincing formula of the opposition between labor and capital (which, in fact, was a colossal, gnoseologically revolutionary move, as it allowed numerous things to be systematized and brought into a single, more or less consistent and dynamic construct). Being a great paradigmatic success, Marxism was very popular and won the minds of the best 20th-century intellectuals. But Guénon put forth an even more fundamental generalization, an even more radical unmasking, an even broader contestation of worldview that puts everything into question.

René Guénon developed one of the most important and paradigmatic intellectual schemes. Of course, it had existed in vague form before him and was used to one or another extent, but only Guénon distinguished it as a language. He did something analogous to what Saussure and other structural linguists did. The most important, inexhaustible category in René Guénon's paradigmatic scheme which he distinguished and which is perhaps the most general and the strongest among all the terms and concepts of our time, is the category of the "language of modernity."

The Notion of "Modernity" and "Modernity" as a Concept

In historical science, it is customary and justified to contrast "New Time" (Modernity), or modern society, and traditional society. In Guénon's words, the word *le moderne* — that is "the modern" and "modernity" — takes on such colossal meaning and significance that it describes the whole meta-language of the world in which we live. In fact, Guénon fits the notion of "modernity" with a notion of paradigms[8] that predetermine a meta-language, a language, and only then the field of discourses belonging to modernity. Can you even imagine such a degree of generalization?!

The structuralists pointed out that, apart from discourse proper — that is diachronically pronounced utterances and arbitrarily developed, verbally logical chains — there is the synchronous, simultaneous reality of constantly existing language, which they studied with the help of a meta-language based on a special philosophic-linguistic methodology.

For his part, René Guénon incorporated this structuralist model, as well as number of other gnoseological paradigms predetermine various more specific languages (in the structuralist sense), and more specific paradigmatic complexes and socio-cultural structures all into one notion; he then enclosed all of this into clearly defined boundaries encompassing everything as a whole, disclosing and revealing the essence of modernity to be a kind of colossal field embracing everything with which we deal, with which we have become accustomed to operating, without suspecting that this is only one thing, and that beyond it exists a whole span of other possibilities

---

8   The Greek word *paradeigma* literally means "that which predetermines the character of manifestation while remaining outside of the manifest" (*para* - "above," "beyond," "through," "around," and *deigma* - "manifestation"). In the broadest sense, a paradigm is the original model, the matrix that comes into play only indirectly, through its manifestations whose structure it predetermines. A paradigm is not manifest in and of itself, bur rather is the structuring reality which is not subject to direct reflection and which, always remaining behind the scenes, establishes the basic, fundamental proportions of human thinking and human being. The specificity of a paradigm consists in that its gnoseological and ontological points are not subject to differentiation as long as the basic intuitions that pass through the paradigmatic grid take the form of one or another affirmation of its gnoseological and ontological character. The term "paradigm" was used in Platonic and Neoplatonic philosophy to describe a certain higher, transcendental form predetermining the structure and form of material things.

and other languages. Guénon included all the languages of modernity, all of its paradigms, into a single notion that relegated "His Majesty," the Language (and Meta-Language) of Modernity, to the level of one possible language alongside others. It could be said that he reduced a reality which pretended to the status of a universal language to a mere accumulation of utterances, structured according to a certain logic and strict, specific rules, having shown that there are other fully-fledged models which are much more universal. He sharply demoted the ontological degree of that which predetermines our entire civilization and all the realities of our world. This is a point of the utmost importance. If we turn to Guénon, considering him as an author who accomplished something analogous to the structuralist revolution, then we can discover a completely new meaning and significance to his works, and we can realize the most important orientation of his mission.

So, what is "modernity"? "Modernity," according to Guénon, is a certain background paradigm, an operating system, a kind of computer language. This analogy with the languages of programming is productive. As computer technology evolves, the basic programming codes advance ever more deeply with computer language into the background sphere. Gradually, languages are appearing which already operate with the original machine language. Then come the "users," who are completely ignorant of both the original language and the secondary ones developed out of it, and now hardly anyone remembers early computer technology. At first, every computer user had to be a programmer to some extent, if only a small one. Gradually, this need disappeared and the idea of how computers operate also changed. Later, there emerged ever newer operating systems until, in the end, even common ideas about the programming process itself and about the existence of a computer language, dissipated. But the original machine language did not disappear as a result of this change. It remains at it was, only from that time on it has withdrawn from the scope of attention into the realm of background realities which are not immediately apparent. We no longer see this language; we do not encounter it as we did before with the first computers. Now we can't even imagine what this language is; it exists on a different layer of computer technology. Ultimately, there are people appearing on the scene who know how to use a computer, master it perfectly, but nevertheless have no idea as to what lies at its technological basis. They are like drivers who have no idea what an engine contains, yet nevertheless drive perfectly and can drive around like this for all of their lives.

In Guénon's teaching, defining "modernity" is a matter of distinguishing some paradigmatic proto-mechanism that determines how our world is structured. We, ordinary people immersed in the process of becoming, tend to perceive our surroundings, what we are, and what is around us, as a given, as a kind of "everything." It is to this "everything" that we defer our cognitive steps. Upon encountering some idea of what was in the past and what will be in the future, we compare such to our "everything." At any given minute, our "everything" is everything for us without quotation marks. Outside of everything, there can only be analogies — analogies of the past (memories), analogies of the future (forebodings, prophecies, plans). Guénon argues that the whole totality of the operating system of modernity, our proverbial "everything," is in fact nothing other than a malicious, anomalous, vicious, deeply inorganic, and inharmonious illusion of artificial origin, an artifact, a simulacrum, a machination imposed upon us, and by no means "everything." Such a simulacrum of an operating system is called "modernity" and "the modern world" in Guénon's teaching. From his point of view, modernity is an anomaly. It is only one model among others, or more precisely, an anomalous model within an infinitely larger set of other possibilities. It is merely one language among others and not a particular universal reality.

In opposition to the notion of "modernity," Guénon introduces the notion of "tradition." Thus arises one of the most interesting points which, from the perspective of philosophical structuralism, is central for Guénon. Guénon affirms that there are two types of languages: the language of modernity, which includes all possibilities inherent in the concept of "modernity" and predetermines all the languages and even meta-languages within the framework of modernity, and the language of Tradition. Here arises the first conflict, the first dividing line: on the one side is modernity, on the other side is Tradition. Other scholars have also employed the notions of "modern society," "traditional society," "New Time," and "what came before New Time," but ordinarily all of us, besides Guénon's followers, tacitly share the norms of the modern paradigm, even if latently. We tend to see the terminology of traditional society as something belonging to the past and, therefore, inferior, while we perceive the modern as something present, or close to the present and, therefore, superior. Against our will, we operate within the operating environment of "the modern," "Modernity," regardless of whether we understand its functioning mechanisms (like programmers) or commune with it simply through inertia (like users).

This is typical of all people of the modern world without exception, insofar as the language of the modern world, its highest and deepest paradigmatic model, predetermines our relation to the process of time, to history, and to terminology. No matter how some people might have criticized modernity, all of them, even Marx, sooner or later stopped (although Marx, it bears noting, was a real revolutionary who questioned entire layers of reality and declared these not to be reality as such, but rather the game of capital – not authentic being, but the machinations of capital – and so his suspicions are akin to Guénon's). But Guénon goes much further than everyone else. Guénon's is already a completely different reality. He contrasts and puts into confrontation two languages: the language of Tradition and the language of the modern world. He is the farthest away from modernity and he is freer than everyone else from the illusions of the modern world. He is to be found at such a gigantic conceptual distance from the very primal element of the language of modernity, that many of his followers have been beset with the question: Who was Guénon, really?[9] Some of his students, with both delight and horror, reason as follows: he cannot be a human being, because a human being is, by definition, a product of his environment (i.e., he is programmed with a basic operating language). Guénon's, on the other hand, is something opposite to a "product of the environment," including the cosmic environment. Such inferences have given rise to what is perhaps one of the most radical hypotheses concerning his avataric nature (scholars have begun to research the location and position of his home, where he was born, the cardinal orientation of the Church where he was baptized in infancy, and the street on which he lived; they have tried to make a kind of Guénonian temple out of his home[10]). This is how compelling have been Guénon's followers' intuitive suspicions over his nature of fundamental distance from the language of modernity as expressed in his theoretical description of this language as something separate, something external to him that did not touch the main paradigmatic levels of his being.

No matter how one looks at it, René Guénon does not fit into our time at all. He was, as Michel Valsan said, "the greatest intellectual miracle since the Middle Ages."

A miracle he may be, but this does not exhaust everything one might say of him. René Guénon was not at all a modern author; moreover, he is perhaps the farthest removed from modernity. But something is still not entirely right with this picture, for rather few astounding personages like René Guénon were known to appear, even in the world of authentic and organic Tradition. Guénon was not simply a messenger of Tradition in an environment based on the rejection of Tradition. As it turns out, everything is somewhat more complicated.

---

9 See Jean-Marc Allemand, *René Guénon et les sept tours du diable* (Paris: Guy Tredaniel/Editions de la Maisnie, Paris, 1990).

10 Ibid.

Traditionalism and Tradition

Guénon himself says that Tradition alone is what is important. Above all, the language of Tradition, as a system of connections and understandings, stands in opposition to the modern world, to the language of the modern world, and has all the grounds for truth – an absolute truth. For Guénon, the language of Tradition is the last and highest echelon which, full of paradigmatic onto-gnoseological possibilities, has the right to pronounce its sentence and pass its judgement on any normal or abnormal fragment of reality, including the paradigm (or language) of modernity. In his book *The Reign of Quantity and the Signs of the Times*, Guénon says that Tradition is more important than Traditionalism.[11] Tradition and the fact of belonging to Tradition place man more seriously, more fully-blooded, and more deeply into the true operating system than any theoretical Traditionalism that is merely some intention or desire to belong to Tradition. A point of great interest arises here: if "Traditionalism" is to be understood as the recognition, adoption, and development of the paradigmatic models put forth by Guénon, then the situation turns out by no means to be unambiguous. The relation between Traditionalism and Tradition will not be as obvious, as Guénon himself wrote, for if Traditionalism is understood to refer not to other "traditionalists," but specifically to the Traditionalists following Guénon – the "Guénonists" – then the picture turns out to be much more interesting.

Guénon did not simply point out that there exists a special reality, the language of Tradition; he also described that language in general terms and on a schematic level. He clarified, revealed, made manifest, and structured the skeleton preceding the formulations of one specific Tradition in its historically fixed incarnation. Therefore, to master the model discovered by Guénon is to do something other than being

---

11 René Guénon, *Le Règne de la Quantité et les Signes des Temps* (Paris, 1995) [René Guénon, *The Reign of Quantity and the Signs of the Times*, trans. Lord Northbourne (Hillsdale: Sophia Perennis, 2001)].

an adept of one of many Traditions; this is something else than understanding, professing, developing, and agreeing with the logic of that Tradition. Guénon took a step which was perhaps generally impossible within Tradition itself, for only in the modern world (whose language is precisely the complete nihilistic negation of the language of Tradition in its paradigmatic core) does the language of Tradition as something unified, complete, and whole become finally graspable in its pure form as an ideal crystal. Therefore, Guénon did not speak on behalf of one specific Tradition, he did not speak its language (as he would have done if he were only a spokesman for one Tradition, advocating on its behalf). Guénon generally spoke his own language. This language is an especially unique one that allows for describing and studying both the language of Tradition and the language of modernity (as a special anomaly that distorts the main parameters of the language of Tradition). Guénon established a special metalanguage that is so universal and comprehensive that it can be used to adequately study the structures of any language (in the most general sense of the term). Unlike the technical metalanguage of linguistics, Guénon's metalanguage is indeed universal and its structure is wholly free from uncritical interferences derived from the operating environment. Guénon rigorously and consciously eliminated and uprooted the influence of the paradigm of modernity in himself. He did this in a situation in which this paradigm was so total that the alternative paradigm of Tradition could only be affirmed from the outside. Guénon's personal fate consists in moving from affirming theoretical Traditionalism to being-in-Tradition. But what is most important is that this process was accompanied by the sharpest reflection, the paradigmatic value of which greatly exceeds the modest limits of human fate.

Guénon's uniqueness lies in the fact that his Traditionalist teaching represents something radically new, something that had never been before. It is a unique conceptual element that, until then, had never been put into operation. Thanks to Guénon and to our ability to internalize his message, we can henceforth understand not only one specific tradition or several traditions (as specific discourses), but also compose an idea of the structure and essence of Tradition as such. It is especially important that this methodologically takes place against the very contrasting background caused by the juxtaposition of Tradition and the language of the modern world. Consequently, Traditionalism (that of Guénon and his followers) is a unique historical opportunity that exists exclusively inside of the language of modernity as an antithesis to this language. Only in our unique (eschatological, by all signs) conditions does the possibility arise to generalize and universalize the traditional paradigm which was previously not possible for a whole range of circumstances. After all, while being within Tradition, we cannot see it from the outside; we exist as part of it. Meanwhile, being within Traditionalism, we are by dint of circumstances outside of Tradition, but we are capable of purifying and crystallizing the idea of its essence, of its skeleton. In methodological practice, this is carried out by rejecting the modern world, by negating the language of modernity. Such negation is not abstraction, but concrete, direct action.

Nobody among the "people of Tradition" could have done this, could have worked out a description of the language of Tradition and bring its universal metalanguage into relief, for reasons which I have already mentioned. Guénon did this. He opposed the language of Tradition to the language of the modern world. In this, first and foremost, rests the colossal, revolutionary significance of Guénon. Whoever follows Guénon and heads in the same direction, into the realm where there is nothing of the modern world. In practice, this path is realized through sacrificing the language of the modern world.

It is also important that, in addition to the radical dualism of the language of Tradition vs. the language of the modern world, there are softened variations still in existence. There are authors (who can hardly be called "Traditionalists" in the Guénonian sense, but who were either directly influenced by him or by similar ideas) who set themselves the somewhat different task of revealing the elements of the language of Tradition within the language of the modern world. They acted in a tactically different manner — not with a head-on confrontation, but by "entryism," "infiltration," by attempting to evolutionarily change the paradigm of modernity in the direction of the paradigm of Tradition.

Among this group are Mircea Eliade, Carl Gustav Jung, etc. This is a soft form of Traditionalism. The orthodox "Guénonists" (Julius Evola, Valsan, or Titus Burckhardt, for instance) opted for harsh confrontation and took the modern world to be an absolutely negative phenomenon and its language a diabolical anti-language. Conversely, the second category of thinkers argued that foundational, paradigmatic norms traceable back to the traditional array have been preserved through inertia within the language of modernity. They insisted that the paradigm of modernity affects the human being only superficially, that the influence of the language of modernity restructures only the exterior plane of the cognitive process, while in the depths of the human being, as before, the paradigms of Tradition continue to operate (Jung called this reality the "collective unconscious"). Between Guénon (and "Guénonism") on the one hand, and Eliade, Jung, and others on the other hands, one finds a relationship similar to that between radical Marxism and European social democracy. Guénonian Traditionalism insists on the irreversible, pathological character of the modern world and its language and holds that the situation can only be fixed with a radical break with modernity, with a "revolt against the modern world,"[12] a "conservative revolution." Eliade and Jung believe that the modern world is not so "modern" at its core,

---

[12] Julius Evola *Rivolta contro il mondo moderno* (Roma, 1969) [Julius Evola, *Revolt Against the Modern World*, trans. Guido Stucco (Rochester: Inner Traditions, 1995)].

and that with some effort (without revolutionary opposition) it can easily be turned back onto the familiar path of the "eternal return."[13] In some sense, this is like the relationship between "social democracy" and socialism.

Guénon's most radical follower, Julius Evola, considered Eliade and Jung to be apostates who "sold out to the Kali-Yuga regime's world occupation." Other Traditionalists approve of the achievements of such softer Traditionalists, who introduced subversive Traditionalist themes, like a kind of conceptual virus, into the modern world and thereby shook the abnormal operating system and brought restoration somewhat closer. Nevertheless, without Guénon, Eliade and other authors' actions would hardly be qualifiable; there would be no adequate terms or categories for defining what exactly it is that Mircea Eliade did in his works. Recognizing the correctness of the paradigms of the language of Tradition, he attempted to catch sight of them in the modern world, to reveal how they are independent, complex arrays, and thereby reinterpret the modern world so as to carry out, in the final analysis, a "seizure of intellectual power." Alas, he did not succeed. In general, this path of compromise yielded a certain positive effect if only because, thanks to Eliade, a huge mass of people (and an even larger mass thanks to Jung) became captivated with studying the language of Tradition, while Guénon remained an author for a narrow intellectual elite, for a very limited circle of heroic, uncompromising radicals. What is better, a quantitative increase in "soft Traditionalists," passionate about the history of religions, although at times not yielding the needed quality, or maintaining the purity of a circle of "strict Guénonists" who at times degenerate into inactive and sterile criticism driven by "*ressentiment*"? This is an open question, just as that of ascertaining who was right: the Communists or Social-Democrats?

---

13   Mircea Eliade, *Le Mythe de l'éternel retour* (Paris, 1949) [Mircea Eliade, *Cosmos and History: The Myth of the Eternal Return*, trans. Willard R. Trask (New York: Harper & Brothers, 1959)].

Qualitative Time, Synchronism, and the Ontology of Eternity

Let us move on to more concrete matters. There are two important elements that will allow us to understand what the language of Tradition is and what the language of modernity is. At the core of the language of Tradition discovered by Guénon lie a number of definite postulates and fundamental principles pertaining to qualities which are so necessary and global for our thinking of paradigmatic categories such as time and space. When we talk about understanding time and space in the language of Tradition and the language of modernity, we find ourselves in the cosmos of these two languages and we begin to recognize their coordinates. We can then mark out some of the axes of coordinates, and out of these two obscure uncertainties everything takes on more complete, more concrete, more distinguishable contours.

Modernity (or the language of modernity) sees unidirectional time as the main reality, the foundational mode of being. This axiom, this postulate is subject to no doubt in the language of modernity. Time flows in one direction, and everything that exists, exists within time. Everything that lies outside of time, if such is conceivable, is some kind of abstraction, an artificial construction that does not have its own being. Such is some kind of imaginary value which may have some grounds for consideration, but in fact is ontologically negative. Consequently, becoming turns out to be the only form of existence, of being, and whatever exists dwells in becoming, in unidirectional time. Strictly speaking, there is no eternity in this language. If eternity is spoken of, then it is a purely non-ontological abstraction. Becoming, left alone by itself and taken as a certain self-sufficient and sole form of existence, of being, with any reality, acquires a fundamental, paradigmatic charge. The process of time becomes a wholly ontologically positive process — obviously positive because there is only being in it, from it, and through it. This positive attitude towards time –

the notion that time is a unidirectional process and the denial of any self-sufficient, autonomously existing eternity – is the most important coordinate of the language of modernity. This language is structured around this ontological axis. The ordinary people of modernity (the language of modernity), whether a philosopher, a scholar, a TV announcer, a banker, a porter, a linguist, a mathematician, a physicist, a bathhouse attendant, or a driver, do not necessarily understand this clearly, nor do they have complete awareness of the matter. The vast majority of people, scientific and non-scientific alike, are completely unaware of just how deeply this concept of being as time — *Sein als Zeit* — predetermines the modern notion of reality. In the language of modernity, being is identical to time, or more precisely to unidirectional time, which is a positively unfolding process insofar as it carries being with and within it. Virtually no one (belonging to the vast majority) ever thinks or even suspects that all of their reasoning, all of their actions, all of their decisions, plans, and opinions on the nature of things stem precisely from this premise, that this is one of the most important vectors of the language of modernity, but that there might and do exist paradigmatic linguistic models (in the structuralist sense) that are arranged in a completely different way.

If we subject to careful, critical examination any philosophical proposition, any physical — indeed, generally scientific — hypothesis, any conception of chemical, social, or cultural processes expressed within the framework of modernity, then we will find the constant of unidirectional time everywhere as one of the basic axes of coordinates of the language of modernity. Unidirectional time, the coincidence of time and being, and the idea that the world is something that exists only in becoming and has a positive ontological (and axiological) character is one of the most important laws of the paradigm of modernity. Such quantitative (or modern) time is conceived as an endless, aimless progression.

If we turn to more concrete manifestations of the language of modernity, to the level of families of specific discourses, we can identify two varieties of the ontologization of time. The most orthodox perspective from the point of view of the language of modernity – that which most accurately reflects this notion of time held within it – is the positivist approach that has been generalized into a worldview by representatives of liberal philosophy (Friedrich von Hayek, Bertrand Russell, Karl Popper, Imre Lakatos, etc.). Here, time has no teleology whatsoever; it flows unidirectionally without aim or predetermination. The positivists' and liberals' purely quantitative time is as close as possible to the paradigmatic, basic version of the understanding of this coordinate within the framework of the language of modernity. The positivist (or post-positivist) approach typical of classical science develops and explicitly discloses one of the most important rules of the language of modernity — the law of identity between being and time. This paradigmatic discourse, a linguistic tautology of $A=A$, informs us about the structure of the language in which it is pronounced. Precisely this current in philosophy comes closest to isolating the parameters of the meta-language of modernity, cleansing its crystalline paradigm from minor and sidetracking details. The works of Karl Popper are supremely revealing in this respect.[14]

Marxism which, without a doubt, also remains within the framework of the language of modernity, represents the opposite pole here. In this case, the historical process (albeit as the process of the "development of matter") is recognized as a kind of teleological predetermination. History flows towards universal rationality and Communism as an eschatological and ontological goal. From the perspective of the paradigm of modernity, Marxism is a kind of "philosophical heresy," even though it remains within the framework of the language of modernity. It is an attempt at "inner emigration" without going beyond. One could express this thought differently: from

---

14 See Karl Popper's *The Open Society and Its Enemies*.

the perspective of the normative rules of the paradigmatic linguistics of modernity, Marxism is the most controversial expression. It is an avant-garde discursive challenge posed to the primal elements of the language in which, with the help of and by means of which it is realized. It is an expression that tries to claim recognition for the legitimacy of the linguistic rules, it threatens a systems failure of the whole language of modernity, and it is a proposal to use a critical model that is maximally foreign to this language's structure in order to comprehend it. Marxism also comes close to passing onto the level of being a meta-language, as it seeks to universally interpret modernity. But if liberal philosophy says a universal and integral "Yes!" to this modernity (and hence the meta-language of liberals is congruent with the very structure of modernity), then Marxism tries to formulate a universal and integral "No!" without going beyond the boundaries approved by modernity (hence the meta-language put forth by Marxism is a radical critique). This clarification allows us to understand René Alleau's proposed "convergence" of Guénon and Marx in a new way. But this similarity operates only up to a certain point. Marx stands on the border of the language of modernity, while Guénon moves beyond this border. Guénon is transcendent in relation to this language.

Guénon's Traditionalism affirms a completely different picture and notion of time as the basic coordinate of the language of Tradition. Guénon affirms that eternity is the form of existence, of being par excellence, and that being, which is eternal being, is invariable, that it does not flow anywhere in the form of emanations. It remains intact, whole, and unaffected by any processes, always and through whatever forms of time remaining self-sufficient, self-complete, full, absolute reality — reality which is simultaneously possible, actual, (in and for itself) necessary, and absolute. Thus, a radically different notion of time is performed in the language of Tradition. Along with the relative form of existence, of being, that is, being in time or being in becoming, there is eternal being, self-sufficient, motionless being unaffected by anything. Thus, we find ourselves within a completely different paradigm.

This is the first step: affirming the existence of eternity, of eternal being, and the logically ensuing notion that time is a process of ontological, existential waning. Time, therefore, is not unidirectional, for it ontologically depends on the unmoving ontology of eternity and revolves around it, flowing from and being absorbed by the primordial, unchaining, supra-temporal instance. Time, as an infinitesimal unit dependent upon eternity like a kind of "other-being" of eternity, has a relative ontological charge. But, taken on its own apart from eternity, it weighs nothing and means nothing; in some sense, it simply does not exist — this is the shadowy aspect of time in the paradigmatic language of Tradition. On the whole, time here is the process of a certain reduction, a gradual descent of eternity from itself, a diachronic dispensation of the qualitative content of eternity in the direction of existential waning. As follows, not only does time have a definite vector, a definite teleology, but this teleology is at once negative: it is a movement from plus to minus, from fullness to poverty. Understanding the process of time as degradation, as a secondary (in some way negative) category of the manifestation of eternal being (since we are talking about moving from the qualitative maximum to the qualitative minimum), gives us an absolutely different world, a different notion of the nature of reality, a different system of coordinates, a different science, a different culture, different art, different everything.

But here we come to another important point about the language of Tradition: insofar as eternity is absolute, constant, and complete, whereas time is relative and waning, time cannot wane eternally or even indefinitely. According to Traditionalist language, time wanes to a certain critical point. Once the sector of reality captured by time reaches a certain limit, eternal being once again discovers itself, and a new cycle begins. In the Traditionalist picture, time is therefore simultaneously teleological (oriented towards a specific qualitative limit) and cyclical. It moves from the fullness of the revelation of being to the diminution of this revelation and ultimately, once it reaches its critical boundaries, its positive part becomes infinitesimal, and the substantive side of time, its ontological slice, the "spark of being" within becoming, is exhausted, dissipates, and there arises the situation of the end times, the apocalypse. The hourglass of the world is turned over, and being once again discovers itself in its splendor, in its eternal fullness, and a new aeon, a new cycle, arises.

So, in the case of understanding time, we have an important illustration of one of the two axes of coordinates central to the language of Tradition. Guénon describes this in detail in *The Reign of Quantity and the Signs of the Times*. The understanding of time in the meta-language of modernity is radically different. It is not difficult to comprehend that both languages describe and predetermine completely different realities, two distinct worlds with radically different ontological structures. Moreover, these differences are not emphases or axiological assessments, nor are they orientations, solutions to ethical problems, preferences, morality, etc. They are the very notion of what exists and what does not. In the language of Tradition, there is no time in pure form, but there is eternity. In the language of modernity, time singularly exists, everything is only in time, and there is no eternity. It is not difficult to imagine the extent to which such a fundamental, paradigmatic linguistic difference impacts all the other forms of existence for beings which act in accordance with the rules of these two very different "operating systems."

What is important to understand above all else? That we are not talking about one or another philosophical school, each of which has its own claims. We are not talking about the opinions of groups or even religious institutions (as if atheists think one way, idealists another, and Christians and Buddhists still some other way). We are talking about deeper and much more serious things of a general order. The language of modernity can, in the most total sense, interpret in its own paradigmatic key, its own interpretive system and conceptual-logical structure; it can interpret diverse doctrines as individual discourses and expressions which are decipherable and assessable in accordance with a particular model. The common language of modernity can use other, more narrowly understood languages (religious, scientific, cultural, secular, etc.), everywhere inserting into them its own basic, invisible, not directly grasped, unpronounceable, but implied elements. This situation resembles what Freudianism calls "complexes." A complex never talks about itself — it lurks in the background, tries to elude direct analysis, and the most complex psychoanalytic practice is needed for a person to remember what frightened them in their infancy, like a rattle or a cat, and turned into their main problem in life. If they can remember, the Freudians believe that can be cured. There are, however, more severe situations: if you don't remember, then you'll die with your complex uncured. It is just as difficult to get down to the bottom of the basic linguistic elements.

In structuralism and in Traditionalism (Guénon's "school"), we are not simply talking about individuals, but whole sciences, religions, and entire continents of consciousness being subject to a different kind of "psychoanalysis". Deep, underwater impulses that predetermine the whole system of ensuing structures and strata are revealed by a special method. The threads of barely distinguishable linguistic primary influences are picked up somewhere on the bottom and raised up, disassembled and unraveled to demonstrate what is at the core of the discursive constructs that deny their own artificiality. There is a relevant term in the discourse of American journalism: "conventional wisdom." Any banal statement is said to be a product of this "conventional wisdom." It seems that this "wisdom" comes from itself and precisely corresponds to the direct and spontaneous voice of human (and non-human) being. In fact, however, this is absolutely not the case. "Conventional wisdom" is crude, mechanical, artificial, and fake, created and discarded by social engineers in accordance with specific tasks for manipulating the patterns of the language of modernity.

Comparing and contrasting the language of Tradition and the language of modernity, studying their internal linguistic patterns, entails the complete destruction of this notorious, proverbial 'conventional wisdom'. It means discovering the deepest paradigms that elude our attention, even during the most serious and careful philosophical study and immersion in the essence of things. Here we will discover those ontological horizons, layers, and landscapes that have a fundamentally different character, a different outline, a different configuration than that envisioned by those who are engaged and immersed, inertially and without critical distance, in the flat and ambiguous process of becoming.

Qualitative Space

Now for a few words about the quality of space. This is the second axis of the language of Tradition on the one hand and the language of modernity on the other. In the language of modernity, space is seen as something that is not homogenous or qualitative, but rather as something quantitative. A particular spatial world exists in the language of modernity. This spatial world of language organizes our perception of space, how we interact with extension as such.

In the spatial world of the language of modernity, all objects consist of interchangeable components, hence the notion of the quantitative nature of space as nothing other than the finite corporeal extension of some presupposed sub-corporeal breadth (pure matter). In fact, one of the first catechizers of the language of the modern world, René Descartes, said that there are only two things, "rational thinking" or "rational discourse" and étendue, "extension," or space. This purely qualitative, homogenous l'étendue is how the modern world understands space. This space is isotropic — right and left, top and bottom – West and East are fundamentally indistinguishable within it. Ultimately, from this follows the notion of "One

World," "globalism," the idea of unifying all countries, states, and peoples into a single commonwealth.

How is this possible? It is not only possible, but necessary from the point of view of the logic of the language of modernity, being that it is only some kind of error or distortion (gravitation or the Louisville field in modern physics) inserted into the essentially homogeneity of space that has resulted in its not being completely identical everywhere. From the paradigmatic point of view of the language of modernity, this fact carries a certain subtly negative load, an unnecessary perturbation, a component that must gradually be overcome in the process of totalizing the paradigm of modernity and the development of "civilization."

As in the case of time, we never think about quantitative space on purpose, but the language of modernity as a whole, all scientific disciplines, methodologies, cultural and everyday activities harbor this deeply rooted idea of homogenous, qualitative space that is concealed from direct critical reflection in the background. It is a kind of "space complex" organized on the basis of Galilean-Cartesian settings. This is localized space.

A completely different idea of space is inlaid in the language of Tradition: namely, qualitative space. It develops out of the notion of the cycle, of the cyclical nature of reality. The cycle arises from the fact of eternity, and spatial heterogeneity arises from the fact that there is a cycle. The so-called "Celtic Cross," a combination of a circle and a cross, is the most ancient, archaic Indo-European calendar, the most ancient model of the cycle. This sign encompasses both space and time as Tradition conceives of them. Time, as it were, passes into space, or space is dynamically animated by time. In this entire cycle, grasped from the position of eternity, we see the beginning and the end not sequentially, as within the framework of becoming, but simultaneously. We see the beginning, the end, and the middle synchronously. Consequently, passing to the representation of the sun's movement, the annual seasons, we can consider a certain part of this figure (the left side) to depict decline, and the other (the right side) ascent. Placed in the matrix of the cycle, space acquires a qualitative significance, a certain symbolic charge. From now on, any object, any form, any configuration of small or large objects with which we deal, whether the borders of a state or a continent, takes on an additional qualitative significance which is seen not as something inserted, but as the voice of qualitative space itself. Here it is unimportant whether spatial symbolism (yantra in Hinduism) is the product of human hands or the work of nature. You can contemplate a tree growing by itself and see the symbolic structure embedded in it, or you can contemplate an icon or a Tibetan mandala, where analogous harmonious symbolic figures are depicted artificially. According to the traditional view, to the language of Tradition, there is no fundamental difference between an artificial symbol and a natural object. A painting of the sun or the real sun equally symbolizes the Primordial Origin, being, and eternity. As a result of this, there exist a whole number of magical transformations and metamorphoses in Tradition. Tradition, accentuating this symbolic charge, dissolves the fact of the presence of a homogenous corporeality, and the idea, the spiritual part, the free, luminous aspect of things, beings, and objects, is freed from the dark quantitative shell. Space is transformed, illuminated, spiritualized, and comes alive. The broadly understood iconography of Tradition, symbolism, and sacred geography are based on this.

The science of geopolitics is one partial application of the spatial language of Tradition. This is the most "modern," technological, somewhat pragmatic application of the principle of qualitative space. As a methodology, geopolitics sharply contrasts the paradigms of the language of the modern world, as it is based on certain mythological and symbolic premises that are actually identical to elements of the language of Tradition. Hence, the most consistent guardians of the orthodoxy of modernity deny the very fact of the possibility of such a science existing. Let us note that the deep philosophical and ontological foundations of geopolitics were not only laid out by Carl Schmitt in his work *Land and Sea*,[15] but are to be found in purest form in René Guénon's book *East and West*.[16]

Post-Guénonism

The language of Traditionalism (especially Guénon's Traditionalism as a kind of meta-language of Tradition, as a language for describing the language of Tradition) is common to all historical traditions. I am not talking about Guénon's most radical theses when he asserts the presence of a metaphysical unity of traditions; there are different views on this question, and I would not like to dwell on them.[17] What is absolutely indubitable is the unity and absolute legitimacy of affirming the paradigm of Traditionalism that Guénon deduced and this paradigm's universal applicability to all forms of tradition, no matter how they are expressed.

All existing traditions, on their paradigmatic linguistic level, conflict with the language of modernity, because their basic settings contain contradictory fundamental ontological notions. They are absolutely irreducible to each other, inconvertible, and mutually exclusive. When we talked about the ontological axes (time and space) and their central role in the language of Tradition and the language of modernity, we tried to show that they cannot peacefully coexist due to their conflicting basic settings, that there is a deep confrontation between them. There exist two "armies," two "parties": the "party" of the language of Tradition and the "party" of the language of modernity.

---

15 Carl Schmitt's *Land and Sea* has been published in Russian in A.G. Dugin, *Osnovy geopolitiki* [*Foundations of Geopolitics*] (Moscow: Arktogeia, 2000) [Carl Schmitt, *Land and Sea: A World-Historical Meditation*, trans. Samuel Garrett Zeitlin (Candor: Telos Press Publishing, 2015)].

16 René Guénon, *Orient et Occident* (Paris, 1983) [René Guénon, *East and West*, trans. Martin Lings (Ghent: Sophia Perennis, 2001)].

17 See Guénon, *The Reign of Quantity and the Signs of the Times*.

So, what is "post-Guénonism"? "Post-Guénonism" is a term that signals a reaction to Guénonism. Guénonists are authors who replicate Guénon, who regard him as a guru, who busy themselves with repeating Guénon's discourse (rather than mastering his language) with very slight deviations, and who regard this engagement as a kind of intellectual hobby. Some people enjoy stamp collecting, some engage in sadomasochism, and others constantly study the crisis of the modern world and the signs of the times: this is a kind of niche for a certain type of European character who perceives Guénon as a type of discourse. In order to distinguish Guénon's Traditionalism as the meta-language of Tradition from simply reproducing Guénon's discourse, from simply repeating with variations what Guénon said, it makes sense to introduce the term "post-Guénonism." This term should be understood to mean a deep assimilation and mastery of Guénon's Traditionalism as a fundamental language which effectively generalizes all other languages. Once Guénonism becomes an assimilated language, a meta-language, a methodological, ontological, and paradigmatic structure, rather than an individual discourse, it can yield a completely unexpected effect.

Post-Guénonism is not simply a position; it is a mission, an imperative, an action, a process. There are two components to this process of assimilating Guénon and understanding Guénon as a language rather than a discourse. The first is studying, knowing, and mastering a specific living Tradition from the position of Traditionalism (Guénonism). This is a very subtle and delicate path. Depending on what tradition or confession we are talking about, there are specificities, pitfalls, nuances, and dead ends to deal with. I will only say that this path is not as smooth as it might seem at first glance, and "Traditionalists" sometimes change confessions like costumes without ever finding a strict correspondence to Guénon's theoretical orthodoxy.

The second component of post-Guénonism is a revision of the language of modernity from Traditionalist positions, that is measuring the exact distance between what is paradigmatic of modernity and the fragmentary remnants of archaic structures, i.e., elements of the language of Tradition that continue to exist through inertia.

Post-Guénonism is realized mainly in two spheres of action. On the one hand, there is applying the paradigm discovered by Guénon to an individual, actually existing Tradition. Doing so is not as simple as it might seem at first glance. When we apply the paradigmatic language of Tradition (the Traditionalist meta-language) to actually existing Orthodox Christianity, Buddhism, Judaism, Islam, Hermeticism, that is to living traditions and their authorities, we are subjecting these domains (and these personages) to a certain conceptual-methodological X-ray which highlights the structure of their defects and their deviation from the pure paradigm. This is a very serious and fundamental test of the adequacy of what figures as Tradition.

Secondly, Guénon described the main characteristics of the modern world, the language of modernity, its pure paradigm (the main contours of which coincide with the corpus of liberal theories), but the modernity actually surrounding us has significant deviations from its own ideal, from its basic model. These deviations are the inertial elements of Tradition ("residues" or "vestiges") with which modernity is still riddled. The actual "modern world" is much more traditional than the ideal "modern world." The specific discourses of this world only strive to aspire to purity, to the correct language of modernity. Accordingly, as a method, Traditionalism allows us to peer into many modern phenomena and reveal the archaic, inertial nebulae within them. After the phase of affirming that the language of modernity is the antithesis of the language of Tradition, the second phase begs introduction, revealing the diverse domains within the modern world which deviate from the language of modernity and, consequently, call for adequate interpretation within the context of the language of Tradition. This is all the more important insofar as there is no approximate equality between the language of Tradition and the language of modernity: the language of modernity presents itself as an extremely distorted, antinomian fragment of the language of Tradition, the latter being primary not only historically, but ontologically and metaphysically. Just as the level of purely quantitative matter is unattainable in principle and attempting to totally reduce it is an unrealizable intention, so too is the absolutization of the language of modernity unattainable in practice.[18] Modernity cannot ultimately purge itself of Tradition, for pure negation is ontically impossible. This line of investigation has been developed by Mircea Eliade, Carl Jung, and their followers.

However, the reverse circumstance is also real. Contemporary traditions (even authentic ones) are in practice much more modern than they might seem at first glance. The fundamental language of Tradition gradually recedes under the onslaught of the operating system of modernity. Where the external facade remains unchanged and traditional, a completely modern spirit might reign right underneath it on the level of exegesis (interpretation, assimilation, and understanding). Of course, uninterrupted traditions always retain the possibility of restoring their true traditional-linguistic dimension, but in certain cases this is not at all easy to do, and a huge percentage of authentic confessions' representatives are not only incapable of doing so, but hinder it in every possible way. This is such a serious situation that in certain extreme cases more archaic, sacred, and ultimately Traditionalist features can be found in exteriorly secular and "modern" currents than in certain confessions which have historical continuity. For instance, Soviet or Chinese Communism contains more elements of the language of Tradition (no matter how paradoxically and contradictorily expressed) than modern Protestant theology.

---

18 See Alexander Dugin, *Metafizika Blagoi Vesti* [*The Metaphysics of the Gospel*] in *Absoliutnaia Rodina* [*Absolute Homeland*] (Moscow: Arktogeia, 1999).

René Guénon: Traditionalism as a Language

In our eschatological conditions, Traditionalism (as Post-Guénonism) turns out to be something greater, something more than mere belonging to a particular tradition. A Traditionalist, even one who does not practice any religion (no matter how rare such is, contradicting as it does the natural logic of Traditionalism), but who has with Guénon mastered and assimilated the language of Tradition, is closer to Tradition (or, in the very least, is more acutely and tragically aware of their distance from it) than a person who externally and formally belongs to an authentic tradition (including an initiatic or esoteric one) but who has not performed the complex, difficult, and painful process of uprooting the linguistic paradigms of modernity.

Guénon said that "Traditionalism" is only an intention, a mere expression of a desire to draw near to Tradition. In fact, everything is much more complex. At our point in the cycle, Traditionalism is precisely what checks Tradition for authenticity and registers the presence (or absence) of elements of the language of modernity within it.

The picture I'm describing is very simple. If it is recognized, assimilated, and made into the substance of your own consciousness, then many things will become clear and intelligible. Everything will be reducible to the simplest formulas, and yet these most simple elements will make it possible to clear out the colossal paradigmatic blockages and drifts in religious, philosophical, ethical, and practical problems. Singling out and comparing paradigmatic languages is a very important operative method and technique. After all, even a real, living tradition can at a certain point simply forget about the fundamental maxims of Traditionalism. For example, the understanding of God and divine reality held by a number of Christian and even quasi-Orthodox thinkers becomes an attitude towards something subject to time. This is how a number of Christian (and even Orthodox) theologians interpret the historical change of epochs as before Christ and after Christ. Everything changes with the incarnation of the Son as man, indeed, but the Divine always transcends history; it may enter history, but it is never identical to it.[19]

For example, the Jesuit Pierre de Chardin said that God and the evolution of the material world are one and the same thing. Without a doubt, this is the language of modernity (evolutionism) dressed up in pseudo-Christian "theological" robes. But the element of identification of being with what is within time can very often be found in even less odious authors. The paradigmatic language of modernity is no simple matter (one cannot hide from it with any number of prostrations, fasts, prayers, and diligent self-improvement). It is like a devil, a spiritual dog that can easily penetrate closed doors — it has somehow even found a way to sneak up upon saints and hermits. The language of modernity is the Devil, the Antichrist, a 'noetic wolf' as the Old Believers say. The language of modernity is capable of invisibly and imperceptibly decomposing the conceptual, ontological, semantic, and metaphysical side of one or another tradition even while partially preserving its external aspects. This is a very serious point. Traditionalism has a colossal religious, spiritual, eschatological significance, because it is directly bound up with the restoration of the substance and the most important side of Tradition. Of course, if Traditionalism is limited only to critiquing the modern world, then it is left inert, impotent, and sterile. A critical Post-Guénonism which deals only with modernity and exposing all of its aspects is important as a preliminary, nihilistic phase, but it is insufficient. A fully-fledged and complete Post-Guénonism presupposes the presence of both of these elements: on the one hand: a positive "critique from the right" of a specific living tradition, entering into, assimilating, and studying this tradition; and on the other hand, a most severe rejection of the modern world on the level of discovering and exposing its deep linguistic paradigms.

---

19 This topic has been covered in detail in Dugin, *Metafizika Blagoi Vesti*.

René Guénon: Traditionalism as a Language

There is a typical errancy among ordinary Guénonists (not Post-Guénonists like us). They repeat the critical motifs against the modern world that Guénon developed with slight additions. Perceiving Guénonism to be a discourse and set of invectives against the meta-language of modernity, they take it to be something frozen, something given once and for all. But the modern world is also changing, qualitatively and substantially. The modern world is deteriorating. Being a complex array of anomalies, it is going from bad to worse in its anomalousness.

What is happening in the process of the progressive "modernization" of the modern world? Whatever turned out to be insufficiently modern, whatever does not fully coincide with the ideal language of the modern world, with its crystalline paradigm, is gradually being shed and overcome. Just look at the dynamic processes in the ideological sphere in the 20th century! This dynamic unequivocally shows how the modern gradually spews out whatever is less modern. This is not to say that what was rejected in this process was genuinely traditional, but rather that within the framework of the language of modernity it was more traditional than the rest. Applying this model of analysis, we can note that the most "traditional" of the "modern" ideologies of the 20th century were those of the so-called "Third Way." Being the least modern, they were the first to fall, overcome by more modern ideological forms. The Communist regimes were more modern than those of "Third Way" ideology, but less modern than liberal ones. Here arises a very important point which has been overlooked by conventional Guénonists' critiques of the modern world. Progressively defeating (and displacing) at first nationalist and then communist ideologies, liberal discourse gradually approached the pure model of the language of modernity, practically becoming identifiable with it.

What Guénon recognized as the core of the language of modernity is most fully proclaimed by radical liberals like

51

Bertrand Russell, Karl Popper, Raymond Aron, Friedrich Hayek, Francis Fukuyama, and George Soros. The modern discourse of the West's militant liberal ideologists and their philosophical servants (Philippe Nemo, Bernard-Henri Lévy, André Glucksmann, etc.) is no longer mere speech expressed in the language of modernity, but practically is this language itself. Hence why they speak of the "end of history," the "exhaustion of any and all discourse," and "Postmodernity." Postmodernity is the beginning of the era of victorious liberalism, the modern world's last dash towards its ideal language. Henceforth, nothing fundamentally new can be said anymore; all that remains is quoting, recycling, and "remixing" expressions uttered at previous stages of history. The "end of history" understood in liberal terms is the final manifestation of the language of modernity in its final, "eschatological" form. Liberals are the ones who understand everything that is going on just as precisely as we followers of Guénon do. Hence the tension of real dialogue between us — the dialogue that is the true intellectual content of the processes taking place in the modern world.

Behind all the events in the world around us (the fall of the ruble, military conflicts, government resignations, new discoveries in archeology, etc.), there is a struggle between two opposing camps. One pole is the tiny camp of Post-Guénonists, almost non-existent, like a grain of sand in the desert, and the other is the gigantic liberal camp of the language of modernity aspiring to and claiming global dominance.

The small camp of Post-Guénonism is, nevertheless, heir to the gigantic ontological heritage concentrated in the language of Tradition. It contains an incredible wealth of meanings, and these meanings are alive, they move like continents, rising up and subsiding. This is real life, which can be of any kind: good, bad, successful, catastrophic, it is life. Traditions come in different forms: there are sinister and merciful ones and they sometimes conflict with one another. But this is not so important, because today it is only in them, in the world of the language of Tradition, in the world of Traditionalism, that the colossal energies of real being with its inner wealth and external poverty contrast the opposing picture of the liberal world, based as it is on the polished and filed language of modernity, where sparklingly abundant advertisement boards cover up a suffocating vacuum of meaning.

Traditionalism and Russia

What can be said of Post-Guénonism (Traditionalism) applied to the conditions of Russia? For us, the realization of the program of Post-Guénonism is the foremost, singular, and foundational state, national, social, and cultural task. We have only one author whom we need to read: René Guénon. We have only one task: to understand what he wanted to say, to make his thinking our thinking and his language our language. Only on this path can one formulate, grasp for, and find things which are truly significant within the general context of a nation and its people. Outside of this, any change in government, cataclysms, and social shifts (even the most positive ones) will be metaphysically tantamount to zero, because outside of Post-Guénonism there is no spirituality, no social justice, no life — nothing.

Here it is worth emphasizing a very important methodological point. Applying the program of Post-Guénonism to the Orthodox tradition, I came to the conclusion that here exists an ideal form which is in fact our "national Guénonism."[20] This is the Old Believer's Right, the Old Orthodoxy, which, since the second half of the 17th century, is in an ontological, eschatological, and apocalyptic state in which the positions expounded by Guénon are crystal clear and intelligible. There is not simply a proximity or similarity of positions (on the level of discourses) here, but

---

20   Dugin, *Metafizika Blagoi Vesti*.

an almost complete identity. In Russia and within Orthodoxy, assimilated Guénonism (Post-Guénonism) is solely the Old Believers' reality, which preserves in general contours the paradigmatic Traditionalist language that underlies the entire Christian tradition. The cyclology (or historical "ecclesiology") of Christianity is adequately represented in precisely this sector of Orthodoxy. The Old Faith is that conceptual reality which comes to the fore upon applying the Traditionalist method to examining the whole Orthodox tradition.

I emphasize that this conclusion is not the result of personal acquaintance with Old Believer circles. On the contrary, following the strict logic of Post-Guénonism convinced me of the authenticity and supreme value of the Old Believers' Rite, and only then to contact (extremely productive and substantive) with Old Believers.

Precisely because this conclusion is purely theoretical and correct on a speculative level, the objective (and sometimes discordant, fragmentary, and problematic) state of today's Old Believers' Rite (far removed, of course, from the gnoseological and eschatological standards inlaid in it) does not change anything with regard to the adequacy of our conviction. From now on, if we correctly seek and use the correct conceptual tools, we will find everything that we need in the Old Faith.

The Apocalypse and Linguistics

Man wastes himself away in the actual. I think the Sumerian language became a dead language the moment everything that could be said in it had already been said, at which point history demanded the Assyrian languages and then others. Language, being potentially inexhaustible in its ontological center, in its synchronic state, becomes exhausted over the course of its diachronic, progressive development. And here a very interesting observation is born: the emergence of Guénon's language, the appearance of Guénon himself, his terminology, his model, and his ontologically revolutionary paradigm, occurred precisely at the very moment once Tradition was already at the edge of existence (with one foot beyond it) in the modern world. Only then did it become possible to see and embrace all of the ontological contours of what had developed and what had been thinned and squandered in history.

We, Guénon's successors, are heirs to a very anxious, very desperate, almost hopeless position. We stubbornly defend what has historically lost and ended. Just as being gradually leaves the process of becoming, extracts itself from it, and in no way increases the scale of its presence as the cycle nears its end, so has Traditionalism itself arisen in the critical, extreme situation of the end.

Post-Guénonism, as knowledge and as the action that follows from such knowledge, is extremely tragic. But the following gives cause to rejoice: we see just how rapidly the substance of the discourses laid out by the norms of the language of modernity is being exhausted.

This allows us to foresee, anticipate, and look forward to the emergence of a new, long-awaited era, when the situation will be somewhat different (indeed radically different). Today, our speech (our Traditionalist discourse) is minimized, maximally concealed. Even when we speak publicly, openly and without hiding, our discourse still resembles sermons in the catacombs more so than proclamations from rooftops. From our camp to the broad collective soul, after filtration by the thought-police, only crackling, whistling, and coughing can be heard — Fukuyama the "last man" has turned on the silencer.

I am deeply convinced that we are not mere powerless witnesses regretfully stating what is happening in this "outer twilight". We are the last small detachment defending the holy vessel in the midst of the abomination of desolation — lost in the winter of the end times, we are the small, militant faculty of the New University ("new" because it belongs to the reality that shines from beyond the final boundary), a department of "fisher kings" studying the laws of linguistics. I began by saying that Friedrich Nietzsche titled one of his works *We Philologists*. I dare to hope that, to some extent, he had us in mind.[21]

Translated by Jafe Arnold, Charlie Smith, and John Stachelski

---

21 The present text was originally a lecture delivered at the New University in Moscow in 1998, subsequently edited and published in Alexander Dugin, *Filosofiia Traditsionalizma* (Moscow: Arktogeia, 2002).

REGARDING THE TERM "TRADITIONAL AUTHORS"

Róbert Horváth

The most eminent among the authors known as "traditionalists" or "perennialists" are called "traditional authors" in Hungary. In this context, this latter expression should obviously be comprehended as contemporary, referring to 20th-21st century traditional authors. From the spiritual perspective – since traditionality is considered here in this sense – Plutarch the priest of Delphi, Plotinus, Pico della Mirandola, Ibn al-'Arabī or for example, Śaṅkara are obviously traditional authors. However, it is not immediately evident why and on what basis René Guénon and others are called the same.

Some may think this is only to avoid the term "traditionalists," because – as is said – a normal person cannot be associated with any "-ism" or "-ists." We do not say there is no truth in this statement, but this approach fails to grasp the essence of the issue. Indeed, there were times in history when we ourselves would have preferred to strictly avoid any form of "-ism." Today, however, in this age beyond any "-ists" and "-isms," when, due to overall spiritual indifference and sluggishness, the quality of thinking is sinking to an even lower level, we should recognize that there is nothing clearly positive behind such avoidance of "-isms." We have more or less the same opinion about avoiding the use of terms ending with "-ist" and "-ism" based on stylistic and "aesthetic" considerations instead of intellectual ones. We would even be ready to call ourselves "traditionalists" if this were the only alternative to the contemporary indifference to ideas. Yet, as we have already remarked, in certain cases "traditionalism" can represent an interim phase in the process of effectively reaching traditional spirituality. Not all "traditionalist" thinkers are "traditional authors," but they may become such. This is an important possibility.

Intellectual and mental commitment is an important human starting point, even if it is merely a starting point, and even if traditional authors represent much more. Therefore, we are not using the term "traditional authors" only to avoid calling them "traditionalists." Nor is this only because in Hungarian the term "traditional" is not as generic as in other languages and can be more specifically linked to "spiritual tradition," while in other languages it may also refer to "customary tradition." The reason why we call them so is that *the most eminent 20th–21st century authors known as "traditionalists" can be effectively considered as heirs and contemporary equivalents of the former traditional spiritual authors.* We are not only talking about the heirs of the Platonic lineage as some may think, but — *mutatis mutandis* — also about those who under the current difficult circumstances are the contemporary heirs of the Aristotelian lineage, whose works preserve not only esoteric approaches but also the key mental, logical, dialectic qualities usually associated with Aristotle. In the following, we will present four major and five further sets of ideas to support the view that some more or less contemporary authors can be called traditional authors just as rightfully as the earlier authors mentioned above as examples.

In the past century, an incredible number of writings from great spiritual traditions were translated and published, and the teachings of a large number of ancient masters became available for study. By now, even teachings that were completely unknown in the West 50 years ago have become accessible to some extent. For example, works by Patrul Rinpoche have been published in Hungary in recent years. Today, we can hear about things worthy of more serious study even from traditions that surpass *Vajrayāna* in terms of emphasizing radical spiritual autonomy – like *rDzogs chen*. Yet all this scarcely has any direct spiritual results. Besides the lack of adequate generic spiritual results in proportion to the weight of these subjects, spiritual results are also scarcely seen at the personal level. It is obvious that several ingredients of the teachings are missing, even if sometimes fairly correct translations exist.

In terms of spiritual results, the situation is not much better for those who have tried to turn to authentic commentators, living representatives, and masters of these teachings, seeking to relate to oral traditions as well. On the one hand, we must observe that the number of authentic commentators is also extremely low today. The number of authentic representatives, of communities whose decline is at least limited, and of persons at the level of a master, is even lower. The decline of traditional organisations – their transition from esoteric to exoteric – or the stagnation of their spiritual intensity should be considered, just as the fact that personal encounters that mainly take place as a result of travelling at the physical level do not necessarily represent *spiritual encounters*. On the other hand, even if more or less authentic transmitters, representatives, or masters of such teachings are successfully found, they do not actually take into account the defects and characteristics of the contemporary Western man when interpreting the teachings. Previously, a detailed consideration of Western characteristics could not have been an obligation for Eastern representatives even if that was what Western people would have needed. Yet, for example, the words of His Holiness Dilgo Khyentse – who also commented on the works of the previously mentioned Patrul Rinpoche – require further commentaries in order to avoid misinterpretations by Westerners. Due to the erosion of the meaning of words and a radical change in mentality, the meaning of countless terms used by commentators has become merely moral. Just to illustrate this with one example: when an earlier author or an Eastern commentator living in a relatively closed environment said "Be of good heart," "good" here – depending on the depth of its context – should not by

59

any means be taken in the moral sense; it does not mean "good-heartedness," but in a given case it can be a call for the disciple to consider the highest spiritual state known to him as his own centre, essence, self. Do we need a more typical example of the ambiguity of old or contemporary Eastern commentators?

Authentic representatives of spiritual traditions have indeed been paying more attention to adequate teaching for contemporary Westerners as of lately, since the number of qualified Eastern disciples is also rapidly diminishing. Undoubtedly, this must be even more so in the future – the more authentic an Eastern representative is, the more so. The question is, however, whether the intensity and mode of this attention will be appropriate. For example, concerning the commentaries and teachings by the venerable Namkhai Norbu, in many instances we could repeat what we said earlier about Dilgo Khyentse. A person who really possesses the ability to teach should be careful about using expressions such as "unprejudicedness" or "equality," which have a non-spiritual sense in the Western world and, like "compassion" or "non-discrimination," simply have a different meaning with anti-spiritual connotations. Familiarity with the actual conditions and mastery of the possible approaches, i.e. their appropriate application, are closely connected to the authenticity of teaching. This is the first (**I**) major key point why the most prominent earlier and present "perennialists" can be rightly called traditional authors and heirs of the wisdom of the former traditional spiritual authors. In the times we are living in, commentaries are required even for the commentators.

Even personal encounters with extremely rare authentic representatives do not become effective spiritual encounters unless *doctrinal preparations* of the widest possible range are made. Actually, the importance of 20th and 21st century traditional authors partly consists in the adequate doctrinal preparations they made and prompted to be made. This is the second (**II**) major key point. We do not want to say that their role is reduced to commenting on the commentators. The scope of *spiritual preparations* is much wider. In addition to explaining traditional teachings in ways that are appropriately articulated for contemporary man, they also include (1) an overall understanding, feeling, and adoption of the mentality of traditional cultures and their characteristics. Similarly, they include (2) formulating an outlook that represents the essence of all spiritual traditions and is fundamentally consistent with each of them, meaning that we look at the world, experience situations in our lives, and see ourselves in accordance with their teachings. Moreover, (3) the most important traditional authors have always paid special attention to and focused on the highest, esoteric and metaphysical class of spiritual teachings.

It is very important that in the works of more or less contemporary traditional authors, as in the case of early traditional authors, there is, besides the above-mentioned key aspects, an almost tangible *spiritual autonomy*, the presence of the principle of *spiritual sovereignty*, which – in addition to the principle of respecting spiritual authorities – was always evident in the greatest traditional works. This is the third (III) major key point. This autonomy, accompanied by intense participation, identification, and vivid understanding in and with the ultimate Principle, and freedom from intellectual superstitions and stereotypes, is regarded by witless scholars and sectarian traditionalists (those only committed to a single tradition) as inauthenticity and personal mysticism. However, we must not care about this. These are the opinions of people who are not familiar with the complete work of the authors concerned.

Concerning doctrinal and spiritual preparations, it must be noted that these require the personal acquisition of several *qualities* (4). The works of modern and contemporary traditional authors indicate that they possess a range of qualities of basic importance. The artistic and logical qualities, rational reasoning, and exact presentation – precise articulation – are clearly present, as well as intuition and a spiritual intellect capable of identifying with high-order realities. These all appear in explanations, expositions, and phrasing that on the whole are the most appropriate for contemporary man, not only for the purpose of purely doctrinal expositions, but also for wider spiritual preparations.

It is well known that the workings of the mind of modern man are incredibly intense – but not in their quality – and unsettled. They are so intense that generally and practically, the mental level cannot be simply overcome or transcended unless thinking becomes qualitative. Due to the nature of his thoughts and the amorphousness of his thinking, modern man must first establish order and bring about a qualitative transformation in these areas before he can transcend the mind (and must also break free from the suggestive influences of modern civilisation producing similarly profane, worthless, and incoherent thoughts). At this point – still in the area of doctrinal and spiritual preparations – there is another argument in favour of contemporary traditional authors (5).

For our part, we find it ridiculous when well-educated Western people with minimal doctrinal and spiritual preparations seek personal relationships leading to initiation while they are not capable of reading through the lines of a book and steadily, assiduously interpreting their meaning. Of course, literacy has not always been a prerequisite of acquiring higher knowledge, but in the case of a contemporary person who otherwise reads regularly and has some ideas about, for instance, "correct" political views, the lack of capacity for conscious reading and thinking is absurd. Today, not only do we have to address the importance of extensive doctrinal preparations, but we must also speak of the importance of the thorough and detailed reading and understanding of the works of the traditional authors of our times. Actually, articles should be written on how to acquire the quality of clear understanding through intense reading. Without the latter, contemporary Western man's aspiration for relationships leading to initiation is practically frivolous.

Regarding the Term "Traditional Authors"

It is often argued that the work of today's authors of traditional spirituality is too "philosophical" and theoretical in nature. There are even some who say that they are "difficult to comprehend" — such people should consider the acquisition of certain skills as we have suggested. Concerning the accusation of being theoretical, we should note that the very reason why these authors can be justly called traditional is that all of them were also "spiritual practitioners" who had authentic *sādhanas*, spiritual methods, and paths they practiced and traversed. This is the fourth (**IV**) major key point. Their ultimate authenticity and traditionality – which is more difficult to describe in detail – is actually due to the decisive importance of the concept of *spiritual realisation* in their work. Let us for now put aside the important question of the exact degree of this realisation in terms of its metaphysical, esoteric or exoteric extent. In the end, all higher traditional teachings are incomprehensible without the concept of spiritual and metaphysical realisation – and not only incomprehensible, but also meaningless. The beginnings of theology and the deep foundations of the human desire for transcendence are incomprehensible, because they are suprarational, mysterial, and magical. We thirst because we are able to drink, and because we know – and on the higher levels of our being, possess – the reality of water. We desire because we can realize our desires, even if they become real in a sense other than the common human sense.

Thus, we have four key orientations for characterising, interpreting, and continuing the works of traditional authors:

I. Interpreting the teachings requires taking into account the defects, characteristics, and actual conditions of contemporary Western man;

II. Having the adequate doctrinal and spiritual preparations;

III. The presence of the principle of spiritual autonomy and sovereignty with the principle of respecting spiritual authorities;

IV. The decisive importance of the idea of spiritual and metaphysical realisation.

In addition, we have disclosed five key aspects involved in, and called for by, the works of traditional authors:

1. An overall understanding, feeling and adoption of the mentality of traditional cultures and their characteristics;

2. Formulating an outlook that represents the essence of all spiritual traditions and is fundamentally consistent with each of them;

3. Paying attention to and focusing on the highest, esoteric and metaphysical class of spiritual teachings;

4. The personal acquisition of significant qualities;

5. Teaching to think.

With these orientations, we may at last draw up a list of traditional authors of our age by name and in chronological order, or more precisely, a list of traditionalists who have matured or have the potential to mature into traditional authors.

René Guénon, the first author on this list, was preceded by several persons in the early 20th century whose work can be considered traditional in spirit but was still permeated by either 19th century occultism or an exclusive commitment to specific traditions, or by authors who did not leave extensive written works behind. Among them, several of whom were also Guénon's collaborators, are **Paul Vulliaud, Louis Charbonneau-Lassay, Albert Puyou de Pouvourville (Matgioi), Léon Champrenaud (Abdul-Haqq), Ivan Gustaf Aguéli (Abdul-Hādī), John Woodroffe (Arthur Avalon)** and **Arturo Reghini**.

The voluminousness of written works clearly cannot be regarded as one of the criteria of spiritual greatness – teaching itself constitutes only one-third of the manifested aspects of the inner Guru –, yet it is natural that it should be considered here. Among the authors more or less parallel in chronology with Guénon, we must also mention **Ananda Kentish Coomaraswamy**, and in some sense, **Leopold Ziegler**. Among the initial followers of Guénon we can find authors with both less voluminous and more extensive written works. The

Regarding the Term "Traditional Authors"

former include **Marcel Clavelle (Jean Reyor), René Allar, André Préau, John Levy, Arthur Osborne, Michel Vâlsan, Jacques-Albert Cuttat (Jean Thamar), Elie Lebasquais (Luc Benoist)**. The latter include **Marco Pallis, Frithjof Schuon, Titus Burckhardt, Vasile Lovinescu, Leo Schaya,** and **Martin Lings**. This "second generation" of 20th and 21st century traditional authors also includes **Julius Evola**, who is prominent in several aspects.

A concurrent, significant line of authors – following or alongside Ziegler – appeared in the 1930s in the German-speaking countries. They were open to other traditions, were characterized by deep thinking and expressiveness, were fundamentally Catholic, and emphasized the need to apply the political and social aspects of the traditional concepts. These authors include: **Othmar Spann, Taras von Borodajkewycz, Walter Heinrich**, and others.

After the initial followers – disciples but not in the formal sense – of Guénon and Coomaraswamy, the first authors under the influence of Schuon also emerged (this influence was already manifested in the works of Pallis, Burckhardt, Lings and Cuttat): **Whitall Perry, Seyyed Hossein Nasr, Kurt Almqvist** (all of whom were also admirers of Guénon). Subsequent followers of Guénon also appeared: **Guido de Giorgio, Roger Maridort, Franco Musso (Giovanni Ponte), Abdul-Wahid Pallavicini, Gaston Georgel**, etc.

As we approach our days, this list – thanks be to God – can be extended with several more authors. A lengthy enumeration again raises the issue of the extent of written works and of other problems, but still we wish to mention the following names: **Lord Northbourne, Brian Keeble, Charles le Gai Eaton, Victor Danner, Wolfgang Smith, Huston Smith, William Stoddart, Rama Coomaraswamy, James Cutsinger, Charles-André Gilis, Jean-Louis Michon, Ernst Küry, Henri Hartung, Jean Borella, Jean-Léon Granger (Jean Tourniac), Christophe Levalois, Bruno Hapel, Renato Del Ponte,**

Regarding the Term "Traditional Authors"

Gianfranco de Turris, Claudio Mutti, Nuccio D'Anna, Tage Lindbom, Antonio Medrano, Federico González, Marcos Ghio, Ernesto Milá, Geydar Dzhemal, Alexander Dugin (in his early works), **Florin Mihăescu, Dan Stanca, Béla Hamvas** and – with special emphasis – **András László**, etc. Since this list also includes persons concerned with a single tradition, it would be unfair to leave without mention authors like **Daisetz Teitaro Suzuki, Eugen Herrigel, Joseph Epes Brown, Philip Sherrard, Jean Hani**, etc.

At the end of this article, with such a necessarily incomplete list of traditionalists, we did not want to enter the world of personal antagonisms. The point was to show the relationship between traditionalists and traditionalist authors, as we have seen above. We are fully aware of the personal differences and disputes and have reservations about some of these authors. But we thought the latter list is useful because it is sufficiently comprehensive and informed to be considered unbiased, and provides a good insight into the relationship between traditionalists and ancient traditionalist authors, provided we delve into the works of all of them. In spite of the enormous differences between these authors, we undoubtedly see the contours of one and the same spiritual current. We intentionally avoid the term "school," since they themselves did not want to create any particular school. Much more is involved: spiritual traditionality – and the variety of its manifestations.

Translated by Gábor Faragó

TRADITIONALISM AS UNDERSTOOD BY RENÉ GUÉNON AND ITS CONTEMPORARY UNDERSTANDING

Maxim Makovchik

Today, a century since the publication of Guénon's first book, the question concerning what "Traditionalism" is and who "Traditionalists" are has only grown in complexity. The cultural and civilizational landscape has undergone significant changes across the world: the civilizations of the East (whose traditional aspects were more noticeable and easier to come into contact with in Guénon's time) have entered a phase of advanced Westernization, at least externally, and a plethora of counter-traditional currents have emerged there, albeit alongside processes and new thinkers opposing them. In this essay, we shall examine the question "What is Traditionalism?" from the point of view expounded in the works of René Guénon – a point of view which can be expressed today by a researcher inspired by Guénon's works[22], which we call "contemporary understanding."

For now, we shall avoid the designation of "Traditionalist" insofar as we wish to analyze the following question: should someone who finds the works of Guénon and related authors valuable agree with such a characterization? For the passive

---

22 To use the phrase "researcher of René Guénon" without qualification poses great difficulties, as he was not the founder of any doctrine or trend in philosophy which one might associate with his name. Certain authors have even contrived to refer to him as a "founder of a movement," but we might ask in turn whether Newton, Laozi, or Thomas Aquinas were founders of movements. Scientists and thinkers may elucidate and develop the truth in one or another form, but they do not "found" any "movements."

observer who operates with the term "Traditionalism" in such a widely disseminated manner, this question will appear strange: after all, it was none other than Guénon, Coomaraswamy, Evola, and other thinkers of their ilk who founded the school of Traditionalism, the fundament of which is considered to be Guénon's corpus. Such is the generally accepted point of view to be found in any dictionary or reference work on the matter. But it goes without saying that a point of view's dissemination signifies nothing other than the mere fact that it has been disseminated.

It would be better to turn to what Guénon said on the matter in his works, in which this question underwent unambiguous examination. But we shall do so briefly and concisely, as such works would obviously have taken on an entirely different form had they been written now, in the first half of the 21st century. For one, Guénon neither created nor founded any doctrine; he merely elucidated knowledge already contained in the living traditions known to him and, what is more, he never associated his works with "traditionalism." From Guénon's position, the very concepts of "tradition" and "traditionalism" can even be viewed as contradictory since, if tradition is a truth that is passed down (*trans* + *dare*), a method by which the purpose of human life might be fulfilled (*puruṣārtha*), or a means of comprehending and realizing eternal principles[23], then traditionalism is nothing more than a striving and aspiration towards its namesake.[24] This striving cannot be considered a comprehension, nor can an inclination towards knowledge be considered knowledge. We are much worse off if striving and inclinations become the replacement for comprehension and knowledge; the former categories then become the antipodes of the latter, a mirage that has distracted the seeker. We employ the term "seeker" instead of "researcher," since knowledge of tradition is not the purview of dry office

---

23 Naturally, it is not our task to provide an exhaustive definition of "tradition," as this concept contains no necessity, and the formulations introduced here serve as nothing more than guidelines.

24 René Guénon, *The Reign of Quantity and the Signs of the Times*, trans. Lord Northbourne (Hillsdale: Sophia Perennis, 2001), 169, fn. 4, 211.

work like the contemporary study of philosophy, but a living intellectual act by a human being.

Put differently, in light of the fact that the true essence and aim of tradition can hardly be understood by contemporary man without prefatory explanations at the very least, we are endangered by a phantom projected by the modern mentality, a phantom which Guénon calls "traditionalism"; such is an aim in and of itself – a self-sufficient doctrine that is enclosed in the framework of a "worldview" or a "sociopolitical program." Traditionalism is sometimes even characterized as a reactionary set of alternative moral frameworks contrasting modernity, which reduces what is traditional to the psychological, social, and cultural plane. However, even this is not a limitation; for some of Guénon's contemporaries, tradition was a complex of habits and cultural models which have stood the test of time; in this case, traditionalists are reconstructors, down-shifters, and partisans of simplification. The concepts of tradition and traditionalism should be strictly distinguished so that they may be treated as objects of consideration. If it is inappropriate to grant a decisive voice and elucidating authority to the representatives of tradition (who, more often than not, act as representatives of one or another traditional form and speak in its name without analyzing the question of what constitutes tradition as opposed to traditionalism), then it is appropriate to grant as much to thinkers who understand the works of René Guénon as well as those of authorities in close proximity to him. It bears paying particular attention to the negative character of the widely known book written on the subject by Mark Sedgwick[25], whose role in explaining traditionalism (and, by extension, tradition) is analogous to that played by Helena Blavatskaya in distorting traditional doctrines.[26]

The mixing-up and complications that arise in the midst of substituting the notion of what is traditional, i.e., that

---

25 Mark Sedgwick, *Against the Modern World: Traditionalism and the Secret Intellectual History of the Twentieth Century* (Oxford: Oxford University Press, 2004).

26 René Guénon, *Theosophy: History of a Pseudo-Religion*, trans. Alvin Moore, Jr., Cecil Bethell, Hubert and Rogini Schiff (Hillsdale: Sophia Perennis, 2001).

which pertains to tradition and its intellect level, with the notion of what is "traditionalist," i.e., that which pertains to traditionalism and its philosophical level, only continue to increase with the passage of time. We constantly observe attempts at dragging things down to inferior levels; for example, in political discourse, one often encounters the concept of "traditional values." Under careful scrutiny, the usage of such a term turns out to be a parody or, in the best-case scenario, an imitation of the external results of traditional principles; ultimately, the concept of tradition is reduced to the level of the social or the political. It is not difficult to notice that the modern world, in the majority of its organized forms (no matter how these might attempt to appear), truly opposes tradition[27]: in so doing, it suppresses and replaces religious forms, customs, ways of life, art, and other manifestations of the traditional spirit.

The further the modern world manages to progress in its suppression of everything traditional, the more difficult it will be for modern man to understand what tradition and traditionalism are in any positive sense. But this also yields a reverse effect: in its uttermost phases, along with the progress which increasingly alienates man from every aspect of his own life, in addition to castrating and denaturing life itself, encroaching modernism does much to drive people toward tradition. One may compare this phase with the end of the Maha-Yuga, after which comes a new golden age[28]; an analogy such as this is fitting, since each person also experiences the Yugas (understood in an internal sense, as opposed to external one) on the various levels of their own personal existence; thus, a person's attainment of the traditional spirit corresponds

---

27 Guénon characterized this opposition more precisely as a "broad collective suggestion" (Guénon, *Reign*, 210). One should take a moment here to consider just what direction calls for "revolt" or "war" against the modern world should take and whether one ought to think in these terms at all (cf. René Guénon, *The Symbolism of the Cross*, chapter VIII on *el-jihâdul-akbar*).

28 One should also recall the far more complex symbolism of the Revelation of John, which relates no less to the inner man than it does to historical realities.

entirely to the arrival of a new golden age.[29] And in this sense, we may amend the understanding of traditionalism as a reaction to modernity by positing the problem to be not modernity itself, but rather, first and foremost, growing disorder and necrosis as such[30]; secondly, this is not a reaction, but rather a natural fluctuation, like a pendulum which ineluctably swings from one extreme position to the other; thirdly, we are speaking here not of traditionalism, but of tradition.[31] And precisely at the moment when such a reversal occurs, it is important for the person who turns in this direction not to encounter a surrogate or a dead-end. It is precisely here that we arrive at the answer to the question of what Traditionalism is (or, more precisely, what it should and should not be) for those making sense of Guénon's utterances in the 21st century.

Guénon himself explicitly described what Traditionalism must not be: it must not consist solely of "a sort of tendency or aspiration toward tradition without really knowing anything at all about it."[32] More specifically, this may be the initial stage of knowledge on the part of a person who was previously unacquainted with anything traditional; in this case, such strivings and inspiration are completely appropriate as an intermediate level of knowledge. But one must overcome this level, as one cannot truly comprehend and enter tradition, leaving "traditionalism" behind, on the sole basis of human drives. For the sake of self-transcendence,

---

29 Naturally, in an example such as this, it is neither obligatory nor necessary to speak of the total attainment of a state corresponding to the golden age, as the human being has its own components on a plethora of levels, at each of which the attainment will be more or less complete.

30 Here it would also be appropriate to recall the image of lost paradise found in Christianity.

31 The notion that traditionalism is a reaction has to do with the philosophical level and those below it, but the even greater problem with this mindset consists in the fact that tradition, simplified into traditionalism, will also be understood as a "new spiritual current" ("new" in relation to modernity and its lack of memory) in a New Age or Theosophical spirit. This comes surprisingly close to Guénon's critical notion of "traditionalism," but is under no circumstances applicable to an understanding of tradition.

32 Guénon, *Reign*, 211

the relative positioning and striving which may arise as a reaction to external factors must be exchanged for an act of personally unconditioned choice which is independent of one's environment; only on this basis can one truly approach the traditional. The freedom that comes with a knowledge of truth is born of the freedom one has to choose it, as though this freedom is drawn to itself. A person will only arrive at an understanding of the necessity of transitioning from imposed motivation to unconditioned choice (if such a transition is unavoidable) only by studying a real, living tradition[33], but not from the surrogates of books and philosophy.

It must also be clearly distinguished that Traditionalism cannot be positively understood as a form of meta-religious ecumenism. Guénon took great pains to caution his readers against mixing various traditions. The approach of *Philosophia Perennis*, with its mode of elucidating traditional knowledge (despite the fact that one may indeed find the same universal principles at the foundation of different traditional doctrines), is conditioned by the epoch common both to us and Guénon, in which the doctrines of the different religious forms, as a result of their obscuration, are ever more frequently perceived as something relative; and, with an eye to restoring a true understanding, it is highly effective to show how, behind this perceived relativity, the seeker may uncover a universal exposition of eternal principles bearing no connection to the secular. Guénon reveals this universality by appealing to the symbolism of world traditions and showing how, in all cases, one finds a unity, void of all eclecticism and ecumenism.

Traditionalism is not a replacement for tradition. One should remember (though this is less perceptible in the most recent centuries) that for anyone who belongs to one of the traditional forms, others who have no relationship to that tradition are outside of his world; and those who have nothing to do with tradition at all are little better than animals, since

---

33   One must not lose sight here of Guénon's insistence on initiation and membership in a regular organization.

what they lack is precisely that divine element which ennobles the animal component of man. It is precisely to this category that a "traditionalist" who has not gone beyond books will be seen as belonging by, for example, a Himalayan ascetic, a Sufi, or an Orthodox monk. In other words, one may follow a definite tradition, and this is a path with an explicitly determined higher goal, but one may not follow "traditionalism," since there is just about nothing which can replace attachment or unification with a traditional organization existing in one form or another.

To distinguish between Tradition and Traditionalism, it is important to pay attention to the means by which traditional knowledge is transmitted – both with regard to traditional texts, whose authority is irreproachable for both Guénon and his pupils, and to the representatives of any corresponding tradition. To take one example, we might recall the varied situation of *śruti* and *smṛti*, in the sense that both types of text, when analyzed separately, are undoubtedly traditional; but the first of them holds great authority in all cases (i.e., should one need to choose the "more" traditional option or simply a traditional source, it will be precisely the *śruti* that are recognized as such). Are Guénon's texts traditional? In the literal sense, they are obviously not. Do they allow one to understand tradition (as that which stands behind traditional texts)? Obviously, they do. One need only reference the example of the Christian theologians who in and of themselves bear no relation to the Christian canon, but who to a great degree allow one to understand that canon and, therefore, are extremely valuable for anyone studying the doctrine.[34]

---

34 As an apogee of our current line of discussion, beyond the bounds of similar analyses, one may recall the words of the Bhagavad-Gita:
śrutivipratipannā te yadā sthāsyati niścalā
samādhāv acalā buddhis tadā yogam avāpsyasi
In Sementsov's Russian translation, this says: "When you, Partha, in samadhi hold your thought motionless and indifferent to the words of the Veda – this means you will attain yoga." These verses speak of attaining not only what lies beyond reflections of traditional knowledge (with which one may associate the entirety of traditionalism), but what lies beyond traditional knowledge (*śruti*) itself, i.e., the secret of secrets, the light of light. But the path leading there passes through the lower-lying levels.

We have yet to answer the primary question: how should someone who comprehends what Guénon said relate to Traditionalism? Firstly, one must understand what such traditionalism is. This notion could stand for a philosophical system, a culturological concept, ethnographic constructions, or some means of introducing one to traditional knowledge. In each instance, one's verdict and relationship to the concept will strongly differ from others. Secondly, recalling all that Guénon had to say about traditionalism and traditionalists (which includes almost nothing of approbation), one should understand that his criteria are set quite high and are almost unreachable for even the sincere seeker who in our times finds himself at the initial stages of his path. Correspondingly, it would be incorrect to treat Traditionalism (in the event that this concept stands for a stage and form of familiarization with traditional knowledge) as something negative even though it is not in itself Tradition. Immersion in Traditionalism can offer a wonderful way for receiving one's bearings and heading in the right direction until, sooner or later, the seeker arrives at their own "Active Door," the "gateway"[35] which marks the passage between such orientations and the true knowledge of the traditional spirit.

Translated by Charlie Smith and Jafe Arnold

---

35 Cf. A.K. Coomaraswamy, *Selected Papers - Volume I: Traditional Art and Symbolism* (Princeton: Princeton University Press, 1977), 521.

THE REALISATION OF THE SPIRIT OF TRADITION AND THE CULTURE OF THE UNREALISED SPIRIT

Jonatán Gődény

> *Indeed, you make me laugh you people of the present! And especially when you are amazed at yourselves!*
>
> — Friedrich Nietzsche[36]

The Situation of Contemporary Man and His World

There is nothing that has not been written about the crisis of Western culture. The most significant works on the subject were published one hundred years ago. If one also includes those forerunners who, as Béla Hamvas remarked, did not recognise the crisis in its entirety but knew about its advent with complete clarity, then this period can be dated back even earlier. The epoch-making works of the eminent traditional thinkers have one thing in common, namely that they are even more relevant and significant today than when they were originally published. To understand this, it is enough to have a glance at the pages of *The Crisis of the Modern World* to see that René Guénon speaks of our time. The driving forces and the background factors of the crisis have remained the same over the course of time. We need not look further for evidence. It is no longer our task to point out hitherto undiscovered truths,

---

[36] Friedrich Nietzsche, *Thus Spoke Zarathustra*, trans. Adrian del Caro (Cambridge: Cambridge University Press, 2006), 94.

nor to come up with fanciful interpretations in order to add a unique colour to the assorted swirl of opinions. One thing is needful: simply to consistently recognise and rephrase the great principal truths about the subject that were lucidly formulated by our predecessors. The enterprise we need to embark upon is not so much about exploration, but rather discernment, that is the realisation of the fact that the theses formulated in the past are also valid today. As an existential concern, it remains for us to rediscover in the present circumstances the schemes which were carefully elaborated in the past. In this regard, Frithjof Schuon's concern for the traditional doctrines can also be applied: "Everything has already been said, and well said; but one must always recall it anew."[37] To put it another way, our concern is to point out, with greater or lesser shifts in emphasis, what has already been elucidated by our spiritual predecessors. It goes without saying that such a venture will not be as lofty, brilliant, or revolutionary as Oswald Spengler's monumental historical study, *The Decline of the West*, or the even more ground-breaking work by Julius Evola, *Revolt Against the Modern World*. Let us hastily add, however, that our own response cannot be and should not be the same as these works. It is our mission, above all, to give testimony for accepting and confirming the truth. Indeed, there is a crisis. What is more, it is the greatest one humanity has ever seen. What is needed now is not eccentricity, but to bring to the forefront those who dared to tell the truth and to honestly confess that the passage of time has also justified what they said.

The subtle tendencies referred to by the spiritual geniuses of the 20th century can now be seen unfolding in full clarity. Those tendencies, which were only in their germinal forms at the beginning of the 20th century, have become tares today. We have the 'advantage' of experiencing what our predecessors

---

[37] Frithjof Schuon, *Form and Substance in the Religions* (World Wisdom, 2002), viii.

were only able to predict. We also perceive those things in their tangible concreteness today, whilst the greatest luminaries of the past spoke of them merely as essential generalities. An increasingly clear picture emerges for us, one which Guénon, at the end of the Second World War, could only formulate thusly: "as for the 'counter-tradition,' we can still only see the preliminary signs of it."[38] And thus, one can obtain further evidence to clarify the unmistakable crisis of modern Western culture.

We say an 'advantage,' of course, only figuratively, since our age can be characterised in many ways but in no way as advantageous. It is precisely today that we can really feel the heavy burden of the crisis of the world resting on our shoulders. This, however, does not suggest that we are better than our ancestors, nor that fate is somehow more unfair to us. One must be careful not to portray oneself as a victim of the time by using his bitter situation to justify himself. No matter in what age one lives, the fatality of the crisis is experienced by everyone. From a certain point of view, there is nothing unique, nothing personal, and nothing exceptional about it. There is no room for self-pity, even if there is no doubt that the crisis is increasing in speed and strength and the descending movement of manifestation is also exponentially accelerating at an ever-increasing pace. For this reason, we can in no way afford to waste our time formulating sterile and hyper-rationalistic speculations. The chaos has been pointed out by many writers in many ways. There are also remedies, thousands of years old, for the way out, even if they cannot be readily adapted to the present circumstances. Once again, our central task is to find, recognise, and point out to our generation the truth that has been transmitted by the greatest crisis experts.

---

38 René Guénon, *The Reign of Quantity and the Signs of the Times*, trans. Lord Northbourne (Hillsdale: Sophia Perennis, 2001), 260.

The Realisation of the Spirit of Tradition

The Delusion of Progress

In *The Crisis of the World,* Hamvas observes that Western modernity is contradictory, because it must contain both respect for cultural values and destructive criticism of them. In light of this, he wrote that "the dramatic situation of modern man is how he establishes and can establish the balance between his complete dissatisfaction with culture and his complete approval of culture."[39] From this it follows that only those who, in addition to possessing the values of European culture, also have a heightened and clear awareness of the crisis, can be considered cultured in the strictest sense of the word. However, it seems that no one intends to take serious account of the recurring observations of the great thinkers of European history. It is not that this knowledge is hidden, since it is readily accessible in our days. However, one has a general impression that it is as if it has never been spoken of. If, in addition, we fail to see the crisis, then we are only partially able to make our own culture. Total blindness to the crisis also precludes the possibility of being able to distinguish between the appropriate values, since it is easy to see that value-awareness is also deficient in the absence of crisis-awareness. This general impression becomes even more impactful if we fail to perceive the fact that our civilisation is heading toward a cataclysm. The lack of insight into the fatal errors and fallacies of our time engenders the possibility of the sudden realisation that one has become incapable of making a meaningful distinction between truth and the illusion of truth, between quality and mere commercial kitsch. Immediately after the First World War, Spengler observed that the "ancient-medieval-modern" scheme in the science of history reveals much more about the myopic and egoistic mentality of its inventors than the intrinsic flow of the nature of history. Spengler himself clarifies:

---

[39] Béla Hamvas, *Krízis és katarzis,* Világválság (Budapest: Magvető, 1983), 37.

The cultures that are to come will find it difficult to believe that the validity of such a scheme with its simply rectilinear progression and its meaningless proportions, becoming more and more preposterous with each century, incapable of bringing into itself the new fields of history as they successively come into the light of our knowledge, was, in spite of all, never whole-heartedly attacked.[40]

Despite the relative popularity of Spengler's remarkable book, this trend has essentially remained the same. What is taught today in almost all European schools is that everything in the world has been inexorably progressing. Despite all the ups and downs and the temporary difficulties experienced in our world, it is always the most current state that is the most advanced and developed. Based on the viewpoint emphasised by Hamvas, this means that public education, even with the most benevolent appraisal, only imparts one half of the cultural knowledge that it needs to convey. According to the narrative of modernity, the disappearance of the guilds, the arrival of the steam engine, the invention of the light bulb, the outcome of the great wars in the world, and the emergence of the internet are all necessarily, even almost automatically, closely succeeding stations on the way to the future golden age. We are told that these stations are something like floors built on top of each other in an infinitely high building, which is reminiscent of the Tower of Babel. When the picture of progress in the world is somewhat nuanced over the course of higher studies, it is too late to make substantial corrections since, by that time, the gilded rhetoric about world progress has already gained a considerable foothold in the minds of those who are trained in modern education.

Even such worldwide turmoil as experienced in the last global crisis in 2020 cannot diminish this utterly unjustified hurrah-optimism that is so characteristic of our popular culture. In the background of the news relaying the number of deaths, economic regression, and bizarre technological

---

[40] Oswald Spengler, *The Decline of the West: Form and Actuality* (Facsimile Publisher, 2015), 16.

innovation, there is always a strange and somewhat inexplicable optimism and self-confidence. No doubt, the crisis today is often depicted as even more terrible than it really is, but it nonetheless seems as if the current situation remains permeated by the delirious atmosphere brought about by the pseudo-mythology of progress that has been hammered into our heads since our childhood. We are told that there is an issue with climate change, our health, public safety, immigration, and the economy, not to mention the constantly growing world population. Despite this, however, there is one thing with which there can be no issue at all: the new form of superstition that has emerged in the guise of progress, which nonetheless bleeds from too many wounds to be worthy of that name.

In a certain sense, of course, current European civilisation does know about the crisis. Nevertheless, it is unable to perceive it in its entire reality. It preaches about the crisis, but only to make its followers even more dependent on its panacea, i.e., progress, the very same progress that is the source of all the turmoil. Thus, contemporary Europe finds itself in a particular state of discordance: it deceives itself into thinking that it knows about the crisis, without having the courage to call into question the main conditions of the existence of this crisis, namely modernity. It has so little creativity that, in order to resolve the crisis, it can come up with nothing but an even more intensified modernity. This is identical to a situation in which we try to veil an earlier lie with an even greater one.

The Traditional Stance

The traditional thinkers have gone to the greatest extremes because they have had the courage to reject modernity completely. There can therefore be no doubt that they enjoy an exceptionally low popularity, since their central aim has always been to destroy with one blow the delusion that has been cherished for centuries. Their ontological status resembles a man who suddenly realises that he is dreaming and authoritatively decides that he no longer intends to participate in the headache-inducing carnival, and thus immediately resolves to wake up. He is a real killjoy. He disrupts the play of modernity in which everyone is searching with great enthusiasm for the missing components that will bring about a great utopia. The search continues through the lens of binoculars, under microscopes, on distant planets, and within the tiniest of particles. It has not been found yet, but soon enough, they say – we still need to wait, but not for long. All research, surveys, and studies indicate the same: it is coming. It is, however, not at all clear what is coming, except for one thing: it is going to be magnificent. As fascinating as this quest may be, the representatives of tradition find no interest in it - so little that all this hocus-pocus bores them to death. They consider it a circus, a humbug, a fraud, and a cheap self-delusion. Tradition provides everything one yearns for in spiritual life: religion, arts, sacred sciences, and a spiritual way of living. Therefore, from the viewpoint of tradition, modernity, with all its achievements, buzzes, and delirious dreams, is very questionable, to say the least.

Traditionalists understand the crisis best, as they clearly see the discrepancy between the way things are and the way they should be. Besides all its boastful inventions, modernity has altogether only aggravated the situation. It has corrupted our ontological relationship with nature, poisoned our ritual way of living, and betrayed God in favour of modern sciences and other materialistic caprices. It has smuggled new ideas into our culture in the spirit of disbelief, denial, rebellion, and destruction. Hamvas has succinctly remarked: "while the perfection of external things has reached a very high level, human beings have not only remained the same, but they have visibly descended into a far lower domain."[41] Schuon

---

41 Béla Hamvas, *Scientia Sacra*, Volume I (Budapest: Medio, 2006), 232.

has similarly noted: "But not only is there the grip of matter on the spirit, of outwardness on inwardness, of dispersion on concentration, there is also the predominance of psychism over the intelligence."[42] Modern man has apparently left his infancy and become mature. In fact, however, he has given way to a darkness that diverts him more and more from his original goal.

Culture means cultivation: the cultivation of man and the cultivation of culture. Man is cultivated by culture and *vice versa*. Culture preserves its high quality when man embraces it in a humble, intelligent, and living way. He can only contribute to it if he does not destroy the already existing harmony. He can construct, develop, subtract, and contribute only if he does not do so in the name of private arbitrariness and only if he does not lose sight of his ultimate goal. According to tradition, this goal is the following: to reunite oneself with one's own primordial nature: *Moksha, Bodhi, Nirvana, Sunyata, Sems Nyid, Salus, Sat-Cit-Ananda*, i.e., liberation, awakening, the arrest of becoming, emptiness, pure awareness, salvation, and being-consciousness-bliss. The particular names depend on a given tradition, but what matters is that one needs to realise one's own true nature. Tradition, or to put it more accurately, the ancient metaphysical knowledge of mankind, orients us towards this goal. As Hamvas says, "culture is the realisation of the spirit preserved by tradition,"[43] and it is precisely modernity that distances us from it.

The stalwart representatives of modernity, however, cannot swallow this bitter pill. In general, modern man has an erudition that is "purely bookish and verbal, one that allows its possessor to speak with assurance about everything, even including what he is most ignorant of."[44] When encountering new ideas, he gets

---

42 Frithjof Schuon, *Roots of the Human Condition* (World Wisdom Books, 1991), 110.

43 Hamvas, *Scientia Sacra*, I., 236.

44 René Guénon, *Perspectives on Initiation*, trans. Henry D. Fohr, ed. Samuel D. Fohr (Hillsdale, Sophia Perennis, 2004), 217-18.

upset, boils over with anger, and considers a counterattack - mostly, of course, under the surface, i.e., merely within himself. It seems that he is not bothered by anything in the world. It is better to pretend as if nothing essential was ever spoken of. Even so, he makes a science out of what has been spoken. He starts to scrutinise under a microscope what Guénon, Evola, Coomaraswamy, and Schuon have said about modernity and its progeny. In his eyes, these authors are only specimens of a specific thought system. Like other fleeting figures, they are only dots, bright spots in the endless web of the history of ideas, i.e., curiosities. People today are hardly concerned with the personage of Jesus, Shankaracharya, or Abhinavagupta, or if they are, then they approach them as would a modern scientist when he encounters a hitherto unknown species of animal: exclaiming 'Oh, how strange it is!', he immediately dissects the lifeless and stuffed being and places it among his other prized trophies. It is neither seen with any consequence nor considered with any genuine reflection, since he does not incorporate the knowledge he gains into his existence. Strange as it may seem, he does relate to the metaphysical doctrines even more seriously than those who take their values earnestly and try to apply them in their lives, but he does so merely on the surface. What he achieves with all this is merely sprinkling water on the truths which burn with great flames in these works. He diverts their straight trajectory and softens their revelatory powers. What is more, he leeches and mummifies them, banishing them all into a museum.

Despite his aversion towards the modern world, the Traditionalist who has spent his life ceaselessly maturing his outlook has no intention of rejecting the knowledge accumulated in the modern age. One cannot reproach modernity for not providing what it cannot provide. Modern man, who has not the faintest idea of the true nature of the crisis, always misunderstands the attitude of the Traditionalist. He is terrified of losing his well-established existence, which, despite its shortcomings, failures, and superficiality, still fills him with satisfaction. He associates with the man of tradition the ferocity of the anarchist and the clumsiness of the fire-starting savage. He sees only recklessness in his radicalism, a lack of empathy and compassion in his severity, and impracticality in his spirituality. The man of tradition, however, as so suggestively described by Hamvas in *Scientia Sacra*, is totally free from this type of rigidity: "The reason why the sacred subject could have been the Master of Life is because [...] he summoned the gods with his personal presence, in him existence was revealed in its quintessence, and his universal being radiated the vigilance of the primordial age."[45]

It is true that the Traditionalist despises modernity; however, his attitude and activities are not determined by confrontation with the *Zeitgeist*, but by the endeavour to realise the spiritual dimension of human existence. He stands firm in maintaining that any loftiness found in modernity from Descartes to the postmodern philosophers, from Dostoyevsky to Krasznahorkai, from Mozart to Black Metal, from Leonardo da Vinci to Tarkovsky, is found merely because it still carries the germs of the traditional spirit within itself. Anything that is inspiring, spiritual, essential, qualitative, and metaphysical in a modern work is precisely because it can still preserve the splendour of the traditional world. This is presumably the reason why he is willing to interact with this layer of the modern world which he tries to transform into his innermost nature. He does so not *because* it is modern but *even though* it is modern.

Among other things, the man of tradition must know the elements of European culture to be able to form an appropriate judgement about it. In the absence of sufficient knowledge, criticism may be justified, but it is by no means convincing. He attempts to make certain segments of modern culture a part of his own. And therefore, although parts of it appear with a different accent in his life, they are still present, even more

---

45   Hamvas, *Scientia Sacra* I, 68.

so since he knows their failings. Thus, he is far from being a person who buries his head in the sand by blindly glorifying the past, and thus far from one who refuses to live in the present to tackle its calamities. It is not his desire to yearn for the past, and even less does he intend to escape from it: what he wants instead is to revive the archaic knowledge so unmistakably exhibited in the past. He demonstrates it in every word he utters, in every thought he writes, and in every action he performs. Be they modern or not, he seeks its reverberations in all cultural phenomena. He is primarily concerned with the voice of the ancestors, the message of tradition, and the manifestation of the spirit, which are the heart and the engine of culture. Such is what makes cultivation effective, actual, and true. It is what makes a culture culture.

Those Who Remained Standing among the Ruins

Amongst the traditional thinkers, it was Guénon who pointed out the crisis most acutely. To read his books is like being woken up at dawn by a bucket of ice-cold water. He is ruthlessly penetrating and straightforward. Those who encounter his writings for the first time and lack the required intellectual qualification will undergo an existential commotion, as if the world we have imagined were suddenly turned upside down; bad is the good, good is bad, progress is regress, light is darkness, and the truth is deception. As he remarks: "We have in fact entered upon the last phase of the Kali-Yuga, the darkest period of this "dark age," the state of dissolution from which it is impossible to emerge otherwise than by a cataclysm."[46] Elsewhere he wrote of the "satanic nature" of "the origin of the modern deviation": "The word 'satanic' can indeed be properly applied to all negation and reversal of order, such as is so incontestably in evidence

---

46 Rene Guénon, *The Crisis of the Modern World*, trans. Marco Pallis, Arthur Osborne and Richard C. Nicholson (Hillsdale: Sophia Perennis, 2001), 17.

in everything we now see around us: is the modern world really anything whatever but a direct denial of all traditional truth?"[47]

Guénon is rigorous and radical in his expressions, in which evasive and myopic speculations play no role at all. It is not surprising that most people have recoiled from his works. Even the loudest climate warriors, who envisage the darkest vision of the future, cannot bear such a radical tone. Moreover, being a highly reclusive man, he is unusually cold and aloof. He gives no room for any individuality, any personal opinion, or sentimentalism. Guénon offers nothing more than what he promises, and he does so with surgical precision, heightened vigilance, and spiritual seriousness. What one can get from his writings is neither more nor less than the bare truth.

The Crisis of the Modern World and *The Reign of Quantity and the Signs of the Times* are like a map. Anyone who has read these two works can no longer go astray in the chaos of the contemporary world. The only thing one needs to do is to substitute the unknowns in the equation of our time with the main concepts laid down in these writings. In so doing, to put it plainly, one comes to deal with descent rather than ascent, quantity rather than quality, individualism rather than unity, materialism rather than spirituality, and modern mechanistic science rather than the sacred. Henceforth, everything that has happened suddenly makes sense. Once we have recovered from the initial shock, we realise that reading Guénon's works looks more like a journey to the top of a huge mountain from where we can survey the landscape stretching below and breathe the immensely clear air. The image of the world, which previously seemed confused, becomes sharper and clarified. Together with the distressing awareness of the crisis, an inner yearning also appears. We have in mind the seed of a spiritual mission that penetrates the heavenly heights and which is masculine, noble, serious, free from sentimentality and modern frippery.

---

47 Guénon, *Reign*, 198.

The Realisation of the Spirit of Tradition

If we look at Evola's writings, it becomes clear that, although he seeks to point out the same spiritual summit, his works are permeated by provocative thoughts that immediately evoke a peculiar feeling in the readers. After a few pages, one would suddenly recruit an army against the modern world, issue declarations, wage war, and make sacrificial offerings to the deities. One feels as if noble blood started to flow through one's veins and one can hear the ever-increasing whispers vibrated by unearthly powers in one's ears. One would most willingly raise one's chin a few inches higher, erect one's posture, and feel tempted to analyse the sharp facial features of the Roman aristocrats. Evola writes: "The only thing that matters today is the activity of those who can "ride the wave" and remain firm in their principles, unmoved by any concessions and indifferent to the fevers, the convulsions, the superstitions, and the prostitutions that characterize modern generations."[48] What a truly invigorating thought! Here, too, one feels the urge to immediately reach for the hilt of one's non-existent sword and, in imagination, start slaughtering the Titans who are about to besiege Olympus.

For Evola, offering a detailed representation of the crisis is at once an excellent opportunity to cast light upon the greatness of the original nobility. He also elucidates features of European culture that have hitherto not received adequate emphasis. For instance, the aristocratic or heroic attitude which was an integral part of the great European culture of the past, and whose features seem utterly incompatible with the latest concepts of culture. In the contemporary world, these spiritual virtues are almost totally neglected. As Evola writes: "There is a well-known intellectual and humanist type who fosters an almost hysterical intolerance for anything referring to the political world - state ideals and authority, strict discipline, war, power, and domination - and denies them any spiritual

---

[48] Julius Evola, *Revolt Against the Modern World*, trans. Guido Stucco (Rochester, Vermont: Inner Traditions International, 1995), xxix-xxx.

or cultural value."[49] According to Evola, this moral decadence is one of the glaring symptoms of the crisis. Modern Western culture is a hotbed for the impotent armchair philosophers and the abstract artists who, as the devil hates Holy Water, abhor the cult of strength, power, masculinity, spiritual superiority, and sacred horizons. Even if Evola sometimes goes too far with his criticism, nonetheless, his arguments are fully valid. Culture has become too flabby, bourgeois, abstract, and spiritless. It lacks loftiness, dignity, and an important element that is more than human. It is devoid of the spiritual fire and power which could devastate the decors of the ordinary and lukewarm life and break through the veil of profanity. We speak of a culture that ideally allows its inhabitants to boldly look into the unknown, and which evokes the awe of transcendence. Culture is not only about the harmonious arrangement of this world, but must open its doors to what is beyond life so as to allow man to rise toward the Absolute. In Evola's works, this principle seems to have appeared with at least just as much force as the amount of resistance that has been aroused against it amongst the vanguards of modern culture.

Béla Hamvas also illustrates the dimensions of the crisis in such a way that often evokes the splendour of tradition. In his masterpiece, *Scientia Sacra*, the stench and darkness of the crisis is barely noticeable. We experience instead the serenity, vigilance, tranquillity, beauty, naturalness, and harmony which characterised the pinnacle of the traditional world. Whilst Guénon and Evola give clear testimony to the indispensable metaphysical truth of tradition, in the writings of Hamvas one discovers the beauty which radiates through the veils of the truth: we love the truth because the truth is beautiful. His writing bespeaks of such a harmony of the traditional world that one feels impelled to sit at the feet of Lao Tzu to listen to his teachings. The images depicted by him entice us

---

49 Julius Evola, *Ride the Tiger: A Survival Manual for the Aristocrats of the Soul*, trans. Joscelyn Godwin and Constance Fontana (Rochester, Vermont: Inner Traditions, 2003), 151-152.

so greatly that we immediately aspire to participate in the labour of the traditional carpenter whose activity intends nothing more than to imitate the creation of the universe. We desire to plough with the peasant who, in the light of our newly transformed views, appears to be wiser than an eminent university professor. From the Egyptian tradition through Hinduism and Buddhism to Christianity, we wish to breathe in the spiritual fragrance of tradition. We would like to hunt for bison with the Native American Indian warriors, help the shamans with performing their ceremonies, and meditate with hermits who have retreated to distant mountains. Suddenly, we desire to know our ancestors and all that they knew. We are stimulated to live like those "who knew and felt beyond themselves the perfection of the infinitely divine existence."[50] Hamvas depicts the beauty of human life in such a dazzling fashion that the dark clouds of the modern world seem to dissipate. The objectively comfortable aspects of our life, which we once considered so important, lose their meaning. In their writings, both Guénon and Evola put great emphasis on the interpretation of the essentially synthetic character of spiritual ideas and symbols, but perhaps it is Hamvas who is the most capable of conveying to us the feeling, thought, colour, smell, and taste, i.e., the reality of that of which mainstream culture today has lost even the faintest memory.

Whilst in the writings of Evola one finds the spiritual significance of the idea of authority and power that dominated the traditional world, Guénon, on the other hand, is greatly concerned with the notion of purity and the neutral superiority that deeply permeated the same epoch. Hamvas, however, is primarily impressed by the spiritual atmosphere arising from the essence of tradition, its all-pervading taste, which, for him, evokes the flavour of ripe fruit. In order, however, to discover those elements of the traditional world which have not been mentioned above, we must turn to other prominent traditional

---

50 Hamvas, *Scientia Sacra*, I, 72.

thinkers, such as Jean Hani, whose works are indispensable for understanding the leitmotif of the relationship between medieval Christians and the crafts. His work is a good place of entry to learn how Christians in the Middle Ages perceived the worldly manifestations of the universal divine activity in writing, cultivation, healing, pottery, combat, fishing, and gardening. One also needs to be immersed in the intuitive and intellective brevity demonstrated by Frithjof Schuon, not to mention the unparalleled knowledge permeated by Brahmanical loftiness presented by Ananda Kentish Coomaraswamy.

In order to understand the true meaning of the holy, it is also necessary to acquire the knowledge presented by Mircea Eliade and Rudolf Otto. Let us here also allude to the writings of Martin Lings, which explore how even such compositions which, at first glance, seem profane, can carry spiritual ideas expressing the truth. Furthermore, we must also remember that Titus Burckhardt's expositions of the sacred arts are essential for understanding the spiritual influence conveyed by traditional architecture. For spiritual guidance about India, one must turn one's attention toward the volumes written by Arthur Osborne and Paul Brunton. As far as Hungarian native speakers are concerned, they simply cannot overlook András László's penetrating thoughts, which always reach the very core of whatever subject he treats.

In studying the writers named above, however, we would only be fulfilling the first part of our spiritual journey, as the Herculean labour would still remain: the need to immerse oneself in the primary traditional sources, such as the spirituality of the Upanishads, the discourses of the Buddha, the spiritual treasuries provided by Padmasambhava, the Old and the New Testaments, the teachings of the Christian saints, the Quran, the wisdom of the Sufis and Confucius, including the Tao Te Ching. But we must go even beyond this line, since a mere theoretical understanding of the teachings has always been considered to be inadequate. In other words, we must cultivate what we have learned from these doctrines. Moreover, this must be accomplished with the greatest vigour, the sincerest humility, and the most profound attitude so that we can approach the spiritual states from which this knowledge emanates. This is how traditional culture, or the true tradition of culture, can be revived in one's life.

The Degradation of Culture

Up until now, we have argued that modern Western culture is experiencing a devastating crisis. In what follows, we shall see the reasons why our assumptions concerning this crisis are only partially true. From one specific avenue of approach, culture as such no longer exists, taken both in the traditional and the modern sense of the word. Given this, its collapse will be imminent. As we have pointed out, in traditional societies, culture meant, above all, the cultivation of the human soul. What we perceive today is precisely the contrary: culture has become a cheap product rather than a means of perfection. Everything has been turned upside down: film is produced for the sake of marketing, newspapers for advertising, and cultural guidebooks for attracting viewers, subscribers, sharers, followers, likes, etc. The point is the continuous increase of numbers. As a product, culture has hence become an excuse, a mere stimulus to attract our attention. By means of its falsification, it has become an empty and worthless content provider. The reason why many people who consider themselves to be cultured speak of culture is because they simply intend to tattle about themselves. It is not an exaggeration to say that we live in an age of cultural prostitution, wherein culture, like a strumpet, is passed from hand to hand by TV channels, book publishers, and influencers who yearn for five minutes of fame. These revealing signs indicate that our era will soon come to an end and that it either may be about to move into postmodernity or, in fact, has already done so.

In spite of this upending of culture, our society could potentially be richer than ever, given that the cultural treasuries of the entire world are now within our reach. Here we have in mind the varying types of cultural forms which could enrich our life, such as Japanese martial arts, tea ceremonies, and landscape gardening, as well as Indian dance, music, scriptures, and exotic food, including the unique statutes, buildings, and teachings of Tibetan Buddhism. This cultural current, however, is also highly contradictory, as it embraces both the most foolish customs and the most beautiful sacred masterpieces of the world. Despite this, or precisely due to what we have said above, culture nonetheless has lost its gravity. The enormous amount of information proliferating today makes contemporary man yearn for new areas of knowledge. However, as soon as he actually encounters a new area, he immediately forgets the previous one, as it is almost impossible to keep in mind the magnitude of available information, a significant part of which is completely irrelevant. This situation entails the accumulation of gigantic amounts of information that rest in the servers of computer terminals and need only one click to be accessed anywhere in the world. Since the knowledge is always accessible on the servers, the convenience of this permanently prevents one from seriously engaging with anything essential. Most of us in our time, however, have failed to foresee how the unlimited information accumulated on machines would bring about the most uncultured society of any era in human history. The following words of Nietzsche also reflect this state: "All ages prattle against each other in your minds; and the dreams and prattling of all ages were more real than even your waking is!"[51]

Contemporary man cannot but marvel at the knowledge possessed by the luminaries of the past. He sees the polymath as immeasurably distant from himself, if he notices him at all. The polymath speaks at least five languages, is well versed

---
51 Nietzsche, *Thus Spoke Zarathustra*, 94.

in the world of art and its history, plays and composes music, hunts, is familiar with a wide variety of geographical locations, can read the signs of the natural environment, is at home in politics and likes dwelling in the world of religions. In the eyes of many, this level of cultural knowledge is a prime example of an unnecessary effort and a complete waste of time, time that should have been used for the infantile enjoyment of freedom, a highly prevalent mistake in the world today. What is the benefit of knowing, for instance, when Caesar was born, if we could find out with a click on our smartphone? Why should we learn languages when we can consult Google Translate, which satisfies our needs, albeit inaccurately? In fact, why should we remember anything at all when the camera footage speaks for itself?

What was once the erudition of man has now become merely the data of the machine, such as the records of Wikipedia, "virtual intelligence assistants" or "knowledge navigators." We have all the knowledge needed to live in the modern world. However, it is an artificial erudition, since genuine knowledge has been replaced by information recorded in machines. This amounts to having nothing, since our cultural knowledge from here on out is preserved by the computer, and thus it is limited to the machine. A man with genuine cultural erudition is not yet a transcendent man, since he is still fallible; however, he possesses a definite and clear supremacy over the world. He stands firmly on his feet, and due to the knowledge he has digested, he can make judgements, decisions, and considerations soberly. He is on the open water like everyone else, but his knowledge rivals the power of a battleship that is equipped with loyal sailors, food, new sails, and weapons. Contemporary man, on the contrary, seems to be a shipwreck, desperately struggling among the huge waves without a life jacket. In the meantime, mesmerised by some strange enchantments, he envisions the pledge of his escape among the wreckage of his former ship. He cherishes a hope that the various automatisms which have always helped him will do so in the future - and therefore, he will be saved.

From the above, it may seem obvious that it is no longer necessary to acquire knowledge insofar as we have our "procedural thinker," namely the machine which thinks for us. But perhaps what is even more astonishing is that it will soon no longer be necessary to be actively engaged in anything at all, since machinery will act for us. It seems to us that one of the main directions of postmodern culture, which has heavily merged with technology, is to bring all human activities to an end, including the activity of the mind, i.e., thinking. The postmodern mentality is no longer characterised by the absurd dictum "I think, therefore I am," but rather by "I surf on the Net, therefore I am." Machinery takes the place of the worker, but it is often forgotten that it also usurps the place of the Creator. Artificial Intelligence writes letters, composes music, makes phone calls, drives a car, orders food, harvests crops, plays chess, cures pain, etc. The way it works is still stumbling, sluggish, and stalling – but it works. Of course, it will never be perfect, although all this is enough to cause destruction, falsification, deception, and usurpation in our life. All this suggests not only that human knowledge becomes unnecessary, but so do expertise and skills. In fact, this is a declaration of war against sanctified ritual work, which is undoubtedly one of the most essential elements of culture. What is more, it is an all-encompassing war in which the goal is the total subjugation of man's spiritual values. In fact, it is nothing but ignorance and denial of the assertion that "to practice a trade is to act upon the world with a view to transform it; it is, consequently, to extend God's work", since "all occupations imitate God."[52] We have immeasurably distanced ourselves from the times in which, as Eliade observed, "Religious man assumes a humanity that has a transhuman, transcendent model. He does not

---

52 Jean Hani, *Divine Craftsmanship, Preliminaries to a Spirituality of Work* (Angelico Press/Sophia Perennis, 2016), 3-4.

consider himself to be *truly man* except in so far as he imitates the gods, the cultural heroes, or the mythical ancestors."[53]

Our time produces many ignorant and helpless amoebas. Besides that, it manufactures machines that take the place of God and the divine action that otherwise raises human insensitivity towards true culture. For some reason or other, amidst a cheerful smirk, we are still persuaded to adore the *Zeitgeist*.

At this point, we have arrived at one of the most characteristic occasions of the modern age, the festivity of all festivity, the contest of untalented and ignorant nobodies in which every new bounder turns out to be the bright star of the day. The recipe has been the same for a long time: every year, many dilettantes are tested in competitions, which continually require less skill and intelligence each year. It is thus not surprising that the low level of the singing contests held a few years ago has also been surpassed already. In certain internet applications, it is enough to pretend to sing a pop song in order to be watched by millions and rewarded with a prize. It is usually followed by an invitation in which the "artist" is summoned to various shows where, we are told, the cacophonous genius of the "star" can change millions of lives. One wonders whether it is really a cheap comedy or a scam and whether we will find a candid camera, but none is found. Advancing at this pace, it is only a matter of time before the fight for popularity begins in the sensational programs of farting, belching, and breathing. "Oh, how you stand there, you sterile ones, how skinny in the ribs!"[54] – the words of the great Zarathustra echo in our ears. How far is this from the traditional artist who "belongs to a type of culture which is dominated by the longing to be liberated from oneself," wherein "human individuality is not

---

53 Mircea Eliade, *The Sacred and the Profane: The Nature of Religion*, trans. Willard R. Trask (New York: Harcourt, Brace & World, 1987), 99-100.
54 Nietzsche, *Thus Spoke Zarathustra*, 94.

an end but only a means?"[55] The modern artist, who has increasingly become separated from the Principle and who, due to his attachment to authorship, i.e., his egoism, is "a man not yet adult,"[56] languishes in the distance from imperceptible spiritual heights. As we have said above, if something is handed down in our time, it is mostly a means and not an end. We can see that, most of the time, it does not demand any significant content. In a corrupted society such as ours, nonentities are cultivated with nothing and made into naught. Because today, "where the process is heading towards, or supposedly progressing towards, is precisely into the naught."[57] The transmitter, if he transfers anything at all, is passing on merely his lack of knowledge about culture. What is transmitted is thus nothing but spectacle without content, humour without originality, and criticism without a message. "It is this empty, inconsequential and powerless activity wherein nothing is realised because there is nothing to be realised."[58] Although what we speak of belongs to the purview of mass culture, it also reflects, even if indirectly, the state of the putative high culture. The cultural elite itself which allows public awareness to sink to such infernal depths is not much different from this state. For the Traditionalist, this should come as no surprise, since this is what happens when one eradicates tradition and spirituality from culture. If the essence disappears, nothing remains, or if anything remains, then only that which is even worse: parody of genuine truth. This nothing which is said to be something is cultivated by the postmodern world under the banner of culture.

---

55 Ananda Kentish Coomaraswamy, *Christian and Oriental Philosophy of Art* (New York: Dover Publications Inc., 2011), 41.

56 Ibid, 41.

57 László András, *Tradicionalitás és létszemlélet* (Budapest: Persica, 2nd edition, 2014), 138.

58 Hamvas, *Scientia Sacra* I, 234.

The Realisation of the Spirit of Tradition

The Key for Transmission

Culture, just like tradition, needs to be handed down. The most vital and effective way to do so is through oral transmission. Culture, or to put it another way, essence, truth, and depth cannot exist without man. Culture cannot be handed down in the same way as one puts a bundle down on the floor, and by the same token, it cannot be simply handed over to someone for safekeeping. It is essential to gain a clear understanding of the teachings laid down in the sacred texts. But this does not mean that the theoretical study of these texts is sufficient in itself. Seeing a master eating a bowl of lentils or tying his shoelaces once is worth more than reading a hundred books. Like a succulent food, the books fill you up, provided only that you sprinkle it with the spice of the life and presence of the master. Being in the presence of a master, one can destroy and rebuild entire worldviews in a second. The master is the one who knows you better than you know yourself. It is, after all, the master himself who triggers one's irresistible desire to know oneself. According to the teachings of tradition, however, this cannot be, or can be only partially, realised without the power of the presence of the master. Something essential is always lost in the transmission through intermediaries, namely an invisible element, an inexplicable magical influence that is quintessential for spiritual empowerment and initiation and which nothing else can replace. Guénon states clearly:

> An oral transmission is always and everywhere considered a necessary condition of true traditional teaching, so much so that putting this teaching in writing can never dispense with it, and this because, to be really valid, its transmission implies the communication of a 'vital' element as it were, for which books could not serve as a vehicle.[59]

Based on the above logic, it is easy to see that the far more fashionable means of communication, such as the computer,

---

59 René Guénon, *Initiation and Spiritual Realization*, trans. Henry D. Fohr, ed. Samuel D. Fohr (Hillsdale: Sophia Perennis, 2004), 32.

the telephone, or the television, are not in the least suitable for anything relative to oral transmission.

One form of initiation in Tibet perfectly shows the importance of how intimacy and immediacy are linked to the transmission of knowledge. In the tradition of Dzogchen, for instance, the master whispers the divine words into the ears of his disciple through a long bamboo tube, so that the secret communication cannot be disturbed even by the wind. The procedure is only successful when the spiritual influences, transmitted during the ordeal, have immediate effects on the neophyte that can only be achieved by the power of the immediate presence.

It appears that our postmodern age tries to completely neglect this traditional law that applies not only to the highest forms of initiation, but also the lower methods of cultivation. The transmission of cultural elements is increasingly transferred to the online space. In other words, the communication of knowledge, which constitutes the essence of culture, is being virtualised. If there happens to be a master who wishes to transfer his knowledge with no ulterior motives, provided that there is a recipient who sincerely accepts it for the purpose of cultivation, the problem still remains that the vibrant immediacy which defines human existence disappears; smartphones, laptops, and virtual glasses are wedged between the transmitter and the receiver of knowledge. It follows that a whole generation of teachers are emerging who will interact with their students only in virtual schools. In the near future, due to the so-called extended reality, the teaching of markedly practical activities, such as electrical work, will be conducted in the online space. More recently, "cybersangha" has become very popular, wherein the aspirants, logged in from their home, perform joint meditation by staring at each other through the computer screen – not to mention the joint Christmas parties on Skype and the tragicomic phenomenon of online masses.

It can be seen from the above that the culture of human contact has become totally corrupted, which makes for fertile soil for mental illnesses and causes personality disorders whose end product is the antisocial person. The "Me Too" scandal, the disintegration of traditional family patterns, the protection measures against the pandemic, the Internet 2.0, condoms, porno – such corrupt healthy human interaction. It is as if all of this is driven by a vengeful rebellion against healthy human contact. If it is not what they intend to achieve, by their very nature it is what they cause. The fact that the sexual orientation of young people today is almost exclusively determined by the increasingly wild, perverted, unrealistic, and spectacle-oriented pornography is not the worst-case scenario; such a person, even if he follows bad patterns, at least attempts to make physical contact. Due to the revolutionary innovations of robotics and virtual reality, however, the presence of a sexual partner is now completely unnecessary. Whilst the sensation of the beloved body is ensured by the mechanically moved plastic limbs and genitals, its spectacle, on the other hand, is replaced by a hyperrealistic three-dimensional software. For those who would see only dystopia in such things, it is worth mentioning that today virtual pornography and increasingly lifelike sex robots are among the fastest growing markets in the world. For an already fragmented society, the cessation of physical touch and person-to-person contact, or at least its reduction to a minimal level, will be the ultimate *coup de grâce*. To create this, current technology has taken the lead; that technology, it is now certain, wants to devour and swallow the entire living space of humanity.

Resolution

Our former statement, namely that the West alone represents decadence, seems to be invalid. Through the overwhelming power of globalisation, corruption has taken over the whole world. Except, perhaps, for a few more remote settlements, the East has been Westernised, i.e., modernised, and by extension, desacralized. Due to the high-speed internet communication that spans the whole world, a current trend or news item can spread across the globe within a minute. There is no place in the world to which one can retire from the threat of modernity. "Moreover, the circumstances make it increasingly unlikely," Evola points out, "that anyone, starting from the values of Tradition [...], could take actions or reactions of a certain efficacy that would provoke any real change in the current state of affairs."[60] The hope for restoring the traditional world is an illusion; the modern world has distanced itself too far from its origin, and its ambition is too strong to give up everything that has been achieved. The locomotive increasingly accelerates; it is heading straight towards the abyss, and those who control it prefer to accept the fatal fall than to repent and admit their fundamental errors.

The external contest will never be meaningless; to take a stand, to point out errors, to oppose corruption, or to resubmit a claim for sanctity are all also forms of culture. A culture is culture when it involves real human beings and mature personalities and entails efforts to link this world with the afterworld. Therefore, as long as there are people, cultured personalities, and metaphysical aspirations, there is culture. If one is able and intends to work on oneself, is willing to go beyond one's own limits, is curious enough as well as intent on knowing spiritual realities – even if the ancient splendour has faded away – there will be culture.

According to the position of the traditional thinkers, in order to return to an existence permeated by the truth of tradition, it is not enough to know the features of European culture. It takes more than simply knowing Greek philosophy, the teachings of Socrates, Plato, and Aristotle. Nor is the wisdom of the Neoplatonists, the Christian Church Fathers, the holy tradition of the Catholic Church, mysticism, astrology,

---

60 Evola, *Ride the Tiger*, 2-3.

alchemy, or magic sufficient in themselves. The brighter gleams of the ancient philosophical tradition of European culture can no longer save contemporary man. Nor can its feats in literature, psychology, sociology, history of art, music, and natural sciences. Whilst these might have been sufficient for spiritual fulfilment 100 years ago, their meaning today has become so misunderstood, lost, misinterpreted, denuded, and vulgarised that it no longer ensures the achievement of the desired cultural standard. Being familiar and well-versed in Eastern cultures and traditions helps not only because it broadens our horizons, but also because, through them, we can better understand certain elements of our culture and tradition. Due to the contrast and comparison, lost analogies can receive meaning again, forgotten truths can come into focus, and statements that have become clichés can regain their former dignity. Putting the methodology of comparative theology into consideration, it can be interpreted as follows: "Comparative theology is not primarily about which religion is the true one, but about learning across religious borders in a way that discloses the truth of my faith, in the light of their faith."[61] This formulation by Francis X. Clooney may also be applied to the fields outside of theology.

Today, the culture of Western man is no longer exclusively the culture of Europe. Since he has access to other cultures, these cultures increasingly have an impact on his own, and so, to a certain extent, he also has a responsibility toward them. In this way, he also has the task of making the most valuable elements that are part of his extended culture. In this regard, there is only one thing that can help one to make a meaningful decision: tradition and spirituality. The goal of culture is to bring people back to religion, the culmination of which is God. Cultivation is not for its own sake: it serves the ultimate truth, which is always attainable under all circumstances, because its reality is not outside of and independent from us, but is inside,

---

61 Francis X. Clooney, SJ., *Comparative Theology: Deep Learning Across Religious Borders* (Wiley-Blackwell Publishing, 2010), 15-16.

i.e., within our essential self. As Lama Shabkar puts it, "The truth is that beings, though they do not know it, have not been distanced even an iota from their original and perfect state over the course of time: this is the reason why they do not recognise the essence, pure consciousness, because it is their home."[62] In the face of pseudo- and counter-cultures or the loss of culture in general, this unearthly quality shines in us forever, in a way that can never be crushed and taken from us.

Translated by Zsolt Sáfián

---

62 Sabkar Lama, *A hatalmas Garuda lebegése*, trans. Agócs Tamás (Budapest: Dzogcsen Fórum, 2020), 32

GUÉNON'S *CRISIS*, "CRISIS LITERATURE," AND NEGATIVE THOUGHT

Giovanni Sessa

In order to historically situate René Guénon's *The Crisis of the Modern World* (1927) — a work of synthesis that presents the theoretical traits connoting the meta-historical vision of "integral Traditionalism" — in any convincing manner, and to highlight its value, it would be good to place it, as Julius Evola appropriately did in his introduction to the Italian edition, within the vast production of what has been defined as the "literature of crisis." Guénon's outlook, centred on a radical opposition to modernity and founded upon references to *pure, superrational intellectuality*, was the only one in those years to place itself beyond the boundaries marked by the idea of the world that was established in the West by the end of the Middle Ages and later became common sense. It did so both in terms of its intellectual instrumentation, i.e., in its diagnosis of the epochal disease, as well as in the therapy identified to recover the Way to *health*. This was pointed out even by Roberto Calasso, the founder of the famous Italian publishing house Adelphi and a scholar who is not a Traditionalist in the proper sense: "While culture critics, even the most radical ones [...] have always kept many ties with the object of their attacks, Guénon is the only one to have eschewed all those ties from the beginning, and to have described the Western world, as if he contemplated it from an outlying distance, as the land where "the ripe fruit falls at the feet of the tree."[63]

---

63   René Guénon, *Il Regno della Quantità e i Segni dei Tempi* (Milan: Adelphi, 1982), back cover description by Roberto Calasso.

It is therefore essential to ask ourselves about the *ubi consistam* of "crisis literature," since the French esotericist's book is, in some respects, involved in it, even though the radicality of Guénon's work's prospects and solutions differentiate it. "Crisis culture," as recalled by Michela Nacci, who has extensively dealt with the subject, had its historical epicentre between the two World Wars, its place of choice in the Musilian *Kakanien* and its reference text in *The Decline of the West* by Spengler.[64] Within the literature of crisis, *deprecatio temporis* became the collective heritage of a generation of intellectuals who were aware of the inanity of progress and of the risks implicit in technology. A generation of thinkers, writers, and artists who argued by oppositions and who soon learned to "move between dichotomies, in which on the one hand there were the characteristics of the present time, and on the other hand there were their positive, opposite [...] epochs of civilisation and epochs of culture."[65] The opposition between *Kultur* (Culture) and *Zivilisation* (Civilisation), which was central to German thought from Spengler to Mann, would have thus become the dialogical object of a significant part of the European *intelligentsia*, among which Guénon himself must be counted. He identified the propulsive trait of *civilisation* as: "the tendency to bring everything down to an exclusively quantitative point of view [...] This tendency is most marked in the 'scientific' conceptions of recent centuries; but it is almost as conspicuous in other domains... so much so that [...] our period could almost be defined as being essentially and primarily the 'reign of quantity.'"[66]

---

64 Cf. Michela Nacci, *Tecnica e cultura della crisi (1914-1939)* (Turin: Loescher, 1982), 9-26.

65 Ibid, 11.

66 Cf. Guénon, *Il regno della Quantità*, 12 [René Guénon, *The Reign of Quantity and the Signs of the Times*, trans. Lord Northbourne (Hillsdale: Sophia Perennis, 2001), 3].

The Restless Spirits of the Eve

The fire of polemics flared up in Europe in the decades between the two World Wars and set *the reign of quantity* as its target. Frightening cracks in the certainties of the *belle époque* and positivism had shown up, well in advance, at the end of the *romantic* nineteenth century. They were heralded, amongst various other symptoms, by Brunetière's proclamation of the "bankruptcy of science" and by the tragic gunshots which interrupted the spiritual, as well as actual, youths of Otto Weininger and Carlo Michelstaedter.[67] These two precocious Central Europeans, facing the existential, social, and political *insecuritas* that connoted the epoch in which they lived, produced *strong* answers that aimed to tear asunder the nihilistic horizon. Their intellectual production,

---

67 Ferdinand Brunetière, teacher at the Sorbonne and distinguished literary critic of the second half of the 19th century, positivist in his formation, at first developed an approach to literature centred on a classifying schematism, which led him to rigidly distinguish literary genres. In the last period of his life he converted to Catholicism and developed a decidedly more critical view of scientific knowledge. Otto Weininger was born in 1880 in Vienna, where he committed suicide in 1904 at the age of twenty-four, in the house where Ludwig van Beethoven had lived. His main work, *Sex and Character*, whose first edition was published in 1903, in 1921 had reached its twenty-second edition. In it, he theorised the absolute Man and Woman as meta-empirical types, of which the first one is positive and the second one is negative, putting forward the idea of spiritual sexuation. The thesis turned out to be explosive in the cultural climate of the epoch. Carlo Michelstaedter, from Gorizia and with Jewish origins — a heritage which he shared with Weininger —, shifted the dichotomy of the literature of the crisis (*Kultur / Zivilisation*) to the contraposition between *rhetoric* and *persuasion*. The first one was identified as the life of correlation, as the continuous deferment of desire, an aesthetic life incapable of knowing the full possession of itself; the second one as the outcome of a mystical journey aimed at self-conquest, an example of *practical Eleaticism*. He took his own life on 17 October 1910, when he was only twenty-three. It is worthwhile to remember that Michelstaedter's positions acted in depth on the philosophical formation of Julius Evola. Cf. Otto Weininger, *Sesso e carattere* (Rome: Edizioni Mediterranee, 1992); Carlo Michelstaedter, *La persuasione e la rettorica* (Milan: Adelphi, 1992); Julius Evola, *Saggi sull'idealismo magico* (Rome: Edizioni Mediterranee, 2006). I take the liberty of referring to my essay, too, *Dal misticismo michelstaedteriano al magismo evoliano*, in *Carlo Michelstaedter e il Novecento filosofico italiano*, ed. Daniela Calabrò and Rosella Faraone (Firenze: Le Lettere, 2013), 173-183.

focused on Lukács's early "Platonism," was in an eminent sense an *ethos*, a practical attitude, an attempt to trace a possible new *Abode* for atomised mankind. Theirs was an intellectual experiment whose antecedent is to be found in Max Stirner, theorist of the *Unique*, who knew that the Absolute, "which admits no mediations, the univocal, is only the concrete, individual phenomenon"[68] — provided that it was assumed in its constitutive nakedness, as a singular presence.

We are referring to that congeries of thought which Massimo Cacciari defined as the "metaphysics of youth" and which embraces the generation born "around" 20 November 1889, the day when Gustav Mahler conducted his First Symphony at the Budapest Philharmonic.[69] It is connoted by a speculative and existential experience marked by the *negative* and by the refusal of any transcendental reference, matured through the exegesis of Stirner and Nietzsche. Our authors were induced to live Socratically, by giving priority to the ethical dimension, taking a decision and choice which with them, unlike what happened to Kierkegaard, was no longer aimed at the religious in the proper sense, but to the *Werk*, to the work which, in such a perspective, should have realised the reunion of life and thought, of the finite and the infinite.

Such authors carried within themselves, as an unacknowledged speculative foundation, the Vaihingerian philosophy of the *als-ob*, of the *as-if*. To put it in Cacciari's words, the theoretico-practical "heroism" to which they devoted themselves: "consists [...] in forbidding us all illusions and, in this state of the soul, in aiming at giving shape to our *in-dividual, as if* we were living in a Culture, *as-if* that in-dividual

---

68 György Lukács, *L'anima e le forme* (Milan: Sugarco, 1991), 76.

69 Cacciari expresses himself this way: «This is the time of memory. All those born "around" Mahler's First participate in it: their "youth" is only a compositional element, a movement in the context of the Symphony, fuguing towards its own *Trauermarsch* (funeral march)». Massimo Cacciari, *Metafisica della gioventù*, in György Lukács, *Diario (1910-1911)* (Milan: Adelphi, 1983), 71-148, here p. 72.

were truly a symbol."⁷⁰ Cacciari further pointed out that in the background of such authors' vision there was Schopenhauer's *World* and, in their perspective, there was Franz Rosenzweig's *The Star*, the latter of which was not coincidentally written amidst the trenches of the First World War.⁷¹ Such culture shares the same polemical goal represented by the aesthetic or rhetoric life, since: "for the aesthete, the world and the I swing in the everlasting *insecuritas* of the *Stimmung*, of the state of the mind."⁷² Many authors of the *crisis* leaned over the *Abgrund* (abyss). This is recalled by Franz Kafka in an apologue he wrote in 1918. In it, the Prague writer confronts the figure of Prometheus, the symbol *par exellence* of that ardent and strong-willed age. Regarding Prometheus, he remarks that there exist four different versions of the myth and that the mythical tale always attempts to explain the unexplainable by placing itself in supra-rational terms: "And since it comes from a background of truth, it must end up again in the inexplicable."⁷³ The Germanist Marino Freschi comments on this passage in the following terms: "The Kafkian unexplainable is a way to narrate that "background of truth" which reason cannot indeed reach, perceive, explain, "clarify" — *er-klären* —, and which signals an essence, which is foundation and salvation beyond the sunset, beyond the West, the land of the evening, and which is still our own."⁷⁴

This statement locates us at the centre of the interpretive problem that we want to address: "crisis literature" has in itself two possible outcomes. The first one holds that the

---

70 Massimo Cacciari, *Metafisica della gioventù*, in G. Lukács, *Diario (1910-1911)*, 97.
71 Cf. Arthur Schopenhauer, *Il mondo come volontà e rappresentazione*, ed. Cesare Vasoli, vols. I and II (Bari: Laterza, 1972); Franz Rosenzweig, *La stella della redenzione*, ed. Gianfranco Bonola (Genoa: Marietti, 1998).
72 Massimo Cacciari, *Interpretazione di Michelstaedter* (Turin: *Rivista di Estetica*, n. 22, 1986), 21-36, here p. 22.
73 Franz Kafka, *Prometeo*, in *Racconti*, It. trans. by Ervinio Pocar (Milan: Meridiani-Mondadori, 1987), 430.
74 Marino Freschi, *1918. Tramonti tedeschi* (Acireale-Rome: Bonanno 2018), 128.

fragmentation is insurmountable, i.e., it interprets presence, actuality, our "here and now," in terms of mere subjectivity, of historicity, of a desacralised and insuperable immanence. From such a perspective, the wistfulness for Order may, at best, tend towards the restoration of a seeming, simulated Harmony. The second one, well exemplified by anti-modern positions, explicitly recovers the *symbol* as the Way to the Origin, to the completeness of the Principle — the *symbol* as *epistrophe*, as transitable return to a bygone situation of substantial Order, founded upon the con-secration of Power descending from above. Probably, as noticed by Massimo Cacciari, the will to save the phenomenon, the lost fragment, that was proper to crisis thinkers, indicates a deeper motivation: the will to rediscover, in any case, the *idea*, the archetype of the phenomenon, its symbolic dimension.[75] Therefore, the two Ways are not so antithetical as such might appear to a superficial approach.

These different proposed solutions bear witness, first of all, to the pervasive scale taken by the crisis in the twentieth century. Such yielded the loss of the "homeliness" of reality, that is to say, the impossibility of mankind recognising the familiar features of reality, the phenomenon described by Weber with the term "disenchantment of the world," which is the ultimate outcome of techno-science, of the *Gestell* (the Enframing), whose logics have dis-animated *physis* (nature) and made it into mere unqualified space, while at the same time reifying human relationships. The *revolt of the masses* of which one important intellectual of the *crisis*, Ortega y Gasset, magistrally spoke, has been nothing but the un-eschewable point of arrival of a path of decadence driven by existential disorder incubated for a long time, even since the autumn of the Middle Ages,

---

75 Cf. Massimo Cacciari, *Metafisica della Gioventù* in Lukács, *Diario (1910-1911)*, 71-148. The Venice philosopher specifies that for the Hungarian thinker, the return to the *symbol* only happens *melancholically*, as a *memory* of what was and no longer is. A negative recovery of the symbolic, therefore, would stride through Lukács' early research, which would be a crossroads of crisis literature.

by European culture and humanity, which finally bursted in the modern epoch in pandemic terms.[76] Michela Nacci hit the mark by pointing out that "crisis culture is shapen towards apocalypticism; since the values that it considers fundamental for a civilisation have disappeared [...] it is possible to get out of this civilisation, i.e., to save oneself by returning to foregoing conditions, otherwise, all that remains is catastrophe."[77] And it is exactly to these aspects that Guénon's *Crisis* draws the reader's attention, putting into the equation the possibility of a possible new beginning.

The End of the World and Cultural Apocalypses

The *World of Yesterday* of which Stefan Zweig left an indelible memory, the world nostalgically longed for across many of the pages of the "literature of crisis," dissolved together with the empire of the two-headed Eagle at the end of the First World War. On what values it was based, and what it meant to live that way, was made crystal clear by Joseph Roth in the epoch-making novel *Radetzky March*. In it, we read: "Thus it was in those days! Anything that grew took a long time to grow; and anything that ended needed a long time to be forgotten. But everything that had once existed had left its traces, and in those days we lived on memories as today we live upon the ability to forget quickly and without hesitation."[78] And yet, within that ordered, placid world — repetitive in the rhythms and rites of everyday life, seemingly natural like

---

76 The understanding of the crisis as the disease of the epoch was very clear to Carlo Michelstaedter, who thus wrote from Florence to his sister Paula in a missive dated 9 December 1906: «As for what concerns mental balance, it is partly individual, and partly the disease of the time, since we are precisely in an epoch of transition in society, when all ties seem to be loosening and the gearing of interests is dispersed, and the paths of existence are no longer clearly traced in every environment (*Epistolario*, ed. Sergio Campailla (Milan: Adelphi, 1983), 158.

77 Cf. Nacci, *Tecnica e cultura*, 12.

78 Cf. Stefan Zweig, *Il mondo di ieri. Ricordi di un europeo*, (Milan: Mondadori, 1994); Joseph Roth, *La Marcia di Radetzky* (Milan: Adelphi, 1987), 28.

the unceasing rain that wetted the daytimes of stationmaster Fallmerayer in Roth's homonymous tale, or like the resounding footsteps of the Directors in the long and silent hallways of the *Kaiserlich und Königlich* High Schools, described with wistful emotion by Elias Canetti, Giani Stuparich and Franz Werfel — there suddenly broke through the devastating drives of *eros* and *thanatos*, almost in a symbiotic bond, to overwhelm the orlays and unswerving lives of skilled and devoted officers.[79] They broke through as a tangible sign of the subtle and perpetually operating action of the entropic forces of life, which is perennially exposed to *crisis*.

The existential trajectory of one of the best-known and widely-read heralds of the Order of *Mitteleuropa*, Adalbert Stifter, testifies to how the apocalypse was present *in fieri* in *Kakanien*. Stifter sang about the rural idyll, yearned for the recovery of the enchantment of a lost childhood, described ordered existences, and built a harmonic prose as the mirror of his contemplative relationship with reality, but, above all, he sensed the tragic essence of life. He vainly tried to silence, repress and stifle it, thus turning it, according to Claudio Magris, into an abstract moralism.[80] Stifter had neither the strength nor the courage to make himself a *posthumous man*, one who, according to Cacciari, "is not only the man who outlives the end of the Subject. It is also the man who begins to listen to the *Ab-grund* (Abyss),"[81] one who confronts the chaotic dimension of existence. The writer did not have the boldness to look at the Origin, the groundless ground, the Principle of Freedom, in its eyes, which would have made him capable of a free and rectifying action towards the oncoming

---

79 Cf. *Il capostazione Fallmerayer*, in Joseph Roth *Il mercante di coralli*, (Milan: Adelphi, 1991), 99-126; Elias Canetti, *La lingua salvata. Storia di una giovinezza* (Milan: Adelphi, 1990); Giani Stuparich, *Un anno di scuola e Ricordi istriani* (Turin: Einaudi, 1961); Franz Werfel, *Anniversario dell'esame di maturità* (Parma: Guanda, 1988).

80 Cf. Claudio Magris, *Il mito absburgico nella letteratura austriaca moderna* (Turin: Einaudi, 1988), in particular 151-161.

81 Cf. Massimo Cacciari, *Dallo Steinhof. Prospettive viennesi del primo Novecento* (Milan: Adelphi, 1980), 17.

end, and he, therefore, surrendered to the growing disorder, to decadence. Thus, he took leave of life prematurely.

In order to understand the modalities through which the idea of apocalypse is implied in "crisis literature," and how the theme of the *end of the world and/or of a world* is also a relevant element in Guénon's *Crisis*, it is worth treating Ernesto De Martino's theses, which have been hastily relegated exclusively to the field of ethnology. The Demartinian exegesis of the apocalyptic phenomenon makes use of complex tools, mainly of a philosophical type, which arise out of a close confrontation with anti-modern and/or crisis authors. In this wake, reference should be made, first of all, to De Martino's posthumous book *La fine del mondo*, which collects greatly diverse and manifold materials.[82] The book is tied together by two fundamental research tracks: the first refers directly to the apocalyptic theme, while the second deals with a reflection on mankind and its cultural destinies. As for the analysis of the apocalyptic theme, it begins "from psychopathological documentation, in consideration of its heuristic efficacy," its demonstrative capacity, to then move to the analysis of the major historical religions and of the festive institutions for the periodical renewal of the cosmos "which host within themselves the theme of the end of the world as a recurring *risk* and ritualise it."[83] The next step leads the scholar to deal with Christian apocalypticism, which places the perspective of ransom beyond the world, and to read the qualifying moment of the Marxian apocalypse, the immanentised variant of the Christian one, as a premise that is "necessary for the construction of an arrangement of reality *ab imis fundamentis*."[84] But, what we most need to refer to here

---

[82] Cf. Ernesto De Martino, *La fine del mondo. Contributo all'analisi delle apocalissi culturali*, ed. Clara Gallini (Turin: Einaudi, 2002). In the introduction written by Clara Gallini and Marcello Massenzio the text is defined as follows: "A workshop, therefore, in the rich sense of a term that refers to the various modes by which a research object may be inspected, exploring its most diverse implications" (p. IX).

[83] Ibid, X-XI.

[84] Ibid, XII.

is that, while analysing thought about the end in contemporary culture, De Martino evokes the image of the "descent to hell," thus grasping how the destruction of the world's homeliness, of the cultural/cultual *Heimat* (Fatherland-Abode) of mankind, made it impossible to transcend life into value, to shift from the natural to the cultural. Because of this, in some of its exponents the "literature of crisis" shares the *impassability*, the existential insuperability which is typical of psychopathological apocalypses. It has no way out: any perspective of reintegration, any New Beginning, is missing. Not so in Guénon, who, on the contrary, in *Crisis* describes the reasons for the *end of a world*, namely the modern one, beyond which he foretells the return of Order. The problem is that such a prophecy is based upon a cyclical view of history and, therefore, on a deterministic vision of the latter.

De Martino makes reference to a particular phenomenon which, decades later, reappeared in the research interests of James Hillman: the "loss of the soul," the *quintessence* of our times — a bereavement that, as can easily be observed, makes it impossible for individuals to have deep contact with the innermost Self and denies communities the recognition of their *ethos*, of their specific modality of encountering the world.[85] According to the scholar, the presence of the *crisis-ransom* nexus constitutes the criterion for attributing the prerogative of "culture" to certain apocalyptic formations; this happens when the end of the world "is assumed not as a fact, but as an impending *risk*."[86] The idea of the *end of a world* connotes Guénon's *Crisis* from within, but it is especially present in Evola's *thought about Tradition*, in that both of them, in the underlying assumptions of their own works, re-propose the essential role of myth and rite *for life*. The ethnologist, while starting from comparative historicism and aiming to build an ethnographic humanism as the ultimate outcome of modern humanism (we are well aware of this),

---

85 Cf. James Hillman, *Fuochi blu*, ed. T. Moore (Milan: Adelphi, 1996), 34-35.

86 De Martino, *La fine del mondo*, XV.

knows that rite complies with the model of the "naked" crisis, that which emerges in psychopathologies, but turns crisis into a "threat" of crisis, that is to say, ritualises it, activating processes of *effective reintegration* by virtue of the mediation exercised by the mythical symbol. In this sense, the exegesis of the Roman *mundus patet* ritual presented in *La fine del mondo* is exemplary. By *mundus* we refer to the pit that in Rome was opened three times a year and which released the dead to roam on earth. Under these circumstances, any human activity was halted, and a temporary "end of the world" was faced. Thus wrote De Martino: "The *mundus* ritual would evoke the risk of the crisis of the end of the world, exorcising and controlling it by limiting it in time and space."[87] Rites are interpreted by the scholar as cultural techniques that humanity, over its history spanning millennia, has employed to solve its own constitutive precariousness, through a "transcendence [...] in value."[88] Contrariwise, in the contemporary historical reality, the radical loss of "homeliness," the "protest" against familiar, traditional reality, ends up in destruction without compensation in everyday life, into which the monstrous, terrifying face of life can always break through. In this sense, the ethnologist considers paradigmatic the pages of Sartre's *Nausea*, with the diaries of its protagonist, Roquentin, from which transpires the loss of any leap capable of valorising existence.

Therefore, despite theoretical and methodological differences, De Martino and anti-modern thinking share a similar judgement about the need for preserving the atavic memory of humanity, one of the places of the emergence of which is the body, the paradoxical synthesis of memory and

---

[87] Ibid, 11. It is worth specifying that something very different reveals itself in the *mundus patet*! That is to say, the eminent sense of *tradere*. Around the *mundus* in Rome, the community of the dead (the Ancestors, the spirit of the *gens*), the living and the future ones ritually gathered, unified by the eternal syntonic action towards the *authoritative precedent* represented by myth, the only thing capable of making the Origin *always possible*, a perennially self-renewing event, a stable appearance in/of metamorphosis.

[88] Ernesto De Martino, *Storia e metastoria. I fondamenti di una teoria del sacro*, ed. Marcello Massenzio (Lecce: Argo, 1995), 101.

happy oblivion (in the sense of unconscious memory): "The experiences of the heartbeat, of the upright position, of the prevalence of the right hand over the left one, are signs of ancestral cultural choices, which are culturally transmitted and daily renovated."[89] It is the overshadowing, obscuring and forgetting of the ancestral precedent that trivialises and reduces the existential depth of a daily life which has become incapable of "sustaining," "supporting" mankind's life. This is the condition described in "crisis literature," to which Guénon's book answered with a radical project of return (*revolvere*) of/to the Origin, with a call to the *philosophia perennis* of Tradition.

The Island of the Free Spirits

Evola, in his foreword to *The Crisis of the Modern World* in 1937, held that Guénon's reference to the principles of Tradition placed him in a dissonant position with respect to the champions of the "crisis of modern culture." All these authors — Spengler, Massis, Keyserling, Benda, Ortega y Gasset, Huizinga, to name a few — spiritually belonged to the same world which they criticised. In this sense, the judgement expressed in 1962 by Delio Cantimori in his foreword to Huizinga's book *La crisi della civiltà* is emblematic. Here, the scholar resumed the critiques that he advanced to the Dutch historian's book after the publication of its first German edition in 1936 (the first Dutch edition appeared in 1935), also recalling the polemical notes written by Carlo Morandi, Eugenio Garin, and Ranuccio Bianchi Bandinelli.[90] The objections expressed by the three of them may be summarised as follows: Huizinga's text lacked theoretical depth in its

---

[89] De Martino, *La fine del mondo*, XXIII. It is not accidental that the centrality of the body as the place of the *beyond*, has been experienced in different ways in contemporary philosophy and art. In this regard, it is enough to refer to Jean Luc Nancy, *Noli me tangere* (Turin: Bollati Boringhieri, 2005); Vitaldo Conte, *Pulsional Gender Art* (Rome: Avanguardia 21 Editrice, 2011).

[90] Cf. Johann Huizinga, *La crisi della civiltà*, (Milan: Pgreco Edizioni, 2012), introductory essay by Delio Cantimori, VII-XXXII; Eugenio Garin, *Introduzione*, in Johann Huizinga, *L'autunno del Medioevo* (Florence: Sansoni, 1985); Ranuccio Bianchi Bandinelli, *Dal diario di un borghese* (Rome: Editori Riuniti, 1996).

diagnosis, and this affected its therapeutic proposal in both intellectual and political terms. In the face of the dissolution of the bourgeois-Christian world, the "free spirits" of the times were invited to an "inner purification": "The champions of a purified civilisation will have to be like people who have just awoken in the early morning. They will have to shake off the sad dreams" about the upcoming barbarism.[91] Thus, it was a professorial solution to the crisis, a hope for salvation placed in a return to liberalism as it was realised in Europe between 1870 and 1914. This meant a return to a time whose idealities (as Guénon claims) had produced the crisis or, in any case, had contributed to it — to a world that was ended by the Great War and that now was reduced to an *Insel*, an Island of (presumed) civilisation for the "free and enlightened spirits" (it is therefore not by chance that Zweig's publishing house was named *Insel Verlag*), for a Proustian *petite bande*, wistful for the *belle époque*, whose idealities had been betokened by Van Gogh in his *Bedroom* painting as "expressions of a deep and strong feeling of refusal for a certain degeneration of civilisation."[92] Some among them saw, in the room with the chair, pipe, and garlic, a reference to existential sobriety, which would soon become the reason, often not supported by spiritual depth, for their convinced adherence to the political positions of socialism and/or of the nascent fascisms. These visions were unable to grasp, as instead happens in Guénon's pages, the eternal and perennial reasons of life which had been forgotten by modernity. The thinkers of the crisis called for a recovery of the fundamental ethical values of Christianity (for some of them, this retroactive action implied the exaltation of the civilisation of the Middle Ages, the last example of social organicism) as the glue for a civic patriotism sometimes founded, in nationalistic terms, upon the taste for language and upon a vague feeling of the value of the European cultural tradition, identified as an ideal fatherland,

---

91 Cantimori, *Saggio introduttivo*, IX.
92 Ibid, XVIII.

cosmopolitan and liberal, for the cultured bourgeoisie of the epoch. But, above all, most of the *Islanders* were linked to the rationalist- and positivist-oriented historiographical and philosophical vein, which, according to the thought about Tradition, is the undisputed cause of the modern *dis-aster*, of the loss of touch with the reality of the cosmos and its eternal rhythms. In short, Huizinga and his associates saw *shadows* spreading over Europe, but they did not understand that what had yielded such shadows was the same humanist, utilitarian, and liberal culture in which they themselves had been formed: they wanted to use as medicine the very same pathogenic germ that had produced the disease. The *exceptionality* of Guénon's *Crisis* has to be found in its referral to a different perspective, to a worldview that is not humanist, but *perennialist*. About this, it is worthwhile to specify, as done by Evola in the introduction to the book, that: "[...] the world of principles as Guénon conceives and shows it at the basis of every true tradition, is much less a bloodless world of abstractions than a world of forces, the action of which, while being invisible, is no less effective."[93]

Of course, despite this, it would be ungenerous to lump all the grass together, since among the thinkers of the crisis there were some who developed a very deep conception of it. Amongst them, we cannot but count Spengler, who, through his morphological vision of history, understood that when a culture achieves the fullness of its possibilities, its blood runs out, its forces are drained, and it becomes a *civilisation*. A culture (*Kultur*), on the contrary, is an ensemble of symbolic expressions which become art, religion, science and language; its twilight corresponds to the waning of its peculiar symbolical expression, the only one which is capable of saving the past from oblivion and of meaningfully transmitting it into the present so as to enlighten the style and destiny of the people who produced it. The positions manifested by Hugo

---

[93] Julius Evola, *Introduzione*, in René Guénon, *La crisi del mondo moderno* (Milan: Hoepli, 1937), 5-6.

von Hofmannsthal seem equally relevant to us; he coined the oxymoron "conservative revolution," and in *The Tower*, at least in its first drafts, he asked himself the same question as Guénon concerning the transitability of the *symbol* and the possibility of *Ordnung* (Order), a question which he answered positively.[94] The central character of the narrative is Prince Sigismund, held captive in the tower for having been designated by the stars as the subverter of the Order. In the throes of wild and brutal passions, his condition exemplifies that of the European man, who carries the crisis of an entire civilisation on his shoulders. A disenchanted view of the Political stands out against the background of the wreckage of modernity, of an Order bereft of consecration and no longer able to realise the *harmonia mundi*, to operate the pontifical and anagogical function of upward thrust, which is reduced to the place of all strifes and sunderings. The Hobbesian-Schmittian modern paradigm of *Dictatorship* establishes a seeming *Peace*. The Greek condition of *argia*, which testifies — in Michelstaedter's sense — to the *persuasion* of the individual and the community, requires the chrism of holiness, of the *Order* from above, which Guénon re-proposes in the pages of the *Crisis*. We are dealing with a "utopic" proposal, but in a classical and Platonic sense, not a "utopian" one, which speaks to the consciousness of the individual so that he takes action in the world while being mindful of the *authoritative precedent* of myth, without stepping into the risk of a *perfectivist* deviation, without yielding to the *titanic* temptation which urges him to build a world thought that is righteous and harmonious in conclusive terms. In order to fully understand this, it is worthwhile to employ the tool of theory for our discourse as well.

---

94 Cf. Oswald Spengler, *Il Tramonto dell'Occidente* (Parma: Guanda, 1991); Hugo von Hofmannsthal, *La Torre* (Milan: Adelphi, 1987), with an essay by Massimo Cacciari, *L'intransitabile utopia*; Giovanni Sessa, *Filosofia della liberazione e Impero interiore: l'utopia evoliana*, in *Studi Evoliani 2008* (Carmagnola: Fondazione J. Evola-Arktos, 2009), 65-81. For a historical contextualisation of the different expressions of the "literature of the crisis" we refer to Michela Nacci, *Tecnica e cultura*, cit.

Symbol and Fragment in Negative Thought

The philosophy of crisis has been the subject of Massimo Cacciari's research since the 1970s. His essential intention was to show the structuration and potential for "re-foundation" that were intrinsic to negative thought as they emerged from the revolutionary breaking produced by the Schopenhauer-Nietzsche duo, as well as from the Nietzsche-Wittgenstein twentieth-century speculative axis. The exegesis of such a historico-theoretical context makes us aware of the impossibility of any synthetical and definitive formulation of the "re-foundation," that is to say, of the impossibility of a full return to the symbolic, to the original and holy Principle, but this does not imply, as remarked by the Venetian philosopher, the nihilistic acceptance *sic et simpliciter* of a context of despair and dispersion. Cacciari points out that this complex of relations "*speaks* its most understandable language [...] through the multiplicity of "dialects" of the *serious Viennese apocalypse*,"[95] that is, through the exponents of the "literature of crisis" who asked themselves about the essential problem: *the end of a world and/or end of the world?* Wittgenstein must certainly be counted among them.

He wanted to speak to "friends scattered to the corners of the world," just like Huizinga who had "free spirits" as his referents, but the difference which separates the two is abysmal. Even the Austrian philosopher and his "friends" looked to the *Zivilisation* (Civilisation) without any sympathy, but from very different depths. He, as Cacciari suggests, had understood that modernity is founded upon a decisive word: Progress. Its form is "[...] *typisch aufbauend* (typical organising, building): it is *constructive* according to its most intimate essence."[96] Progressing and progressivist *reason* actualises itself through increasingly large and articulated structures, and it widens, from time to time, the perimeter of the known world. It is

---

95 Cacciari, *Krisis. Saggio sulla crisi del pensiero negativo da Nietzsche a Wittgenstein* (Milan: Feltrinelli, 1976), 8.

96 For all of this, see Massimo Cacciari, *Dallo Steinhof*, 51 ff.

a designed and built world which continuously extends its exclusively materialistic-quantitative borders in a ceaseless race. It is a titanic assault upon heaven: the expansion of the technical domain into an environ that is valorised exclusively through the dynamics of exploitation. The Wittgensteinian detachment from such an idea is a sidereal distance from its productive-constructive essence. The "scattered friends," like the *posthumous men* of the Viennese apocalypse, constitute a diaspora from the Modern, in that they are foreign to its *ratio*. Their otherness from Modernity is induced by their having memory of the *originally* destructive character (and not constructive as every positivist claims) of the dialectic which, as Colli remarked, manifested itself in Zeno in a striking form. In dialectical thinking, every object, be it sensible or abstract, may be interpreted under the sign of either being or non-being, and may be regarded as either possible or impossible. In the *Viennese*, such a situation is no longer a structuring certainty but finally returns to being felt as a *problem*, as they were aware of the power of *negation*. Modern *reason*, which is forgetful of the allusive dimension grasped by Greek philosophy, has done nothing but remove the auroral intuition which says that the world is the *expression* of an *otherness* that is untouchable and unattainable in itself, but which *enlivens* the entities. Therefore, while the clarity of *ratio* is functional to production, constructive-productive calculation, the *Klarheit* (clarity) to which Wittgenstein refers, is only in honour of "God" (for us, of the *dynamis*), in honour of that unspeakable, unthinkable background to which thinking can only hint. It urges reason to "constantly return to that same thing which represents its problem, to unveil the non-constructive," non-manipulative foundation which constitutes reason itself.[97] Such *clarity* refers to a thinking which is *other-non-other* from logocentrism. The Modern needs to recover the "backward gaze" of the Benjaminian Angel, so as to see re-envision the groundlessness of the Principle, the Freedom-Potency of the

---

97 Ibid, 55.

Origin, the original Negation which Julius Evola was able to grasp with extraordinary philosophical strength in his most properly speculative works and which shows itself in Musil's prose or in Schönberg's musical grammar.

Reality needs *re-animation* through the periodical and rhythmical self-giving of the unspeakable within it. Such a process, in the thought of the French Traditionalist, is based upon the indubitable, contemplative recovery — in a higher sense — of the *symbol* which gives itself in given moments of the historical path as an irruption of super-history into history, of super-nature into nature, assisted by the action of the *intellectual elite* upon which the Blois thinker counted for the re-establishment of the Order. Needless to specify, the *intellectual elite* anticipated by the Traditionalist has nothing to do with the abstract intellectualism of modern "clerics," but rather hints — by analogy, as Evola clarified — to a form of participation, of realisation and of contact with "powers" lived according to the modality of a lucid consciousness and distant from any irrationalism and/or mysticism.

In the Viennese Apocalypse — it is still Cacciari who accompanies us in this *ex-cursus* —, *fragmentation* dominates the scene of the world. It is a human and social condition of *incompleteness*, of existential laceration, which yearns nostalgically for completeness. Ultimately, a *fragment* still reminiscent of the *symbol* finds a voice in it — a *fragment*, an actuality, which is an *unhappy consciousness* of the symbol, to which it would like to return due to its own constitutive insufficiency. This condition may be better understood by making reference to two "figures" produced by intellectuals of the crisis: the doll described by Rilke, and Kleist's puppet: "The doll dwells in places of oblivion, remote hideouts, and when it resurfaces from them on occasion [...] it teaches us to recognise that leaning of our soul, which no childhood may exhaust, towards what is impassable and unovercomeable. The doll's absolute lack of imagination betokens the silence which envelops us."[98] Kleist holds that what manifests itself in the puppet, the *animated* doll, is the utopic grace that we might savour anew upon once again coming close to the tree of knowledge: "Kleist's wistfulness for it is the nostalgia for man as still cosmically 'inwoven,' about which Plato spoke in the *Laws*, as an ensemble of inner strings and threads through which the gods drag and drive him."[99] The doll represents dejection and historicity, it is a metaphor of the current human condition, the modern one. The puppet represents utopia and "finding its figure once again is possible only by filling the absolute hollowness of the doll's silence with nostalgia."[100] Take heed well: this means filling the emptiness of Modernity with the soul of Tradition, which is always metamorphic and *at work*.

Tradition and Crisis

Between the two extremes represented by the return to the rock crystal of the Guénonian symbol and the fragment reminiscent and nostalgic of the *Arche* (Principle), *tertium non datur?* Is there no further possibility of redemption? Maybe yes. There exists an intermediate position, and it seems to us that it is precisely that indicated by Evola. It was proposed in brief in the foreword to the *Crisis* and, in a more thorough way, in the whole Evolian *iter*, an example of a philosophy *at work*[101] which, as far as we are concerned, is the highest moment of the *thought about Tradition* produced over the course of the twentieth century. In the Roman thinker's works, the idea of Tradition is articulated in a dynamic, active way: the *tradere* is historically structured, induced by the encounter between

---

98 Ibid, 121.

99 Ibid, 122.

100 Ibid, 123.

101 Cf. Romano Gasparotti, *L'individuo assoluto e la magica potenza dell'immagine*, introductory essay to Julius Evola, *L'Individuo e il divenire del mondo* (Rome: Edizioni Mediterranee, 2015), ed. G. de Turris. In these pages, the prefacer conducts a meaningful reading of Evolian philosophy as an example of thinking which is always *at work*.

the ideal-typical and archetypal *traditional* heritage with the metaphorical reality of the world, within the *event*, within the historical and/or natural datum. As pointed out in the editorial note to the Italian edition by Gianfranco de Turris, Guénon's *Crisis* becomes a *Revolt* in Evola's thought. This means that the Roman thinker indicates the *practical* way by which to fill the void of modernity with the *animus* of Tradition. In other words, Evola answers the question that Guénon put forward with the *Crisis* by presenting the traditional world beyond any symbolic staticity, beyond any scholastic and merely contemplative dogmatism. The life *humus* that connotes the specificity of his research has to be read beyond any literalist barriers.

In this perspective, Evola's treatment of the idea of time is decisive. In many places of his works, it is possible to find how the cyclical and deterministic conception is made true through a further intuition, that of *spherical* temporality, in which the three ecstasies of the oedipal-chronological time are in one. For this reason, Tradition, in the Evolian exegesis, is untied from the idea of the past, and instead refers to the Origin, which he, being mindful of the lesson of the *Romantics* of Heidelberg (with whom he corrected the gnoseological limit of actualism), understood as *in force*, as effectively subsisting within time, and *always possible*. Provided, of course, that our actions in the world have as their reference the *authoritative precedent* witnessed by myth, the golden thread by means of which we can order and give shape to reality, allowing the *fragment* to propose itself and to be experienced and lived as a *symbol*. This pertains to the *Crisis*. Is not the cyclical vision re-proposed by Guénon to contemporaries, together with the regression of the castes, an attestation that the world entropically tends to disorder? The crisis is always latent, at some times disruptive, and mankind must incessantly implement a rectifying action against the forces of heaviness, of *regressio*, of reduction to mere materiality, which are at work both inside mankind itself and within reality.

Why does all of this happen? In short, why is the world a perennial crisis? Evola had understood this back in the 1920s, and with him a few others, once again with foresight. Amongst these was Andrea Emo, who, to this question, answered: because being is *nothing*, in the sense that the Origin is neither a datum, nor an entity, nor a *positum*, but is an absolute Subject (in the Schellingian sense), thus no-thing, no-entity. Everything that is, is as such for its original denial of that *non-ens* which shows itself in the metamorphosis of the world, perennially nailed to the succession of life and death. This position is decidedly more radical than that expressed about the crisis by *fin de siècle* literature as discussed hereinbefore, while it shares assonances with and proximities to the latter.[102] Emo, like the Central Europeans, attached great significance to poetry and word. He held that poetry "is always present in the world, which it dominates, governs and leads... Hindered from appearing in a form, it reappears immediately in another form... The art of a few is to find it precisely where no one was looking for it."[103]

Unlike some malevolent and recent critics of Tradition, who have interpreted the definition of "work of art" attributed by the philosopher Manlio Sgalambro to *Revolt Against the Modern World* in terms of *diminutio*, we espouse it *in toto*, on the basis of this Emian quote. Tradition contains within itself the secret of Hermetism: the *possibility of the impossible*, to achieve which, throughout the quest, we must equip ourselves with the necessary *courage for the impossible*.[104]

Translated by U.X.A.

---

[102] About this particular aspect cf. Massimo Donà, *Andrea Emo e la cultura mitteleuropea*, in Andrea Emo, *Quaderni di metafisica*, ed. Massimo Donà and Romano Gasparotti, foreword by Massimo Cacciari (Milan: Bompiani, 2006), 1549-1556.

[103] Ibid, 1552.

[104] On the possibility of the impossible cf. Massimo Donà, *Un pensiero della libertà. Julius Evola: filosofia e magia al cospetto dell'impossibile*, in Julius Evola, *Fenomenologia dell'individuo assoluto* (Rome: Edizioni Mediterranee, 2007), 13-33.

ANTI-TRADITION IN THE AGE OF IRON

Troy Southgate

> *We are the golden men, who shall the people save:*
> *For only ours are visions, perfect and divine.*
> *For we alone are drunken of the last, best wine*
> *And very Truth our souls have flooded, wave on wave.*[105]
>
> – Lionel Johnson

Whilst the twentieth century played host to some of the most cataclysmic events in human history, the twenty-first century threatens to be just as tumultuous and destructive as its predecessor. During the course of this essay I intend to present a study of the continuing attack on Tradition in light of the information provided by some of the leading authorities in the field; namely, Ananda K. Coomaraswamy (1877-1947), René Guénon (1886-1951), Julius Evola (1898-1974), Lord Northbourne (1896-1982), Frithjof Schuon (1907-1998), Abu Bakr Siraj Ad-Din (1909-2005) and Whitall N. Perry (1920-2005). I will also examine the timeless wisdom contained in the sacred Hindu texts. It should be noted, however, that the word "Tradition" – after the Greek *paradidomi* and Latin *traditio* – relates to the transmission of that which is sacred and does not, as in the case of the lower-case "tradition", indicate that it is no more than a broad umbrella term for the maintenance of those national and cultural values which are found in the comparatively more profane sphere. Jean Borella defines Tradition as something which humanity has not invented but received, and which

---
105 Lionel Johnson, "Munster: AD 1534," quoted in Nicholas Drake (ed.), *The Poetry of W. B. Yeats* (Penguin Books, 1991), 44.

thus finds its starting point, in the final analysis, in the superhuman origin of all things. This tradition is identical to the Logos of humanity; it is the expression of its law and the standard of its earthly existence. Thus, normal life is what takes place according to this standard – by which all moments, all acts, all works are accomplished according to its rule and its light.[106]

Another expression for Tradition is *philosophia perennis*, or the perennial philosophy, something defined by Frithjof Schuon as "the totality of the primordial and universal truths – and therefore of the metaphysical axioms – whose formation does not belong to any particular system."[107] Schuon preferred the term *sophia perennis* ("perennial wisdom") to that of *philosophia perennis*, because the latter is considered to be more closely associated with the realm of the profane. But regardless of the differing terminology that one finds among its chief advocates and spiritual teachers, Tradition alludes to something that was

> given to humanity at the beginning of time: it constitutes the primordial tradition which manifested itself in the 'arctic cradle' of humanity, that is, in the 'earthly paradise'. Afterwards it took on multiple forms – which are all the world's religions given by God's revelation – according to the times and mentalities; but, despite this diversity, there remains the essential unity of the truth.[108]

One of the main sources which sets out the perennial struggle between the opposing worlds of Tradition and Anti-Tradition is Julius Evola's *Revolt Against the Modern World*, which was first published in 1934, when Europe was finally beginning to recover from the disastrous consequences of the First World War whilst hurtling towards a second conflict of similar magnitude. Evola was certainly not the first to note that human history represents a vast field of conflict upon which competing spiritual forces with diametrically opposed interests

---

106 Jean Borella, "René Guénon and the Traditionalist School" in Antoine Faivre & Jacob Needleman (eds.), *Modern Esoteric Spirituality* (SCM Press, 1993), 340-341.

107 Frithjof Schuon, "The Perennial Philosophy" in Martin Lings and Clinton Minnaar (eds.), *The Underlying Religion: An Introduction to the Perennial Philosophy* (World Wisdom, 2007), 243.

108 Borella, "René Guénon and the Traditionalist School", 341.

wage eternal war. The Catholic Church – or at least its more traditional wing – blames the Protestant Reformation for the rapid decline of religiosity since the sixteenth century, holding it directly responsible for the rise of atheism, humanism, scientism, liberalism and various other modern ills.

Evola, himself a leading thinker in the Traditionalist School, also views the distinguishing 'lunar,' 'motherly,' 'telluric' and 'non-Aryan' characteristics of Christianity with a large degree of suspicion and believes that the origins of Anti-Tradition can be located as far back as the ancient world. Not in the sense that the decline of Tradition can be traced to a common point on any historical (or pre-historical) time-line, of course, because the process of degeneration has taken place within different civilisations and at different periods. The actual rate of decline also differs from civilisation to civilisation and, in some instances – the United States being a case in point – the fabric of a civilisation can begin to unravel almost immediately.

What most civilisations have in common is the fact that each of them have, at one time or another, experienced some kind of Golden Age, or Satya Yuga. This, predictably, is followed by an all-too-familiar and recognisable pattern of spiritual decay which results in the collapse of the social hierarchy and foments widespread disorder. Evola tells us that a Satya Yuga is something which

> corresponds to an original civilisation that was naturally and totally in conformity with what has been called the 'traditional spirit.' For this reason, in the periods that the Golden Age is associated with both historically and meta-historically, we find symbols and attributes that characterise the highest function of regality – symbols of polarity, solarity, height, stability, glory, and life in a higher sense.[109]

Alternatively, in *Ride the Tiger: A Survival Manual for the Aristocrats of the Soul* (1961), Evola describes the events which

---

109 Julius Evola, *Revolt Against the Modern World* (Inner Traditions International, 1995), 184.

take place at the other end of the scale – the Kali Yuga – as a "climate of dissolution, in which all the forces – individual and collective, material, psychic, and spiritual – that were previously held in check by a higher law and by influences of a superior order pass into a state of freedom and chaos."[110]

For the ancient Aryans, the beginning of the end was represented by the fierce conflict between the luminous deities (*deva*) in the north-east of India and their demonic adversaries (*asura*) to the south; for the Egyptians it was a crucial shift of power that finally resulted in the gradual triumph of the priestly caste over its regal opponents; for the Sumerians it was partly the reinterpretation of the myth of Gilgamesh by the Hebrews, who later cast him as Adam the primordial sinner; and for the ancient Greeks, meanwhile, it was the victory of the Dionysian spirit over that of the increasingly sterile Apollonian society. And so the list goes on. But despite the intermittent revival or reintroduction of the solar principle by way of notable exceptions such as Zoroaster, Ahura Mazda, Mithras and even the Safavid dynasty (1501-1722), the rot always sets in eventually and the long and protracted war against Tradition is now well under way and has become the very hallmark of the modern world.

The move away from Tradition, however, must go through two further stages before it enters the Age of Iron, or Kali Yuga. These are the Age of Silver, or Treta Yuga, and the Age of Bronze, or Dvapara Yuga. The metallic terminology is mostly used in relation to the West but, nevertheless, the three stages which follow the Satya Yuga result in a gradual loss and decline of primordial and spiritual truth. The four maha yugas, or age-cycles, are said to accord with 1,728,000 (Satya), 1,296,000 (Treta), 864,000 (Dvapara) and 432,000 (Kali) years respectively. Collectively, the four human cycles are known as Manvantara, or Breath of Life.

---

[110] Julius Evola, *Ride the Tiger: A Survival Manual for the Aristocrats of the Soul* (Inner Traditions International, 2003), 9.

Anti-Tradition in the Age of Iron

The French intellectual, René Guénon, one of the fiercest critics of the present epoch, spent a great deal of his time analysing the signs leading up to the Kali Yuga. In his acclaimed *The Crisis of the Modern World*, first published in 1927, Guénon suggests that mankind has already been living in the Age of Iron for over six thousand years and that during this period

> the truths which were formerly within reach of all have become more and more hidden and inaccessible; those who possess them grow fewer and fewer, and although the treasure of 'non-human' (that is, supra-human) wisdom that was prior to all the ages can never be lost, it nevertheless becomes enveloped in more and more impenetrable veils, which hide it from men's sight and make it extremely difficult to discover.[111]

The Kali Yuga is equivalent to just one-tenth of the entire Manvantara, which gives us an insight into precisely how arrogant and puffed-up modern civilisation has become. Paraphrasing *Metamorphoses* by the famous Roman poet, Ovid (43 BCE – 17 CE), Roy Walker wrote:

> *Of iron*
>
> *Is the last*
>
> *In no part good and tractable as former ages past;*
>
> *For when that of this wicked age once opened was the vein*
>
> *Therein all mischief rushéd forth, the faith and truth were fain*
>
> *And honest shame to hide their heads; for whom stepped stoutly in,*
>
> *Craft, treason, violence, envy, pride, and wicked lust to win.*[112]

The main primary source which provides us with most of the detailed information about the nature of the Age of Iron, the period in which the people of Western civilisation now find themselves, is the *Vishnu Purana*. This Hindu text, which amounts to a total of 23,000 verses, is one of eighteen

---

111 René Guénon, *The Crisis of the Modern World* (Sophia Perennis, 2004), 7.

112 Roy Walker, "The Golden Feast (1952)" in John Zerzan (ed.), *Against Civilisation: Readings and Reflections* (Feral House, 2005), 12.

Anti-Tradition in the Age of Iron

Mahapuranas. According to Srimad Bhagavatam, the Puranas themselves are

> supplementary explanations of the Vedas intended for different types of men. All men are not equal. There are men who are conducted by the mode of goodness, others who are under the mode of passion and others who are under the mode of ignorance. The Puranas are so divided that any class of men can take advantage of them and gradually regain their lost position and get out of the hard struggle for existence.[113]

Meanwhile, returning to the matter of the Kali Yuga, or Age of Iron, the *Vishnu Purana* – which functions in a manner not dissimilar, perhaps, to that of the Christian Book of Revelation (*apokalupsis*) – informs us that Kalki, the tenth and final avatar of Vishnu himself, will arrive on a white horse to bring to an end the chaos and disorder that will have enveloped the entire planet in darkness:

> When the practices taught in the Vedas and institutes of law have nearly ceased, and the close of the Kali age shall be nigh, a portion of that divine being who exists of His own spiritual nature, and who is the beginning and end, and who comprehends all things, shall descend upon earth. He will be born in the family of Vishnuyasha, an eminent brahmana of Shambhala village, as Kalki, endowed with eight superhuman faculties. By His irresistible might he will destroy all the mlecchas (Barbarians) and thieves, and all whose minds are devoted to iniquity. He will re-establish righteousness upon earth, and the minds of those who live at the end of the Kali age shall be awakened, and shall be as clear as crystal. The men who are thus changed by virtue of that peculiar time shall be as the seeds of human beings, and shall give birth to a race who will follow the laws of the Krita age or Satya Yuga, the age of purity. As it is said, 'When the sun and moon, and the lunar asterism Tishya, and the planet Jupiter, are in one mansion, the Krita age shall return.'[114]

The Traditional civilisation of the Indo-Europeans, according to *Vishnu Purana*, will fall into the hands of barbarians and the established monarchies will abandon their responsibilities and go on to rule with an iron fist. The prevailing caste will be that

---

113 *Srimad Bhagavatam*, 1.2.4.

114 *Vishnu Purana*, Book 4, Chapter 24.

of the Shudra, or lowly artisans and labourers, whilst those in the Vaishya caste will abandon farming and agriculture and find themselves treated like serfs. Elsewhere, the warriors of the Kshatriya caste will plunder the land and property of their own people, instead of protecting them, whilst the priestly Brahmins will lose their inner piety and self-respect and be treated like ordinary men. The struggle between the Kshatriya and Brahmin castes has also been expressed in a European context, something discussed in Guénon's 1929 work, *Spiritual Authority and Temporal Power*:

> This opposition of the two powers, this rivalry between their respective representatives, was depicted among the Celts as a wild boar and a bear locked in combat, a symbol of Hyperborean origin and thus connected to one of the most ancient traditions of humanity (if not the oldest of all), the primordial tradition.[115]

It is also said that women will rebel against their husbands and parents, following a path of indecency and immorality. The *Bhagavad Gita*, another crucial mainstay of the Aryan tradition, tells us that Kalki Avatar will appear to re-establish the spiritual order: "Whenever there is a falling away from the true law [religion] and an upsurge of unlawfulness, then I emit myself. I come into being age after age, to protect the virtuous and to destroy evil-doers, to establish a firm basis for the true law."[116]

It is important to note that, whilst the prophetic verses of the *Vishnu Purana* were written in relation to future events set in the context of Ancient India, we – as the descendants of those Aryans who left the civilisation of the Indus Valley and travelled westwards into Europe – are, in many respects, an ongoing consequence of the overall shift away from Tradition. In other words, the warnings given in the Vishnu Purana can also be applied to those Indo-Europeans who now reside in the West. In Europe, therefore, at least prior to the Reformation,

---

[115] René Guénon, *Spiritual Authority and Temporal Power* (Sophia Perennis, 2001), 10-11.

[116] *Bhagavad Gita*, 4: 7-8.

the so-called Enlightenment, the French Revolution and the concomitant rise of the bourgeois Third Estate, a few remnants of Tradition continued to endure through the divine right of kings and in the tripartite structures of feudalism. In time, however, these remaining scraps of Primordial Tradition were systematically erased by the arrival of the modern world.

For Guénon, the war against Tradition – like all other forms of subversion – is being directed from behind the scenes and most of its success is the result of 'counter-initiation'. In other words, although Tradition requires the help of 'suprahuman' intermediaries dedicated to the furtherance of primordial truth, the forces of Anti-Tradition – arranged in groups and associations with highly questionable or fraudulent hierarchies – attempt to parallel the genuine initiatic chains of transmission and further their own dangerous agendae.

The first step towards an attack on the final vestiges of Tradition in European civilisation, Guénon argues, involves effecting

> a change in the general mentality and at the destruction of all traditional institutions in the West, since the West is where it began to work first and most directly, while awaiting the proper time for an attempt to extend its operations over the whole world, using the Westerners duly prepared to become its instruments.[117]

In agreement with Evola – as well as the exponents of orthodox Catholicism – Guénon believes that the humanism of the Renaissance, the rationalism of the Enlightenment and the bourgeois nature of Protestantism each conspired to bring about the overthrow of the more Traditional and sacred aspects of the Middle Ages. The role of Enlightenment philosophy led, by way of Thomas Hobbes (1588-1679), to the mechanisation of Aristotelianism and helped pave the way towards full-blown materialism. Rationalists such as René Descartes (1596-1650), too, helped to sow the seeds for the rise of profane science and man – stripped of his spirit – was

---

[117] René Guénon, *The Reign of Quantity & the Signs of the Times* (Sophia Perennis, 2004), 193.

Anti-Tradition in the Age of Iron

soon reduced to little more than a numerical unit of economic production. Quantity, if you will, over quality.

Interestingly, however, Guénon notes that whilst the aim of this Anti-Traditional current was solidification, it soon resulted in dissolution. This is because a thoroughly discontinuous phenomenon had attempted – and failed – to attach itself to the continuity of the past. A new humanist platform had been established, only for the whole process to lead to dehumanisation and degeneration. Nevertheless, there is a second phase in the Anti-Traditional strategy:

> After having enclosed the corporeal world as completely as possible, it was necessary, while guarding against the re-establishment of any communication with superior domains, to open it up again from below, so as to allow the dissolving and destructive forces of the inferior subtle domain to penetrate into it.[118]

Replacing spirituality with materialism, then, gave the forces of Anti-Tradition an opportunity to wipe the slate clean and fundamentally alter the course of Western civilisation. But that which began life by radically opposing Traditional values, gradually emerged from the shadows to become a counter-initiatory threat that sought to imitate – through inversion – the character of Tradition itself. This has been achieved through a combination of deviation and subversion, although it is important to note the distinction that exists between them:

> [D]eviation can be regarded as comprising an indefinite multiplicity of degrees, so that it can go to work gradually and imperceptibly; this is exemplified by the gradual passage of the modern mentality from 'humanism' and rationalism to mechanism, and thence to materialism...[119]

Deviation, in other words, has led to what Guénon describes as 'the reign of quantity'. Once it has replaced the Traditional order, however, this tendency evolves into a form of active subversion, which "is but the last stage of deviation and is

---

118 Ibid., 195.

119 Ibid., 197.

its goal, or, in other words, that deviation as a whole has no tendency other than to bring about subversion."[120]

Like the irreparable rift between God and Lucifer, therefore, the forces of Anti-Tradition set themselves up to replace the very Tradition that they so vehemently oppose. Subversion, then, is akin to a 'satanic' denial and represents a negation of primordial truth. Continuing with this analogy, Guénon says

> that 'Satan is the ape of God', and also that he 'transfigures himself into an angel of light'. In the end, this amounts to saying that he imitates in his own way, by altering and falsifying it so as always to make it serve his own ends, the very thing he sets out to oppose: thus, he will so manage matters that disorder takes on the form of a false order.[121]

Reality is fundamentally distorted and one of the main tactics of the Anti-Traditionalists is to compare the true state of nature with some form of basic animality. This leads people to dismiss their instinctual resistance to rationalism and mechanisation, allowing the Anti-Traditionalists to lull them into a false sense of security and then seduce them with a false 'egalitarianism' and a contrived 'democracy'. This leads, as Ananda Kentish Coomaraswamy has suggested, to great confusion:

> There are types of society which are by no means 'above,' but on the contrary below' caste; societies in which there prevails what the traditional sociologies term a 'confusion of castes'; societies in which men are regarded primarily if not, indeed, exclusively as economic animals, and the expression 'standard of living,' dear to the advertising manufacturer, has only qualitative connotations.[122]

Beyond all this, of course, lies an inverted 'spirituality' which relies on the wholesale reinterpretation of Traditionalist symbolism and, inevitably, leads – as we have already seen with the Theosophists and more recent attempts involving

---

120 Ibid., 198.

121 Ibid.

122 Ananda Kentish Coomaraswamy, "The Bugbear of Democracy, Freedom and Equality" in Harry Oldmeadow (ed.), *The Betrayal of Tradition: Essays on the Spiritual Crisis of Modernity* (World Wisdom, 2005), 126.

syncretism, ecumenicalism and multi-denominational worship – to the promotion of a profane and baseless world religion. As Mark Sedgwick explains: "The theory of cyclical time and Kali Yuga complete one aspect of the Traditionalist philosophy by providing the explanation for the state of affairs explored by Guénon elsewhere: inversion is a characteristic of the Kali Yuga."[123]

The natural response from Traditionalists must be to remain faithful to the primordial source, although we must also ensure that we are following the right course. As Schuon contends, before

> it is possible to envisage any kind of remedial activity, it is necessary to see things as they are, even if, as things turn out, it costs us much to do so; one must be conscious of those fundamental truths that reveal to us the values and proportions of all things. If one's aim is to save mankind, one must first know what it means to be a man; if one wishes to defend the spirit, one must know what is spirit.[124]

As the famous story about Krishna and Arjuna in the *Bhagavad Gita* demonstrates – when the latter hesitates in battle and is reminded by the former that he must perform his destiny as a warrior – we must each fulfill our particular *sva-dharma*, or 'own duty'. This, of course, is the function appropriate to one's status, or caste. Consequently, therefore, the individual must embark upon his specific *karma-marga*, or 'path of action'. Once combined, the *sva-dharma* and *karma-marga* indicate that we must act, not through ambition or desire, but according to duty. In addition, however, we need to ensure that action is founded upon truth and justice. Lord Northbourne reminds us that the most

> important thing about any statement is not whether it is general or particular, but whether it is true or untrue. Unless the truth can be grasped in its broad essentials it is unlikely that specific action

---

123 Mark Sedgwick, *Against the Modern World: Traditionalism and the Secret Intellectual History of the Twentieth Century* (Oxford: Oxford University Press, 2004), 28.

124 Frithjof Schuon, "No Activity Without Truth" in Jacob Needleman (ed.), *The Sword of Gnosis: Metaphysics, Cosmology, Tradition, Symbolism* (Penguin Books, 1974), 27.

will be soundly based. In the end, therefore, everyone must seek for himself the application appropriate to himself.[125]

Schuon believed that Anti-Tradition must be countered with the truth and not, as some have suggested, by establishing a new ideology. It is enough for Traditionalists to highlight the false nature of the materialistic opposition that we face, and not to imagine for one moment that Tradition itself is somehow incapable of meeting the challenge.

With the iron grip that materialism has upon our schools and universities, however, the struggle to retain one's intellectual autonomy is becoming more and more difficult:

> To think and act without the constraint of any knowledge and values other than those of the modern scientific mentality is to commit oneself to a tyranny of an unprecedented maleficence. This is why the freeing of ourselves from subservience to this mentality constitutes the second condition whose fulfilment is a prerequisite of our survival as human beings.[126]

But lest we find ourselves wringing our hands in despair at the increasing chaos of the contemporary world, Guénon provides us with some words of divine justice:

> Modern civilisation, like all things, has of necessity its reason for existing, and if indeed it represents the state of affairs that terminates a cycle, one can say that it is what it should be and that it comes in its appointed time and place; but it should nonetheless be judged according to the words of the Gospel, so often misunderstood: 'Offense must needs come, but woe unto him through whom offense cometh.'[127]

Finally, despite the unfathomable damage that has been caused by the Anti-Traditionalists, the few of us that remain loyal to Tradition must seek to nurture and promote its timeless values both within our own communities and in our own lives.

---

125 Lord Northbourne, "Modernism: The Profane Point of view" in Lings and Minnaar (eds.), *The Underlying Religion: An Introduction to the Perennial Philosophy*, 16.

126 Philip Sherrard, "Epilogue" in Oldmeadow (ed.), *The Betrayal of Tradition: Essays on the Spiritual Crisis of Modernity*, 361.

127 Guénon, *The Crisis of the Modern World*, 20.

Anti-Tradition in the Age of Iron

Whitall N. Perry says that "it is imperative that some sort of traditional restoration take place and the nucleus of an elect be formed with the dual role of reclaiming perennial values, and of acting as a counterforce to the aberrations of the modern world."[128]

In the opinion of Martin Lings, who was also known as Abu Bakr Siraj Ad-Din, this activity can take place in a social context and the "hope of communities must lie, not in 'progress' or 'development,' but in 'renewal,' that is, restoration."[129] The distinction that Lings makes between 'development' and 'renewal' rests on the fact that the natural vigour of our Traditional societies is already present and the key is to realign it with original principles. Here are a few closing remarks from Robin Waterfield:

> Traditional society will not be achieved by a nostalgic attempt to re-create a vanished past. Guénon was always warning against this kind of misapprehension. There is no way back, there is equally no way out, but there is a way through. Man's infinite worth lies solely in his freedom to become what he is, to realise his potential. Traditional social order helps him in this spiritual task.[130]

Despite the fact that we can act on the microcosmic level, the role of the Traditionalist élite is to allow things on the macrocosmic scale to take their natural course. Those who live in accordance with the primordial, therefore, will not be disappointed.

---

128 Whitall N. Perry, "Afterward: The Revival of Interest in Tradition" in Lings and Minnaar (eds.), *The Underlying Religion: An Introduction to the Perennial Philosophy*, 317.

129 Abu Bakr Siraj Ad-Din; "The Spiritual Function of Civilisation" in Needleman (ed.), *The Sword of Gnosis: Metaphysics, Cosmology, Tradition, Symbolism*, 105.

130 Robin Waterfield, *René Guénon and the Future of the West: The Life and Writings of a 20th-Century Metaphysician* (Sophia Perennis, 2002), 85.

THE ANTITHESES OF MODERNITY

Gianfranco de Turris

> "The desert grows: woe to him who harbours deserts."
> — Friedrich Nietzsche

From what does the actuality or unactuality of a philosopher derive? What does it mean when we talk about a thinker, or no longer talk about him, after more than 110 years have passed since his birth and more than 40 since his death? It depends not so much on the worth that the cultural establishment, the intellectuals in power, and journalism — which, for better or worse, mould and condition public opinion —, assign to his ideas, but, I believe, rather on the capacity of his system of thought, philosophical categories, tools of investigation, and metaphysical and metahistorical reference points *to suitably interpret and satisfactorily explain Reality in multiple aspects, thus providing the necessary methodology to carry out such an operation to those who make reference to him.*

Julius Evola, precisely because he is often defined as "inactual", i.e., not belonging to the present world, but still being operational, active within it (which is different from being "unactual", i.e. outdated, no longer relevant for the present world), possesses such capacities and succeeds in bestowing them upon others. He is therefore not a name outdone by facts and other positions, his opinions are not obsolete (in their foundations, obviously, not in their contingent and circumstantial aspects), and consequently he is not to be relegated to the high and unreachable shelves of a library or to the no-longer-frequented basements of a house as certain Italian politicians did in order to be admitted to well-to-do circles and to make sure that their past is forgotten. His "worldview" is actual, current, relevant for the present, and, even more importantly, it is worthwhile for dealing with the reality which surrounds us and in which we act.

All those who reason with their own heads and are not tricked by contemporary political and ideological pipers are well aware of the general situation through which we are living in our epochal times, and are therefore aware that it is necessary — at least for personal and thus inner survival — to hold clear and firm points of reference. Whatever may be said and whatever irony may be made about it, only a model that is at once philosophical, existential, and spiritual allows us to provide such points of reference. One cannot move in disarray, haphazardly, unless one wants to live only occasionally, on the wave of events and not opposing them, as so-called "weak thought" proposes.

Only those who have elaborated an overall "worldview" and have delved into the various aspects, both theoretical and practical, of our life *here and now*, can be of use when needed. Julius Evola is precisely such a thinker who has provided such points of reference. Let us try to briefly identify the nodal points of the current *modus vivendi*, the one with which we claim to have opened the 21st century, and thus give an answer to why it is necessary to refer to the thought and *Weltanschauung* put forward by Evola over the 50 years of his activity. The key to understanding the present that he offers to us, which is based upon an analysis of the past and highlights its obvious outcomes, also helps us to deal with such a present with full knowledge of the facts: it is precisely his essential function today that also explains why it is necessary to discuss him and his ideas whenever there is the occasion for it, and then to critically reprint his works, recover his dispersed texts, analyse his multifaceted thought, read it, meditate on it (since every time one rereads Evola's writings, one discovers new and different aspects, unexpected anticipations, and downright "prophecies" about our times), and refer to it whenever possible.

In practice, to every position, option, choice, point of view, attitude, value, principle, and watchword that is most popular today as imposed by the "masters of Single Thought", endorsed and confirmed by the megaphones of enslaved mass media, standardised by conviction or servility, and thereupon ultimately deemed "normal" and accepted without discussion, there exists a counter-position, a counter-principle in Julius Evola's ideas, based on his overall philosophical, historical, political, and existential vision. This is the reason why his thought can be taken as a point of reference for a *positive attitude* that opposes the contemporary drift, at least on a personal level.

The examples of these two opposing perspectives are innumerable, but some stand out for their intrinsic importance.

Uprooting

Today, as psychologists, sociologists, and anthropologists practically unanimously say — albeit remaining systematically unheard —, mankind is utterly uprooted, no longer has any point of reference in national, local, and even familial traditions, which are not only forgotten, but tend to be destroyed, if not denigrated, and, at the very least, condemned and made objects to be ashamed of. Forgetful mankind floats on the Naught, sails on the Lethe. It is very difficult to prove that this is not the case, independently of the opinion one may make thereof.

Julius Evola bases his own "worldview" on the existence of a metahistorical Tradition, which, however, from time to time and in different ways, has descended into History, and he makes reference to this Tradition, although not with sentimental nostalgia, but in an attempt to re-propose and re-actualise its perennial teachings for the present times. Through values and symbols, attitudes and mentalities, mankind is no longer at the mercy of historical becoming, without any foothold, bereft of any ideal anchorage. This also means a reference to particular and local traditions, without however falling into a ridiculous small-town skitting. The connection to one's own history — made up of episodes and characters, behaviours and affirmations of principles — prevents one from being overwhelmed by the cancellation of any specificity, the latter being what the new model that goes by the name of "globalisation" would like, on both a worldwide and European scale.[131]

Single Thought

Today, a soft dictatorship is consolidating itself. While not resorting to classical autocratic instruments, it tends to impose, in a "democratic" manner, not only what has been defined as Single Thought, but also Single Behaviour: the same way of reasoning as a matter of course, the same "values", the same feelings, but also an identical style of speaking, clothing, and even eating - whatever is defined as "politically correct", enforced by a cultural, ideological and religious lobby through the worldwide *mass media*, which has generalised and "globalised" an exclusively subjective point of view, making it objective, and lowering and imposing it from above in the name, nonetheless, of "democracy".

Evola, on the contrary, affirms the value of differences and individual specificities, both personal and national. We often forget his words against dictatorship, totalitarianism, Bonapartism, Caesarism, the "military station state", which would like to regiment everything, regulate everything, to foresee and forbid everything: the State, he says, in the wake of Walter Heinrich, is *omnia potens* and not *omnia faciens*, as some would still like today despite widespread talk about "liberalism", the "light state", and "federalism". The counterpart to all of this is, instead, an "organic state", which has a strong ideal and — why not? — spiritual central power of direction, based on the recognition and acceptance of diversities, intermediate bodies,

---

[131] Cf. Evola's *Rivolta contro il mondo moderno*; *Gli uomini e le rovine*; *Il ciclo si chiude*.

the delegation of the power of realisation from this ideal and spiritual centre to the periphery, all connected by synergies and by a fidelity to common and shared principles which prevent leaps forward and derailments. In short, it is how the great traditional empires were once constituted and functioned.[132]

Liberal Democracy

Today, the "end of history" is theorised in the sense of a definitive victory of the democratic West over the East of "real socialism". Even if the events of the last 20 years show that this has not been exactly the case, we continue to debate about an intrinsic supremacy of liberal and liberal-democratic thought, liberism and the free market, to be imposed with what have been hypocritically defined as "humanitarian wars", whose consequences have been disastrous, worse than the "evil" which they wanted to defeat.

Evola, instead, explained in detail what the origins and responsibilities of liberalism are, its Enlightenment roots, the birth of socialism and communism from its womb, what of it can be accepted in the extreme case, and what instead must, in any case, be rejected even today, beyond any infatuation. We are not dealing with a new universal panacea.[133]

Moralistic Do-Goodism

Today, we are in the grip of a "do-goodism" that is even imposed by decree, mandatory by law, according to an attitude typical of French Revolution-style Enlightenment *philosophes* and of the Soviet post-Bolshevik Revolution "engineers of the soul", that is an unrealistic attitude wished for by intellectuals detached from reality, which has its roots in the utopia

---

[132] Cf. *Rivolta contro il mondo moderno*; *Orientamenti*; *Gli uomini e le rovine*; *Introduzione al Tao Te Ching di Lao-tze*; *Fascismo e Terzo Reich*, *Mito e realtà del fascismo*; *Lo Stato organico*; *Civiltà americana*; *Il ciclo si chiude*.

[133] Cf. *Rivolta contro il mondo moderno*; *Orientamenti*; *Gli uomini e le rovine*; *Idee per una Destra*; *L'arco e la clava*; *Civiltà americana*; *Il ciclo si chiude*.

of the innate goodness of the human being ruined by society, thus tending towards the implementation of a downward levelling, the forced manifestation of a jubilant and prosaic sentimentalism, only to then inflict very harsh penalties, both concrete and of social blame, on the transgressors of these behavioural laws, while multiple murderers are justified and free to roam around Italy.

Evola, in his ruthless analysis of contemporary society, is completely realistic; he recognises its evils and faults and if he proposes a change, which is *at first inward and only later outward*, he proposes it as oriented upwards, in the direction of those more arduous values, difficult to achieve, which are nowadays forgotten and replaced only with "ethics" and "morality" generically understood. Such values include loyalty, honesty, a sense of responsibility, understanding and valuing personal and collective differences, honour, truthfulness to the given word, absence of compromises, dignity, disinterestedness, active impersonality, inner spiritual realisation.[134]

System of Lies

Today, as a consequence, we live ensnared in a sheer System of Lies (to resume a definition by Fausto Gianfranceschi from an essay dating back to about 40 years ago) and, therefore, of sheer de-responsibilisation. On the one hand, words no longer correspond exactly to the subjects which they refer to, but constitute a ridiculous "do-goodistic" euphemism thereof; on the other hand, the information that reaches us through the new mass media is increasingly filtered, selected, manipulated, ideologically polluted, and does not correspond at all, or it does only minimally, to what happens in Reality: in this way, it not only gives a completely distorted depiction of the latter, but also tries (and largely succeeds) to sway the great mass of the public towards specific and biased interpretations.

---

134 Cf. *Cavalcare la tigre; Orientamenti; Gli uomini e le rovine; Maschera e volto dello spiritualismo contemporaneo; Introduzione alla magia; La Tradizione ermetica.*

Evola, on the contrary, is in favour of the affirmation of a Truth, first internal and then external, private and public, for a rigour which is not moralistically and hypocritically consisting merely in words and not in facts, but an expression of the superior feeling of the human being in accordance with the place that he occupies in society. A truth that is a direct consequence of the principles in which one believes, and which one professes in the context of a society, that refers to a spiritual and metaphysical centre that is, at the same time, "political" above all parties - and it cannot be otherwise. The System of Lies exists and proliferates precisely because dignity, honesty, responsibility, honour, refusal to compromise, fairness, and truthfulness to the given word have nowadays vanished from common sense.[135]

The Reign of Quantity

Today, we are living in the Guénonian "reign of quantity", an undifferentiated mass in which number rules and everything is levelled too much below an *aurea mediocritas*, thus penalising the best ones, the emerging ones, in which everyone must necessarily be alike in body, soul, and spirit, in which whoever proclaims existing differences between men and between cultures is accused, opposed, even criminally convicted in the name of *ad hoc* laws — i.e., laws against freedom of thought —, deprived of the possibility of speaking and writing. In the name of "democracy" — liberal and progressive, nonetheless —, his books are forbidden, seized, burnt at stakes not much different from those still attributed to the Nazis. "Biodiversities" are protected, while cultural and intellectual diversities are opposed. Evola is not afraid to affirm and explain how our world is one in which differences exist and persist *despite everything and everyone*, in which not everyone is equal at all, in which there may be even very profound unevennesses, but

---

[135] Cf. *Rivolta contro il mondo moderno*; *L'arco e la clava*; *Orientamenti*; *Gli uomini e le rovine*; *Metafisica del sesso*; *Cavalcare la tigre*.

he also explains that what is ultimately important are spiritual differences, on the basis of which he theorised a hierarchy of values, to the point that he wrote that there is no difficulty in admitting that a "Yellow" man or a "Hindu", an "Arab" or a "Red" man, may be spiritually superior to a "White" man.[136]

Massification

Today, we have entered a psychological mucilage, a pre-personal regression to the naturalistic, almost animalistic level, into an absence of true character, into sentimentalism, into a blending of multiple individualities. Massification, yielded by the uniformity of thought and behaviour, extends further and further, unnoticed and without causing any concern. Contrariwise, Evola opposes to it a "worldview" in which at the centre stands a well-established *person*, which is a further step from, and an adaptation of, his initial concept of *individual*. Only in this way is it possible to resist the overwhelming and seemingly unstoppable advance of Modernity. Just think of very current tools such as the Internet, Virtual Reality, the multiplication of interconnections and the addiction, conditioning, and pathologies which they — as is now proven — produce, not to mention their ludic application as videogames. Only a well-steady I, a formed personality, a "differentiated man", as Evola defines him, that is to say, an individual who distinguishes himself from the mass by his psychic and inner characteristics, can survive by not losing his uniqueness, his identity along the way, by not melting, so to speak, into the electronic, cybernetic, digital, mass-mediatic *mare magnum*.[137]

---

[136] Cf. *L'arco e la clava*; *Fascismo e Terzo Reich*; *Cavalcare la tigre*.

[137] Cf. *Teoria dell'Individuo assoluto*; *Fenomenologia dell'Individuo assoluto*; *Cavalcare la tigre*; *Introduzione alla Magia*; *Maschera e volto dello spiritualismo contemporaneo*; *I "placebo"*; *Il maestro Dioniso*; *L'infezione psicanalista*.

Pansexualism

On the one hand, what Evola, already in the 1970s, defined as "pansexualism" is rampant nowadays: an obsessive and pervasive presence of sex that degrades and trivialises it to such an extent that, despite appearances, it now has little effect, so much that psychologists and sexologists sound the alarm for an increasingly widespread "decrease of desire". On the other hand, eroticism becomes virtual: unreality is preferred to reality not only through pornographic magazines and websites, which is not even a new thing, but above all through surrogates such as erotic telephone services and eroticism via computers. In these contexts, verbal and written relationships are held with interlocutors who are not seen, whose *true identity* is not known, who can thus be very different from what one thinks, and who are only imagined (think of false profiles on Facebook). On yet another hand, we are witnessing an ever greater confusion of the sexes, and not only in their tasks, roles, and responsibilities, but also in their physical essence: this is the victory of transsexuals and homosexuals over heterosexuals and the disappearance of the concept of "normality".

Faced with all of this, Evola always indicated, as a consequence of his conception of *person*, of the human being, what makes a man a *man* and a woman a *woman* without ambiguity, without confusion. With the theory of the intermediate stages of sexuation, he explained the reasons for certain situations and preferences, and thus put things in their place instead of demonising them. His magnetic theory of eroticism then demonstrates how the more manly a man is and the more womanly a woman is, higher levels can be reached going beyond mere pleasure: in this way, sex and eroticism are redeemed from any moralistic accusation, and "pansexualism" is criticised not from a bigoted and sexophobic point of view, but, instead, in the name of a conception that can transform eroticism into a way of knowledge, saving it from its increasing trivialisation.[138]

Relativism

Today, in the manner of a conclusion and synthesis of such a bleak panorama, everything that has to do with ethics, society, and community is relativised, every behaviour is "understood" and justified, evaluated only according to permissiveness, unless politics and ideology are involved, and in this case one becomes intransigent and iron-clad: everything is granted, tolerated, justified, as long as it falls within the vast category of "progressivism" and "democracy", and only those who are perceived as foreign to such a category are cast as villains and reprobates, towards whom one can rightfully act as the unwavering guarantor of any rule.

Evola teaches that there cannot be "two weights and two measures", that there must exist true justice, strong but not blind, that there must be rules — *primarily* inward — that should not be forgotten and that must be followed, that we must have respect towards others if we have respect for ourselves, that we should not expect from others what we ourselves are not capable of obtaining. In short, one must not be driven by a "political" bias in choices and decisions, but by a superior concept of fairness. The *example* must be worthy.[139]

Technocracy

Today, the tools and means of modern living are being exalted. Technology, which ultimately often exploits us, makes us thralls and servants, transforming itself into a downright Technocracy.

---

138 Cf. *Metafisica del sesso; Cavalcare la tigre; Maschera e volto dello spiritualismo contemporaneo; Il mistero del Graal; La tradizione ermetica; L'infezione psicanalista.*

139 Cf. *Gli uomini e le rovine; Cavalcare la tigre; Fascismo e Terzo Reich; Teoria dell'Individuo assoluto.*

In the wake of Jünger, Evola teaches that Technology, the Machine, is not neutral and therefore one must always be present to oneself in making use of it. He does not preach or urge its abandonment (he never wrote anything about this) or closing oneself off in an intellectualistic and ultimately sterile "ivory tower": on the contrary, he suggests throwing oneself *dans la melée* in order to test oneself and come out of it unscathed.

But this can be done only if one is well protected, shielded behind one's own non-utopian, non-sentimental, but *realistic* and *objective* "worldview"; this allows one to look at the hostile world in front of oneself with a cold and aware gaze, and thence eventually to overcome it, at least in the inward dimension, by understanding it.[140]

Neo-Spiritualism

Today, we are facing the fallout of the spread of the so-called New Age, which since the 1960s has been preaching what has been called a "do-it-yourself religion". It is nothing other, however, than a heterogeneous mix of many strands which were already individually present in the past: old spiritualism, then redefined as "channelling" in English; belief in Invisible Masters and in a religion of universal brotherhood, which are nothing else than the Unknown Superiors of Theosophy and its doctrine; the trivialised rediscovery of Celticism, which results in a return to naturalism; the refashioning of Eastern doctrines — in themselves serious and important — such as Buddhism and Tantrism, complete with billionaire gurus, paid seminars, advertisements in magazines, actors and footballers as sponsors, forgetting what they actually are (philosophies and ways of living which are hard and difficult to be practised, not the pretence of following paths which in the West have actually become easy and within everyone's reach); the preaching of a fundamentalist animalism and of a "politically

---

140 Cf. *L'"Operaio" nel pensiero di Ernst Jünger*; *Superamenti*; *Cavalcare la tigre*.

correct" vegetarianism up to the extreme of the proselytism and intransigence of vegans, who have Anglo-Saxon rather than Franciscan and Buddhist roots; not to mention religions coming down from outer space, contact with the Afterlife through modern technologies, the revival of Satanism, and so forth. All of this is nothing more than that "second religiosity" characterising the epochs of decadence described by Oswald Spengler at the beginning of the 20th century in his *The Decline of the West*.

Evola criticised all of this already in the 1920s and 1930s, calling it "neo-spiritualism", a dark mask of true spiritualism and almost more dangerous than explicitly recognisable and concrete materialism and atheism. He warned of the appearance of "cracks in the Great Wall", as René Guénon himself did, and the infiltration of dangers from below, from "hell" if you like. To this he opposes, on the one hand, reference to a metahistorical Primordial Tradition, and, on the other hand, a personal but lofty and uncompromising spirituality, preferring religions of spiritual realisation characterised by a metaphysical and esoteric background to devotional ones. And since, as previously mentioned, the Primordial Tradition has historically manifested itself from time to time in different ways, Evola also admits a reference to specific Traditions, as in our case would be a Catholicism of a particular type, of an active strain in the vein of medieval Catholicism, even though, as he said several times, this would mean being "only half Traditionalists". His vision was indeed a Ghibelline one.[141]

In short, what is expected from a philosopher in order to be able to usefully refer to his thought? An interpretation of Reality and History, an answer to the fundamental questions of our *hic et nunc* existence, ethical and existential directions, a perspective for the future and for the Aftertime. Julius Evola — and he was certainly not the only one — provided points of reference for all these needs. Perhaps his "recipes" might not

---

[141] Cf. *Maschera e volto dello spiritualismo contemporaneo*; *Introduzione alla Magia*; *Cavalcare la tigre*; *Il mistero del Graal*; *La tradizione ermetica*.

be to one's liking, maybe they might seem inconsistent or even dangerous to some, and outdated and useless to others. The fact is, however, that they are there, they exist, they can be found in his books, and, because of the position which he takes towards the contemporary world, they are an *unicum* in the panorama of a 20-century philosophy thrown towards the future. It is for this reason that such an "in-actual" thinker ultimately turns out to be very "actual", and it is not possible — in the most absolute way — to ignore him, especially on the part of those who feel strongly at unease (without understanding the deep reason thereof) in the Modern World, in a certain sense feeling alien to it, and in some confused and uncertain way wishing to try to survive, or rather continue to live, within modernity's most explicit, showy and engaging form from which one cannot flee: Technocracy.[142]

Translated by U.X.A.

---

[142] The present text originally appeared as the first chapter in Gianfranco de Turris, *Come sopravvivere alla modernità* (Idrovolante Edizioni, 2016).

THE TEMPORALITY OF THE TIGER: SOME NOTES ON THE EVOLIAN 'RIDING THE TIGER'

Giovanni Damiano

> "Not everyone is given to approach extremes"
> — Lautréamont

In an article published in *Il Popolo italiano* in April 1957, Julius Evola wrote the following about "riding the tiger": "the figure of riding the tiger has Eastern origins. It is a Far Eastern saying that 'he who rides the tiger cannot dismount' since, naturally, the animal would pounce on him. However, if he keeps his grip, it may be that he gets the better of the animal."[143] Thus, in an epoch of crisis and decline, which, according to Evola, the modern age is, riding the tiger would represent first of all an assumption of responsibility, in the sense that not opposing the flow would not signify yielding to it, but rather steadfastly following the wave, waiting for a possible future action capable of changing the course of things. Evola describes such an image in his book *Ride the Tiger* (*Cavalcare la tigre*) with more or less the same words, reiterating that "one should not become fixated on the present and on things at hand," but rather "keep in view the conditions that may come about in the future," thus "letting the forces and processes of this epoch take their own course, while keeping

---

[143] Julius Evola, "Cavalcare la tigre", in Id., *Il Popolo italiano (1956-1957)* (Rome: Fondazione Evola-Pagine Editrice, 2014), 96. On the same page, Evola also defines riding the tiger as one amongst the "true traditional symbols."

oneself firm and ready to intervene when 'the tiger, which cannot leap on the person riding it, is tired of running.'"[144] To the contrary, in *The Path of Cinnabar* (*Il cammino del cinabro*), Evola not only disconnects riding the tiger from the doctrine of cycles, but limits riding the tiger solely to the inner sphere; he discourages us from entrenching ourselves in riding the tiger for the sake of deferring the closure of the cycle itself to an indefinite time, which annuls any reference to the future (which, as we shall see, actually ends up opening it). In the 1957 article, however, Evola made clear references to the level of "collective" and "political forces."[145] In Evola's words in *The Path of Cinnabar*: "the formula 'riding the tiger' merely applies to the inner problems of the individual…and in no way pertains to either external goals or to the future."[146]

The immediate aim of this short essay is to analyse, in a very summary and circumscribed way, the image of the Evolian tiger in relation to time, that is to say, what it represents, or, better said, of what the tiger is an image and symbol with respect to time. It seems indisputable to me that the tiger is an image of the modern era. Given that *modernus* has since its inception had the meaning of "current," a word which, properly speaking, describes everything that is in the present,[147] I believe that it is equally irrefutable that the temporal dimension of the Evolian tiger is identifiable precisely with the *present*.

But — and this is the first decisive point — what type of present is this? It is certainly not the present entirely

---

144 Julius Evola, *Cavalcare la tigre* (Milano: Scheiwiller, 1971), 17. [Julius Evola, *Ride the Tiger: A Survival Manual for Aristocrats of the Soul*, trans. Joscelyn Godwin and Constance Fontana (Rochester: Inner Traditions, 2003), 10].

145 "Cavalcare la tigre", 97. To be more explicit, Evola affirmed that riding the tiger "is susceptible to multiple applications: to the inner life of the individual, but also to historical and collective situations" (96).

146 Julius Evola, *Il cammino del cinabro* (Rome: Mediterranee, 2018), 409. [Julius Evola, *The Path of Cinnabar: An Intellectual Autobiography*, trans. Sergio Knipe (London: Integral Tradition Publishing, 2009), 223].

147 About this, see the fundamental study by Walter Freund, *Modernus e altre idee di tempo nel Medioevo* (Milan: Medusa, 2001).

The Temporality of the Tiger: Some Notes on the Evolian 'Riding the Tiger'

projected towards the future as a mere anticipation thereof, as is intended by utopian-progressivist thought, which would be a present emptied of any meaning and value as it is entirely sacrificed to the future, a present reduced to a simple necessitated moment of a future which is inevitably destined to take place, "obviously" in the name of progress. Therefore, this linear, vectorial vision of time abrades, so to speak, the whole specificity of the present, "diminishing" it to a reifiable moment within a process which tends toward a "progressive" end, a processuality that is consequently made up of moments which are all equally homogeneous and empty, that is to say, homogeneous in their emptiness. In short, "today" is utterly bent to the reasons and the goals of the (progressivist) "tomorrow." To put it with Fachinelli, we are faced with a vision of time "as an irreversible flux, as a one-way totalisation in which all previous processes are reabsorbed."[148]

The Evolian tiger, however, is also something other than what Hartog calls *presentism*, which is a condition of the dereliction of time once it is bereft of both the past and the future; practically, we are dealing with a radically impoverished, one-dimensional time, an "irremediably present" time.[149] It is no coincidence that Beonio-Brocchieri, while underscoring the "omnipotent and omnivorous character of the present" and the "suffocating tyranny exercised by it,"[150] comes to speak of "a paradoxically de-temporalised time,"[151] precisely because a present which is utterly compressed and shrunken in presentism makes any ideas of temporal articulation, any

---

148 Elvio Fachinelli, *La freccia ferma. Tre tentativi di annullare il tempo* (Milan: Adelphi, 1992), 182.

149 François Hartog, *Chronos. L'Occidente alle prese con il tempo* (Turin: Einaudi, 2022), 244. Giacomo Marramao also focuses on the passage from the "colonisation of the future" (due to 'progressivist' philosophies of history) to the "eternalisation of the present" in *La passione del presente* (Turin: Bollati Boringhieri, 2008), 9.

150 Vittorio H. Beonio-Brocchieri, *Immagini del tempo e della storia nella modernità. Uno sguardo critico* (Rome: Carocci, 2022), 13.

151 Ibid., 12.

chronotype — to use Elvio Fachinelli's terms — disappear.¹⁵² In such a case, generations that were once almost contemporary with one another are now condemned to belong exclusively to their own time, with the result that the past is looked upon as a sort of *terra incognita*, an alien and foreign "landscape" which no longer belongs to us and of which we do not feel like heirs at all. The obvious outcome of such a dynamic is the observation that, in the absence of "intergenerational stability," "generations live virtually in 'different worlds,'" thereby causing a veritable "collapse of the symbolic reproduction of society."¹⁵³ In sum, what takes place is a transformation of time capable of upsetting the ideology of progress itself, which is "futuro-centric" by its own nature. Indeed, while progress brings with itself a detachment from the past, whereby — as Koselleck expounded in memorable pages — the set of foregoing experiences becomes useless within a context that is entirely devoted to a future which is thought of as having radically *new* characteristics compared to the past,¹⁵⁴ in the "today," with presentism, such a dynamic ends up disengaging itself from the future too, so as to become an end in itself precisely *in the present*. In summary, it is a "temporality 'stranded' in the present," and therefore no longer able to "move between the different dimensions of present, past and future."¹⁵⁵ A present that is forgetful of the richness of the times will therefore be "inhabited" by a multitude of history-less beings, since the removal of the past and of its plural memories (since the past is not monolithic and uniform) can only lead to such an outcome. It bears clarifying that speaking about an "eternalised" present does not at all mean thinking of it as something motionless

---

152 Cf. Fachinelli, *La freccia ferma*, 186-188. In corroboration, Heidegger suggested that we think of time not in the abstract as singular, but as "there are many times" - Martin Heidegger, *Il concetto di tempo* (Milan: Adelphi, 1998), 49.

153 Hartmut Rosa, *Accelerazione e alienazione. Per una teoria critica del tempo nella tarda modernità* (Turin: Einaudi, 2015), 83.

154 Cf. Reinhart Koselleck, *Futuro passato. Per una semantica dei tempi storici* (Bologna: CLUEB, 2007), 309-322.

155 Beonio-Brocchieri, *Immagini del tempo e della storia nella modernità*, 99.

The Temporality of the Tiger: Some Notes on the Evolian 'Riding the Tiger'

and inanimate, as if some sort of eternal present of an almost "Parmenidean" type were resurfacing in the heart of modernity. Quite the opposite: presentism is connoted by an unruly, messy, and feverish haste, by a continuous, unceasing agitation, combined with an eagerness for novelty, which, however — and this is the essential point — do not escape the present, but are all consumed within it. It is a Narcissus-time, mirroring only itself and impermeable to any other temporality.

Nonetheless, the Evolian tiger does not look to the past with nostalgia either; in it, there is no turning back to an idealised and uncorrupted past, to a true golden age compared to a present which is perceived as perpetually in crisis, in radical decline, and the victim of a tumultuous and blind movement. Instead, there is a convinced and decisive acceptance of the challenge represented by one's own time; in the Evola of *Ride the Tiger*, there is full awareness of the fact that modernity is unbypassable, and therefore of the necessity of coming to terms with one's epoch, without trying easy illusionistic shortcuts (since they are ideologically oriented), and without even taking refuge in comfortable "inner citadels" from which to observe the convulsive events of history with aloofness and scorn. In sum, the tiger's present is not interpreted as an absence or a lack to be filled by looking back towards happier times.

So, what type of present does the Evolian tiger go together with? The answer seems very clear to me, and it is to be found in the very nature of the animal chosen by Evola. The tiger is the present, but a constantly moving present, not deadened but uproarious, alive and lively, aggressive and, above all, untamed; it has nothing to do with Adorno's tigers, neither with the one locked in a cage nor with the other one which moves freely but only in its impassable enclosure.[156] Moreover, as already said, this is not an "eternalised" present, which would paradoxically

---

[156] Cf. Theodor W. Adorno, *Minima moralia. Meditazioni della vita offesa* (Turin: Einaudi, 1994), 132.

therefore be basically pacified, even in its agitation, as a present continuing in its empty repetition, i.e., in the vacuous quest for something new that is always ephemeral and superficial. Nor is it a present that is virtually reduced to a fossil, a mere station on the way to future "progress." In fact, Evola himself reminds us that the tiger can both run and tire, which, joined with the animal's untameable character, represents, in my opinion, the real key to understanding this "formula": the impossibility of enclosing time in a forefixed and foreordained scheme, of harnessing it into a linear and homogeneous movement, of subjecting it to a single dimension. The tiger's time is made up of swerves, sudden deviations, abrupt changes of direction; likewise, it can know continuous thrusts forward as well as unexpected quietings. Equally important, and indeed essential in order to free time from the meshes of necessity, is the untethering of the tiger-present from the doctrine of cycles as done by Evola. Indeed, at the moment in which the tiger's movement is taken away from cyclical readings, and above all from the reference to the closure of the currently dominant cycle, the *kali-yuga*, time and history are opened once again, i.e., they are emancipated from a suffocating grip and returned to a free becoming, which is an immense reserve of possibilities. To recover a nice image by Fabrizio Desideri, the present is once again exposed "to the *clinamen* of possibility."[157] In other words, not only is it good that the cycle does not close, but above all it is good that the whole cyclical system is put into question, so as to avoid the risk of diminishing the power of riding the tiger, bending it to an unavoidable and unescapable *telos*. In other words, it is decisive that the power can flow freely without being constrained in the snares of Ananke.

To recapitulate: the present of the tiger is *free*. It is a present which is not subjected to a fatally forewritten future, be it cyclical or linear, and it is not forgetful of the richness of the times, since it is not closed into a mere replication of itself.

---

157 Fabrizio Desideri, "Postfazione" a Louis-Auguste Blanqui, *L'eternità attraverso gli astri* (Milan: SE, 2005), 94.

The Temporality of the Tiger: Some Notes on the Evolian 'Riding the Tiger'

Therefore, precisely by virtue of being free, the tiger stands at the intersection of all times, and, let it be said *en passant*, also of the time of the origin (not intended metaphysically), which can be started once again in the present only by "an act of breaking" towards the latter, and therefore with an act "of radical non-correspondence towards contemporaneity,"[158] and this because "the origin truly manifests itself only when it builds a completely different actuality,"[159] i.e., a distancing from a particular present, nonetheless operated always *in the present* and in view of *another present*.

Once again: the free present is the point of confluence of all times. It is not by chance that Heidegger, over pages of intensely critiquing the equation of Parmenidean being with eternity, notes that "the present is so much time that the past and the future are usually understood only and above all by starting from it."[160] In other words, if the present is disregarded, there can be neither past nor future, but - attention - all of this is only from the perspective of an authentic present, i.e., a present that is taken away from whatever necessitating bond and that is capable of marking a radical discontinuity with philosophies of history (be they reactionary or progressivist, here such a distinction is not important) as well as the presentism which reigns today; only in this way is it possible, for example, for there to be what Walter Benjamin — in his fifteenth thesis about the concept of history and with a language not too dissimilar from the Evolian one — called "the tiger's leap in the past,"[161] which, in turn, is bound to the key term *Eingedenken*, to be read as the "threshold between the event (the sudden surfacing of a darting image from the past) and the praxis which may correspond to this event (or

---

[158] Francesco Marchesi, *Ritorno ai princìpi. Concezioni della storia da Machiavelli alla Rivoluzione francese* (Rome: Carocci, 2022), 175.

[159] Ibid., 187.

[160] Martin Heidegger, *L'inizio della filosofia occidentale. Interpretazione di Anassimandro e Parmenide* (Milan: Adelphi, 2022), 207.

[161] Walter Benjamin, *Sul concetto di storia* (Turin: Einaudi, 1997), 47.

The Temporality of the Tiger: Some Notes on the Evolian 'Riding the Tiger'

miss it)."[162] Ernst Bloch also speaks about this when he links the "remembering" to the "not-happened" which is to be sought for "in the already-happened,"[163] but in order to extract new constellations of sense (which, for this German philosopher, are revolutionary) from the latter. In sum, we are dealing with a "setting in motion" of both past and future at once, but still starting from a present precisely within which it is possible to make such a sudden leap (an eventuality which is precluded wherever it is subject to conditions which make it unfree). Indeed, it is only *in this present* that the decisive moment which transforms the past can take place; the past, apparently left behind as something inert, immobile, something definitely gone, is thence transformed into something which is once again alive and lively, in order to then be projected into a future which is not already predetermined, but which has to be written anew every time.

One last remark; riding the tiger is often associated with the concept of acceleration, as if Evola, through such an image or symbol, had aimed to shorten the times that would separate us from the end of the dark age, almost as a calque of the *pressing time* of Apocalyptic literature. Now, in my opinion, such an interpretation should be radically rejected, and for at least three reasons; the first one is explicitly indicated by Evola himself when, as already said, he unlinks riding the tiger from any reference to a cyclically intended future; then, of course, the tiger moves quickly, but there are no textual footholds to justify its accelerated motion; but, above all, the clearest disproof of the accelerationist reading is to be found

---

162 Stefano Marchesoni, "Flashback-Forward. L'immemorare tra Bloch e Benjamin", introduction to Ernst Bloch-Walter Benjamin, *Ricordare il futuro. Scritti sull'*Eingedenken (Milan-Udine: Mimesis, 2017), 20. Expressions singularly resonating with the conceptual plexus of *Eingedenken* are present, in my opinion, in the volume by Antonio Damasio, *L'errore di Cartesio. Emozione, ragione e cervello umano* (Milan: Adelphi, 1995), where he speaks about "memory of the possible future" (p. 325) or of "memories of the future" (p. 353).

163 Ernst Bloch, *Thomas Münzer teologo della rivoluzione* (Milan: Feltrinelli, 1981), 33. Hence, Bloch says, "the dead turn again, in a new way of acting, in connections of meaning that show the new" (*ibid.*).

The Temporality of the Tiger: Some Notes on the Evolian 'Riding the Tiger'

in the behaviour of the one who rides the tiger, who neither incites nor spurs it to run more rapidly, not to mention that he does not guide it and even less so can master its run. Briefly said, riding the tiger has very little humanism in it. It is by no means whatsoever an umpteenth example of the triumph of man capable of governing time and the events that occur within it. It is not an image of man as the lord of time. Quite the contrary, he who rides the tiger finds himself in the most radical insecurity, as he can always be thrown off and trampled by the animal; in other words, his condition is constitutively exposed to risk, to danger. The only true attitude of he who is on the back of the tiger is rather that of *estote parati*, that is, keeping hold, while staying watchful and ready to take action when the tiger shows signs of exhaustion.

Without wishing to resort to very risky parallels, the reference to the gospel warning to *estote parati* and to be ready at the right moment so as to grasp the *kairós*, recalls some pages by Heidegger which seem to me not too far from what Evola is talking about, if not on a doctrinal level, then certainly for the existential condition they describe. In one of those rare books in which philosophy seems almost on the verge of "understanding" life, Heidegger, speaking about the attitude of the early Christians towards the *parousia*, writes that they lived in a "constant insecurity" which is — and this is an essential point — "the characteristic trait of all those things that have a fundamental meaning." Furthermore, the exhortation — Pauline in this case — addressed to the early Christians is "to be watchful and sober," that is, to keep cool, clear-headed, without being contaminated by enthusiasm or, even worse, "by the eagerness to fantasise of those who, sniffing out questions such as that of the 'when' of the *parousia*, speculate on it,"[164] so as to "stay steady" without wavering, since the *parousia* is also the "time of verification," of the either-or which marks a distinction from the "lost ones."[165]

---

164 Martin Heidegger, *Fenomenologia della vita religiosa* (Milan: Adelphi, 2003), 146.
165 Ibid., 202-203.

The Temporality of the Tiger: Some Notes on the Evolian 'Riding the Tiger'

At this point it would be appropriate to broaden the perspective a little with regard to the issue of acceleration as such, which seems to me to deserve some further reflection. Although it has found its most congenial field of application in modernity, the category of acceleration, from the genealogical point of view, decidedly harkens back much earlier in time, in some ways further confirming the well known theses of Karl Löwith on the religious origin of many concepts which later became secularised with the birth of the modern epoch. Indeed, when Koselleck notes how the 18th-century philosophy of progress has amongst its essential characteristics precisely that of marking a formidable historical acceleration, which then finds its culminating moment in the 1789 revolution, he adds that such an "acceleration of time" was already an "eschatological category," foreign to the classical world and now immanentised within the dimension of an "earthly, worldly planning."[166] It is a decisive passage; it was precisely the missed coming of the end of the world that made possible the birth of the Church and "the establishment of a static time that can be experienced as tradition."[167] Tradition, as the reassuring barrier to the Apocalyptic irruption and to its "*very soon*," is born precisely out of the catastrophe of the messianic idea. The imminence of the end of the world is literally "frozen" so as to allow the Church to turn into a triumphant worldly institution destined to perpetuate itself over the centuries. This is why Jacob Taubes cannot fail to recognise that "Apocalypticism is revolutionary,"[168] precisely because it questions the ordered flow of the time of tradition, hoping for its violent break. Hence the resurfacing of Apocalyptic prophecy in the great revolutionary conjunctures of the 16th-17th century, for instance in the Germany of the Protestant Reformation with the world upheaval preached by Thomas

---

166 Koselleck, *Futuro passato*, 26.

167 Ibid., 25. Hartog too underlines the very close link between Apocalypse and acceleration, insisting on images of God who "hastens the times", of the "pressing time" and of messianic *urgency* (Cf. François Hartog, *Chronos*, 17, 19).

168 Jacob Taubes, *Escatologia occidentale* (Macerata: Quodlibet, 2019), 36.

The Temporality of the Tiger: Some Notes on the Evolian 'Riding the Tiger'

Müntzer for the purpose of establishing the kingdom of God on Earth, or during the English Revolution with the Fifth Monarchists.[169] Hence, again, the converging, the meeting, of acceleration and the revolution of 18th-century France within a common "futuro-centric" vision. Therefore, the purpose of revolutionary acceleration is the conquest of a future considered to be undoubtedly better than everything coming before it, in full respect of its progressive character, or even a future of absolute perfection, almost the secularised version of Müntzer's dream, as in the case of Jacobinism.[170]

But the discourse becomes quite more complex with the emergence of the awareness that no one ends up belonging "completely, without residues, to their own time" when the latter "undergoes sudden accelerations, as in the case of revolutions,"[171] so much so that revolutionaries themselves experienced this directly, such as when they were devoured by the Saturn-revolution, as Georg Büchner had understood in his *La morte di Danton*. This is why the risk of the heterogony of ends, of serving uncontrolled forces which are abysmally distant from one's intentions and projects, is always lurking, whereby the operator and his actions might turn into what Carl Schmitt, in very clear pages, called *involuntary accelerators*, which are bent to dynamics extraneous or even opposite to them. In short, the gap, the temporal asymmetry, that is created as a result of the accelerationist interruption, the feeling of no longer being wholly part of the current times, may lead to a series of sundry ruinous behaviours, from withdrawing into an idealised past to falling into *occasionalism* (Schmitt again), or to the attempt, unsuccessful by its own nature, to steer one's times with the weapon of ideology, thus ending up — recovering the Evolian image — thrown off by the tiger-

---

169 Cf. Mario Miegge, *Il sogno del re di Babilonia. Profezia e storia da Thomas Müntzer a Isaac Newton* (Milan: Feltrinelli, 1995), respectively 35-40 and 137-151.

170 The line that goes from Müntzer to Robespierre, passing through the English Fifth Monarchists, is traced in the text by Miegge, 151.

171 Beonio-Brocchieri, *Immagini del tempo e della storia nella modernità*, 94.

present and therefore defeated by it. Nonetheless, this point, albeit only cursorily treated here, is connected to another, yet more essential note. Acceleration always responds to a finalistic logic, is always teleologically directed, and therefore has a one-sided trend, filling the course of time and history in its entirety. And even when it seems to move according to the logic of unpredictability, when, therefore, it seems to "run off course" as in the case of the involuntary accelerators, this does not mean that it loses its finalistic nature. It indeed undergoes a twist, but in the sense of the heterogony of ends and certainly not that of a radical ateleologism. In other words, the finalistic system remains unchanged, and this puts such a perspective into frontal collision with that of the *open* vision of historical time, which, on the other hand, by definition does not place mortgages on the future, the latter having to be intended, rather, as a free field of tensions between compossibilities. Accordingly, a catastrophist acceleration is nothing other than a reproduction of progressivist teleologism, obviously inverted in its meaning, as well as a "filiation" — just equally if not even more faithful to the original —, of apocalyptic acceleration. In sum, I believe that the genealogical matrix of such a philosophy of history — which is precisely an Enlightenment-type teleology — is very clear, and it is a matrix whose outcomes are merely inversed while its vectorial nature remains unbroken. In short, the linear and finalistic trend of history is by no means abrogated or put into question, only its sign is changed.

Yet, the discourse is even more complex, since there are, in my opinion, at least two different accelerationist variants. One is what we have examined hereinbefore as corresponding to the "futuro-centric" disposition, which is typical of "progressivist" philosophies of history, on the basis of which acceleration is precisely aimed at achieving certain objectives, making them, so to speak, "within reach," bringing them ever closer in an ever faster motion. And this obviously applies to its negative copy too, given that catastrophic acceleration itself tends towards the realisation of an end. The other typology, on the other hand, has to be traced back to presentism, the Christian origin of which (albeit obviously twisted and radically transformed) was exposed by Hartog, in that presentism "resolves itself in the instant and has no other horizon than itself," not perceiving itself as "an intermediate time,"[172] as instead happened to Christian time. Compared to Rosa's thesis, which detected the cycle of acceleration, understood as "a self-perpetuating closed system,"[173] in the interweaving of the three dimensions of the acceleration of the pace of life, social changes, and, obviously, technological acceleration, Hartog not only has the merit of having highlighted the Christian background of "presentist" acceleration, but above all he has underscored its ineliminable finalistic characterisation, for instance when he writes that such an accelerative form, based on the exaltation of instantaneity, simultaneity, rapid obsolescence, continuous innovation, and so on, finds "its purpose in itself."[174] Therefore, I believe that only this type of autotelic acceleration can be correctly defined as *accelerationism*, that is to say, as a conception hinged upon the valorisation of acceleration in and of itself, of acceleration as such, having precisely the end in itself, and thereby tending to a closed self-reproduction, since it has no other possible outlets. An alternative to accelerationism — barely hinted at here and requiring much more space to elaborate —, one that is in line with the open vision of time and history and is very distant from both sterile nostalgia for lost "slowness" and "futuristic" wishful thinking, will then have to dismiss acceleration in its centrality and reduce it to merely one among plural and possible temporal dimensions, one that is always in question in the unpredictable game of freedom. This is yet another confirmation, if we still need it, of the freedom of the Evolian riding the tiger.

Translated by U.X.A.

---

172 Hartog, *Chronos*, 262.

173 Rosa, *Accelerazione e alienazione*, 32.

174 Hartog, *Chronos*, 250.

TRADITIONALISM AS THE TREE AND THE ARK OF THE RADICAL SELVES FOR THE RESTORATION OF THE ERST PHILOSOPHY

Uligang Xanth Ansbrandt

Introduction

The present essay tries to chart routes that may be taken by Traditionalism in the contemporary epoch, exploring what Tradition and Traditionalism are, who their representative agents — the Traditionalists — are, whither Traditionalism may fare as a movement, and how it may be employed as a methodological praxis. Traces and hints left behind by the early Traditionalist authors René Guénon (1886-1951) and Julius Evola (1898-1974) are connected to frameworks of ideas wrought by contemporary Traditionalist thinkers, including Aleksandr Dugin and Yevgeny Nechkasov, as well as in the wake of my own work *Eurasian Universism: Sinitic Orientations for Rethinking the Western Logos*, in order to then outline ways of concrete development within the contemporary Eurasian setting. More in detail, Traditionalism is understood as the gnosiological and onto-theological tree-like structure of the holy itself, and is allegorised as a means, vehicle — an ark — for gathering qualified agents, Traditionalists — whom Dugin calls the Radical Selves —, who are its operators and whose task would be that of navigating cultures and opening interactive hermeneutical "passages" between them, for stimulating a rebirth of the structure of the holy into reality, especially within the degenerating reality produced by Western modernity-postmodernity, in order to outlast it. Traditionalism is ultimately characterised as an "orthological" hermeneutical methodology for setting in operation new manifestations of the Erst Wisdom — otherwise called the Eternal/Perennial Tradition/Philosophy — into matter.

1. Cues of Hermetic Alchemical Cosmology

Summarising an idea that underlies my book *Eurasian Universism* (2022) in its entirety, we can affirm that the history of human civilisation tells of the struggle of mankind to rise above brute matter, and to mould it by following spiritual models, and it is especially in the cosmological systems of the vast expanse of Eurasia that we find a deep inspiration for the ascension of the human soul from the Earth below to the constellations of Heaven above through the way of the spirit, which comes down as a ladder to the Earth from the constellations of Heaven themselves.[175] Mankind operates within the tensional dimensionality straught atwixt the North Pole of Heaven and the South Pole of the Earth, between spirit and matter; the human entity itself is in fact a microcosmic reproduction of the macrocosmic polar drama, and can take the side of either the one or the other of the two poles. Mankind has therefore a twofold nature, which, according to the Italian Traditionalist philosopher Julius Evola (1898-1974), is represented by the twofold World Tree

---

[175] The cosmological, esoteric and ritual theme summarised in the present essay is underseen from various outlooks in my book: Xantio Ansprandi, *Eurasian Universism* (Tucson, Arizona: PRAV Publishing, 2022). Other works that behandle it from still other perspectives are: Joscelyn Godwin, *Arktos: The Polar Myth in Science, Symbolism, and Nazi Survival* (Kempton, Illinois: Adventures Unlimited Press, 1996); and Peter Levenda, *Stairway to Heaven: Chinese Alchemists, Jewish Kabbalists, and the Art of Spiritual Transformation* (New York City, New York; London, England: Continuum International Publishing, 2008).

or *Axis Mundi* of Good and Evil.[176]

Regarding the nature of mankind, Evola thus writes in his *The Hermetic Tradition* (1931), citing the *Corpus Hermeticum*, IX, 4 / X, 24-25:[177]

> Man is not lowered to have a mortal part, but, on the contrary, such mortality increases his possibility and his potency. His twofold functions are possible to him only because of his twofold nature: he is constituted so as to embrace at one time both the terrestrial and the divine [celestial]. / We are not afraid to tell the truth. The true man is above them [the celestial gods], or at least equal to them. Since no god leaves its sphere to come down to the Earth, whilst man goes up to Heaven and measures it. Whence, we dare to say that a man is a mortal god and that a uranic [celestial] god is an immortal man.

The ascensional way of the spirit consists of seven phases, states or levels, also represented as steps of a ladder, which are the reflection of the Seven Sprits, Lights, Eyes, Deities or Archangels of the supreme God of Heaven — the One. They "are simultaneously internal and external, abide in mankind and in the world, in the visible and in the invisible aspects of

---

176 Julius Evola, *La tradizione ermetica*, ed. Gianfranco de Turris (Rome, Italy: Edizioni Mediterranee, 1996 [1931]), 40. About the ambivalence of the symbol of the tree, Aleksandr Dugin writes that it may give way to an "optical-ontological illusion": on the one hand, at first impression, the tree may be interpreted as growing from the Earth without the intervention of Heaven, and therefore it may be interpreted as a symbol of materialism (the Greek concept of *hyle*, one of the terms for "matter", literally means "wood, forest"), the conception of the world from below, which explains the superior through the inferior and the birth of the son only through the mother without the father's intervention (matriarchal view); on the other hand, it is well known that the tree grows from the seed, from the power of life which comes from Heaven to the Earth, and life is not given to the seed by the Earth itself, but the latter only welcomes and nurtures it (the concept of *khora* in Plato's *Timaeus*), and therefore the tree is, in this case, a symbol of the son which is borne by the mother through the intervention of the father (patriarchal view). The second view is often also represented, for instance in Jewish Kabbalah, as a tree which grows from above, from Heaven, towards the Earth. See: Aleksandr Dugin, *Soggetto radicale. Teoria e fenomenologia* (Milan, Italy: AGA Editrice, 2019), 204-205; Aleksandr Dugin, *Platonismo politico* (Milan, Italy: AGA Editrice, 2020), 106-107. N.b. *Soggetto radicale* is the Italian edition of *The Radical Subject and its Double*, and is augmented with an appendix dedicated to Julius Evola (323-351) written by Dugin himself.

177 Evola, *La tradizione ermetica*, 40.

them both", they work as "astral fecundations of the terrestrial womb", each of them identified as one of the traditional Seven Planets of the Solar System, their bodily "petrifications" — Sun, Saturn, Jupiter, Mars, Mercury, Venus, Moon —, and they are each associated with a colour, a metal, given animals and plants, as well as a human temperament and the seven centres of the human body throughout which the energy of the supernal God flows and goes up through the World Tree towards the Seven Stars of the North Pole, which are the uppermost celestial bodies corresponding to the Seven Planets and are gathered into the two *Arktos* asterisms, the fixed stars — Ursa Major and Ursa Minor, also known as the Big Chariot and Small Chariot.[178] Concepts such as the Vedic Sanskrit *Rita* (or *Dharma*,[179] which in the most ancient Vedic literature defines any particularisation and specialisation of the *Rita*), the Greek *Orthotes* (in later Hellenic philosophy equated with

---

[178] The various phenomenal associations of the Seven Spirits are not deepened in the present essay. For detailed analyses, it is suggested to refer to: Evola, *La tradizione ermetica*, 52, 72-81, then 100, where Evola speaks about the human body as a "stem" through which the divine energy flows and lights up various "qualities", associated to various colours, sprouting from the stem itself as "buds", then 129, note 75, where Evola cursorily mentions that the seven metals are associated to seven human types, each of which has its own medicine; Heinrich Cornelius Agrippa von Nettesheim, *Three Books of Occult Philosophy*, trans. James Freake, ed. Donald Tyson (Woodbury, Minnesota: Llewellyn Publications, 1993), 72-104, 274-275, 315-328 & passim; Peter James, Marianus Anthony van der Sluijs, "Ziggurats, Colors, and Planets: Rawlinson Revisited", *Journal of Cuneiform Studies*, 60 (Chicago, Illinois: University of Chicago Press, 2008), 57-79. These sources are by no means exhaustive, and it is worthwhile to clarify that different religious and esoteric traditions propose different associations. Regarding the human body as a microcosmic "stem" or "tree", reflecting the macrocosmic World Tree, it is represented, for instance, in the Germanic tradition by the rune *Algiz*, "Elk", precisely representing either a stem/tree, or a man with raised arms, or the branched horns of the elk animal (Evola, *La tradizione ermetica*, 100), and in the Mesopotamian tradition by the *Duranki*, the "Link of Heaven and Earth", which is at the same time the cosmic tree, the human body and the temple as the place of encounter between the powers of Heaven and Earth, and ultimately represents the order of manifestation of God in matter. About these meanings of the cosmic tree in the Mesopotamian tradition, see: Simo Parpola, "The Assyrian Tree of Life: Tracing the Origins of Jewish Monotheism and Greek Philosophy", *Journal of Near Eastern Studies*, 52(3) (Chicago, Illinois: University of Chicago Press, 1993), 173.

[179] From the same Indo-European linguistic root of the Sanskrit *Dharma*, which is *d[h]er*, also comes the Latin *Firmus, Firma*.

the *Logos*), the Latin *Ratio* (and *Ordo*), the Germanic *Irmin*, and the Slavic *Prav* — all meaning "Right" and "Rightness" — identify at once both the starry divine operational order of the North Pole, the seven-levelled axis of ascension to and imitation of it, and, in some cultural contexts, the God of the North Pole itself, which is the First Principle, the outset of the starry divine order and of the ladder for ascending to it, and the destination to which the ladder and the stars lead the soul of the awoken seeker.

In the Eurasian cosmological systems, matter is viewed as the metaphysically low, female and passive part of the cosmic drama, and corresponds to the thick and tendentially cold Earth-stuff and Water-stuff which gravitate towards the South Pole of the Earth, the *Infernus* and the *Hypochthonion* ("Under-Earth"). Such is *Chaos* in its unordered state, onto which the metaphysically high, masculine and active part of the cosmic drama, the spirit, penetrates; the latter is associated with the thin and tendentially hot Air-stuff and Fire-stuff, but also, before entering matter, with the firststuff Aether, also known as the metaphysical Fire, which in the manifested world coalesces into the form of whatever one of the other four stuffs. The active, fiery spirit, coming from the North Pole of Heaven, the *Paradisus* and the *Hyperuranion* ("Over-Heaven"), and being the same as the *Nous* which begets the ordering *Logos*, elevates and sublimates material reality in an ascending process. The *Nous–Logos* is the same as the self-manifesting First Principle, the aethereal metaphysical Fire of the Erst Male, which is different from the hot Fire-stuff of physical reality and is often characterised as a Cold Fire in Hermetic alchemical symbolism — Evola elucidates that Hermetism represents one of the offshoots, amongst the purest ones according to him, of the unitary Erst Philosophy, or Erst Wisdom[180] —, a Fire which is Ice at the same time, acting by a sharp and terrible harshness which does not set the

---

[180] Evola, *La tradizione ermetica*, 25. Evola uses the definition "Unitary Primordial Tradition"; I prefer to use "Erst Philosophy" or "Erst Wisdom" throughout the present essay.

flow of matter ablaze but freezes it, enlivening but at the same time dominating, steering and shaping it until it culminates in the miracle of self-awareness, the birth of the I.[181] It is a Fire internal to beings, that is present in them in higher or lower degrees, and is cultivable; it is an inner heat which "washes", that is to say, purifies, matter.[182] This Fire-Ice, which burns-yet-freezes matter, which steers and shapes it, setting marks, edges to it, is also symbolised by the shining sword, which in turn also represents the World Tree which connects Heaven and Earth, and on which, at the point of the intersection of the two dimensions, the verticality of Heaven and the horizontality of the Earth, a rose — or, in general, a flower, such as the lotus in Egyptian and Eastern traditions — blossoms as the symbol of the perfect realisation of the spirit within matter.[183] This Cold Fire corresponds to the ancient Germanic concept of "Brand" (Proto-Germanic: *Brandaz), the "Fiery Sword".[184]

The interpenetration of the forces of the two opposite poles is well represented by the "Paradigm" from *De coniecturis* by the Rhenish German mystic Nicholas of Kues (1401-1464) as interpreted by the Russian Traditionalist philosopher Aleksandr Dugin in conjunction with the Hermetic alchemical symbols of Sulfur with Gold, Mercury with Silver, and Salt: Sulfur symbolises the Superior Waters, Air-stuff, and is associated with Gold, which further symbolises the Sun, masculinity, light and qualitative distinction, and in Kues' Paradigm is represented by a white triangle descending from above; Mercury symbolises the Inferior Waters, Water-stuff, and is associated with Silver, which further symbolises the

---

181 Ibidem, 62, 65.

182 Ibidem, 144-147.

183 Ibidem, 98-100.

184 "Brand" originally means both "fire" and "sword", or "shining sword", "flaming sword", and, in particular, it refers to the double-edged sword. A flaming or double-edged sword is the weapon of the archangels Michael and Uriel, as well as of the Coming One in the Jewish Biblical tradition and in John's *Apocalypse*, and is also the weapon of *Kalki*, the embodiment of God which ends the Iron Age (*Kali Yuga*), according to the Hindu tradition.

Moon, femininity, darkness and quantitative indistinction, and in Kues' Paradigm is represented by a black triangle ascending from below; Salt, instead, symbolises the Earth-stuff, as well as the myriads of living creatures which emerge from the commingling of the two opposite principles, and in Kues' Paradigm is represented by the grey rhomboid space resulting from the interlocking of the two triangles.[185] The terrestrial surface, the *Epichthonion* ("Upon-Earth"), which is matter, or the Earth-stuff, in its solid and thus workable state, hosts the myriads of living creatures as the embodiments of the *Logos*, whilst the *Hypochthonion* is a conceptualisation of liquid and thus still unmasterable matter.[186] The perfection or imperfection, the purity or impurity of "metals" — that is to say, individual beings which emerge from the Earth-stuff, according to the Hermetic vocabulary — depends on the degree of presencing in them, or the strength of action in them, of Sulfur in its most pristine state, that is to say the aethereal metaphysical Fire of the Erst Male with minimal contamination by Mercury, by fluid matter, i.e., materialised to the least degree.[187] It is worthwhile to indicate that the Greek term for "Sulfur" is *Theon*, the same term which also means the abstract, unpersonal, unparticularised "Divine".[188]

"Matter" is "Mother" — these two words, being variations of the same etymological theme, are almost synonymous, and carry with themselves the whole semantic complex expressing what is not or not yet shapen by the celestial *Logos* of the First Principle, by the spirit of the Father God of Heaven. This is the private dimension *versus* the public dimension, apolity *versus* polity — with all the semantic implications of these

---

185 Aleksandr Dugin, *Il sole di mezzanotte. Aurora del soggetto radicale* (Milan, Italy: AGA Editrice, 2019), 7; Dugin, *Soggetto radicale*, 157-158; also see: Evola, *La tradizione ermetica*, 58-71.

186 For the distinction between *Epichthonion* and *Hypochthonion* see: Aleksandr Dugin, *Noomachia. Rivolta contro il mondo postmoderno* (Milan, Italy: AGA Editrice, 2020), 123.

187 Evola, *La tradizione ermetica*, 65-66.

188 Ibidem, 49, note 66.

two concepts, namely the unorganic, unorganised "unpolished" state and the organic, organised "polished" state.[189] Given that everything in the physical dimension is made up of matter, which is pervaded and given form by the spirit, in this dimension the feminine and quantity tend to prevail over the masculine, that is to say *Chaos* over *Logos*, the latter being in a constant movement and struggle to qualify and sublimate the former with its forms — so that the *Logos* is ongoingly, victoriously reborn out of *Chaos*; the logic of thinking shapes itself out of the chaotic primordial matter through ordered embodiments.[190]

The flowing waters of matter are the "Woman of the Philosophers", the material to be shapen with the grounding of the divine work of Heaven; this flowing, not yet shapen matter is also symbolised by the *Katholikos Ophis*, the "All-Whole Serpent/Dragon" — corresponding in meaning to the *Jormungand* of the Germanic tradition — which, according to Gnostic teachings, slithers across everything. This ouroboric primordial Serpent duplicates itself into another female and a male serpent, symbolising Earth below and Heaven above, Moon and Sun. The female serpent retains the character of the primordial Serpent — indeterminate possibility of qualification, chaotic transformation and multiplicity, represented by a further multiplication of the female serpent itself into other female serpents, "green and wanton dragons", like the ones foughten by solar heroes in many traditions. The male serpent embodies the *Logos* itself as the "Philosophical Basilisk" of Oswald Croll (1563-1609)'s writings, which, in the guise of a thunderbolt — the weapon of *Marduk*, "Son of the Sun", in his fight against the draconic all-mother *Tiamat*, the

---

189 Ansprandi, *Eurasian Universism*, 38, for the common etymological origin of the concepts of "politics", "politeness", "polishedness", and even "polar", and their cosmological, axial implications.

190 The birth of the primordial duality of Sun and Moon, of *Logos* and limited *Chaos*, from the primordial waters of unrestrained *Chaos*, which, in Hermetic alchemical symbolism, is ultimately the same as the primordial One, the *Nous* of Heaven, is well explained in: Evola, *La tradizione ermetica*, 48-60, 70.

"Sea", in the Mesopotamian tradition —, acting as an ordering centre of irradiation, can dominate and mould the chaotic waters.[191] It is the Fiery Dragon, which, once awoken within the heart, enlightens the entire human entity as a sevenfold lightning energy, freeing the entity itself from the coils of the female watery serpent, and ascending as the freed solar principle to the brain, where it contemplates the world within a clarified mind.[192] If separated from the masculine, solar centre, the feminine, lunar flowing matter would be mere blind impulse and wild precipitation, a whirlwindish waterfall.[193]

To describe the macrocosmic drama of the self-unfolding of the universal God, which is *Nous* and *Logos*, Evola quotes from the *Corpus Hermeticum*, I, 9 as follows:[194]

> The intellectual entity, the God male and female, that is Light and Life, begets with the *Logos* another creative intelligence, the God of Fire and Fluid, which in turn constitutes seven ministers, which enclose the sensible world within their circles. Their domain is called Orlay.

This macrocosmic drama reflects itself in the microcosm of mankind and the individual, in which the God of Heaven can become aware of itself as the Golden Sun of the fiery I, and of its own penetration into the material Earth, which is *Chaos*, to spiritualise and sublimate it, so that, as Evola writes:[195]

> [The] intellectual entity [...] is the Sun and the Gold in man. It is the centre, the principle of a spiritual, radiating and not inert stability, first origin of whatever through the Superior Waters [Sulfur; Gold; Air-stuff; celestial Sun; blood in the human body] and the Inferior Waters [Mercury; Silver; Water-stuff; celestial Moon; human nerves and glands] comes down to the telluric compound [Salt; Earth-stuff; human skeleton, cartilages, tendons] to move and enliven it in a superior sense. Supraindividual in itself,

---

191 Ibidem, 56-59.

192 Ibidem, 133, note 93.

193 Ibidem, 59.

194 Ibidem, 72.

195 Ibidem, 70, and 66-70 for the associations in the squared brackets.

it gives rise to individuality, to the I-function. It is the *Nous* [...] the foremost power of Fire.

2. Essentials of Traditionalism

2.1. *Sophia Perennis*, the Western Inversion, and the Theory of the Cycles

Following the Dutch scholar of esotericism Wouter Hanegraaff, according to whom Traditionalism is a revolt against the modern Western world but is born with Western modernity itself, and based on a correspondence with the English poet Kathleen Raine (1908-2003), the English historian Mark Sedgwick sees ideas similar to those of Traditionalism already in Renaissance Platonism, especially in the thought of the Italian philosopher Marsilio Ficino (1433-1499), who sought to re-create the Platonic Academy in Florence and wrote about a *Prisca Theologia* ("Original Theology"), later also yclept *Philosophia Perennis* or *Sophia Perennis*, that is "Perennial Philosophy" or "Perennial Wisdom",[196] by the Italian philosopher Agostino Steuco (1497-1548), which underlies all historical religions and is aimed at heightening the human soul from the senses and matter to the enlightening divine source, to God, through the spirit, whereby the human mind acquires from God the knowledge of the divine order of the universe and of how to reproduce it within reality, establishing vertically oriented, divinely inspired and celestially wended civilisations.[197] Ficino, however, still operated within the fold

---

[196] "Perennial" means that such Wisdom ongoingly manifests itself in time in the form of the year — the Latin adjective *perennis* is a compound of *per annus*, meaning "before/above/over the [cycle of the] year[s]". It is worthwhile noting that the Latin *annus* is likely related to the Sumerian *An*, which in the Mesopotamian tradition, one of the earliest iterations of the pristine Erst Wisdom, means the supreme "God" as "Heaven", whose centre is the North Pole and whose manifested form is the cycle of the year.

[197] Mark Sedgwick, *Against the Modern World: Traditionalism and the Secret Intellectual History of the Twentieth Century* (Oxford, England: Oxford University Press, 2009), 15, 23.

of Christianity,[198] which many Traditionalists regard as the main cause of the loss of Tradition in the modern world because of some mistaken metaphysical outlooks it came to embody.[199] Howbeit, the origins of Traditionalism may be unmistakably traced back to the work of the French metaphysician René Guénon (1886-1951), commonly regarded as the very founder of Traditionalism, in which the idea of a *Philosophia Perennis* is one of the three fundamental cores as identified by Sedgwick, forwhy Traditionalism has often also been termed "Perennial Traditionalism" or straightforwardly "Perennialism".[200]

---

198 Ibidem, 23.

199 Ansprandi, *Eurasian Universism*, 58-62. According to Evola, the main fault of Christianity, which has wroken catastrophe on the civilisation of the ancient Western Eurasian world, is of having universalised a false way of realisation, that is to say, initiation and access to truth and immortality, or eternal life, indiscriminately to all humanity, thus trivialising these concepts which originally belonged to the metaphysics of traditional religious mysteries, accessible only to qualified individuals. The mistake, which began in some degenerative forms of Orphism, was globally expanded by Christianity, and ongoes in modern spiritualisms (i.e., those doctrines according to which there is a distinction between metaphysical or spiritual and physical or material reality, understood as two separate worlds or dimensions where "the dead ones" and "the living ones" exist apart, albeit such worlds are interconnected in rare circumstances and on rare occasions, or by the works of certain specialists or media), has resulted in the widespread idea that the souls of all human beings are unconditionally eternal, immortal. In traditional mystical doctrines, otherwise, the souls of the vast majority of human beings are mortal, in that they are destined to continuous mortal lives in matter, i.e., ongoing cycles of incarnation and dissolution, or "survival", in matter, characterised by unconsciousness about the truth of the cosmos; Olympic (i.e. heavenly) immortality is a condition attained only by those individuals who, during their mortal lives, have been able to direct their consciousness, through processes of "initiation" and *anamnesis*, i.e. "remembrance", to the metaphysical origin and truth of the cosmos and of their own particular being, which is the mystery of Heaven and of the North Pole. Individuals thus initiated cease to be human and are reborn, already during their lives, to the same level as the Olympic deities, and co-work with them to the great mystery of the cosmos, and are freed from the bonds of the material world, and they see the multitudes of uninitiated human beings as rambunctious masses in need of being ordered and educated. With Christianity, cosmic truth was terrestrialised and perverted into the life experience of any human being, universally "globalised" initiation lost any metaphysical meaning and operational usefulness, and rebirth was reduced to either thoughtless and sentimental delirious detachment from reality or blind and moralistic abiding by doctrinal precepts. All of this is explained in: Evola, *La tradizione ermetica*, 107-109.

200 Sedgwick, *Against the Modern World*, 22-23.

In the words of the Romanian Islamic scholar and diplomat Michel Valsan (1907-1974), a close follower of Guénon:[201]

> The supreme condition of the human being is metaphysical knowledge, which is the knowledge of eternal and universal truths. The value of a civilisation lies in the degree to which it integrates such knowledge and in the consequences that it draws from such knowledge for the applications related to the different domains of its structure; such an integration and internal irradiation is possible only in those civilisations which are called traditional, which are those deriving from non-human and over-individual principles, and are founded upon forms of organisation which are themselves the incontestable expression of the truths which they should open participation to. The task of any traditional form is indeed to offer humanity, which is given order by it [by said traditional form], the teaching and the means which allow to realise the abovementioned knowledge and to take part in it either from near or far, in accordance with the different possibilities of the individuals and of the specific natures.

Besides *Philosophia Perennis*, the second core idea of Traditionalism, which is the gist of its opposition to the modern Western civilisation, is that modernity, since the Renaissance, is built upon a cosmological inversion which places Earth above Heaven, the physical principle above the metaphysical principle, matter above the spirit, quantity above quality. Such an inversion, for which everything comes from matter, has become fully realised in the Western civilisation, grafted upon the latter's postulate of linear time, and has reached a stage in which the spirit and the metaphysical knowledge of Tradition are utterly denied and forgotten — everything develops merely from material mechanics in a linear technological progress.[202] The idea that everything derives from matter and only from matter also bears with itself the idea that everything is made up of material atoms, that the atom is the ultimate foundation of reality, a conception which, when applied to human society,

---

[201] Michel Valsan, "La funzione di René Guénon e il destino dell'Occidente", *Oriente e Occidente*, 1 (Milan, Italy: 2010 [online version]), 2. Originally published as "La fonction de René Guenon et le sort de l'Occident" on *Études Traditionnelles*, special 1951 number dedicated to René Guénon.

[202] Sedgwick, *Against the Modern World*, 24-26.

gives rise to the concept of individualism, the other postulate of Western modernity, which, according to Guénon, is a twisting of the traditional concept of individuality as maturing within a collectivity, and is ultimately doomed to disintegrating the latter and therefore human society itself.[203]

As I have tried to demonstrate in *Eurasian Universism*, the postulates of linear time, materialism and individualism upon which Western modernity is built, are the secularised versions of postulates which were historically chiefly embodied by Christian theology, made possible by its separation of the human mind (*phren* in Greek; *mens* in Latin) from the Mind of God (*Nous*; *Intellectus*), of human reason (*arete*; *ratio inferior*) from the teleologically vertical Reason of God (*Orthotes* and *Logos*; *Ordo* and *Ratio Superior*) which manifests itself in the cyclical rhythms of the starry skies and is embodied in the cycles of earthly natural lives, and the fixation of the latter, of the divine reason, exclusively in the historical person of Jesus of Nazareth. This separation gives way to the omnipotentisation and hypertrophy of the human being within matter and along the horizontal teleology of Christian eschatology, which is a "paradoxy" of time,[204] although all of these causes and effects might rather be symptoms of the stiffening and decomposition which any civilisation — thus also the Western civilisation built upon Christianity — thoroughgoes in the final phases of its life and death cycle.

The theory of cyclical time and of cyclical phases undergone by civilisations, and by mankind as a whole, as the opposite of the idea of linear time and continuous progress and material growth which have been fully realised by the

---

203 Ibidem, 28.

204 Ansprandi, *Eurasian Universism*, 58-62, 245-257. In the words of the Italian anthropologist and historian of religion Ernesto de Martino, the Christian operation of fixation of the *Logos* in history introduces a "paradoxy" in time, since the latter's ultimate solution is placed in the linear vector which spans between the historical life of Jesus of Nazareth and his return at the end of times, and thereby abolishes the traditional spiral conception of time and the tool which is traditionally used for ever-renewing, re-throwing it, which is the symbol, comprising myth and rite (see 60).

Western civilisation, is the third core idea of Traditionalism,[205] and continues in the Traditionalist Eurasianism of Aleksandr Dugin, who recovers the olden esoteric concept of the *translatio imperii* — "transferral of the empire", *imperium*, i.e., of the divine and spiritual power constituting a civilisation from within[206] —, which throughout history would have shifted from the Babylonian Empire (corresponding, in terms of the cycle of human civilisation, to the Golden Age) to the Persian Empire (Silver Age), then to the Greek Empire of Alexander the Great (Bronze Age), then to the Roman Empire (Iron Age; thenceforth becoming also known as the "Roman Idea"), then to the Byzantine and the German Empire (the "Twoth Romes", the former being the legitimate one, whilst the latter being the illegitimate one created by the "false emperor" Charlemagne, crowned by Pope Leo III in Saint Peter's Basilica in the Vatican on Christmas day in the year 800), and finally to the Russian Empire (the "Third Rome", which both closes the Iron Age and restarts the cosmic cycle, opening a new Golden Age).[207]

As bespoken in *Eurasian Universism*, the Italian scholar of religion Ernesto de Martino (1908-1965) similarly identifies an "inversion of sign" taking place during the stage of a civilisation's death, when the same words, symbols, and institutions upon and through which a given civilisation was built and blossomed are garbled and overturned, and appropriated by disrupting agents to bring the given civilisation to its complete decomposition.[208] In Middle Eastern (Sumerian, Semitic and Jewish Biblical) symbolism, such a process of ascension and later inversion and fall of civilisation is represented by the concept of Babylon (*Babilu*). In its original Akkadian meaning, *Babilu* is the "Gate of God" or "Gate of Heaven", i.e.,

---

205 Sedgwick, *Against the Modern World*, 28.

206 Ansprandi, *Eurasian Universism*, 185, note 497.

207 About the cycle of the empires as told in the *Book of Daniel*, and Russia as the "Third Rome", as a "geopolitical ark" of the Russians as the "bearers of God", see: Aleksandr Dugin, *I templari del proletariato. Metafisica del nazional-bolscevismo* (Milan, Italy: AGA Editrice, 2021), 71-73; Dugin, *Soggetto radicale*, 142, 150, 152-153.

208 Ansprandi, *Eurasian Universism*, 91, 160, 246-247, 265.

the "Bearer of God" and the "City of God", the civilisation populated by those who are born from her union with God, symbolising matter when it is sublimated by such union, personified as *Inanna/Ishtar*, the "Lady of Heaven" in the Mesopotamian tradition, since God manifests itself by uniting with it and imprinting its ordering *Logos* into it. This concept may otherwise become the whore "Babylon the Great" of the *Apocalypse of John*,[209] the civilisation populated by monsters, harlots and abominations born from her intercourse with the "kings of the Earth", thus symbolising matter which liquefies when it separates itself from God, returning to being the primordial untamed dragon *Tiamat* with the wuthering horde of her serpentine abominable offspring begotten without the order of Heaven.[210]

Julius Evola, acknowledged as the second founding father of Traditionalism,[211] also developed a spiritual racial theory in connection with the doctrine of the cycles of civilisation.

---

209 Ibidem, 267-268.

210 The "Gate of Heaven", *Ianua Caeli* in Latin, otherwise yclept "Mystical Rose", *Rosa Mystica*, is Mary in esoteric interpretations of Christian symbolism, such as Rosicrucianism (Evola, *La tradizione ermetica*, 99, note 276). The symbols of the Erst Philosophy indicate that the fate of civilisation is linked to human breeding and to the Woman of the Philosophers, to the kind of female with whom the masculine principle unites and through whom it reproduces itself; a type of heavenly woman generates the sons of civilisation, whilst another type of earthly woman generates the sons of perdition, wherewith civilisation degenerates and dissolves. In *Eurasian Universism* (271-273), I betokened how the switch of the celestial woman into the terrestrial whore within Christianity, thus the turning point of the degenerescent phase of the Western Christian civilisation, might have been represented by the worship ceremony to the *Pachamama*, "Great Mother" in Quechua, officiated by Pope Francis in the Vatican in 2019, an event which is comparable to the officialisation of the cult of the Anatolian mother goddess Cybele in the last, dissolutory phase of the Roman Empire, and of the associated cult of Cybele's self-emasculated lover Attis, the "ear cut when it is still green" symbolising premature death (Evola, *La tradizione ermetica*, 90), which in turn may be likened to the beatification of the prematurely died bourgeois youth Carlo Acutis in 2020. A Hermetic rule reads: "Whiten the black Earth before adding the Yeast [the active, red principle] to it [...]. Sow your Gold in whitened Earth" (Evola, *La tradizione ermetica*, 135, note 105).

211 Later important early thinkers of Traditionalism include the Indian British historian and philosopher Ananda Coomaraswamy (1877-1947) and the Romanian historian of religions Mircea Eliade (1907-1986).

According to him, civilisations that are true and normal, that is to say those built upon traditional metaphysics and the corresponding spiritual hierarchy of society, are all originally founded by racial elites of men, the Aryans, enlivened and shapen by a spiritual connection to celestial, divine forces — a connection which is characterised as a spiritual tensionality, almost in terms of electricity. Such spiritualised races and the civilisations that they establish tend to degenerate, decompose and die whenever they gradually lose their divine connection and blend with animalistic races of hominids, which are either materialised and brutalised remnants of races of previous civilisational cycles, which have long since lost their spirit and divine connection, or apelike hominids which have always lived on Earth alongside the divine races, or a mixture of both the cases. At the same time, Evola recognises that modern humanity is almost entirely racially mixed, and therefore the strife between the spiritual tensionality of divinity and material animalism takes place within the individual itself.[212]

Yet another outlook, which is certainly not unrelated to those expressed afore about the cycle of the empires, the inversions of sign, and the roles of different human races, is that civilisations undergo, just like individuals, the phases of the Great Work (*Magnum Opus*) as codified in the Hermetic alchemical tradition, that is to say, the descent of their godhead into matter and then its ascending transmutation into a perfected form out of matter itself. Starting from brute matter, or rough, undominated and unorganised Earth-stuff, the phases of the Great Work are: *nigredo* or *melanosis*, "blackening" or dissolving putrefaction in the Water-stuff; *albedo* or *leucosis*, "whitening" or awakening purification in the Air-stuff; *citrinitas* or *xanthosis*, "yellowening" or enlightening

---

[212] These matters are explained in detail in Evola's books on race, the main of which is *Sintesi di dottrina della razza* (Padua, Italy: Edizioni di Ar, 1978 [1941]). It is worthwhile to add that Evola identifies the divine men as primarily represented by the Aryan elites of the white races of the north, and the animalistic races of hominids as the black races of the south. The concept of "Aryan" will be clarified further onwards in the present essay.

deification in the Fire-stuff; *rubedo* or *iosis*, "reddening" or recoagulation in the new, now dominated and organised Earth-stuff.[213]

2.2. The Roots, Trunk, and Boughs of the Tree of Traditionalism

The Russian Traditionalist thinker Yevgeny Nechkasov (alias Askr Svarte), the ideologue of "Pagan Traditionalism", says that "Traditionalism arose as an ideology advocating a complete and uncompromising return to the values of the

---

[213] Evola, *La tradizione ermetica*, 43-44, plus 97, where the author also cursorily mentions the doctrine of the cycles, plus 165, note 218. Throughout the book, Evola undersees the Great Work as the Hermetic path of regal initiation — *ars regia*, "royal art" —, an initiation based on the reflection of the individual's microcosm in the universe's macrocosm and aimed at the spiritual awakening of the I without rejecting the body, but using it as the raw material for the work. According to Evola, this path would have been lost with Christianity, which would be based on a theistico-devotional corrupted form of the other possible initiatic way, the sacerdotal initiation — *ars sacerdotalis*, "sacerdotal art". The book contains some errors, betokened by René Guénon and others, above all the subordination of the sacerdotal way to the regal way, of the spiritual-noetic to the animic-psychic, the overturning of white and red, and the characterisation of the former as the "lunar" and "feminine" path and of the latter as the "solar" and "masculine" path, which does not find correspondence in any traditional culture, in which the sacerdotal way is always superordinated to the regal way. See the forewords to Evola's book by Gianfranco de Turris (7-13) and Sayyed Hossein Nasr (15-21). Evola himself (179) recognises that in traditions other than Hermetism the relationship between white and red is the exact opposite, and he also recognises (147) that white indicates the "state of active ecstasy which suspends the human condition, regenerates, gives back the memory [of the origin], reintegrates the personality in the non-corporeal state", the "intellectual rebirth", and (159) the "attainment of immortality", the "standing upright of the consciousness", whose continuity is no longer associated to the body but to higher states of existence which do not belong to the material world. In *Eurasian Universism* (248-257) I myself explained that the overturning of the two roles is part of the corruption represented by Christianity, especially by the institution of the Catholic Church, whose priests have always been cadet and illegal sons of aristocratic families and social outcasts rather than true *sacerdotes*, an inversion of the roles of the two leading castes of the traditional social hierarchy — an overturning of being (sacerdotal way) and becoming (regal way) — which sets in motion the processes which lead to the destruction of any traditional civilisation. This is well elaborated in: René Guénon, *Spiritual Authority and Temporal Power*, trans. Henry D. Fohr, ed. Samuel D. Fohr (Ghent, New York: Sophia Perennis, 2001 [1929]), 20-24. To use Evola's own alchemical vocabulary, we may say that a *sacerdos* is already born with a golden I, and does not need to manufacture it.

traditional era and treating the modern world as an absolute negation of higher, traditional principles", and qualifies that it is "not a religion [in itself, of its own] and is neither new nor old", and it is not even "Tradition" itself with the uppercase T.[214] The latter, the Eternal and Perennial Tradition, or what we have hereinbefore termed the Erst Wisdom, is the source in Heaven in which Traditionalism is rooted and from which it springs out as a tree towards the Earth. According to Dugin, this source is personified as the Gnostic *Sophia*, the primordial Woman of the Philosophers, an "exclusive instance in which all of world wisdom, independently of historical peripeteias, is present and preserved in its 'paradisal', primordial state", and those philosophers who find and love her obtain access to "Absolute Wisdom".[215]

Nechkasov defines Tradition with the uppercase T, the Erst Wisdom, as the "common root of all individual ethnic traditions [with the lowercase T] and religions", which in their esoteric (i.e. inner) core all reflect the One, the unique Divine Beginning, the God of Heaven, adapting it to the peculiar expressive forms and languages of the folks on Earth.[216] It is "the indivisible unity (*synthema*) of the sacred, the dutiful, and the hierarchy, which are manifest in different forms in the social and human being of different peoples".[217] Knowledge of such a heavenly common esoteric core, which is eternal and perennial in the sense that it exists metaphysically outside and above time and yet ongoingly manifests itself in physical time, as the cycle of the year, is handed down in the various earthly particularised cultures through chains of "codification" (from Latin *codex*, *caudex*, which originally meant the "stem" and "branch" of a tree, and by extension a writing on material derived

---

214 Askr Svarte (Nechkasov), *Polemos: The Dawn of Pagan Traditionalism* (Tucson, Arizona: PRAV Publishing, 2021), 38.

215 Aleksandr Dugin, "Traditionalism as a Theory: Sophia, Plato and the Event", trans. Jafe Arnold (*Eurasianist Internet Archive*, 2019), passim.

216 Nechkasov, *Polemos*, 38.

217 Ibidem, 39.

from it, a book), whence derives the concept of "tradition" itself, which means "what is transmitted" — etymologically from the Latin noun *traditio*, "transmission", verb *tradere*, "to transmit".[218] Again, Nechkasov defines Tradition with the uppercase T as "the Primordial Principle, the Source, and the common foundation of all traditions with the lowercase T, which constitute the natural faiths of given peoples and the manifestations of the sacred in forms unique to a given *ethnos*, the very language in which the Divine reveals itself to the people (the *ethnos*), and through which, in the form of myths, rituals, cults, dutiful behaviours, customs, cultural forms and, finally, language itself, peoples engage in contact with and return to the sacred unity and participate in the transmission (*tradere*) of this knowledge".[219] He also quotes a definition given by Evola of what the manifestation of Tradition in reality means, that is to say, "the victorious and the creative presence in the world of that [mystical force] which is 'not of this world', i.e., that of the Spirit, understood as a power that is mightier than any merely human or material one".[220]

We can say that "Traditionalism", with the suffix "-ism" (from Greek *-ismos*, Latin *-ismus*), which means a "style", a way of being, thinking and doing, defines the very process and network of gnosiological communication, of hermeneutical (i.e. interpretive and communicative) passages, between the roots in Heaven, the Erst Wisdom, the Eternal and Perennial Tradition with the uppercase T, and the various codified, particularised and localised traditions with the lowercase T, the many branches on Earth and their leaves, blooms and fruits. Traditionalism is the self-doing/self-making of Tradition and the doing/making of Tradition; we can therefore give a first definition of the "Traditionalist", of the one who does/makes Tradition, as the operator of said process and network of communication, of the trunk, the rod of transmission, of

---

218 Ibidem, 38.

219 Ibidem, 40.

220 Ibidem, 39. Quotes: Julius Evola, "On the Secret of Degeneration", *Deutsches Volkstum*, 11 (Hamburg, Germany: Hanseatische Verlagsanstalt, 1938).

said tree of communication, mediating between the roots and the branches, between Heaven and Earth. Using Martin Heidegger's concepts, we can say that the Traditionalist is the "keeper", the "caretaker" of the tree of Being, the opener of passages and the codifier of communication of the tree of Traditionalism.[221]

Short-circuiting deadlocks may occur within the tree of Traditionalism, and this is precisely what has generated Western modernity. Dugin, in his work *The Radical Subject and its Double*, explains how sedimented "traditions" with the lowercase T, the branches on Earth, may take the role of "Tradition" with the uppercase T, the roots in Heaven, when mechanised, lifeless wonts sundered from the utmost source are sold as divine expressions by the ideologies which have characterised the trajectory of the Western world — think of the so-called "Catholic Traditionalism": the codified web of wonts, which, having lost its link to the One, has gotten cold and has become deathening mechanised formalism; first it begot Western modernity as the secularised iteration of Christian theology, and then it conformed itself to its own product. This is the "Great Parody", the "Great Simulation" of automatised "psychic corpses" as described by Guénon.[222] Such "fake Tradition", a rhizomatic weed which grows from the Earth without intervention from Heaven, understands neither itself nor the modernity that it has yolden, and tries to kill everything that is alive, everything that has kept its connection to the One and to the Erst Wisdom — it tries to choke and kill the tree of Traditionalism, which is reborn in postmodernity as a hot fire within the freezing cold of fake, sclerotised Tradition and modern nonsense to fight them both.[223] Traditionalism,

---

[221] About man as the "custodian of Being" see: Ansprandi, *Eurasian Universism*, 182, where I mentioned the concept while analysing Martin Heidegger's speech and essay "The Thing" (1949-1950).

[222] René Guénon, *The Reign of Quantity and the Signs of the Times*, trans. Walter E. C. James, 4th Baron Northbourne (Hillsdale, New York: Sophia Perennis, 2001 [1945]), 185-190, 267-274.

[223] Dugin, *Soggetto radicale*, 123-129.

on the other hand, "perfectly understands [fake] Tradition, a thousand times better than [fake] Tradition itself, being itself also fully aware of what modernity is [that is to say, the offspring of fake Tradition]"; opposed to both fake Tradition and modernity, Traditionalism "is aware of the structure of the traditions on which it focuses [its studies], having developed a magnificent historiographical, methodological, and terminological equipment, a sort of meta-language which correctly describes the general lines of the most diverse kinds of traditional society".[224]

2.3. The Orlay of the Western World and the Task of Traditionalism

> And then the old world will no longer be world; a new one will be made in its place, and the planets will spiritually consume one another, so that the stronger ones, having eaten up the others [it is the reduction of the subsolar planets by the higher ones], will be the only ones left, and two and three [two expresses the generic principle of opposition, whereas three is the number of planets in each group: Saturn, Jupiter, Mars and Venus, Mercury, Moon] will be won by one alone [it is the final simplicity, corresponding to the state beyond the Seven]. // The lich raises again, with a new body of a sheen white hue [...]. Matter is slow to resolve itself, and once it has become desirous again [...], the Sun rises within it [...] at the centre of Saturn, with Jupiter, Venus and the seven forms. And it is a new creation, solar, white and red, majestic, bright and igneous.
>
> - Basil Valentine // Jakob Böhme[225]

The chains of transmission of the Spirit linking to the One have been broken in Western modernity, and the various particularised traditions, having lost connection with the metaphysical Erst Wisdom, have been reduced to mere sets of despiritualised, mechanised manners and habits.[226] In Kathleen

---

224 Ibidem, 127.

225 Evola, *La tradizione ermetica*, 170. The quotes are taken by Evola from: Basil Valentine, *Le dodici chiavi dell'alchimia*, 59 (IX); Jakob Böhme, *De Signatura Rerum*, XII, 23.

226 Nechkasov, *Polemos*, 39.

Raine's words as reported by Sedgwick, the *temenos* — the Greek concept for the sacrally delimitated space, the Latin *templum*, the sacred centre where the divine and the spiritual are determined and enshrined, "contemplated" (from the Latin verb *contemplare*), the Heideggerian "Ord" (*Ort*), the "place" as the "tip of the spear", which functions as an "ording" (*Ortung*), a divinely ordered "localisation", for "aording" (*Erörterung*), i.e., spiritually gathering in ordered "argument" all the forces at play in a given context thus putting them in communication with the One, which is essential to mankind's existence and civilisation — has vanished from the Western world, and, in its absence, everything falls apart and pulverises in a fidgeting anarchy. This is not merely anarchy as intended in the field of modern politics, but a deeper understanding of *anarkhia* in the etymological sense, the "negation" and "missingness of the *Arche*", of the divine "Beginning", of the One itself.[227] Valsan bewrites the state of the Western world as follows:[228]

> The modern West, with its individualistic and materialistic civilisation, is in itself the denial of any intellectual truth properly so called, as well as of any normal traditional order, and as such presents the most glaring condition of spiritual ignorance that humanity has ever reached to date, both as a whole and in whatever one of its parts. This situation finds an explanation in the forsaking of the non-human and universal principles which the human and cosmic order is founded upon, and it characterises itself in a peculiar manner beginning from the breaking of normal relations with the East.

The abnormal Western civilisation — built upon the aforesaid severing of the transmissions of knowledge, on the aforesaid cosmological inversion of Earth and Heaven, and on the denial of the *Arche* itself —, and all the nefarious influences that it has spread across those parts of the world that it has coaxed and Westernised with its technological wonders throughout

---

[227] Sedgwick, *Against the Modern World*, 16. The concepts of *Ort*, *Ortung* and *Erörterung* are cursorily treated in: Ansprandi, *Eurasian Universism*, 188-189, 222.

[228] Valsan, "La funzione di René Guénon", 2.

history, would be doomed to a fall into barbarism,[229] after "the reaching of a given limit, likely marked by a civilisational catastrophe", the failure and arrest of the Christian-derived linear teleology and conception of time along which the whole process of the Western civilisational entity has been thrown since its beginning.[230]

Traditionalism, which, as we have already said, is not Tradition in itself, arises in the modern epoch, in the situation of broken transmissions of knowledge and civilisational collapse, when sacred representations of the world in terms of myths and rites are missing, and acts as "an orientation towards traditional principles" and as the "philosophical expression of their prioritisation in the conditions of the modern world", trying to re-establish the language of the holy in the latter,[231] re-wiring and re-grounding the tree which manifests Tradition. According to the French Traditionalist author René Alleau, Traditionalism has a revolutionary power comparable to that of Marxism, since in its fundamental radicality it queries society about the "principles" upon which it is built.[232] According to Valsan, after the arrest and collapse of the Western and Westernised civilisation, "a change of direction appears inevitable, and traditional knowledge, both of the East and of the West, indicates that there will be a restoration of all traditional possibilities that present-day humanity still comprehends, which will coincide with a new manifestation of the primordial spirituality, whereas, at the same time, the anti-traditional possibilities and the human elements who embody them will be repulsed outside of this [restored] order and definitively degraded", and yet, the orlay

---

229 Sedgwick, *Against the Modern World*, 26.

230 Valsan, "La funzione di René Guénon", 3.

231 Nechkasov, *Polemos*, 41.

232 Ibidem, 40. Cites: René Alleau, "De Marx á Guénon: d'une critique «radicale» a une critique «principielle» des sociétés modernes", *Les dossiers H* (Lausanne, Switzerland: L'Âge d'Homme, 1984). About Marxism and Traditionalism, also see: Jafe Arnold, "Marx and the Indo-European Mode of Production" (Belgrade, Serbia: Center for Syncretic Studies, 2018).

of Western indigenous traditions, almost completely twisted and lost throughout the process of modernity, is uncertain, and will depend on the mental state of Western humanity at the moment of its civilisation's breakdown; in any case, "the reawakening of the intellectual possibilities of the West may only take place under the influence of the teaching of the traditional East, which always keeps intact the deposit of holy truths".[233]

Guénon envisioned three hypotheses about the fate of the West after its civilisational collapse, depending on Western humanity's mental state at the moment of the event: the first scenario is that the Western anomaly is abandoned to its degeneration, falls completely into barbarism, and simply dies and withers away; the second scenario is that representatives of Eastern traditional civilisations try to save what lingers of the Western civilisation by assimilating it either by consent or force, either as a whole or in parts; the third scenario is that the West does not give up completely to its own characteristics — as it would happen in the second scenario of assimilation from outside, and therefore does not disappear entirely either, as it would happen in both the first and the second scenario —, and a restoration of normal intellectuality and authentic Western traditions, European and beyond, is accomplished spontaneously by the West itself, from within itself.[234] Different parts of the Western and Westernised world might also take different paths, corresponding to the one or the other of the three possible scenarios.[235]

Both Guénon and Valsan, however, already considered the mental state of Western humanity too compromised for an actualisation of the third hypothesis, that of a "spontaneous awakening of latent possibilities" from within the West itself.[236] Guénon emphasised the advisability of relying on existing

---

233 Valsan, "La funzione di René Guénon", 3.

234 Ibidem, 5-6.

235 Ibidem, 10.

236 Ibidem, 6, 10-11.

organisations, and on the Roman Catholic Christian Church in particular, for a restoration of the metaphysics of Tradition in the West from the inside — this would have entailed a rehabilitation of Roman "Catholicism" (Greek *Catholicismos*, i.e. "Totalitarianism, Way to the Whole") in its original, etymological sense, that is to say, unification of the multiplicity from above, from Heaven, from eternity.[237] As noted by Valsan, however, these possibilities have not come into being, and Catholicism has ongone in its degenerative trajectory,[238] which began to accelerate — as Evola remarked — with the Second Vatican Council (1962-1965) under Pope John XXIII and Pope Paul VI, and reached a final stage — I add — under Pope Francis in the 2010s-2020s, channelling regressive forces in a movement of unification of the multiplicity from below, from the Earth, on the temporal and material level.[239]

I would say that the latter is the unavoidable end for a religion which has never been a true expression of the eternal and perennial Erst Wisdom, but a totalitarian aping of it. As Evola says, a tradition which is a true emanation of the Erst Wisdom acknowledges the same worth of other spatiotemporally particularised manifestations of it, so that "no single tradition, as such, can claim to possess the monopoly on absolute truth", but Christianity is founded upon the claim that it is the only and absolute truth, founded by God's one and only historical earthly incarnation; as such, Christianity is actually debarred from any mutual assimilation with other traditions from above, since this "stems from the acknowledgement of the One Tradition that exists beyond its various particular and historical forms".[240] According to Evola, this issue is also evident in the fallacy of Christian mysticism,

---

237 Ibidem, 7.

238 Ibidem, 17.

239 Julius Evola, "The Myth of East and West and the 'Meeting of Religions'", *The Bow and the Club*, trans. Sergio Knipe (Budapest, Hungary: Arktos Media, 2018), passim.

240 Ibidem.

which stops at the phase of concentric realisation, whereby the mystic objectifies perfection as an external and unreachable personified image of God; this phase of inner work does not proceed towards a vertical realisation, or identifying union with God, so that the mystic collapses unto himself, as he "passes from the level of metaphysical and intellectual realisation to that of sentimentality, love, devotion", thus regressing into merely human impulses and even sub-intellectual complexes, which in true mysticism are otherwise burned off on the vertical path of the mystic towards deification.[241]

Valsan also onlooked the situation of the Eastern European world of mixed Orthodox Christian and Islamic traditional culture as deeply penetrated by the anti-traditional spirit of Western modernity, although not as bleak and compromised as the situation of the West proper, so that "the conditions of the spiritual climate and mentality [in these cultural complexes] have [...] remained [...] particular, and [...] the modalities of a future restoration will be to a certain extent different [than in the West], whatever be the qualitative significance that might be attributed to this difference".[242]

Given the impossibility of a restoration of the Erst Wisdom within the framework of existing organisations, Guénon, and Valsan in particular, admitted the possibility of the metaphysical elite creating new traditions for re-grounding the Erst Wisdom in the Western world; this would be more difficult and would take place in the longer term, since the elite would have to create new theoretical and practical tools by itself, albeit with the support of the Eastern elites, and even formulate new modalities of true spiritual realisation, i.e. initiation, for the members of the elite itself and for the lesser orders of the hierarchy of society.[243] In Valsan's own words:[244]

---

241 Ibidem.
242 Valsan, "La funzione di René Guénon", 13.
243 Ibidem, 21-23.
244 Ibidem, 22-23.

There still remains the possibility that a truly Western initiation, which no longer exists in the West, will be re-enacted in a favourable intellectual environment, with appropriate means. What might this initiation be and where could it be found? It may only be the ancient, regular and effective initiation of the traditional West, which has long since withdrawn to the place where every initiation which no longer has the possibility of maintaining itself in its normal umbworld, when cyclical conditions are unfavourable, withdraws. [...] This concealment, when it concerns the fundamental initiatory form of a tradition, coincides with the concealment of the spiritual centre of said tradition, which retreats towards the point of origin of the centre of each particular tradition, that is to say, towards the supreme spiritual centre, in which it belives in a latent state and from which it can sometimes manifest itself anew when cyclical conditions allow it. [...] When, for various reasons, a reactualisation is no longer possible within the framework of existing organisations, and yet essential conditions are satisfied in an undefined ambit, a re-manifestation can take place, with regards to the latter [the undefined ambit] or certain "qualified" individuals, and then the necessary initiation and the corresponding means can reappear. However, in this case, the initiation and the means of the work of realisation would present relatively new modalities, linked more strictly to the qualifications of the field of reactualisation; it is after all through these qualifications and according to their measure that would be elaborated the work tools which would subsequently thus come to appear, as a sort of creation of the elite itself, according to the opportunities of the latter's effective development.

At our point in history, corresponding to the final phase of the Western and Westernised world, that of the arrest, collapse and dissolution of its latest historical civilisation, which is to say the post-Greco-Roman, Germanic civilisation infused with the theology and teleology of Christianity, the task of Traditionalism should be precisely that of constituting the metaphysical elite of qualified intellectuals envisioned by Guénon, the Traditionalists, capable of operating a re-grounding and restoration of the Erst Wisdom into new configurations, new forms of tradition, possibly inspired by Eastern doctrines, in order to induce the rise of a new civilisation, or multiple new civilisations, from the wasteland which will be left after the breakdown of the whilom configuration of the West.

3. Styles of Traditionalism

3.1. Hard and Soft, Guénonian and Pagan-Only Traditionalism

Nechkasov, using categories established by Sedgwick, distinguishes between a "hard Traditionalism" and a "soft Traditionalism", of which the former completely rejects and directly opposes the modern Western world and is represented by Guénon and Evola, themselves representing, respectively, the two possibilities of contemplative-theoretical challenge and active-practical change of Western modernity at its core, whereas the latter uses "soft power" methods and "does not urge revolution or radical revolt against the modern world", but rather tries to hijack it and use its own institutions and weapons against it, while "striving to consistently, steadily develop its own space with its own orientations within academic disciplines, culture, literature, and public life", as represented, for instance, by Mircea Eliade and by the contemporary Russian Traditionalist philosophers Aleksandr Dugin and Ilya (alias Veleslav) Cherkasov, the former of whom is the ideologue of Traditionalist Eurasianism, which considers Eurasia as the heartland where the Erst Wisdom is preserved in its purest forms, and the latter of whom is a leading ideologue of Rodnovery (Slavic Neopaganism).[245] Hard and soft Traditionalism are complementary to each other and may concur in the methodology of the Traditionalist, since "soft Traditionalism establishes alternative spaces, vectors, and centres of attraction within the system and develops questions and knowledge in the fields of philosophy, the study of culture, and the study of religion which, without a doubt, can be of use to the path of hard Traditionalism", while the latter "can translate such 'soft' theories into religio-communal, social, and political practice (ranging from systemic to radical) and can

---

245 Nechkasov, *Polemos*, 44-46.

serve as the source of fiery inspiration for 'soft' scholars and thinkers".[246]

Another interesting distinction operated by Nechkasov in the wake of the French historian Dominique Venner (1935-2013), is between Traditionalism in the broadest sense, corresponding to Guénonian Traditionalism, and what Venner termed "Traditionism", a type of Traditionalism which devotes itself exclusively to indigenous European cultures and religions and as such rejects the religions of the Abrahamic textual revelation, and corresponds to the Pagan Traditionalism formulated by Nechkasov himself.[247] Guénon's Traditionalism includes the Abrahamic religions in its scope, and the French metaphysician's thought has often been regarded as strongly influenced by Abrahamic dualism, so that he even converted to Islam and became a Sufi master, and suggested other Traditionalists to follow the same path.[248] Evola's Traditionalism, otherwise, rejected Abrahamism and aimed at resisting and fighting degenerative Western modernity while remaining anchored to the divine ideas on high, riding the flux of modern degeneracy just like the sage of the Chinese saying "rides the tiger", waiting for the re-manifestation of the divine ideas into reality. Nechkasov declares to have taken inspiration mostly from Evola's thought, aside from Venner's, for the formulation of his Pagan Traditionalism.[249]

3.2. The Dark Logos of Orplatonism

Yet another perspective on both the historical origins, the style and the role of Traditionalism, is put forward by Dugin — elaborating from Sedgwick's ideas — in his writing "Traditionalism as a Theory: Sophia, Plato and the Event", a chapter in his 2013 book *In Search of the*

---

246 Ibidem, 46.

247 Ibidem, 43-44.

248 Ibidem, 42.

249 Ibidem, 41, 44.

Dark Logos: Philosophico-Theological Outlines.[250] He says that both Traditionalism and Renaissance Neoplatonism with Hermeticism ultimately go back to Late Antiquity Neoplatonism and Hermetism, and therefore to ancient Greek Platonism. Scientific rationalist humanism, which is the reduction of everything to human reason and its scientific knowledge and was the founding cornerstone of Western modernity, arose as a demetaphysicisation of Renaissance Humanism — which, elsewise, was originally a magical and sacral understanding of the "perfected man" corresponding to the Platonic philosopher, to what Dugin calls the "Angel-Initiator" in his writing —, and such a demetaphysicisation was maybe aimed at accommodating it to the rationalistic mainstream of Christian theology. Given this, Traditionalism reveals itself as "one of the most important philosophical currents to emerge in the critical moment of the exhaustion of the agenda of classical scientific rationality [...] and with the formation of the first post-modern theories subjecting modernity to deconstruction".[251] While Renaissance Neoplatonism was born together with modernity, and even contributed to its very foundations, Traditionalism rejects modernity, challenges it and strives to change it.[252]

Undoubtedly a forerunner of Traditionalism, Late Antiquity Neoplatonism — elaborated by Plotinus, Porphyry, Iamblichus, Proclus, and Damascius —, synthesised Plato's thought into a unified noocentric cosmology with Hellenistic and Middle Eastern philosophical, religious and mystical systems, including Aristotelianism (reinterpreted through the Platonic lens), Stoicism, Orphism, Pythagoreanism, Egyptian Hermetism, as well as Syrian and Mesopotamian magico-

---

250 Dugin, "Traditionalism as a Theory", passim.

251 Ibidem. Notice that, according to a terminological convention established since around the mid-2000s — which I have used myself in this paragraph, and throughout the essay —, "Hermetism" defines the Late Antiquity religio-philosophical schools based on the *Hermetica* writings, while "Hermeticism" defines its later revivals since the Renaissance.

252 Ibidem.

religious systems (theurgy, the *Chaldean Oracles*, Chaldean astrology) and Iranian dualist doctrines (Zoroastrianism).[253] This continued in the *Corpus Dionysiacum* and, through it, it was transmitted into the Christian Middle Ages, resurfacing in the mystical theology of Scotus Eriugena, Eckhart von Hochheim, Henry Suso and Jacob Böhme, and also continued in Jewish Kabbalah, while in the Middle East it was central to the development of Islamic theology (the mystical current of Islamic theology, rivalling rationalist schools), with Al-Ghazali, Ibn Arabi, Ishraqism and Ismailism.[254] It onwent also in the Byzantine Empire with Michael Psellos, John Italus, and Gemistus Plethon, the latter of whom directly influenced Marsilio Ficino, and then onwent in Ficino's contemporary Giovanni Pico della Mirandola.[255] Later, the same stream of thought resurfaced in Giordano Bruno, and further onwards in nineteenth-century occultism, which directly influenced Guénon, in whom, according to Dugin, "all of these numerous streams come together to compose the most modern, capacious, and systematised worldview".[256]

The "paradigmatic matrix" employed by Guénon, and by the Renaissance Neoplatonists before him, to treat and interpret all historical religions, theologies, and philosophies is not drawn from any single one of them, but is from the metaphysical source from which all of them have ultimately outsprung.[257] Such a paradigm is the same as the original Platonic theory (*theoria*), that is to say, the "divine observation" of Heaven, and especially the divine contemplation of different phenomena to find their common source forms, ideas (*ideai*), in Heaven, but it is neither reduceable to ancient Greek Platonism nor to the mytho-historical personage of Plato

---

253 Ibidem.

254 Ibidem. About Ishraqi mysticism, a cursory description is found in: Dugin, *Soggetto radicale*, 343-344.

255 Dugin, "Traditionalism as a Theory", passim.

256 Ibidem.

257 Ibidem.

himself — who was the "Event", in the Heideggerian sense of "Aeyeness" (*Ereignis*), who executed the foundational act which would have given rise to Platonism and to the stream of thought which would have led, ultimately, to the Western civilisation. Such a paradigm comes from the Erst Wisdom, and Plato might have been just one amongst the initiates of a golden chain which goes back to the Terrestrial Paradise at the dawn of creation, a re-transmitter, re-translator of the metaphysical truths of the Erst Wisdom, one of the multiple manifestations of the Angel-Initiator in different contexts,[258] much like Zoroaster in Iran and Huangdi in China.[259]

According to Dugin, the stream of thought hitherto described, which has flowed into Traditionalism, may be defined as a "Dark Logos", because it is founded on the awareness of the pre-existential — i.e. unmanifested; not yet manifested — One; it is an unshakeably vertical *Logos*, unswervingly opened upwards, towards the source of all things, and yet it works by constantly upturning the strict laws of Aristotelian rationality: instead of working through consequential linear logics, it works by paradoxes, aporias, and super-rational ambiguity; it is evasive, dialectic, and leads the thinker through the "dizzying chain of insights and initiations" up to the Erst Wisdom, to the One itself.[260] It might also be yclept "Orplatonism" (*Urplatonismus*), with the prefix "or-", the English cognate of the German *ur-*, which indicates a yondermost origin, source, thus expressing the Platonism of all Platonisms, the Eternal Platonism.

Platonic theory, as Dugin says, is simultaneously enlightenment and absorption of the rays of the One, the ideas which rush to meet the excelled philosopher, the theoretician

---

258 Ibidem.

259 The concept of Huangdi in Chinese religion and philosophy is treated in: Ansprandi, *Eurasian Universism*, 185-205. About Plato and Zoroaster as a transmittable "office", a "function" (judging by the chain Plato-Plotinus-Gemistus Pletho), also see: Dugin, *Platonismo politico*, 82.

260 Dugin, "Traditionalism as a Theory", passim.

who has ascended to Heaven, and become embodied in his mind and in the unfolding of his thinking. It is the "theory of all theories".[261] The thinker thus performs the philosophical rite, the "rite of all rites", which unites the noetic cosmos with the aesthetic cosmos, seeing the One which reflects itself in the multiplicity of reality, which is its manifestation, and co-working with the One by opening ways of connection, passages to the One itself within the multiplicity which is the One's body — this is the rite that the Neoplatonists called theurgy (*theourgia*).[262] Theory is the blissful work of the gods of the One, and to take part in it already means to exist on a higher plane of reality, the Celestial Paradise, where being and thought are bundled up more tightly together; it is the philosophical "Orland" (*Urland*), "Orhome" (*Urheimat*), where the Woman of the Philosophers, *Sophia*, the personification of the Erst Wisdom itself, abides.[263] The entire historical chain of Platonism, or Orplatonism as I have called it, which is ultimately an iteration of the very same source upon which Traditionalism draws, may be interpreted, according to Dugin, as a stairway which leads the thinker to the aforesaid higher synthesis of being and thought, to the celestial Orhome, which is the North Pole with its constellations. At the top of the stairway, the theoretician must take a further step into the utmost Heaven, uniting with *Sophia* and becoming like the deities in Heaven, becoming the Angel-Initiator.[264] Such a stairway to Heaven can be discovered and trodden only independently by chosen individuals, since access to it is not given by anyone else but the God of Heaven, the One itself.[265]

---

261 Ibidem.

262 Ibidem.

263 Ibidem. The author uses the locution "philosophical Homeland", while "Orland" is my coinage and "Orhome" is the precise rendering in English of the German *Urheimat*.

264 Ibidem.

265 Ibidem.

3.3. Orthodox Universism

My work *Eurasian Universism* may be regarded as an exercise of both soft and hard Traditionalism, as it tries both to open unprecedented passages, spaces and vectors through which thought may move so as to question the very foundations of Christianity and of the Western modernity it spawned, to unhinge them, and also to propose models for religio-political reconstruction of the world, especially drawing upon Chinese examples, after the breakdown of the Western civilisation. While decidedly outspeaking a rejection of Christianity — which I believe together with other Traditionalists to have exhausted its life cycle and its erstwhile function as the spiritual, verticalising shaft of the Western civilisation and to have become the nest of horizontalising forces of dissolution which are bringing said civilisation to its end —,[266] and supporting a spiritual renewal of authentic European cultures within the frameworks of Neopaganism,[267] I do not fully share Nechkasov's utter rejection of the Abrahamic religious traditions of Judaism and Islam, holding that spiritual renewals might be possible even within their paradigms, and that useful tools for spiritual ascension are yolden by their esoteric currents, Kabbalah and Sufism, and by Gnostic interpretations of their doctrines. This is especially possible within the fold of Islam, which is a religion of direct relationship with the One, linked neither to any ethnic identity nor mediated by any earthly power, and representing the conclusion of the whole Abrahamic revelation. It is worthwhile to underline that, in addition to Guénon, all the immediate forerunners of

---

266 Ansprandi, *Eurasian Universism*, 247, 265-275.

267 Ibidem, 275-281. At 277-278 I mentioned the major movements of: Mesopotamian-Canaanite Zuism (Sumerian-Semitic Neopaganism) and Egyptian Kemetism (Egyptian Neopaganism) of the Near East; Celtic Druidry (Celtic Neopaganism) and Germanic Heathenry (Germanic Neopaganism) of Northern Europe; Baltic Druva (or Baltuva, or Romuva; Baltic Neopaganism), Slavic Rodnovery (Slavic Neopaganism) and Scythian Assianism (Scythian Neopaganism) of Eastern Europe; Greek Hellenism (Greek Neopaganism) and Roman-Italic Traditionalism (Roman-Italic Neopaganism) of Southern Europe.

Traditionalism converted to Sufi Islam: Isabelle Eberhardt, Ivan (John Gustaf) Aguéli, and Rudolf Glauer.[268]

Regarding the Abrahamic traditions, my view is therefore in line with Guenon's and Dugin's, and I think that the pacifying understanding (*al-islam*) of the universal God (*Allah*) of the North Pole (*Qutb*) should be at the core of Traditionalism, and even generally polytheistic Neopagan religions should be oriented according to such vertical understanding of reality, given that many of their groups struggle to develop high theological systems and tend to unorganised, rambling, horizontal polytheism, intended as belief in multiple gods as equal independent supreme principles, often worshipped in syncretism — this mistaken view is what Islamic doctrine defines as *shirk*, i.e. the "association" of equal partners to *Allah*,[269] and has never been characteristic of high civilisations, which have always been shapen by monistic-pantheistic-panentheistic theologies, conceiving the various gods as a vertical immanent hierarchy of hypostases emanated by the One, the only transcendent supreme principle, which becomes manifested in its own, said emanation.

The error of *shirk* arises in the degenerative phases of civilisations. As we have already understood from foregoing explanations, the closer the initiate gets to the central One, the more the differences between particularised iterations of the utmost Tradition fade in his eyes, and he perceives them as rays descending from and ascending to the central One, the Erst Wisdom itself.[270] Given this, according to Nechkasov, in the wake of Guénon, the various particularised traditions do not and may not communicate, in normal conditions, on the plane of their most external forms, but only on the plane of their common source, which is nonetheless unspeakable by the means of formal language but only through symbolism.

---

268 Dugin, *Soggetto radicale*, 124.

269 Regarding the Islamic concept of *shirk*, see part 2, note 7 of: Daniele Bianchi, "Julius Evola e il cristianesimo", 3 pts. (*EreticaMente*, 2020).

270 Nechkasov, *Polemos*, 116.

Communication on the level external forms happens, on the other hand, in the abnormal conditions of degenerate populations and during the decay of whilom high civilisations, when the Erst Wisdom, the One, is no longer perceived, withdraws its rays from reality, and the particularised traditions become empty, mechanised wonts, swappable and blendable with each other, so that what ensues is the collapse and decomposition of the mystical and religious yearning into the confused, senseless horizontal polytheism and syncretism described hereabove. In abnormal conditions, the vertical hierarchies of gods and their rites, which in normal conditions are a representation of the procession of the hypostases of the One reflected in the rhythms of spatiotemporal contexts, crumble and shatter into dust.[271]

Verticalisation may indeed be imparted to Neopagan religions also directly through their Platonisation, without hosting them within the fold of Islam. In writing about Late Antiquity Neoplatonism, Dugin betones its noocentricity, i.e. its focus on the *Nous* of God and its *Logos*; he says that it "conceived itself to be a universal tradition on the basis of which one could interpret all existing religions and philosophical systems. It was the religion of the *Logos*, a noocentric cosmology and apophatic metaphysics claiming the ability to interpret any and all forms of polytheism, symbolism, and theurgic rites", from above, from the outlook of God.[272] Dugin also makes reference to the reform program of the Byzantine Neoplatonist Gemistus Plethon (1355/1360-1452/1454), which consisted in a restoration of Platonic theology as a whole and a return to a vertical polytheism within the fold of Eastern Orthodoxy, while Guénon, in his earliest phase, proposed a restoration of true, vertical Tradition in the West on the basis of its forms as preserved in Hinduism, *Sanatana Dharma* (Sanskrit locution meaning the "Eternal Firmness/Rightness").[273]

---

[271] Ibidem.

[272] Dugin, "Traditionalism as a Theory", passim.

[273] Ibidem.

Traditionalism as the Tree and the Ark of the Radical Selves

The North Pole of Heaven with its spinning constellations (Ursa Major and Ursa Minor, the Big Chariot and the Small Chariot) is the Orhome or Orland bewritten hereinbefore, both the subject and object of the theory of all theories, and is the theory of all theories itself, and is likewise the verticalising steering of human mind thither, where it can get holy ideas to be put into practice on Earth so as to attune the entire life of the human being, of the human civilisation, with Heaven, in the rite of all rites, an "Ordering" (*Ordnung*), a rectification which is ultimately a reproduction of Heaven itself.[274] Throughout *Eurasian Universism*, I have emphasised the centrality of this action of rectification of reality towards Heaven as the quintessential foundation of any normal civilisation, which is always a celestial civilisation, and I think that this should be the main goal of Traditionalism and of all individuals and streams of thought which claim a Traditionalist identity; such an action of rectification is what makes possible the verticalisation and synthesis of multiplicity from above which I have yclept "Universism", distinguishing it from "universalism", which has mostly turned into a synonym of horizontal homologating, all-enwrapping globalism in modern Western thought.[275] It is worthwhile recking that the religious term "Orthodoxy" may be interpreted as referring to the hitherto described rectifying action and to its destination: it comes from Greek *Orthodoxia*, *Orthos* plus *Doxa*, meaning "Right Way", in which its root concept, *Orthotes*, "Rightness", is the Greek form of the reconstructed Indo-European root *Ar* — from which descend the Vedic Sanskrit concept of *Rita*, and the Persian and Avestan *Arta* or *Asha*, which are ultimately the same as the late Hellenic concept of *Logos*, the Latin *Ratio* —, meaning at the same time alignment with the North Pole with its constellations, and the North Pole itself, the Orhome. "Orthodoxy" may therefore also be onlooked as a synonym of "Aryanism", in which "Aryan" (Greek *Arios*;

---

[274] The concept of *Ordnung* is cursorily treated in: Ansprandi, *Eurasian Universism*, 222.

[275] Ibidem, 16, note 11.

Latin *Arius*; Germanic *Herr*) is a spiritual concept, like the ancient Vedic Sanskrit *Arya* and Persian and Avestan *Ariya* or *Airya*, which refers to those humans who are attuned with the North Pole and its starry order, and work for the latter's reproduction in human life and civilisation.[276] In a single notion, comprehending both the rectifying action and its destination, that is to say, the unity from above, into the One, we can therefore speak about an "Orthodox Universism" to define the philosophical dissertation that I wielded in *Eurasian Universism*, which might be yet another of the possible configurations for contemporary Traditionalism.

Besides my emphasis on the importance for Traditionalism of setting for its projects the celestial, polar scope bewritten hitherto, i.e. Orthodox Universism, which is the "theory of all theories", I agree with Dugin that contemporary Traditionalism might take on the same role that Late Antiquity Neoplatonism had in its time, functioning as a means for opening horizontal passages between various particular traditions, interpreting their elements, reconnecting them to their common sources in order to reactivate them, as they have lost meaning in modernity and have become mechanically self-repeating and sclerotising wonts, and even for creating new meaningful syntheses of different traditions or new traditions from scratch. The Traditionalists might collect and configure old and new traditions into new circuits of sense, new "religions" — from the Latin noun *religio*, "relinking", verb *religare*, "to relink"[277] —, whose purpose should be that of connecting and fastening them, through a vertical passage, to the utmost source of everything, to the One, to the Erst Wisdom which is the North Pole. Such theurgic passages, vertically atwixt the noetic dimension and the aesthetic expressions of different particularised cultures, and horizontally among these differing particularised cultural expressions, take place across the tree of Being, which I have identified forthwith as the tree of Traditionalism, contribute to

---

276 Ibidem, 66-69, 222-223, note 595.

277 Ibidem, 43, 122.

4. Paths of Traditionalism

4.1. Vertical and Horizontal, Dry and Damp Initiations

Ilya Cherkasov allegorises that "true Tradition is the transmission of living fire, not the preservation of ashes".[278] The French Traditionalist philosopher Alain de Benoist betones that Traditionalism "is not a question of 'returning' to the past, but of connecting with it", and, quoting directly Jean-Pierre Vernant, "the effort to remember the primary purpose of everything is not the construction of the individual past of a man who remembers, the construction of his individual time, but conversely it is what allows him to escape time".[279] In *Eurasian Universism*, I highlighted how these precepts, in the Chinese tradition — which functions as the book's outlook and lens from which and through which the Western world and its foundational ideas are critically queried —, are not mere sayings but obvious facts. The equivalent of the Western concept of "Tradition" is, in the classical Chinese language, the concept of *Dao*, which in Taoist theology (the mostly *yin*, esoteric aspect of Chinese religion) outspeaks both the metaphysical principle of all reality and the physical flow of reality itself, anchored in its metaphysical beginning. In Confucian theology (the mostly *yang*, exoteric aspect of Chinese religion), the principle and its order of manifestation are *Tian* ("Heaven") and the *Li* ("Reason"), the latter being reproduceable by mankind through particularised *li* ("rites"), which are not to be mechanically and emptily repeated but are aimed at "realising the new by reviewing the old", that is to say, at re-actualising in the present meaningful elements inherited from the past and adapting them to present contexts and to the

---

278 Nechkasov, *Polemos*, 132.

279 Ibidem, 263-264. The author quotes from Alain de Benoist's *On Being a Pagan*.

forces at play in these contexts.²⁸⁰ The etymological analysis of the Chinese grapheme which represents the concept of *Dao* itself gives the meaning of "being in the present while leading forth the essential threads coming from the past for realising the future".²⁸¹

In the critical stage of postmodernity — which began after the Second World War as a gainsaying of the scientific rationalism of Western modernity seen as a lingering vestige of the hierarchical structures of traditional society, and which aims at "freeing" humanity from whatever structure, thus revealing itself as the final "unmasking" of modernity, the program of inversion taken to its very end, that is the utter withdrawal of the divine forms of God from reality and the deluge of return to shapeless matter²⁸² — Nechkasov argues that what is crucial is not so much to resort to the chains of "horizontal initiation" embedded in traditional societies, which in many cases, as we have already explained before, have ossified into meaningless repetitive wonts since their links to the Erst Wisdom, and to the One itself, have long been severed, but rather to reconnect directly and immediately to the primal source of divinity and of all particularised traditions through a "vertical initiation".²⁸³

Unlike horizontal initiation, "lower initiation", or "metamorphosis" as Guénon also clept it, which shrithes through the social orders and institutions of a traditional society, vertical initiation is the attaining of the highest metaphysical dimension itself, the North Pole, accessible only to those who should constitute the uppermost elite of a society; it is a direct transmission of wisdom from God above to the individual being below.²⁸⁴ Evola in particular betones the vertical type of initiation and the "rupture of

---

280 Ansprandi, *Eurasian Universism*, 103-104, 279.

281 Ibidem, 103, 279.

282 Nechkasov, *Polemos*, 203-207.

283 Ibidem, 114-116.

284 Ibidem, 128-129.

levels" of reality which is necessary to obtain it, given by wild experiences or existential trauma which open the individual to the metaphysical overworld. In alchemical terms, such can happen either through the "fiery" dissolution of the self in the divine manifestations of the surrounding reality, which is possible in traditional societies in which the holy is seen everywhere, and whereby the individual is ignited by becoming part of the greater fire of God, or through "icy" separation from the umbegoing reality, bekent as unholy and degenerated, as radically different from the individual's divine self which is therefore set alight as an inner fire.[285] Vertical initiation may be regarded as a self-initiation, although it is always given by the intervention of a transcendent force which engrafts itself upon the individual who has broken the levels of his own reality and opened himself to the metaphysical overworld, and it consists in a "departure to a level that is different from purely human, individual consciousness".[286] According to Cherkasov, vertical, or "higher initiation" — or "path to insight" as Cherkasov himself clepes it — through the icy type of existential trauma is the most efficacious form of initiation in the modern degenerate world; it is the shortest path to insight, but also the riskiest one.[287] In the modern world, all the possibilities for true horizontal, lower initiation have been broken, and therefore the spiritual thrust to ascension moves within the individual itself, which is sunken into "the thick of the ice of modernity". True initiation, according to Cherkasov,

---

285 Ibidem, 129-132.

286 Ibidem.

287 Ibidem, 132. Icy-type vertical initiation, which takes place completely in the interiority of the individual, through a descension to one's innermost self, and identification with it and only with it, is comparable to the "descent to the *Merkabah*" (i.e. the "Chariot", referring to the Chariot asterisms of the North Pole) in Jewish Kabbalah; it is the riskiest type of initiation as it may lead to madness and death if the initiate is unable to withstand the sight of God and the infusion of total wisdom, as told in the Jewish story of the four rabbis (Ben Azzai, Ben Zoma, Ben Avuya and Rabbi Akiva) who "entered Paradise", only one of whom (Akiva) came out of it without becoming mad or dying as happened to the others.

is thus only possible within oneself, and true insight is only possible in the here and now.[288]

In Hermetic alchemical terminology as expounded by Evola, vertical or higher initiation and horizontal or lower initiation are also known respectively as the "dry way" and the "damp way", the "washing with fire" and the "burning through water", the former giving access to the eternal and perennial Erst Wisdom through a technical use of the faculties of the inner spiritual fire for a direct ascension to God, and the latter through a preliminary descent into the material waters aimed at finding and kindling the inner spiritual fire — heed, if it is not clear enough, that the dry and the damp path are a different thing from the fiery and the icy path described afore, which are two approaches to vertical initiation only.[289] The dry way and the damp way are addressed to two different types of man: the former to those whose centre is already in the realm of white Sulfur, or in their already sublimated, sulfurised Mercury, yclept Fiery Mercury or Fiery Water, in the mind, who are already born with a golden self of active awareness and mastery over their psychic and bodily functions, and do not need to go through the black phase of the Great Work; otherwise, the latter is addressed to those whose centre is in the realm of black, common Mercury, in the body, and who need to go through the whole process of the Great Work to verify whether they have the golden self, whether they can kindle their inner spiritual fire, in order to acquire an active awareness and mastery over their psyche and body.[290]

The two types of initiation also correspond, respectively, as bewritten by Guénon, to the "sacerdotal art" (*ars sacerdotalis*) and the "royal art" (*ars regia*), that is to say, the "greater

---

288 Ibidem.

289 Evola, *La tradizione ermetica*, 124-126.

290 Ibidem, and about the two types of Mercury see 68. Interestingly, in some iterations of the Hermetic alchemical tradition the two types of Mercury, common Mercury and sulfurised Mercury, are also respectively yclept "western Mercury" and "eastern Mercury" (see 71, note 148).

mysteries" which concern the possibilities of the overhuman, supernatural and metaphysical macrocosm, the "Celestial Paradise", and the "lesser mysteries" which concern the possibilities of the human, natural and physical microcosm, the "Terrestrial Paradise". In traditional societies, the former was reserved for the initiation of those men who were chosen for the sacerdotal, magico-religious ranks, for "spiritual authority", whilst the latter for the initiation of those who were chosen for the aristocratic, politico-military ranks, for "political power", who were always subordinate to the former, by whom they were actually initiated and endowed with those parts of the divine knowledge — the "divine right" — necessary to exert political power in harmony with the God of Heaven.[291]

Dugin, in his book *Rusia, el misterio de Eurasia* (1992), also writes that the vertical or dry and the horizontal or damp ways correspond to the two itineraries of development of the utmost Tradition through time (history) and space (its historical sacred centres), starting from the North Pole, the Celestial Paradise or Northern Agartha, seat of the pristine Erst Wisdom of which all later centres are projections. The damp way is the lengthy and gradual path which goes from north to south, where it becomes saturated with materialism, then shrithes from south to west, where it fragments itself into individualism, and finally shrithes from west to east, where it ends at the Eastern Agartha or Shambhala, the Terrestrial Paradise which most faithfully reflects the North Pole; otherwise, the dry way is the shorter, quick but also dangerous path which goes from north to north, or, more precisely, from a point in the northeast between the two Agarthas to the North Pole forthwith.[292]

The damp way, saturated with the materialism of the south, is the "curved track", overabundant and pompous in its discursive and symbolic expression, but which then,

---

[291] Guénon, *Spiritual Authority and Temporal Power*, 20-24.

[292] Aleksandr Dugin, *Rusia, el misterio de Eurasia*, trans. Arturo Marián (Madrid, Spain: Grupo Libros 88, 1992), 121-133.

as a reaction, becomes rigidly individualistic in the west, and these two facets of it would correspond to the cultural complexes established by the southernmost and westernmost Eurasians, namely the Greco-Romans, the Egyptians and the Semites in the south, and the Celts and the Northern and Western Germanics in the northwest of Eurasia.[293] The dry way, succinct and laconic in its discourse and simple and essential in its symbolism, is otherwise the "right track", whose holy centre would be Siberia, and which would correspond to the cultural complexes produced by the northernmost and easternmost Eurasians, namely the Turanians (Uralo-Altaics, to whom according to Dugin also the Sumerians belonged), the Eastern Germanics, but also the earliest cultural forms of the Slavs and the Sino-Tibetans.[294] The damp way is horizontally developed, mythologically elaborated and applied to every aspect of life, but such horizontal "culturalism" often loses its metaphysical content, thereupon becoming mere lifeless mechanical repetition, as it is happening once again in the Western and Westernised world, and just as happened in the late Roman Empire. The dry way uses vertically condensed words and sketchy symbols, and this is why, when the peoples who were carriers of it met with the peoples of decadent damp ways, they were perceived as unsophisticated yet morally pure gents — think of the "barbarians" in the late Roman Empire.[295]

Traditionalism should gather the vertically initiated individuals, those who have been taken up by God and by the seven deities to their seats at the North Pole of the sky, those who are loners on their path to liberation from human bonds and acquisition of overhuman wisdom, as its main representatives, and make of them the civilisational elite which Guénon hoped would bring new order to the decaying Western world. According to Guénon, such qualified individuals are always a minority among men: "all men are in a sense 'called'

---

293 Ibidem, 127.

294 Ibidem.

295 Ibidem.

Traditionalism as the Tree and the Ark of the Radical Selves

by reason of the 'central' position the human being occupies among all the other beings found in the same state of existence, but few are 'chosen', and in the conditions of the present age there are indeed surely fewer than ever".[296]

Nechkasov writes that these chosen individuals, bearers of a "golden" self who in the hierarchy of normal, traditional societies would constitute the highest, sacerdotal, magico-religious order endowed with the task of drawing divine ideas directly from the Mind of God in Heaven, from the metaphysical overworld, to instill them into the lower orders of society — i.e., the "silver" and "bronze" aristocratic, politico-military order and the "iron" economico-productive order, which have the task of putting the divine ideas into practice —, are thrown into the marginal periphery in the abnormal, overturned modern societies, in which the leading positions have all been encroached by a blend of the silver/bronze and iron elements, and in which this mixture lastly prevails as the representative in physical reality of shapeless matter, the Earth itself.[297] Dugin says that, in the marginal periphery, the chosen ones are a kind of "lost angels", who live among the worst outcasts of modern-postmodern degeneracy but do not identify with them, keeping intact their divine inner quality while everything around them changes in the final dissolution of all forms.[298] Similarly, Evola beteaches that these superior beings, which in normal civilisations are born embedded within chains of horizontal tradition which are appropriate to their nature, often come to incarnate within degenerate, abnormal civilisations, in which they will find themselves in forlorn to unlucky, uneasy and dangerous situations and unfavourable

---

296 Nechkasov, *Polemos*, 133. Quotes: René Guénon, *Perspectives on Initiation* (Hillsdale, New York: Sophia Perennis, 2002 [1946]).

297 Nechkasov, *Polemos*, 143. The three orders of traditional societies, here expressed through the symbolism of metals, also correspond to the cycle of the ages undergone by civilisations; in the Hellenic tradition such cycle is expressed in this very symbolism of metals: the Golden Age, the Silver and Bronze Ages, and the Iron Age. The entire cycle and the characteristics of each age are well explained in Nechkasov's book, 62-81.

298 Dugin, *Soggetto radicale*, 226.

contexts, as if they were on a fighting line in a risky battle, with the precise mission of re-establishing order, boundaries and shapes to reconnect the underworld of matter unto the overworld of the spirit.[299]

The purpose of Traditionalism, and of the selected elite of vertically initiated Traditionalists, should ultimately be that of going back to the beginning of the entire universe itself, to the initial One, to the God of Heaven. This is the deepest meaning of the term "initiation", from Latin *initiatio*, verb *initiare*, which means "to begin, to start". In turn, as we have already seen in other terms, this would at the same time re-establish connection with the Erst Wisdom, which is eternal (i.e. outside and above time), so as to re-produce the latter's divine order, which is perennial (i.e. ongoingly manifesting itself in time, in the form of the year), into the waters of reality, in the here and now, through new configurations of ideas and formulations of language, codifying and embodying them into the form of new initiatic lines of tradition, new philosophical discourses, new religious doctrines, new religious churches (religious groupings).

4.2. The New Metaphysics of the Radical Selves

> [...] It is exactly when the transmission of forms ceases that the Radical Subject appears. [...] Maybe, Tradition has disappeared only to give way to the Radical Subject. From this point of view, paradoxically, Traditionalism is more important than Tradition itself. [This] does not imply, therefore, the restoration of things how they were in the past, but the discovery of aspects which in the past did not even exist. We do not want to restore anything, but return to the Eternal, which is always fresh, always new: this return is thus to be understood as a shrithing forwards, not backwards.
>
> - Aleksandr Dugin[300]

Dugin calls for the creation of a "New Metaphysics" starting from the "ontological situation of maximal despair,

---
299 Evola, *Sintesi di dottrina della razza*, 144-146.

300 Dugin, *Il sole di mezzanotte*, 30.

in a world utterly forsaken by God",[301] whose protagonist is the Nietzschean concept of the "Overman" (*Übermensch*), "winner over both God and the naught", as re-readen by Evola, which is to say that the Overman accomplishes a double overcoming, of both God — of the external Absolute Otherness that at the same time pervades everything, corresponding to premodernity — and the naught — the desacralised reality, corresponding to modernity, which has rejected and forgotten God.[302] The Overman prevails over them both whenever it has interiorised and identified itself with the Absolute Otherness, finding the holy source within its own self. Such newfound holiness must be affirmed in a spontaneous and independent way, after having thoroughgone the trial of the utter emptiness, of the naught, and this step of new expression of the holy takes place in postmodernity, in which the Overman exerts its creative action.[303] As we have already seen, postmodernity arose after the Second World War to bring the processes started with modernity to their extreme consequences, against modernity itself; while modernity may be compared to the evening, to the twilight, the sunset and dusk, since it preserved, albeit stiffened, residues of premodernity — desacralised subjectivism, rationalism, hierarchies —, postmodernity is comparable to the night until the midnight, during which the residual structures of modernity dissolve in what Zygmunt Bauman defined as "liquid society", which "is not even a society, but a chaotic destruction of the structures which releases a large amount of energy, quickly dissipated in an entropic process".[304]

The Overman's "main attribute" is the concept, wrought by Dugin himself, of the "Radical Subjectivity", or "Radical Self", which is "the agent (*actor*) of the New Metaphysics, its most extreme and polar point", which "appears when it is too late

---

301 Dugin, *Soggetto radicale*, 65.

302 Ibidem, 66-67.

303 Ibidem.

304 Dugin, *Il sole di mezzanotte*, 13.

and everything else has vanished",³⁰⁵ at the midnight of the process of dissolutive downfall of postmodernity, at the end of the descent of the civilisational cycle, shimmering as a glow for a "New Beginning".³⁰⁶ The Radical Self re-establishes the holy into reality, precisely in that part of space which during the process of modernity was bereft of God, in which Being was disowned, and in which the entropic whirl of non-Being was triggered, dragging everything into its twist — the Western world, the "Evenland" (*Abendland*), where the Sun sets, and its stretchings, the Westernised world. However, the Radical Self does not identify with the holy itself, and inaugurates a pan-eschatological "Endless End" within an "Ecstatic Empire", or "Rapturous Kingdom".³⁰⁷ The Radical Self takes the side of the Eastern world,³⁰⁸ the "Morrowland" (*Morgenland*), where the Sun rises again, that is Shambhala which best reflects the North Pole and where the Erst Wisdom is best kept.

The New Metaphysics arises in postmodernity and has deep bonds with it, but it is neither a byproduct of nor a synonym for postmodernity itself; despite its name, "New Metaphysics", it is something old as mankind itself — it has always been present throughout the centuries in a transversal and perpendicular relation with them.³⁰⁹ What Dugin means by "New Metaphysics" is therefore a new configuration of the Erst Wisdom itself, the *zenith*, which manifests itself anew at the most critical point of a cosmic cycle, the *nadir*.³¹⁰ It is rather a project of reactualisation of the holism which characterises the premodern experience of space-time, an ecstatic, self-producing, living, elastically energetic multidimensional whole in which everything is an opening towards something

---

305 Dugin, *Soggetto radicale*, 68-69.

306 Dugin, *Il sole di mezzanotte*, 13, 18.

307 Ibidem, 13; Dugin, *Soggetto radicale*, 68-69.

308 Dugin, *Il sole di mezzanotte*, 14.

309 Dugin, *Soggetto radicale*, 70.

310 Ibidem, 117.

Traditionalism as the Tree and the Ark of the Radical Selves

else.[311] Dugin says that the premodern holy space-time is ecstatic in the sense that it is indeed framed within the four directions of north, south, east and west, and alternates night and day, but these move in circles, are interconnected and are multidimensional in themselves, passages to other worlds. This space-time is like a tree, and its axes are not perpendicular as in the Cartesian system of orientation, but irregular and move like branches whipped by the wind — it is a system of living and ecstatic coordinates, and in every particularisation of the Erst Wisdom it is a reflection of Heaven, i.e. of God, on Earth, i.e. into matter.[312] According to the Dutch-German philologist Herman Wirth (1855-1981) the most archaic symbol of holiness in human representative systems is a simple irregular broken line, bough or twig[313] — like the plant of immortality sought for by Gilgamesh in the eponymous Mesopotamian epic.

The New Metaphysics bespoken by Dugin is therefore the very structure of Traditionalism itself, which is representable as a tree, as we have seen from our reading of Nechkasov's formulations. As we have already said, the task of the Traditionalists, who may now be identified as the Overmen gifted with the Radical Self, should be the recreation or reactivation of such arborescent, living and ecstatic, intercommunicating system of spatiotemporal coordinates within different cultural contexts, in a form suited to each given context; in some cases, it has been completely destroyed and lost, and is therefore in need of being reconstructed from scratch, while in other cases it has been only hidden and forgotten, and buried under the processes of modernity, and it just needs to be rediscovered and reawakened. Regarding such spatiotemporal structure, and the objective of its reconstruction or reawakening, Dugin writes: "our action is not temporary but fundamental, based on an immense multiplicity of ontological 'planes' situated

---

311 Ibidem, 96.

312 Ibidem, 100-101.

313 Ibidem, 99.

in the depths of Being, each of which leads to the centre of the world. [...] [It] frequents heights and abysses, it is the point of intersection between the vertical metaphysical axle and the horizontal one of historical actuality".[314]

The New Metaphysics is a "metaphysics of the end" of the cycle of Being, and, according to Nicholas of Kues' Paradigm, it arises at the moment when the tip of the white triangle, representing Sulfur, intersects with the base segment of the black triangle, representing Mercury; this is where the Radical Self, and the fiery I, is born.[315] The white triangle progressively shrinks until it becomes a "mustard grain" or "white dot" which, while being extremely small, is bequethen with the "infinite light" which was prevalent in the previous phases of the cycle of Being. The Radical Self is not a single entity, it is the quality of a small number of human beings, the Overmen capable of restoring the broken link between mankind — and through it all earthly creatures — and the God of Heaven, re-establishing the "saving pillar of the bright presence" for the "luminous reabsorption from the heights" of the North Pole,[316] i.e., the tree of Traditionalism. They are the various "particles of the bright man", scattered across the dense flux of the decomposing reality of Western postmodernity, like the limbs of Dionysus mauled by the Titans.[317] At the end of the cycle of Being, the Radical Self undergoes an insurmountable trauma: the white dot, the divine spark, is broken off completely from the divine source, from God, and is left alone with itself, and time is suspended, duration vanishes and collapses in the present; however, new metaphysical questions, possible only at this stage of the cycle, arise.[318] The Radical Self affirms its absolute difference from the base of the black triangle, from the many black dots of the dark bottom of the historical process, but at

---

314 Ibidem, 293.

315 Ibidem, 156.

316 Ibidem, 159.

317 Ibidem, 319.

318 Ibidem, 160-161, 169

the same time it does not have the ontological certainty to be the vertex of the white triangle; the New Metaphysics springs from the perspective of the Radical Self on reality.[319] The core of Being itself sends "new rays" to the Radical Self to build the New Metaphysics; rays of incombustible Sulfur (in Hermetic terms) which penetrate the oceans of Mercury unleashed by the melting of the Salt of the world of yestertide.[320]

Dugin betones, however, that the construct of the Western world and its process of development and then degeneration, the cycle which leads to the "Great Midnight" of Being when God is utterly withdrawn from reality and only the flux of dissolved, amorphous matter remains, have been triggered by the Radical Subjectivity itself, and by the supreme One with which the Radical Subjectivity identifies itself, willed as a "trial and purification",[321] after which the Radical Subjectivity becomes aware of its role as the "Midnight Sun".[322] As the "winner over both God and the naught", the Overman has denied God and begotten Western modernity in order to test itself, diving into the tumultuous abyss of dissolved matter, of a temporal becoming bereft of anchorage in the eternal Being, into the tangle of serpents of the primordial watery Woman of the Philosophers — the selfish demons of the godless, false rigid hierarchies of modernity and then, when modernity expires, of the ensuing flowing dissolution of postmodernity — in order

---

319 Dugin, *Il sole di mezzanotte*, 23.

320 Dugin, *Soggetto radicale*, 316, 320.

321 Ibidem, 319.

322 Dugin, *Il sole di mezzanotte*, 9-11. Dugin equates the Radical Self, which he identifies as the "Midnight Sun", with Dionysus, who in the Greek mysteries was titled the "Night Sun". It is the Black Sun which is the root of the diurnal Sun; it therefore shines both during the day and during the night, at midnight, at the culmination of the exile of the Sun, but does not identify itself with the night and its darkness. Analogically, the Radical Self is the root of the ordinary self, immortal root of the positive subject, which survives even in the case of the destruction of the latter. In Aristotelian terms, the ordinary self is equated by Dugin with the passive mind (*nous pathetikos*), which is the same as the Cartesian subject and merely reflects the outer reality and operates within its given edges, while the Radical Self is equated with the active mind (*nous poietikos*), which does not perceive reality, but creates it.

to rediscover its Radical Self, its divine sparkle, its inner fire of identification with the supreme One, and to reaffirm it as the Midnight Sun across the complete dissolution of reality at the end of the cycle, the Great Midnight.[323] The Overman has triggered the cycle of degradation from the Golden Age to the Iron Age, and has generated the infernal abyss of an increasingly spiritless and thick matter in order to forget its own divine origin, and then rediscover, reawaken and reaffirm it as the inner steely fire of the Radical Self as a new *Logos*, ontologically distinguishing itself from the hordes of demons bereft of awareness of the end of the cycle,[324] vanquishing them and remoulding the primordial waters of *Chaos* into a new order, instituting a new "Ord". The Radical Self is the "preman", the "root of mankind", of divinely-ordered humanity, and waits for the restoration of the latter at the time of what Dugin, taking a phrase from Arthur Rimbaud's *Hortensia* (interpretable as the Woman of the Philosophers, *Sophia*), clepes the "fiery hygiene of the races",[325] the separation of the wheat — the Overmen endowed with the Radical Self — and the tares — the "Undermen" (*Untermenschen*) bereft of the Radical Self — and the destruction by fire of the latter.[326]

The Overman is the same as the Evolian "Differentiated Man", immersed in the modern world but keeping itself utterly aloof, without organic connections, emotional complicity or communion of values with the umbegoing degeneracy, and aiming at the subversion of modernity from its very groundwork.[327] The Radical Self is therefore the same as the Evolian concept of the "Watcher", the "inner transcendence" which, once attained through a complete "abstraction" from material reality, becomes the new "overhuman essence" of the individual who thus becomes an Overman, allowing

---

323 Dugin, *Soggetto radicale*, 307-311.

324 Ibidem, 310.

325 Ibidem, 229.

326 Dugin, *Il sole di mezzanotte*, 26.

327 Dugin, *Soggetto radicale*, 324.

it to overcome the boundaries of the human being, becoming what Evola otherwise called the supra-rational "Absolute Individual".[328] The Overman, the one who has become a Watcher, or Radical Self, through an abstraction, "separation", or "rupture" from the level of material reality, is no longer human, i.e. a being of the Earth, but is not a deity of the God of Heaven either; it is rather a "Twixt" (*Zwischen*, a Heideggerian concept), an intermediate being who dwells in an intermediate region of space-time — an "atwixt" or "intwixt" (*inzwischen*) —, an intermediary between the human and the divine, and between space and time, which do not have any influence on it.[329]

Hereinbefore, I emphasised that the task of Traditionalism in postmodernity should be the recreation and/or reactivation of the tree-like system of spatiotemporal coordinates which is the embodiment of the Erst Wisdom in material reality, which brings Heaven down to Earth; the central actor of this structure is the Watching Overman of the Radical Self, the vertically initiated individual, the "Traditionalist without Tradition" whom is the "essence of Traditionalism".[330] Separating itself from materiality and humanity, and from the deathening formalisms of the "cold traditions" sundered from the supreme One, the Overman becomes a fiery Watcher, identifying itself with the supreme One, with the hot Erst Wisdom which is itself separated from the degenerating reality which has repudiated and forgotten it; the Overman thereby becomes capable of catching, channelling and grounding into reality the rays of the One, thus instituting new "hot Traditions".

The Watching Overman, bearer of the Radical Self, affirms itself as a *Homo Novus*, or even *Homo Novissimus*, dancing within the primordial waters to beget a new "Dancing Star",[331] the New Metaphysics of and for a new phase of Traditionalism

---

328 Ibidem, 325, 329.

329 Ibidem, 326-327.

330 Ibidem, 328.

331 Ibidem, 320.

which channels it. Aimed at building new embankments to convey the waters of matter, the New Metaphysics should be organised into "new ontological vectors", built into a "golden network" or system of new, overhuman metaphysical words and concepts.[332] This construction work would be the "new task of philosophy", and Dugin puts forward the creation of an "Eschatological Council of Solar Drops" for gathering the Watching Overmen of the Radical Self, the "submerged lights" scattered across a degenerated reality which is "indifferent if not hostile to them",[333] and even the celebration of a rite for the Midnight Sun of the Radical Self, likened to Heidegger's *Deus Adveniens*, the "Upcoming God"; such a rite would not constitute a new religion, but rather a trans-religious "Ecstatic Eschatology" for standing upright throughout the Great Midnight without blending with it and for propitiating the rise of the Radical Self.[334]

4.3. The Ecstatic Orthology of the Ark of the Radical Selves

> It is of little importance if the European Middle Ages or the Hyperborean "Golden Age" really were as Evola described them. These abstract "pasts" will determine a concrete future. [...] Ettled this way, the empire is what thrusts us to impose the living reality of the ecstatic Celestial City onto matter; it is an angelic praxis. In a certain sense, it is a differentiated empire, thus a holy and inner empire. It is the Empire of the Awoken Ones.
>
> - Aleksandr Dugin[335]

Guénon envisioned the creation of an intellectual, metaphysical elite in the Western world to guide its civilisation, which has lost any connection to the Erst Wisdom, through the aforediscussed possibilities about its future: either towards an assimilation by Eastern civilisations, or towards

---

332 Ibidem, 175-176, 322.

333 Ibidem, 319.

334 Dugin, *Il sole di mezzanotte*, 18.

335 Dugin, *Soggetto radicale*, 335.

a restoration of traditional Western cultures, in any case through a collaboration with Eastern elites in order to recover true metaphysical, holy models.[336] Guénon's entire work was intended for the preparation of this elite, which he envisioned as a small group of the best minds capable of standing on the same plane as the Eastern elites and of understanding and mastering the metaphysical truths of the Erst Wisdom as transmitted by Eastern doctrines, in order to operate a rightening of "the general mentality [of the West] towards the true sources of intellectuality, imparting to it a direction which, on the other hand, would not need at all to be conscious on the level of the masses", acting as a "ferment" for the re-grounding and rebirth of the Erst Wisdom, of the Eternal and Perennial Tradition, into new forms in the desacralised wasteland of the Western world.[337] Even when the Erst Wisdom will have been restored in the Western world, thus forming a new Western traditional civilisation, the role of the metaphysical elite would continue: it would be a new sacerdotal order, the highest echelon of the hierarchy of society, which would provide permanent communication with the sacerdotal elites of other civilisations.[338] The French metaphysician allegorised such an elite as carried by a vehicle, an "Ark" floating on the waters of the flood of the Western civilisation,[339] that is to say, on the currents of thought of the disintegration of the Western world, while knowing the laws of such currents so as to master and channel them into the moulds of new traditions.[340]

Guénon's Ark would correspond to Dugin's Council of Solar Drops, that is to say, of the Overmen of the Radical Self: they are those who are able to ascend to the North Pole, to the eternal Being of which they are a reflection, and abstract themselves from the flux of temporal becoming, acquiring the

---

336 Sedgwick, *Against the Modern World*, 26.

337 Valsan, "La funzione di René Guénon", 5-7.

338 Ibidem, 9.

339 Sedgwick, *Against the Modern World*, 26.

340 Valsan, "La funzione di René Guénon", 7.

outlook of the fixed stars, the seven star-deities of the *Arktos* asterisms, uniting with the maiden *Sophia* and the supreme God of Heaven itself[341] — the uttermost "worldonshowing" (*Weltanschauung*), literally the view "on the self-showing world", the outlook of the supreme Creator and of the seven creators over the myriads of creatures. Through a series of quotes appended with his own considerations, Evola in *The Hermetic Tradition* describes the race of the "Watching Philosophers", what we have defined as the Overmen of the Radical Self, keepers of the knowledge of the ages, hermeneuts (i.e. interpreters; sons of Hermes[342]) as gifted with the sight of the eagle, capable of measuring Heaven and bringing its order down to Earth, showing the way back to their celestial abode, to the Orhome:[343]

> Traced back by tradition to the Watchers — *Egregoroi* — to those who stripped the Tree and tamed the "Woman", [...] "autonomous, immaterial and without kings" is how Zosimus [of Panopolis] qualified the race of the Philosophers, "keepers of the knowledge of the ages" — [...] superior to fate [...]. "Superior to men, immortal", says Pebechius [...]. "Free and master[s] of life", having the "power to command over the angelic natures", would have been the further tradition up to Cagliostro. [...] Such is the truth of the "new race" [...] that the "sons of Hermes" constitute on Earth, [...] giving the fixed and impassible gaze of the "eagle" to the eye stricken and blinded "by the flash of the lightning"; bestowing Olympic, yet

---

341 After the ascension beyond the seven star-deities, one's soul withdraws from the "outer constellation" to turn to "God in its interiority"; on the boundary between the natural external world and the godly inner world, the soul is engaged in a "relentless work", a "Herculean toil" of "separation" which requires "sweat of blood", since it has to fight against both God (to keep itself from melting into the divine light) and humanity (to overtake at the same time the human condition). Up there is the celestial virgin, *Sophia*, who is Venus, and Mary in Christian-themed esotericism, the Gate of Heaven, the Light of God itself, who "takes the soul across a sea of fiery water"; the Fiery Dragon is thereby fully awakened and "breaks the bond created by the ancient Dragon around the Sun principle" abiding in the heart. See: Evola, *La tradizione ermetica*, 133, where the author elaborates on various quotes from Johann Georg Gichtel's *Theosophia Pratica*.

342 It is worthwhile to recall that in the *Interpretatio Romana* of the Germanic deities, Hermes, which is the Greek name for Mercury, and for the Egyptian Thoth, corresponds to Odin.

343 Evola, *La tradizione ermetica*, 38-41.

regal, dignity [...]. [They are] "the mysterious race of the perfect men, unknown to the foregoing generations" [...]. And it is said: at first there is the blissful nature of the [Heavenly] Man up above; then the mortal nature down here; thirdly, the race of the Kingless Ones who have ascended up there, where is Mariam [i.e. *Sophia*], the sought one. This blessed and incorruptible being — Simon Magus explicitates — inwones every being: it is hidden within them, in potentiality and not in actuality. It is precisely the one who stands upright, who stood upright, who will stand upright: who stood upright there above, in the infinite uncreated potency; who has standen upright down here, having been generated by [reflected] image in the flow of the Waters; who will stand upright there above, nearby the infinite potency, when it will have made itself perfectly similar to [the infinite potency].

As for the polar Orhome, and the path to reach it, ascended by those solar sparks, light flares, who overcome the watery flux of becoming and the nature of mortals thus obtaining the absolute divine wisdom and the nature of immortals, becoming part of Being itself, Evola writes, drawing upon the *Corpus Hermeticum* and various other sources:[344]

> Once it has detached itself from the irrational nature, the Soul retraces the planetary spheres, "divesting" itself of what belonged to these, overcoming them, [...] [transcending] the masters of the Orlay [...]; reaching — "clad only with its power" — the eighth state of which the region of the fixed stars is symbol, said the sphere of "identity" or of "being oneself" [...] as opposed to the overpassed spheres which are said of "alteration" or "difference" [...]. There, beyond the Seven, is the seat of "those who are" and no longer "become". There one attains the possession of the transcendental Science. There occurs the "rebirth according to the essence" [...] and one "becomes a god". One transforms into those beings, becomes them. Likened the "necessity" which reigns in the inferior spheres to the current of the Waters, symbols for such a realisation would be the figures of the "Saved from the Waters", of those who "walk on the Waters", and likewise the "crossing of the Sea" or of the "flow" (whence also all the varieties of the symbolism of "navigation"), and the pushing back of the flow. The latter [...] is the direction for reaching the state of "those who are in the *Gnosis*".

---

344 Ibidem, 77.

The Ark itself is one of the symbols of the *Arktos*, otherwise known as the asterisms of the Chariot, also visualisable as a Ship. In early Christianity, which emerged as a new configuration of culture, of thought and social reality within the waning and degenerating phase of the Roman Empire, the same idea of a new system aimed at ferrying worthy men towards the new civilisation, sailing on the waters of the dissolution of the one of yore, was symbolised by the "Ship of Saint Peter" — which is yet another name for the astral Big Chariot[345] —, which has beliven as a symbol of the Christian Church over the centuries, and which even the structure of premodern Christian temples is modelled after. As already cursorily explained hereinbefore, it was Christianity itself, because of postulates contained in its theology, that generated Western modernity and its ensuing degeneration — which may be regarded as just the secular flip side of Christianity itself —, and Christianity and the Western world which it yold have now exhausted their life cycle, are dead, and are dragging every form of being that they engulfed into the whirlpool of their decomposition.

The asterisms of the Chariot at the precessional North Pole, thus of the Ark, are also the "Celestial City" or "City of God" of various Eurasian traditions, including the Mesopotamian *Nibiru* (the "Polar Station" or "Polar Crossing") of the seven *Anunnaki* (the "Offspring of Heaven and Earth"), and the "Celestial Jerusalem" and the "Ark of God" of the Jewish Biblical tradition (which is a fragmentary textual sedimentation of the Mesopotamian tradition),[346] which is already a temporal reflection of the eternal *Babilu*, the "Gate of God" or "Gate of Heaven" at the ecliptic North Pole. It is also the precessional *Asgard*, the "Yard of the Spirits" of the

---

345 Richard Hinckley Allen, *Star Names: Their Lore and Meaning* (Mineola, New York: Dover Publications, 1963), 436.

346 Ansprandi, *Eurasian Universism*, 157, 260, note 689. About the identification of the constellations of the precessional North Pole with the Celestial Jerusalem, also see: Evola, *La tradizione ermetica*, 73.

Germanic tradition, which reflects the ecliptic *Valhalla*, and the *Elysium* which is a reflection of the *Empyrium*, the celestial Empire, in Mediterranean Latinate terms,[347] and the Orland and Orhome of the Erst Wisdom mentioned afore. Dugin clepes it *Angelopolis*, the "City of the Angels", which reflects the *Noopolis*, the "Stronghold of the Mind", perched at the summit of the *Nous* of God, and the *Angelopolis* is the subject of what he calls "transcendental politics", the "architectural plan of political ontology".[348] It reflects itself in terrestrial civilisations, in immanent politics, but these terrestrial imitations of it tend to divert from the celestial model and to degenerate into twisted monstrosities of *Chaos*, nests of demons — as in the Jewish Biblical myth of the Whore of Babylon, interpretable as a perversion of the supernal *Babilu*.[349] Dugin clepes *Platonopolis* the terrestrial city built upon Platonic theory whose gates are opened to the rays of the North Pole, and clepes *Diabolopolis* the terrestrial city which diverts from the North Pole and whose gates are open to the South Pole.[350] The *Angelopolis* is therefore an intermediate state between the *Nous* of God at the ecliptic North Pole of Heaven and the human mind and human life on Earth — it is the *Logos* of the precessional North Pole; Dugin also calls it the "City of the Watchers" or "City of the *Kshatriya*", of the mediators between Heaven and Earth, God and humanity,[351] between the *Noopolis*, the "City of the *Brahman*" in itself, and its terrestrial copy, which I would clepe, in general, the *Geopolis*, the "City

---

347 Ansprandi, *Eurasian Universism*, 282. While *Empyrium* derives from the Greek *Empyrion*, meaning "Inner Fire" or simply "Fiery, Afire, Burning", also evidently related to the Latin concept of *imperium* ("empire"), *Elysium* — Greek *Elysion* — likely comes from the Semitic *Elisha*, meaning "God is Salvation", or *Elisheba*, meaning "God is Seven, Seven Gods", from which also derives the female name "Elizabeth".

348 Dugin, *Soggetto radicale*, 331. *Noopolis* is my coinage.

349 Ibidem, 331-332.

350 Dugin, *Platonismo politico*, 76.

351 Dugin, *Soggetto radicale*, 332.

of Earth", or *Anthropopolis*, the "City of Humans", otherwise callable the "City of the *Shudra*".

The role of the Watching Overmen of the Radical Self should be that of harmonising the terrestrial civilisation according to the celestial, divine model, rectifying the terrestrial civilisation whenever it goes astray, or even destroying it in the case its degeneration has reached an irreversible stage. It is an active "heavenly politics", a "vertical politics", the "only type of politics which is worthy of being realised".[352] Such vertical and rectifying political discourse and action is what in *Eurasian Universism* I have yclept "Orthology", from *Orthos* plus *Logos*, i.e. "Right Order, Right Word, Right Law", and a "Discourse on Rightness", in which "Right" means the alignment with the North Pole, i.e., an "Ecstatic Orthology" consisting in the active strife for the reactualisation of the tree-like structure of the holy — hinged at the North Pole, which is reached by the Overman through ecstatic, mystical journeys of detachment from matter — into terrestrial reality, into various cultural contexts, in order to verticalise (or re-verticalise), that is to say, to rectify (or re-rectify), them towards the sky,[353] making (or re-making) them into "Orthodoxies", "Aryanisms", i.e. "Right Ways". The ancient Indo-European, Vedic and Avestan concept of "Aryan" precisely corresponds to the Overman, "the superior man, who realises the presence of the Watcher within himself — as himself".[354]

It is precisely with the spiritual and existential re-birth of the Overman atwixt Heaven and Earth, after a rupture from the level of humanity, that "the political, social and religious hierarchy originates" as it was in ancient Indo-European societies. Being an Aryan means to be a *Dviya*, a "Twice Born" (in Sanskrit), of whom the first birth is the corporeal one, while the second birth is the spiritual one, the re-birth on the plane

---

352 Ibidem.

353 Ansprandi, *Eurasian Universism*, 276-281.

354 Dugin, *Soggetto radicale*, 334.

of the spirit, of the abstraction atwixt Heaven and Earth,[355] attuned with the North Pole of Heaven. The Aryan is therefore the "Twixt" (*Zwischen*) mentioned afore. In his writings on the doctrine of race, as we have cursorily seen before, Evola says that the Aryans are those elites who, by being in connection with the divine powers of Heaven, constitute divine, celestial "superraces" who organise, on Earth, civilisations hierarchically attuned with Heaven. They establish a vertical communication with the divine powers, with transcendental superconscious forces, and spiritually infuse them from "ayond and above" into the entire layered body of an organic society, joining and vertically sublimating the demonic, genial forces, the vitalisms or subconscious forces, of the subraces of the inferior layers.[356] It goes without saying that if the Aryan elites disappear, the individuals of the subraces are acted upon by the unbridled demonic forces of the subconscious, which haunt the civilisational structures, now emptied of their higher, vertical meanings, and use them for low, horizontal ends, bringing the entire civilisation to fragmentation and dissolution.[357] The connection to the celestial forces is described by Evola almost in the terms of an electrical current; this makes his conception similar to that of the German esotericist Jörg Lanz von Liebenfels (1874-1954), founder of the branch of Ariosophy known as Theozoology, and supposedly the coiner of the term "Ariosophy" itself: Liebenfels bewrote the Aryans as "electrical men", bearers of the cosmic electron of God, a concept similar

---

355 Ibidem.

356 Evola, *Sintesi di dottrina della razza*, 24-25, 27-29, 31, 52.

357 Ibidem, 31. The chthonic spirits, or genies, or demons, which generate human races from below may also be accompanied by the spirits of other animals. These forces of animality, especially of terrestrial animals which are unclean, never belong to the celestial, divine powers from above, but may be mastered and co-opted into the latter's work. When not framed by celestial powers, and if a relationship with them is established passively, these forces of animality give place to the phenomenon of totemism, in which the human personality is overwhelmed, and "a man then finds himself to be, in some way, the embodiment in human form of the 'spirit' of a given animal species" (185-186, plus note 283).

to that of the *Fohat*, the cosmic electricity of the God which is One and Seven bespoken in Helena Blavatsky's Theosophy.[358]

The Orthology described afore, practised by the Watching Overmen of the Radical Self, that is to say, the Traditionalists, is ultimately, as already said in slightly different terminology, a hermeneutical methodology consisting in the re-actualisation of the Erst Philosophy into reality, and it is "onto-theological". It is theological, as it implies the communication with God and the seven deities of Heaven, and it is ontological, as it is aimed at realising their verticalising order into the reality of entities on Earth, "Orthodoxising" reality, rectifying it towards the North Pole. It is practised by navigating over the waters of the flood of the decaying Western and Westernised world, exploring different cultures for opening interactive hermeneutical passages between them, stimulating exchanges of ideas and models for abetting either the continuation of those cultures which are still living and have preserved their link to the Erst Wisdom, or the reconstruction and construction from scratch of cultures which have lost their connection to the Erst Wisdom. The latter are no longer "cultures" but empty, lifeless mechanisms, since the Latin term *cultura* derives from the Indo-European root *$k[w]elh$, *$kolh$, which means what is "high, aloft, excelled", what is "dwelt, inwoned, cultivated" by having been "turned" to towards the sky,[359] a "culture" thus being something which heightens, verticalises terrestrial entities towards the sky. Hence, these cultures are dissolving, as is the case of European cultures and all those non-European cultures which have been swallowed by the colonialist globalisation of Western modernity and postmodernity, which, let us repeat in slightly different terms,

---

358 Jörg Lanz von Liebenfels, *Theozoology, or the Science of the Sodomite Apelings and the Divine Electron* (Europa-House, 2004 [1905]). The comparison of Liebenfels' "divine electron" with Blavatsky's *Fohat* is made in the commentaries to the Italian edition of the book: *Teozoologia. La scienza delle nature scimmiesche sodomite e l'elettrone divino* (Rome, Italy: Thule Italia, 2008), 23.

359 Ansprandi, *Eurasian Universism*, 124. To corroborate, also see: Michiel de Vaan, *Etymological Dictionary of Latin and the other Italic Languages* (Leiden, Netherlands: Brill Academic Publishers, 2008), 105, 124-125.

arose from European cultures themselves under the sway of the ideas of Christianity.³⁶⁰

With the exhaustion of Christianity and its rapid decline in the current, final phase of the Western civilisation, within the metastasis of Western modernity and its dissolution in postmodernity, Traditionalists should also work for the creation of fields for the re-grounding of the Erst Wisdom in the godless wasteland of the Western and Westernised world. Traditionalists might, as already mentioned before, stimulate a correct development of Neopagan religions, as well as new religious syntheses and discourses under the auspices of Islam — which is spreading widely athwart the Western world and represents a fulfilment of the entire Abrahamic religious tradition, solving all the ethnic supremacies and theo-eschatological monopolies on truth of the previous forms of the tradition (respectively, Judaism and Christianity) —, as new living traditions of the Erst Wisdom suited for the peoples and contexts of Europe and of the broader Western world but at the same time providing them a spiritual link with Eurasia.³⁶¹ Eurasia, according to Dugin's Traditionalist Eurasianism, has to play the role of the protagonist in the restoration of the Erst

---

360 It is worthwhile noting that the beginning of the modern epoch is conventionally set in 1492, marked by the discovery of America by the Genoese explorer Cristopher Columbus (1451-1506), which opened the way to the colonial expansion of the European potentates over the Earth's globe — justified by the teleological plan of worldwide Christianisation — and therefore to all the technological and anthropological processes of modernity — and of postmodernity since the second half of the 20th century, coming after the exhaustion of modernity —, which in the long run entailed the erosion of the European *ethne* and cultures themselves, first by metastasising with their own colonial expansion, and then by imploding under the pressure of the anthropological outcomes of their own colonialism, precipitated by their own technological achievements.

361 Islam might be adapted to the spirit of the European peoples in the same way as Christianity, after having taken part in and outlasted the dissolution of the Roman Empire, of the ancient Greco-Roman civilisation, was shapen by the Germanic peoples to become the gist of the civilisation of the Middle Ages, by means of quintessentially European peaks of thought, especially Rhineland mysticism. About this, see: Adriano Romualdi, *Sul problema d'una Tradizione europea* (Palermo, Italy: Vie della Tradizione, 1996 [1973]), 39-45. Regarding specific projects for indigenising Islam in Europe, interesting outlines are those drawn by the English scholar Timothy Winter (alias Abdal Hakim Murad).

Wisdom after the end of times — a Duginian theme which I myself followed and emphasised in *Eurasian Universism*, as the title of the book itself implies —, being the place where the aforesaid Shambhala is located.

Regarding the question of finding a new mould in which to catalyse the restoration of authentic European cultures, even with the wherewithals provided by modernity, Evola's follower Adriano Romualdi (1940-1973) thus writes in his essay *Sul problema d'una Tradizione europea* (1973):[362]

> The problem of a European tradition is that of finding a spiritual form capable of containing three millennia and more of European spirituality. A form that would not represent any syncretistic hotchpotch but that would rediscover the foundation of the white man's own spirituality. [...] A modern European spirituality might not but configure itself as essentially active in a world whose central theme is that of the mastery of the elementary forces. The invasion of the elementary — techniques, distances, excitements — seems to be characteristic of our epoch. It requires an ability of discipline and simplification which is alien to whatever spiritualistic smudge. A style which would catch, in the white, still, and metallic lights of a certain modernity, almost a foreboding of a new classicism. The style of a metaphysics of the effort and formation of oneself.

Dugin says that with the conclusion of the current Iron Age, when the King of the World, the new *Manu* — the legislator of a new mankind, in Vedic terms —, will be revealed and will give rise to the new Golden Age, in the aording of the Aeyeness of the Twixt's "Therebeing" (*Dasein*) — to put it in Heideggerian terminology —, "the east will once again tend to unite with the north, and not only symbolically but in a concrete, absolute manner" which will directly affect Siberia, the land of the bearers of God.[363]

The new *Manu*, the Watching Overman of the Radical Self, the Aryan Twixt, the actor of Traditionalism, and the

---

362 Romualdi, *Sul problema d'una Tradizione europea*, 51.

363 Dugin, *Rusia, el misterio de Eurasia*, 133. About the Therebeing, which corresponds to the state of the Twixt, and about the latter's etymological connection with the early Germanic concept of *Tuisto-Manno*, and therefore with the Vedic Sanskrit *Tvashtar-Manu*, see: Ansprandi, *Eurasian Universism*, 127-128, 186.

new mankind awakened by the metaphysico-hermeneutical operation of its Ecstatic Orthology, stands at the centre of the cross of the tree of Being, between Heaven and Earth, north and south, east and west, in a state of consciousness which is not that of a particularised being, but which comprises and outdoes the possibility of multiple individual manifestations, and is united with the stars, and with them draws the Orlay of the whole reality.[364] I clinch with another description of such a state of being provided by Evola, who further identified it as the state of being of the "hero":[365]

> He for whom neither this shore nor the other one, nor both together, exist anymore, who, without any fear, has abandoned the human bond, has overcome the divine bond and has redeemed himself of every bond, is a *hero*, whose path is known neither by the gods, nor by men. [...] Autonomous, superior to destiny, kingless (as it is kingly in itself) is [...] the "race of the Hermetic Philosophers". [...] Nobler, greater, mightier than his cosmic parents, Heaven and Earth, is said recurrently in the texts the Child begotten by the Art. He is called *magnipotens*. Bearing in his hands the insignia of both the spiritual kingdom and the temporal one, he has become the subject of himself, and has conquered the wulder of the world.

---

364 Evola, *La tradizione ermetica*, 180, 183.

365 Ibidem, 179-180. The concept of "hero" (from Greek *heros*; Latin *herus*), may be, according to a convention on which also Evola relies upon, another iteration, at least functionally and possibly even etymologically, of the concept of "Aryan" itself. The equivalence is mentioned, for instance, in: Julius Evola, *Rivolta contro il mondo moderno* (Rome, Italy: Edizioni Mediterranee, 2003 [1934]), 272; Evola, *Sintesi di dottrina della razza*, 178-183. However, another etymology traces the word "hero" back to the Indo-European root **ser*, meaning "to watch [over], to protect".

HEART AND CENTER IN RENÉ GUÉNON: ON THE USAGE OF SYMBOLS

Jean-Pierre Laurant

René Guénon made abundant use of the related terms "heart" and "center," in relation to the microcosm as well as the macrocosm, with the aim of articulating a spiritual approach which goes beyond the multiplicity of the states of being to the principial unity.[366] In effect, these terms constitute a cornerstone of the architecture of Guénon's oeuvre, but this doubling seems, at first glance, to generate more difficulties than it resolves, as these two notions are not of the same order. Of what is the heart the center? How can the point, the center *par excellence* of the state of abstraction, be sensible? Depending on the perspective one takes, heart and center are neither metaphors nor synonyms for each other, or they are always synonyms.

Some Remarks on Guénonian Epistemology

The argumentation developed over the whole of Guénon's oeuvre had the aim of opening up a way of access for bringing back to conscious thought that which otherwise seems to arise only out of the domain of intuition or spiritual discernment. His work is about returning to clear ideas that were accessible to all at the origins of the world. However, the method put

---

[366] René Guénon, *Les États multiples de l'Être* (Paris: Véga, 1932). More than 150 references for "heart" and 180 for "center" figure in the bibliographical index of André Desilets (Quebec: Les Presses de l'Université de Laval, 1977). But "Initiation" in different variants (chivalric, masonic, feminine, etc.) occurs more than twice as often, and we count around 130 different occurrences of "Tradition."

in place denied being a personal creation, it wanted to be an archaeology of traditional knowledge, universal and timeless.[367] Symbolic thought on the one hand, and mathematics on the other, constituted the last authentic elements of the original knowledge, and they were naturally articulated in this vision of a sacred traditional science as being able to transform our lives, in a veritable *metanoia*. The symbol, in itself or in act, is therefore conceived by Guénon as carrying a real spiritual influence to the extent that it expresses an absolute truth and is able to be expressed in "horizontal," dialectical reasoning. These truths are given "to live," "to be lived," and are therefore the testaments of the very fact of the millennial experience that has borne them. Reference to history, including Guénon's personal history, is unavoidable.[368] For him, Tradition had sense only as living and lived.

How does the "charged" symbol assure passage from one order to another? By induction, by drawing its authority from an authority other than itself, as Shankarâchârya affirms in relation to the Brahma-Sutras based on the Vedas; induction can, "according to Hindu logic, serve as proof" and "be legitimately employed in the realm of sensible knowledge."[369] The symbol is by nature never alone. It functions in a chain associating by "analogy" the heart to the cave or the center to the temple. Guénon clarified in "Symbols of Analogy"[370] the sense in which he utilized this term: "We mean here analogy exclusively in its most rigorous sense, that is to say, following the Hermetic formula, as the relationship of 'that which is

---

367 However, Guénon considered himself to be the only known holder of this method and knowledge, the one chosen to assure its transmission.

368 Guénon was very young when he made his definitive spiritual choices; the whole of his writings are to be understood as an oeuvre of fighting for the truth.

369 *L'Homme et son devenir selon le Vêdantâ* (Paris: Éditions traditionnelles, 1941), 22 and note 2. This is the only reference to "induction" in Guénon's ouvre. [René Guénon, *Man and His Becoming According to the Vedanta*, trans. Richard C. Nicholson (Hillsdale: Sophia Perennis, 2001), 14 and note 5].

370 *Études traditionnelles*, January 1939.

below' with 'that which is above.'"[371] The geometric figures of the inverted triangles in the seal of Solomon, the six-spoked wheel, and the chrism illustrate this referral to induction and passage.[372]

Heart and center thus naturally found their place in the arrangement of a posthumous work that brought together more than seventy of Guénon articles on symbols, the plan of which was conceived by Michel Vâlsan.[373] The eight chapters of the plan all refer to the two notions, starting with the first on the nature and function of the symbol. However, the chapters proceed in different symbolic chains associated with the eye, the egg, and the cave for the first, and the tree, the axis, or the flower for the second; as geographic symbols, the two are intertwined.[374] The whole is articulated around particular aspects of cycles, of passage or of cosmic form, but the last, entitled "Symbolism of the Heart," might surprise: as if the end of a path leading to the "supreme principle," beyond being, the symbol *par excellence* of this last chapter could take the place of a conclusion. This *"pas de deux"* does not refer to a point of doctrine, but to the historical conditions in which these articles were written: firstly to the conquest of an institutional public, that of the journal *Regnabit: revue internationale du Sacré-Cœur* (1921-1929), and secondly in response to questions or objections from "Guénonian" networks.[375]

---

[371] René Guénon, *Symboles fondamentaux de la science sacrée* (Paris: Gallimard, 1962), "Tradition" collection, 319-323 [René Guénon *Symbols of Sacred Science*, trans. Henry D. Fohr and Samuel D. Fohr (Hillsdale: Sophia Perennis, 2001), 308].

[372] Désilet notes around 25 references to "analogy."

[373] This refers to the title (the adjective "fundamental" in particular), the plan, and the notes. The introduction justifies the enterprise as continuing the master's will.

[374] See "Les têtes noires," *Études traditionnelles*, June 1947.

[375] The articles of this chapter date from 1927 and 1948-1950. Michel Vâlsan found himself in a comparable situation in 1961 facing Frithjof Schuon.

The Heart in All its States

The question of "cardiocentrism" has been debated in Western thought since its origins; Aristotle placed the center of the soul there, at the body's point of equilibrium between the upper, the lower, the right, and the left.[376] The *Concordance biblique* (TOB) lists more than 900 references translated from the Hebrew *Lev* (heart/center — interiority) or *Nefesh* (soul) in the Old Testament, and in the New Testament from the Greek *Kardia*, *Psuchè*, *Dianoia* (in Plato, the interior conversation of the soul with itself) or *Sôma* (heart, soul, and body). Both approaches attribute to the heart functions of an intellectual, sensible and "decisional" order, proper to the human soul. The first Biblical mentions make it the seat of thought and judgment (Gn 8:21); it is the seat of the will to return to Yahweh in *Samuel* (1 Sam 7:3).[377] It is also the place of affectivity and love in 1 Sam 2:1 and Songs 8:6: "Put me like a seal on your heart." It is this combination of functions, corresponding to the respective plane upon which places themself, that gives meaning. Hardened when it is led astray, the heart is strengthened when it is turned toward God, or it "melts like wax" (Ps 22:15).

The Alexandrian Fathers, such as Origen at the beginning of the third century, insisted on this essential point, taking up Saint Paul's comparison of the body of man to a tent (the tent of Witness): "we will say that the part concealed by the veil, where inaccessible objects are enclosed, is the master faculty of the heart, which alone can receive the mysteries of the truth and conceive of the secrets of God."[378] Two centuries

---

376 See Aristotle's History of Animals, a little embarrassed by the shift to the left in humanity. The harmony of the soul in Plato is found in the equilibrium of the head, the heart, and the stomach.

377 On the exegesis of the heart in the Christian tradition, particularly in Catholic tradition, see Édouard Glotin S.J., *La Bible du Coeur de Jésus* (Paris, Presses de la renaissance, 2007). The author was responsible for the sanctuary of Paray-le-Monial from 1982-1997. His work is in the catechetical line of the Jesuit Fathers of Paray.

378 *Homélies sur les nombres*, X, 3 2, vol 1 (Paris, Cerf, 1996), 287. The Latin text has: *arcanorum Dei*.

later, Saint Augustine will legitimize all the senses of the heart in a commentary on the Psalms, identifying the heart with Scripture, but he will add that the rending of the Temple veil at the death of Christ had opened access to the Scriptures to all.[379] The localization of the "supreme" central point that Aristotle placed in the third ventricle of the cavity of the heart is now seen as the part struck by the soldier's lance, from which flowed blood and water, the fountain of the spiritual life.[380]

The mystics of the late Latin Middle Ages and the Renaissance, driven by the autonomization of the person and the separation of functions, many of which were moved toward the brain, concentrated on direct access to the heart, to the neglect of the face or the name, and exalted the affective, the suffering of the body on the model of the "Pieta."[381] Like the Apostle Thomas placing his hands on the wound of Christ (Jn 20:27), Catherine of Sienna (1347-1380) is invited to enter into the cavity of his heart. But it is with the Visitandine of Paray-le Monial, Marguerite-Marie Alacoque (1647-1690),[382] that the dolorist devotion to the heart of flesh presented by the Savior in a series of visions beginning in 1675, will give its full measure along with the request for the consecration of France to the Sacred Heart that the nun would make to Louis XIV. This radicalization of cardiocentrism, under the pressure of the advance of the sciences — with Descartes dissociating the biological heart from the soul and seeking the central point of life in the pineal gland of the brain — was replaced by the line of heart-brain-hand as Philippe de Champaigne painted it in his "Saint Augustine." The flaming heart on the hand of "doing," inspired the radiance of the brain "thus speaking."

---

379 *Ennaratio in Psalmos*, 21, 15.

380 John 19:24 is the only Gospel mention; the word "heart" is absent, the lance struck him "in the side."

381 To the contrary, in Eastern Christian Hesychasm the peace of the heart is sought by the invocation of the Name. Direct access to God, without passing through a priest, was particularly attractive to women.

382 See Glotin, *La Bible du Coeur de Jésus*, "chap. 6 L'expérience du cœur de Jésus," 279-354.

After the revolutionary earthquake, the Sacred heart symbolized reparation of the misfortunes of the time,[383] the Church reliving the sufferings of the Passion. In 1856, Pius X extended the Feast of the Sacred Heart to all of the Catholic world, Marguerite-Marie was beatified in 1864 and two encyclicals followed, crowned by the *Haurietis Aquas in gaudio* of Pius XII in 1956. The idea of a plenitude of Revelation underlying and inspiring the above-cited work of Édouard Glotin soon raised the question: if the new heart was eucharistic, then *what* of the Eucharist? The reduction of meaning by the banalization of the sentimental approach was nonetheless inevitable.[384]

Father Anizan, Charbonneau-Lassay, and Guénon

The founder, in 1921, of *Regnabit: revue universelle du Sacré-Cœur*, the organ of the "Society of the Intellectual Radiance of the Sacred Heart" (*Société du rayonnement intellectuel du Sacré-Cœur*) Félix Anizan (1878-1944), the Oblate of Mary Immaculate, was animated by the desire "to go to the end" of this new reading of Revelation in fighting against the sentimental drift. Cardinal Dubois (1856-1929), archbishop of Paris, sponsored the group and introduced him to Charbonneau-Lassay (1871-1946), a close friend of Guénon. The enterprise, open to pre-Christian traditions, was in the line of Hiéron de Paray-le-Monial (1873-1926), was dedicated to Christ the King and "reframed" in Catholic orthodoxy after the departure of its founder, Alexis de Sarachaga (1840-1918).[385] Guénon

---

383 The banner of the Vendée revolt against the Convention displayed the emblem of the Sacred Heart.

384 The "Prayer of the Heart" of Eastern Hesychasm extends the Eucharist without replacing it. A seminarian's joke in the 1950s in Soissons called the Sacred Heart the "Godin," from the name of the stove made in the Familistère de Guise. The mediocrity of the plasterwork decorating the churches is just as obvious.

385 Sarachaga and Victor Drevon, S.J. had attempted to promote a sort of Catholic Hermetic Masonry. Esoteric exegeses flourished. The activities were followed by a number of ecclesiastics.

entered the executive committee alongside clerics, painters like Chabas, and the editor-in-chief of *La Croix*, Jean Guiraud.[386]

Anizan elaborated his symbolic theology upon a hierarchic structure of the universe: man is the link between the created worlds, the God-Man between the Creator and Creation, and he is summated in a central point, his heart. His arguments borrow from the Catholic traditionalism of the beginning of the century, particularly the iconography and study of the radiant heart of the Charterhouse of Saint-Denis D'Orques (17th century) by Charbonneau-Lassay.[387] This was Guénon's first collaboration, with twenty articles: "The Sacred Heart and the Legend of the Holy Grail" was preceded by a short piece by Anizan saluting these "beautiful emissions of the primeval tradition" (*"beaux rejets de la tradition primitive"*).[388] The theme of heart/center was approached here in its mythological and universal states with the presence of the cup/vase in the terrestrial Paradise lost by Adam, chased from the place and exiled in time. Doubly, it was the center of the divine plan with the consecration of the Last Supper and the blood and water collected by Joseph of Arimathea from the side wound on the Cross. The legend of Seth undertaking to recover the cup echoed the notion of hidden transmission that underlies Guénon's entire work. Above all, he insisted on the universality of the symbol, verified by the Hindu tradition, his basic point of reference, which makes the heart "the center of integral being" to which the "sense of eternity

---

386 Interested by Masonry, he had published on the "primitive Rite of Narbonne" under the pseudonym Benjamin Fabre.

387 See *Le centre du plan divin* (Paris: Lethielleux, 1925).

388 August-September, 1925. Anizan refers to the visions of Saint Mechtilde to whom Christ had extended a golden cup from which all the saints had to drink. The meeting with Guénon was reported in a letter from the latter to Charbonneau dated 18 June 1925: "I had received, before your letter, a word from P. Anizan, and I went to see him on Tuesday of last week; he is very happy to know that you and I have arrived at the same conclusions on many points, and by very different methods. I hope to give him a first article before going on vacation; we are moreover entirely in agreement on the essential ideas."

must be reattached."[389] The condemnation of modern excesses since Descartes or Pascal is omnipresent in two articles are devoted to them: "The Radiant Heart and the Flaming Heart" and "Heart and Brain."[390] Some fundamental analogies finally nourish the argument: heart/world tree, heart/cave, etc.

This complete exposition of the symbolic method as "sacred science," the key of Guénonian epistemology, in a journal which was the "spokesman" of an ecclesiastical institution, conferred on the heart a particular status. "Considerations on Symbolism" (Nov., 1926), "The Holy Land and the Heart of the World" (Sept.-Oct., 1926) were completed with "The Word and the Symbol":

> If the Word is Thought interiorly and Speech exteriorly, and if the word is the effect of the divine speech uttered at the beginning of time, then all of nature can be taken as a symbol of supernatural reality ... The primordial Revelation, the work of the Word as Creation, is also incorporated, so to speak, in symbols which have been transmitted over the ages since the beginning of humanity, and this process is analogous, in its order, to that of creation itself. On the other hand, can we not see in this symbolic incorporation of the 'non-human' tradition ... a prefiguration of the Incarnation of the Word? And does this not also make it possible to perceive, in a certain measure, the mysterious relationship that exists between the creation and the Incarnation which is its crowning ... If symbolism in its essence strictly conforms to 'the divine plan' and if the Sacred Heart is the 'center of the divine plan,' as the heart is the center of being, really and symbolically all together, then this symbol of the Heart, by itself or by its equivalents, must occupy in all doctrines issuing ... from the primordial tradition, the central place ...[391]

But beyond a relative unity of the anthropocentric vision of creation and of the nature of the symbol expressed in

---

[389] Pier Luigi Zoccatelli has assembled the articles in *Écrits pour Regnabit* (Milan: Archè / Turin: Nino Aragno, 1999), 4-9. The connection to the Old Testament was developed in "Le cœur du Monde dans la Kabbale hébraïque," July-August 1926.

[390] April 1926 and January 1927, in Zoccatelli, *Écrits pour Regnabit*, 59, 133. with references to Aristotle, to Islamic esotericism and to the vertical and horizontal axes of the cross.

[391] January 1926, Zoccatelli, *Écrits pour Regnabit*, 40-41

the journal, Guénon was a stakeholder in a project of social renovation, justifying "a cult of the Sacred Heart;" he gave to Hiéron's militant journal, Christ the King (May-June 1927), "Christ the Priest and King."

The Center Seen from the Heart

The Eastern aid necessary for the traditional restoration was expressed in Guénon's first doctrinal book, with the evocative title: *Man and His Becoming According to the Vedanta*.[392] The central role of the heart is described in chapter three as "the vital center of the human being, the seat of Brahma"; it is the place of the living soul (*Jîvâtmâ*), the issue of the "Self" (*Âtmâ*), and it has a physical location: "This vital center is considered to correspond analogically to the smallest ventricle (*guhâ*) of the *hridaya* heart) . . ."[393] The titles published during this period of 1925-1927 — *The Esotericism of Dante* (1925), *Saint Bernard* (1926, in a collection directed by Jacques Maritain), and *The King of the World* (1926) — kept the course of addressing the Christian West. This latter work contained a number of passages identical to those in *Regnabit*, notably on the Grail, except that Guénon now linked his commentary on the cup with the "Eucharistic sacrifice of Melchizedek," which is far from the classical exegesis of "types and figures."[394] This personage was identified with the "King of the World," which is to say the real presence of the representative of the "supreme spiritual pole," superior to Abraham, whom he had blessed[395], and whose function was transmitted from generation to generation until our days. His seat is in the mysterious *Agartha* of Mongol legends. The project was strictly parallel to that

---

392 René Guénon, *L'Homme et son devenir selon le Vêdânta* (Paris, Bossard, 1925).

393 Ibid., 48-50 in the 1941 edition. Referring to this state as common to all traditions, he cites Aristotle. The vocabulary utilized is transposed into Thomistic terms in particular: "possibility," "potentiality."

394 Chap. VI, p. 62-73 in the 1929 edition.

395 Genesis 14:18.

of Anizan for the Eucharistic heart, but of another order, so Guénon carefully evaded the expression in his book.[396]

Aware of the importance of the step taken, he justified himself by citing Saint Paul: "About this we have much to say which is hard to explain, since you have become dull of hearing."[397] The disclosure was justified by urgency in the face of the disasters which were announcing themselves, perhaps "the immense event" of which Joseph de Maistre had spoken and which served as a conclusion. The rupture would have affected equally his relations with the Hindu masters for whom he would have said too much; Guénon's biographer and editor, Chacornac, was convinced of this, citing a correspondence of Tamos evoking a "vision" of the latter, in Bengal, of an aged man raising a veil before his eyes and ceasing to write to him.[398]

Charbonneau-Lassay was the key figure in this collaboration; from 1924, their correspondence focused on the development of the themes that Guénon was to address in the journal: the chrism, Melchizedek, the Three Magi-Kings already mentioned by Charbonneau in an earlier article, and the latter had agreed to illustrate the subsequent articles of his correspondent and proofread them before sending them to Father Anizan. They exchanged suggestions. The meetings with Anizan in Paris on the strategy of *Rayonnement intellectuel* were summarized for his absent friend who lived in Loudun.[399]

---

396 The strike of the lance here is said to be to "the side," citing Saint John (John 19:34).

397 Hebrews 5:11.

398 Paul Chacornac, *La Vie Simple de René Guénon* (1958), 78-80. The double rupture justified, in his eyes, his conversion to Islam. Georges Thomas/Tamos (1884-1966), was editor-in-chief of the *Voile d'Isis* under the pseudonym Argos; Guénon had recourse to his mediumistic gifts regularly.

399 Letters from R.G. to Ch. dated 24/11/1924, 2/12/1924, 25/2/1925, 18/6/1925, 28/101925 (Anizan confirms their identity from the perspective of the original unity of all traditions), 2/12/1925, 25/2/1926 (radiant heart and flaming heart). We are thankful to the archives of the Guénon Foundation for the latter. Guénon's confidence in Charbonneau was total, but they were not of the same generation, hence he addresses "*Cher Monsieur et ami*" in June 1928.

It was at the request of the Father that he would devote his last work to the notion of the center in ancient traditions.[400]

Their correspondence also reported negative reactions from priests disquieted by the boldness of their theological positions. In August 1926, he assessed the opposition they encountered from "competing" institutions and from the negative influence of Maritain.[401] He soon became aware of triangular exchanges revealing a change in Anizan, who now "cites Saint Thomas in each phrase" and seemed to have not read his books.[402] The complete rupture, proof of a "double game," is reported to his friend in the following spring. The latter, having mentioned Anizan's request to "clarify his intellectual and religious position" and to resign discreetly, received a solid clarification: it would be enough to read his books and "above all to understand them," something of which the Father seemed incapable, like all the theologians no doubt. The misunderstanding arose from the fact that "they were not talking about the same thing," Charbonneau agreed, and argued that the Father was a stranger to such maneuvers, but, according to Guénon, it remained the case that his manner of proceeding was unqualifiable, and thus he included a letter bordering on insult and said that he had already lost enough time. The affair confirmed what he had always thought and written:

> Catholicism is the only thing, in the current Western world, with which I have sympathized and declared respectable, and the Catholics are also, thus far, the only ones who have addressed to me insults and threats. We can conclude whatever we like; as for me, I conclude from this above all that the Westerners, taken collectively, are "possible" only when one shows them the stick . . . For the rest, I see no appreciable difference between the spirit of domination that is affirmed in the letters of Father Anizan and

---

400 Letter dated 23/1/1926, "Le centre du monde dans les traditions extrême-orientales," published in May 1927.

401 Letter dated 26/8/1926, the Society of Saint Jean de Maurice Denis in particular.

402 Letter dated 18/10/1927. The Maritain group was referred to as "the band of Meudon."

that which presides over the colonial conquests; there is very little "spiritual" in all this!⁴⁰³

Curiously, it was to the publication of *The Crisis of the Modern World* (1927) and not *The King of the World* and the "Eastern centers" that he attributed the crisis; he understood that the Father had been in a delicate situation with the censors of the Oblates in Rome but that did not change anything fundamentally.⁴⁰⁴ By contrast, his relations with his friend changed little. In his eyes, he remained the authority on the matter of Christian symbolism, henceforth he avoided the question of the heart.⁴⁰⁵ The topic of the survival of "societies" of Christian esotericism, under the influence of the Guénonian conception of transmission, was suggested in their exchanges with the mention of *L'Estoile Internelle* and the Knights of the Paraclete, and apprehension over Eastern matters was implied with the "strange visit" received from a representative of ancient Mazdaism in 1925.⁴⁰⁶ Their closeness echoed in the nearly intimate relation over the break with his family and the departure of his niece Françoise, which was taken to be a conspiracy by ecclesiastical milieux.⁴⁰⁷

---

403 Letter dated 8/6/1928.

404 See Marie-France James, *Ésotérisme et christianisme autour de René Guénon* (N.E.L, 1981), 235-299. The Roman dossier studied by Pier Luigi Zoccatelli shows the censors' complete incomprehension of the symbolism.

405 Except for the iconography of the heart of Saint Denis-D'Orques; see the letter dated 30/1/1929.

406 Guénon returns to this several times, see the letter dated /6/8/1928; the person in question, Saï Taki Movi, was identified by Éric Phalippou in *Politica Hermetica* (Laussane: l'Age d'Homme, 2003), 171-216: JJ Modi, a Parsi traveller and intellectual, invited to France by the orientalist Darmesteter in 1925. His cane, decorated with interesting symbolism and given to Charbonneau, is located in the Museum of Loudun. Gauthier Pierozak offers a description of it in the preface to Louis Charbonneau-Lassay, *Le Vulnéraire du Christ: La mystérieuse emblématique des plaies du corps et du coeur de Jésus-Chris* (2017).

407 Letters dated 8/2/1929 and 18/2/1929. "I learned things that surpass all that one can imagine: I was surrounded, without suspecting it, by a veritable network of espionage and treason. The most frightening thing is that the child herself was playing a double game . . ." He asked his friend to no longer speak of them.

The "One" Word, but for Other Ears: The Ouevre's New Orientation

The Symbolism of the Cross constitutes the doctrinal continuation of *Man and His Becoming According to the Vedanta*. The essential remains:

> The human being has, in the domain of individual existence that is his, a role that one can truly qualify as 'central' in relation to the other beings that are similarly situated in this domain; this role makes of man the most complete expression of the individual state...[408]

But here the heart loses its *aura* of real spiritual presence in favor of a rigorous demonstration that borrows its mode of exposition from geometry. "The Universal Man" described here is prior to the Fall and the Incarnation, and the symbol of the cross summarizes him in all his possible extensions, vertical and horizontal. It is by virtue of this metaphysical sense that Christ died on a cross, at the central point where all the contradictions are resolved and not the inverse. Guénon cites in a note *The Epistle on the Manifestation of the Prophet* by Sheikh Mohammed ibn Fazlallah El-Hindi who identifies the Prophet with the Universal Man, and adds the "Word itself," i.e., the word that shows the absence of any divergence between Christianity and Islam at the core of "the esoteric doctrine."[409] The axial symbolism of the "Tree of the Middle" and the concordance between the modes of expression of the central point, "the Great Peace," Shekinah, in the Kabbalah and in the Far East occupy the following chapters. The potential contradiction between the "geometric representation of the states of existence" (chap. XI) and the affirmed centrality of the human state is lifted if one considers the inevitable relativity of the "place from which one speaks."[410]

---

[408] René Guénon, *Le Symbolisme de la croix* (Paris, Véga, 1931), 31.

[409] Ibid., chap III, "Le symbolisme métaphysique de la croix," 32. He takes the chance to slip in on the authority of an Islamic figure that "if the Christians had the sign of the cross, the Muslims had the doctrine of it."

[410] The words "heart" and "creation" (5 times) are avoided for "center" (45 times) and "manifestation" (12 times).

As is well known, Guénon found refuge in Egypt after his violent rupture with Catholic milieux and would henceforth "lean on Islam," i.e., live as a pious Muslim without changing anything in the doctrine expressed in his books, which had carefully dissociated the esoteric from the religious.[411] Nevertheless, the weight of the experience would continue to weigh on his works, his readers being in the West, immersed in a Christian culture, and he demonstrated his choices by dedicating his book to "the venerated memory" of Sheikj Elish, the founder of his chosen Sufi branch; nevertheless, the references to Islam were few compared to the Vedanta or to Taoism (see below for the notions of breadth and exaltation). "Heart" henceforth disappeared from his doctrinal books, namely *The Multiple States of Being* (1932), his post-war work on the cycles of involution, *The Reign of Quantity and the Signs of the Times* (1947), and then *The Principles of the Infinitesimal Calculus* (1948), but over the years it returned in force throughout his articles, the majority of which were responses to questions from readers.

Although more "hushed," the rupture with the learned world was just as real, *The King of the World* was considered an occultist resurgence, and its anti-modernity was no longer accepted since his rejection of and by the nationalist right after *Spiritual Authority and Temporal Power* (1929). In fact, Guénon would regain grand Parisian publication only after 1945, addressing himself until then to networks destined to form the future elite, and not to institutions. Mentions of the heart recur in his articles in response to questions or in reaction to interpretations which were either erroneous in his eyes, such as the reduction of the Grail solely to its Christian dimension by Arthur Waite, or which reinforced his positions, such as Coomaraswamy on the Hindu vision of the passage through the three worlds toward the center.[412] Guénon's

---

411 "Spiritual propriety" being necessarily "inconvertible to anything" — "À propos de conversions", *Études traditionnelles*, Sept. 1948.

412 "Le Saint Graal," *Le Voile d'Isis*, Feb-March, 1934 and "Janua Coeli", *Études traditionnelles*, Jan-Feb, 1946, then "Lumière et pluie," idem, May 1946.

rewriting of "The Radiant Heart and the Flaming Heart" between *Regnabit* (1926) and *Études Traditionnelles* (1948) allows us to measure the interceding experience: the first was founded on the sacrality of a symbol that was anterior to Christianity, its universality regarded as highlighting relevance of his "esoteric" approach," while the second legitimized, in the name of esoteric doctrine, the sacred heart in the late medieval version (or from the early sixteenth century) of Saint-Denis-d'Orques at most.

This situation was to compromise doctrinal reflection on the "heart" among many of his "followers," who were anxious to add the dimension of experience to their engagement. Charbonneau-Lassay, whose Catholic faith did not waver, endeavored to align the criteria set out by his friend with his project concerning Christian esoteric societies. On the other hand, he multiplied the obstacles facing Vasile Lovinescu (1905-1984) on the point of his choosing Hesychastic asceticism in 1935 upon his return from Athos, and all the signs invoked as proofs of Orthodoxy were, according to Guénon, only memories, reduced solely to "the religious."[413] He was inattentive to the fact that Orthodoxy commonly designates the heart as "bossom," the bossom of the Lord on which Saint John heard his heart beat (John 1:23). Excluding the dolorist path and living in the plenitude of Sufism, he considered Hesychasm to be incomplete or decadent.

It is therefore the reemergence of the religious that will characterize the last part of the Master's work and life and involve those who claimed it in a quest for culmination.

---

413 Guénon had written to Schuon on 5/6/1931: "As for Eastern Christianity, I do not believe that very much in terms of profound understanding subsists there. The Syrians are hardly worth more than the Greeks, and the Copts themselves are generally very ignorant. There are still a few old monks who constitute an exception, but they are retired in a nearly inaccessible region, and they no longer admit newcomers among them; it is therefore a tradition that is dying and which has lost all its vitality." On the Lovinescu/Guénon correspondence, see Hans Thomas Hakl (ed.), *Octagon* (Gaggenau: Scientia nova Verlag, 2018), 130-135. On Hesychasm and Sufism in the light of Guénon and Eliade's perspectives, see Enrico Montanari, *La Fatica del Cuore* (Milano: Jaca Book, 2003), 83-179.

The Heart Overflowing

Sufi practice as Guénon experienced it in Cairo used different Koranic terms to designate the heart, *qalb*, in its multiple functions with respect to whether they refer to the place of mystical union, to the knowledge of divine things, or to spiritual combat (the "chest," *sadr*), that is to say the set of "cognitive faculties" accompanying the "mystery of love" that is inseparable from the process and which one finds in the texts of the great Sufi masters.[414] Guénon's practice was totally different from the context of his initiation in 1912, shortly before turning to the Catholic Church, considering that one could be a Sufi without being a Muslim. In 1947, he remarked on what his new life implied in "The Necessity of Traditional Exotericism"; noting that the religious question concerned the West alone, as the Eastern social context remains traditional, he added what was in his eyes a decisive argument: "and also for another reason: there [in Islam] exotericism and esotericism are directly linked in a traditional form, so as to be in a way only two sides, exterior and interior, of one thing."[415] This late clarification weakened the border between the two notions that had been a pillar of his work, even if he had put things in order regarding his personal case in September 1948 in "Concerning Conversions."

All of Guénon's care went to the groups in formation that he had inspired. In the case of initiations of professions, a conclusion was necessary: all the religions were compatible in principle — which supposed that the dissociation always held in this way ("The Three Rings" lodge uniting the religions of the book was created in this spirit) —, but the attitude of the Catholic and Orthodox Churches was not very encouraging.

---

414 See Pierre Lory, "Le coeur dans la mystique soufie" in *Pour une civilisation du cœur* (Paris: Éditions de l'Emmanuel, 2000), 157-163. He cites texts by Rumi, Ibn Arabi, and Ghazali.

415 *Études traditionnelles*, Dec. 1947. Reprinted in René Guénon, *Initiation et réalisation spirituelle*, chap. vii, 60-61. Jean Revor insisted in his widely circulated *Document confidential* on the reticence that had accompanied this publication.

The heart reappeared in his correspondence with Denys Roman (Marcel Maugy, 1901-1986) on the occasion of changes in the ritual of the "Three Rings" on March 6 1950:

> For the reversal of the table of the third degree, I do not see any other way of proceeding than the one you say, but I do not know if one can really make a connection with the 'displacement of the lights' of the Kabbalah, which seems related in reality to the transfer of the center of consciousness from the content of the heart.

Reyor, who was the master's eyes for *Études traditionnelles* after the relative estrangement of Tamos, oriented the journal after his death in 1960 toward a Christian Kabbalah and demonstrated little appetite for Hesychasm, the "prayer of the heart" being reduced to a vestige, in contrast to the view of the Romanian Michel Vâlsan.[416] The latter had participated in the religious effervescence of Romania in the 1930s, troubled by the prophecies of the shepherd of Maglavit in which Hesychasm was an issue. Oriented by Reyor, then integrated in 1937 into the branch of the *tariqah Alawiya* that Schuon had founded, he separated from it in 1950, followed by those who had hoped to live a Sufism strictly conforming to Islamic exoteric orthodoxy. Persuaded of the spiritual mission of Guénon in Romania, he pursued he debate with his master's correspondents in the 1930s and '40s: V. Lovinescu, Marcel Avramescu (1909-1983), a Jew converted to Orthodoxy by the work of Guénon, and Anton Dumitriu (1905-1992) who, after a complicated journey, had joined the group of the "Burning Bush," *Rugul Aprins*, in a monastery near Bucharest with the wish to revitalize Orthodoxy through Hesychasm in the face of Stalinist repression — these correspondents provided Vâlsan with documentation and clarifications on the nature of the invocation of the Name.[417] The latter

---

[416] On this question see Montanari, *La Fatica del Cuore*, chap. 2, "Esicasmo e sufismo," 111-115. See Reyor, "Ésotérisme et exotérisme chrétiens," *Études traditionnelles*, March 1952, reprinted in idem, *Pour un Aboutissement de l'Oeuvre de Rene Guenon* (Milano: Archè, 1991), 34.

[417] See Claudio Mutti, *Eliade, Vâlsan, Geticus e gli altri, la fortuna di René Guénon tra i Romeni* (Parma: Ed. a l'insegna del Veltro, 1999).

informed Guénon of struggles with Schuon's choice in the text "Christic Mysteries" (*Études traditionnelles*, August 1948) on the question of the heart and the invocation of the Name in relation to Sufi *dhikr*.[418] He had argued from Symeon the New Theologian (949-1022), an adept of the transfiguration of the sacraments and of "direct access" to the uncreated light. Guénon had found his work perfectly solid.

The crisis provoked by Schuon pertained to contradictions of the same order experienced by the master at the time of *Regnabit*. The problem remained latent. As early as 1935, he had cautioned Schuon, who had become a Muslim attached to the *Tariqah Alawiya* and *moqqadem* for Europe, against such confusions:

> For the rest, you will do well to always hold firmly to the fundamental distinction of the two points of view, religious and initiatic, and to specify clearly if necessary that, insofar as you are concerned, you intend to devote yourself entirely to the second.[419]

The article from 1948 contradicted the idea of an initiatic Christianity having been reduced to the state of a religion after opening itself up to all. The invocation of the name of Jesus, "the path *par excellence* of spiritual realization," is transmitted not by Scripture, but by Tradition, and the sacraments of baptism and confirmation correspond to the lesser and greater Mysteries, to the return to the primordial state and "the virtuality of the Christic state, therefore supreme."[420] One finds in the Eucharist these two aspects with the bread/body and the wine/blood. What more could there be than the real presence of God? The master responded in the following year in three installments in "Christianity and Initiation."[421]

---

418 Letters dated 5/4 and 22/6/1950, Montanari, *La Fatica del Cuore*, 115.

419 Letter dated 17/4/1935.

420 The full text is given in Parrick et Jean-Baptiste Aymard (eds.), *Dossiers H* (Lausanne: Âge d'Homme, 2002), 432-439. He concludes with an analysis of the invocatory character of the Rosary.

421 Sept., Oct.-Nov., and Dec. 1949.

The Eye of the Heart[422] completed Schuon's thesis, developing the theme along the same axes as Guénon in "The All-Seeing Eye" (April-May 1948), except by insisting on the special place taken by this symbolic association in the revealed religions. He argues for a Christianity from the heart which "then identifies itself with the intellect, with the EYE that sees God and which, by consequence, 'is' God." This uncreated intellect, as Meister Eckhart defined it, is grasped by the third eye which is turned to the uncreated Light, the scriptural reference being Saint Paul's Epistle to the Ephesians.[423] For Islam, it is the great Sufi texts referring to *Hadiths* that he principally uses; the eye of the heart sees God, and through it God sees his creation (Schuon writes "manifestation" emphasizing the universality of the symbol), hence the center of "the supreme identity." Al-Hallaj (858-922) had synthesized this doctrine in these terms: "I saw my Lord with the Eye of my Heart; and I said: Who are You? He said to me: You!"[424] Moreover, the book begins with the association of "hearing, sight, and the heart," which are conspicuous in the Koran in the sense of the heart designating "the spirit or intelligence of man."[425] He had addressed the question of Hesychasm previously in the last chapter of *On the Transcendental Unity of Religions*, "Of Christic Initiation."[426]

On the other hand, the direct heirs of the endeavor attempted with Charbonneau-Lassay to dodge the subject. The abbe Gircourt (1907-1977), for example, devoted a short

---

422 Frithjof Schuon, *L'Oeil du coeur* (Paris: Gallimard, 1950), "Tradition" collection."

423 Ibid., 20; "May it illuminate the eyes of your heart," Ephesians 1:18 (The Jerusalem Bible, the concordance *TOB* gives "May he open your heart to his light").

424 Ibid., 25.

425 Sura 50, *Al-Mu'Minûn* (The Believers), verse 78. See Mohammed Ali Amir Moezzi and Guillaume Dye (eds.), *Le Coran des historiens* (Paris: Cerf, 2019), 859. The commentary reports six occurrences in this sense. Schuon does not give a reference.

426 Frithjof Schuon, *De l'unité transcendante des religions* (Paris: Gallimard, 1948), "Tradition" collection.

passage in notes published posthumously[427] to the symbolism of the Cross, recalling the arguments of the master against ambient insipidness and citing the term only once with a little treatise of two pages on the Feast of the Sacred Heart situating the theological problem in the notion of the "Eucharistic heart." The abbe Jean Châtillon (1912-1988), who had also written his thesis on Richard of Saint Victor and taught philosophy at the University of Nancy and the Catholic Institute of Paris (member of the philosophy commission of CNRS), published on prayer of the heart, "little cited in his bibliography for fear of being accused of 'intellectual vagabondage.'"[428] The abbe Nicolas Boon (1920-1981) is an exception, close to this milieu but also to Masonry, inasmuch as he elaborated a Kabbalistic exegesis of the Eucharistic heart confirming the classic relationship between Ezekiel's vision of the source of living water on the right side of the Temple and the spear thrust into the right side of Christ.[429] He added here a bundle of symbolic relationships inspired by Guénon and used the expression "eye of the heart."[430]

It fell to Michel Vâlsan, by virtue of his proximity to the Roman milieu, to develop at length his vision of Hesychasm

---

[427] Collected by François Chenique and given to read under the title Abbé Henri Stéphane, *Introduction à l'ésotérisme chrétien* (Paris: Dervy, 1979), preface by Jean Borella. The abbe was a professor of mathematics at Sainte-Geneviève de Versailles. He had created groups of "preparatory" students around the work of Guénon.

[428] Biography in *Rev. Etudes Augustiniennes*. 34-1989, 3-11. The edition of Richard of Saint Victor was the great work of his life. *L'Oraison cordiale* of Le Gall de Querdu, 1670, had been regularly reprinted throughout the 19th century. In 1950, the abbe had moved away from these milieus, see Zoccatelli, *Écrits pour Regnabit*, 139.

[429] *Au cœur de l'Écriture, Méditation d'un prêtre catholique* (Paris: Dervy, 1987), 35.

[430] Texts presented by Monique André-Gillois in *Au cœur de l'Écriture Méditations d'un prêtre catholique*, published in the collection "Initiatory paths of the Western tradition", directed by Gérard de Sorval. The short biography recounts the drama experienced in Amsterdam by the future priest when faced with the persecution of the Jews by the Nazis. She refuses to speak of other possible spiritual orientations, a refusal which is reiterated in the back cover description.

in response to an article by Marco Pallis (1895-1989), who in "The Veil of the Temple" had reprised Schuon's positions on the effacement of the opposition of esotericism and exotericism in Christianity.[431] Supported also by Symeon the New Theologian, Vâlsan showed that the Christic baptismal effusion was operational only in those who were "firm in the faith," that is to say in possession of spiritual influences of "another order." He returned at greater length to the heart and *Regnabit* in the introduction to *Fundamental Symbols*, citing Bossuet on the "plenitude" of sense in the Church.[432] In his translation of the *Futûhât* of Ibn Arabi, ch. 20, "The Science Proper to Jesus," he attributes to Jesus, *Aïssä*, the science of letters:

> It is for this reason that Aïssä had received the power of the insufflation of life (*an-nafkh*) which consists of this 'air" (*hawâ*') which comes from the bottom of the heart and which is the spirit of life ..." the exhaled breath makes pauses to which are given the name of "letters.[433]

Conclusion

Anizan's project at Paray-le-Monial also saw continuations, crowned by Edouard Glotin's above-mentioned *Bible of the Heart of Jesus*; they had in common with Guénon and his successors a similar conception of the symbol of the heart as the supreme center and an identical goal: to transform, *Hic et nunc*, a misguided society through its spiritual power, a power that was comprehensible to all in one cultural zone. The heart encompasses for Glotin "the Name" or "the Face" as well as "the

---

[431] Pallis, July-August, 1964. Responses in *Études traditionnelles* May-August 1964, *L'initiation chrétienne* and May-August 1968, *Études et documents sur l'hésychasme*.

[432] Three letters exchanged with Philippe Guiberteau, a specialist on Dante, published in *Science sacrée* (Sept. 2001-April 2002), 21, return to this doctrinal plenitude: "The heart of Christ is the epitome of all the marvels of Christianity" (Bossuet).

[433] *Études traditionnelles* March-April and May-June 1971.

I" in its actual sense.[434] The universal value of the symbol is also common to them, as is the necessity of an interpretive guide or, in other words, an institution, faced with the risk of the loss of the spiritual sense, but the shared vision ends there: it is not the same guide. Father Glotin saw the Revelation of the heart as progressive, and he retraces its history from Saint Justin and the thrust of the lance to Saint Augustine, Catherine of Sienna and direct access to the heart. Contemporary theologians concurred. For Karl Rahner, it was a source word, *Ur-Wort*, which symbolizes the unity of the human body, and Glotin referred to the Omega Point of the cosmic vision of Teilhard de Chardin.[435] The Second Vatican Council also defined the human heart as the principle of a person.

The Guénonian perspective was the opposite, founded on ineluctable estrangement from the "Principle;" it considered the institutions conserving these truths to be a refuge, a "camp of the saints" facing shipwreck in Quantity, incompatible with the notion of the fulfillment of Revelation. The attachment to Sufism was possible for a non-Muslim only by separating esotericism from exotericism and, in the case of conversion, it was the distinction between the mystic and esoteric paths which was effaced. The purely doctrinal reliance on the Vedanta which had entirely nourished Guénon's reflection was, according to him, not problematic on the level of experience: one was born a Hindu, one did not become one. Contradictions of the same order awaited the project of Paray, which was marginalized by the institution of which it was the champion.[436]

---

[434] Ibid., 242-243. He validates an oral transmission anterior to the redaction of the Gospels.

[435] He denounced in a letter to his cousin the insipidity of devotion to the Sacred Heart, hoping that it would instead be "the object of a nearly esoteric cult reserved to those who truly want to be Christians to the foundation, with all their heart." *Genèse d'une pensée* (Paris: Grasset, 1961), 250.

[436] The Father attributes the excess of the neo-gnostics to Saint Irenaeus, as well as Gilbert Durand, and totally ignores Guénon, just as the latter no longer wished to hear talk of the Catholic Church.

In the end, time, which runs to our loss, has disfigured the landscape in which Guénonian reflection once flourished. The heart of Christ no longer shines in the eyes of the Christian world, and the Sufi brotherhoods are often suspect in the land of Islam, where Masonry is banned almost everywhere. Whatever these divergences may be, the religious has reappropriated the field of esotericism.[437]

Translated by S. and Jafe Arnold

---

437 The present article was originally published in French in *Liber, le coeur glorieux* 5 (Marseille: Alcor éditions, 2020).

METAPHYSICAL SOLIPSISM — A FUNDAMENTAL PRINCIPLE OF TRADITION

Tamás Bencze

Tradition, in our concept, is not merely one of the innumerable cultural, religious or family traditions which are upheld to avoid "social entropy" or to furnish the members of a community with a sense of security and belonging by providing continuity "in today's fast-paced world"; it is not a custom, like decorating the Christmas tree as a family; it is not a custom which can be established and kept going, it is not a kind of tradition which can be changed to another one; it is not heritage of just any kind; it is not something that has anything to do with duality — in this sense, even the etymological sense of the word is misleading, as the Latin *trans* + *dare* presupposes two persons, one who gives and one who receives. Moreover, it is not only giving or passing down through generations that is of primary importance here. Tradition is upholding a set of principles of a supratemporal nature. In view of this, we must use the attribute "metaphysical" to discuss *metaphysical tradition*. The word *metaphysical* is used in a higher sense than it is used in philosophy, a use which, from our point of view, can be described as preparatory-introductory. The word *metaphysical* refers to what is beyond Being and Non-Being. Also, one needs *metaphysical tradition* (or Tradition capitalised according to the Guénonian use) as it represents Truth—in this sense, it is similar to a "raft" which is "for crossing over." Furthermore, even though there are a number of particular forms of metaphysical tradition, there is essentially only one Tradition, the Super-Tradition, in which the particular forms have their original and transcendent unity. Cultural, religious, and family traditions can be old and time-honoured traditions, but metaphysical tradition, it may be said with little exaggeration, has nothing to do with time in this respect. A metaphysical traditional school can be founded in the morning and it deserves to be called "traditional" in the afternoon more so than any widespread beliefs or established customs, because it aims at the Subject, the Centre, to which it is also closer than the others.

By the term *solipsism* (from Latin *sōlus* + *ipse*) we mean *metaphysical solipsism*, even if from now on we will use the noun only, which, as a matter of fact, should be enough every time it is mentioned throughout the world, but since it is nearly always misinterpreted, we need to make this clarification. Now, solipsism, which is one of the basic principles of Tradition, is the forceful affirmation of the assertion that—and this can be formulated in the first person singular only—solely I Myself am; only I Myself as Subject am; besides Me, essentially and ultimately there is not anything or anyone else, any "absolute Otherness"; there never has been and never will be. Here 'I Myself' and 'Me' is not the ego; solely I Myself am, not as a person, but as the one and only Subject (Sanskrit *Ātmā*, German *Selbst*) ruling over Being and Non-Being, alone all by My very Self. This definition implies, on the one hand, that I as a person and the Universal Subject are essentially one;[438] and, on the other hand, it also implies that I am everything—in particular modalities, in the sense of modified products of consciousness.

The Subject—my true and valid Self—can be reached through my very own Person, through the individual who I am, through my everyday I-ness; in other words, *ātmā* can

---

[438] Regarding this self-experience, see András László, *Tradicionalitás és létszemlélet*, (Nyíregyháza, Hungary: Kötet, 1995), 39–67; idem, *Solum Ipsum: Metafizikai aforizmák* (Nyíregyháza: Kötet, 2000), passim; idem, *Tradíció és metafizika: Kérdések és válaszok* (Debrecen, Hungary: Kvintesszencia, 2007), 42–46, 73–79, 97–108; idem, Solum-egomet-ipsitas, in *A szolipszizmus igazsága: A nyolcvanéves László András köszöntése* (Budapest: Aktémosyné, 2022), 35–95.

Metaphysical Solipsism — A Fundamental Principle of Tradition

be reached through *aham* (Sanskrit, meaning 'I'). In this sense, spiritual realisation conjoins solipsism comprehended and solipsism realised. There can be any number of persons, but there is only one my-own-person. Solipsism is the idea without which neither spiritual realisation nor any sacred doctrines, do not make any sense. Anyone who will not or cannot accept this, might as well sell cotton candy at funfairs to the same extent as they deal with traditional doctrines—it will absolutely be all the same.

When discussing most subjects, one has to go below the level of solipsism, because the issue does not come up sharply and explicitly, but solipsism is still there at the heart of any adequate doctrinal discussion. In the same way, solipsism is not there in traditional doctrines explicitly, but it is very much there implicitly in the highest forms of Tradition, for example in Hinduism, in Buddhism, in Taoism, in Sufism or in Gnostic Christianity.[439] At the level of solipsism, at the summit of traditional ideas, one can only discuss ideas—with the help of symbols and the human language—like freedom, immortality, or the question of the absolute aim.

*

Human language and human cognition are permeated with metaphors: if you want to understand a phenomenon, whether already existing or new, you think and talk about it using a known metaphor system; the more metaphor systems you use to understand the same phenomenon, the deeper the comprehension and understanding of the phenomenon will be. Julius Evola's writings are strikingly rich in the presence of metaphors which throw strong light —with the strength of *Zen koans*—on the association of concepts and domains that are seemingly far from each other, be it metaphysics, mythology, philosophy, etc. Writing about linguistic carriers in connection

---

[439] The following study has collected most such passages and doctrines from sacred scriptures: Róbert Horváth, "A szolipszizmus igazságai", in *A szolipszizmus igazsága: A nyolcvanéves László András köszöntése* (Budapest: Aktémosyné, 2022), 323–355.

with the decay of words (*sfaldamento delle parole*), he says words exposed to the ravages of time weather, disintegrate, crumble, fall apart into layers, and then they are almost completely pulverized like rocks (*sfaldamento*); mixed and soaked with modern mentality, they are exposed to spiritual and semantic impoverishment (*povertá delle lingue moderne*); they suffer from erosion and waning depth (*un processo di erosione e di appiattimento*); they shift from being three-dimensional to two-dimensional (*le lingue moderne sono bidimensionali*); words are subject to corrosion (*il tempo ha agito in senso corrosivo*); they become practical (*pratiche*) and dissolved, liquescent in a figurative sense, making a fluent, yet diluted (*fluide*) style possible to the detriment of their organicity (*organicità*); one can observe a drop in level (*una caduta di livello*) in the case of words, which become distorted, twisted and bent (*distorto*), outworn, hackneyed, commonplace and banal (*banalizzato*). Words also have a history, Evola continues, and the extent of the loss of their content is an accurate barometer of corresponding changes in their speakers' general sensibility and world-view, because the two are correlated with each other. As Hungarian traditional author Béla Hamvas says, the decline of things has a common source.

As far as the history of the word *solipsism* is concerned, even its birth happened amidst trials and tribulations. The first occurrence of the compound is likely to be connected to a discord caused by a worldview crisis: the literary work in question is *Monarchia Solipsorum: ad virum clarissimum Leonum Allatium*, a satire related to the geocentric versus heliocentric world model debate and Galileo's trial in 1632. This satire was written entirely in the Latin language by an author under the pseudonym Lucius Cornelius Europæus in Venice in 1645, and he published it in the same year. The pseudonym is thought to be that of the Jesuit historian Giulio Clemente Scotti. A French translation of the work by Melchior Inchofer (Menyhért Inchofer) was published in Amsterdam in 1722.

Metaphysical Solipsism — A Fundamental Principle of Tradition

It was after this that the word *solipsism* was introduced into Western philosophy, not as the carrier of the Eastern idea of *kaivalya* and *kevalādvaita*, however, but—mostly—as the generator and "counter-raft" of non-understanding and confusion, in the opposite direction to the understanding that prepares for transcendence from individuality upwards. Hence, the word was almost immediately "dethroned," so much so that the word is now associated with concepts such as narcissism, overemphasis on the thinking subject, subjective detachment of the individual, self-centredness, the end point of a mental introversion, autistic introversion, even mental disorder (*solipsistic dementia*). Here it should be noted that even Frithjof Schuon holds to the latter value judgments when, in discussing the subject, he sees solipsism as a simplification of Hindu doctrines and a deduction of absurd conclusions, and disagrees with Schopenhauer that solipsism is logically irrefutable, but agrees with him that "solipsists are ripe for the lunatic asylum."[440]

*

In the word *solipsismus* (*solus* + *ipse* + *-ismus*), the component *ipse* itself is a compound. The Old Latin forms *eumpsum, eampsam* are combinations of the stem *eio-* with *som, sam*, where the *p* speech sound and letter is a glide consonant, as in the case of *sumpsi* from *sum-si* — see, for example, the word *assumptio*, meaning "taking up" in Christianity (*Assumptio Mariae*). "From the accusative forms a stem *-pso, -psa* was extracted which appears in nominative feminine *eapsa*, masculine *ipsus*, etc. The latter was assimilated to *iste* and *ille* and so gave rise to the normal declension *ipse, ipsa*,

---

[440] Frithjof Schuon, *Gnosis: Divine Wisdom*, trans. Mark Perry, Jean-Pierre Lafouge and James S. Cutsinger (Bloomington, Indiana, USA: World Wisdom, 2006), 56. However, there is one exception where Schuon uses the term solipsism in a positive sense, calling it "inevitable." See Frithjof Schuon, *From Divine to the Human*, S. 1 (World Wisdom, 1982), 136. ("The foundation of the 'logical subjectivism' of believers lies in what we may term 'religious solipsism'".) In the edition of Seyyed H. Nasr this is *"what we call 'religious solipsism'"* - *The Essential Writings of Frithjof Schuon*, (Shaftesbury–Rockport: Element, 1991), 73.

ipsum."441 The second part of the compound *ipse* is the same as Sanskrit *ātman* and *sva*. The term solipsismus implies a double emphasis, since the first member (*solus*) and the second one (*ipse*) go back to the same root; *-ismus* is the suffix which, in philosophical language, is ordinarily attached to the names of beliefs or attitudes.

Despite the fact that the word *solipsism* was born in time — and what is more, in the end times — and in spite of its unfortunate fate, the idea of solipsism is eternal (obviously in the "case" of "the God" or *Gottheit*). The true sense of the term is also eternal, since it is an aspectual, perennial designation in human thought and language of that which was not born and will never pass away. The word, despite its difficult birth, is not artificially fabricated, not made-up, not contrived, but generated by manifesting powers from the Centre, through a *glottogenesis*, ruled over a *glottogenius*, and, as a synonym of Eastern *Brahma-pūra, kaivalya, advaita, kevalādvaita* or the Great Saying *aham brahmāsmi*, it is a linguistic carrier of one of the highest dignities for the West. The virtue of the word is loyalty of the highest order, its dynamism is a combative imperative.

The fate of the word *subiectum* is no less difficult, as the first known meaning of Latin *subiectus* is "the submitted one" or "a person under the dominion of another"— the obvious, literal meaning being 'thrown under'— and only later would it become the "foundation or subject of a proposition" as a loanword and translation of *hypokeimenon* used by Anaximander, Anaximenes, Democritus, Plato and Aristotle. Subsequently, the term came to carry the meaning of "subject matter of an art or science" as the short form of Medieval Latin *subjecta materia*. Even later, in the wake of Cartesian philosophy, it became the "subject of knowledge." In metaphysical Traditionalism, it is the Ground of everything, of all that exists, of all that does not exist, and of the central ruling over that which transcends their unity; it is the Ground

---

441 L.R. Palmer, *The Latin Language*, (London: Faber and Faber, 1906), 257.

Metaphysical Solipsism — A Fundamental Principle of Tradition

of the latter, the "That" which is the Ground of all, but which has ground in nothing. It is the "That" which multiplies Itself, yet Itself remains non-dual (*advaita*).

This automultiplication is called "sacrifice" in Hindu tradition, and the *Brāhmaṇa*s, when writing about the animal sacrifice, say the following: "They carry a torch before it [i.e. the victim, thinking] 'The victim is, in essence, the sacrificer' (*Aitareya Brāhmaṇa*, II.2)."[442] I am the multiplier, I am multiplication and I am also the result of multiplication. Recognizing, understanding, accepting and willing this is the *condicio sine qua non* of spiritual realisation. I must get my act together and tighten my grip on myself in a metaphysical sense as well. Two kinds of paths are outlined in this metaphor: the way of dispersion and the way of gathering.

Gathering-collecting is expressed in the Greek language by the verb *synagó*, "*ho mé synagón, skorpizei*"—"*qui non congregat, spargit*"—"he that gathereth not, scattereth abroad", according to the evangelical formula.[443] This gathering is based on the virtue of loyalty to myself, and it is interesting to note that the meaning of the Proto-Indo-European root **leg-* harboring the idea of loyalty means "to collect," "to gather," which is the same root one can find in the word *religion*. He who does not gather, is disloyal to himself.

"A thousand heads hath *Puruṣa*, a thousand eyes, a thousand feet", so says a Vedic hymn.[444] Expressed in numbers, this is 3x333+1, and since the number 3 is one of the most important symbols of sacredness, superiority and excellence in Hindu, Taoist and Catholic symbology, the sentence can be interpreted like this: multiplicity, the worlds, the cosmoses, the totality of manifestation, can be and is from the central will of unity, and the sum of multiplicity forms a single unit. The same number indicating completeness appears in the

---

442 *Rigveda Brahmanas: The Aitareya and Kausītaki Brāhmanas of the Rigveda* (Cambridge, Massachusetts, USA: Harvard University Press, 1920), 142.

443 *Matthew* 12:30.

444 *R̥g-Veda* XC.1

uppermost *cakra*, the thousand-leafed *sahasrāra-padma*, the one that rotates everything, but does not rotate itself.

*

Thus, there is "something" that is—also *hic et nunc*—indivisible and cannot be multiplied, that is not sacrificable, cannot be split in half or scattered, that is not atomizable and immutable—and this is the doubtless, obvious and indisputable experience of "*I am*." This feeling fluctuates and swings; there are faster or slower, more or less significant significant changes in experiencing it caused by emotions and the different hours of the days; the experience of it is often broken and interrupted, but these characteristics follow from the *saṃsāric* nature of being—in the sense of Sanskrit *bhava* or *astitā*, Latin *adesse*, German *Dasein*—of existence, of the life bound to the body, of the circumstances of the I-ness. I am in a specific situation in existence: my Person is underneath a vast realm of consciousness of eminent rank, from which, for example, traditions originate, but the root of this self-experience in existence is above and behind everything. To put it into the first person singular, everything results from Me. This, of course, is stated at the highest degree, at the degree of solipsism realised, the "synonym" of *pratyeka-bōdhi*, at the degree of the awakened self withdrawn into the one (*eka*), into unity (*pratyeka-buddha*), that is at the degree of *parinirvāṇa*, but it is confirmed by the intuition penetrating the individual consciousness, entering my existence being generated here and now.

Another "synonym" of solipsism is in the teachings of *vedānta*. *Vedānta*—the most important one of the six *darśanas* (*nyāya, vaiśeṣika, sāṃkhya, yoga, mīmāṃsa, vedānta*), the viewpoints within the doctrine of the Hindu teachings—deals with pure metaphysics; indeed, *vedānta* is in many respects metaphysics *par excellence*. The literal and conceptual translation of the term is "end of the *Vēdas*": "end" here means both "conclusion" and "aim." Its basis is the spirituality of the

Metaphysical Solipsism — A Fundamental Principle of Tradition

Upaniṣads. The teachings of the Upaniṣads are aimed at the final and most important goal of traditional knowledge in its entirety; its primary and central theme is ātmā, identical with Vedic brahman, absolute God and Gottheit.

Many different schools approaching vedānta took shape, some of them focusing on the unity of brahmātmā, others on the dividedness and non-dividedness of Being, and they all exerted a decisive force within Hinduism as a whole. Now, according to dvaita-vāda, which is connected to Madhvācārya's name, there is definitely a duality between a being and brahmātmā, and within the dividedness innumerable dividednesses come about. The meaning of dvaita is "dual", and it also means the dividednesses following from it. Dvaita-vāda accepts the very ultimate unity of Puruṣa and prakṛti, of Godhead and nature, of paramātmā and jīvātmā, of Nirvāṇa and saṃsāra, but it is duality that is given preference and stressed.

Viśiṣṭādvaita-vāda, associated with Ramanujācārya's name, teaches the essential unity, but takes dividednesses into consideration as well, this is the "moderate or qualified advaita doctrine," in which non-duality, non-dividedness (advaita), is not radical, but presented in a nuanced and temperate manner.

The highest degree is Śaṅkarācārya's advaita-vāda, the doctrine of non-duality, non-dualism, undividedness. According to this school, dvaita, dividednesses, is a wrong, false and degraded view. Its teaching is that there is nothing else but brahmātmā, and that jīvātmā (the manifestation of ātmā in the living individual) and brahmātmā are identical. You could also say that mahā-parama-brahmātmā, the (my) universal-highest-brahman-self and jīva are identical. Jīva is identical with jīvātmā, and jīvātmā is identical with mahā-parama-brahmātmā.

Kevalādvaita-vāda is the "doctrine of the sole(ly)-undivided," the "doctrine of the sole(ly)-non-duality." The doctrine of the sole(ly)-non-dual takes a stand on the most radical and most extreme advaita. It refers to the teachings of Ādiśaṅkarācārya beyond his *māyā-vāda* and "cosmological" teachings. The meaning of *kevala* is "sole" or "solely," the same as Latin *solum*. The doctrine in question is the equivalent of the philosophical, supra-philosophical, or metaphysical solipsism that crowns Western philosophy.

The Tantric current of Hinduism goes even further: *dvaitādvaita-vāda*, the "doctrine of the dual-nondual," is the teaching concerning the joint idea of duality and non-duality. This school includes and unites the most radical *dvaita*, the most radical *kevalādvaita* and the views between them, keeping their distinctive and characteristic features articulated, and viewing all these from above. "From above" must be emphasized, as it refers to transcending: it means that it is more, higher-and-deeper than the views it includes. *Dvaita*, *advaita*, *kēvalādvaita* and *dvaitādvaita* are not only modes of viewing, but realities of being as well, in other words, they speak of the different degrees of experiencing Being and Non-Being moving away from or approaching the Centre.

*

If we assume that the truth of solipsism does not hold, then, after a short argument, it is not upwards, not in the direction of *nirguṇa brahma*, that I leave the starting point of my striving, but downwards, through *hypokosmia* and *nirguṇa-mūla-prakṛti*, aiming at Nothing, of which there "is" also one, but one that is none other than the counter-image of my true self.

The phenomenon called the "uncertainty of terminology" that affects many fields of life has been around for a long time now; a term is supposed to be well-de*fin*ed with a specific meaning, a boundary where it ends, terminates, *fin*ishes, and academic papers use such in a repetitive manner, avoiding the use of synonyms to prevent any confusion. As far as metaphysics is concerned, Guénon, for instance, writes about the mental disorder of our time (*le désordre mental de*

Metaphysical Solipsism — A Fundamental Principle of Tradition

notre époque), mentioning two collocations he calls *evidently absurd*: "metaphysical anxiety" (*inquiétude métaphysique*) and "metaphysical anguish" (*angoisse métaphysique*).[445] Here, we can witness a confusion of two different levels, which is the result of either lack of understanding or fear. Of the latter, Guénon says that the fact that it is permanently settled in the "psyche" of a being is *"une 'disqualification' à l'égard de la connaissance métaphysique"* — "a 'disqualification' with respect to metaphysical knowledge."[446]

Likewise, the lack of understanding or fear prevents someone from fully comprehending the idea of solipsism and forces someone to make collocations like "solipsistic isolation."[447] Or there is "solipsism syndrome," in which, according to psychologists, periods of extended isolation may result. It is said to be a potential challenge for astronauts on long-term missions. No one would deny this effect, but it has nothing to do with metaphysical solipsism. An individual can feel isolated, but emotions do not concern the Subject of Being, as the essence of solipsism is well above attitudes and experiences. Just as an astrologer is not identical with the Pole Star, a solipsist is far from being the reason why solipsism is articulated.

Another type of error which lends itself to a lot of confusion is the false view of "objective reality." The general misconception is that "it is independent from my consciousness." It is because of *māyā* that I tend to think it is so; there is no other world but what I experience: if this is my present experience, I can transmute the experience of being exposed to *māyā* to the experience of ruling *māyā*—which is precisely spiritual realisation; hence the attribute *magical* solipsism. Wittgenstein says that "at death the world does not

---

445 René Guénon, *Initiation et réalisation spirituelle* (Paris: Les Éditions traditionnelles, 1952), 29.

446 Ibid., 34.

447 Georges B. J. Dreyfus, *Recognizing Reality: Dharmakirti's Philosophy and Its Tibetan Interpretations* (Albany: State University of New York Press, 1997), 427.

alter, but comes to an end." He also says in the same work: "what solipsism means, is quite correct, only it cannot be said, but it shows itself."[448]

Solely I am, there is no one and nothing besides me. Evola says, "the subject as such is something immediate, a pure, naked 'I am', a direct experience: now immediate can never be an ἕτερον, but always an αὐτον" ("*il soggetto come tale è qualcosa di immediato, un puro, nudo 'sono', una diretta esperienza: ora immediato non può mai essere un ἕτερον, ma sempre un αὐτόν*").[449] Auton (αὐτόν) is *ahamātmā*, and anything *in* it is heteron (ἕτερον), modified Auton, which is Auton from the viewpoint of the Subject, but seems "something else" from the viewpoint of a being. The acceptance and joyful willing of the ontological solitude, like its analogy, the solitude and willing of contemplative life, requires *ārya* qualities and attitudes. The Buddha illuminates this with many images, such as metaphors of fire, wind, tree, lotus, bamboo, fish, deer, elephant, rhinoceros. Finally, we should mention the symbol of the net (Sanskrit *jāla*), which symbolises the non-understanding and non-acceptance of solipsism. According to the Buddha, wrong views are similar to a net cast in a small pond, and the fish in it—that is, those who hold false views (*diṭṭhi*)—are caught in it anyway, which expresses the unconscious wandering in *saṃsāra*. However, pointing out and exposing wrong views makes the "net of views" (*diṭṭhijāla*) the "net of the highest order" (*Brahmajāla*).[450]

Although the Buddha denied the existence of the self, the *ipsum*, on some occasions, He spoke in verse, and the following lines are worthy of summarising what has been said, referring, at the same time, to the adequate attitude: "Having burst apart the fetters, / like a fish that tears the net and swims free, / Or

---

448 L. Wittgenstein, *Tractatus Logico-Philosophicus*, trans. D. F. Pears and B. F. McGuinness, (London: Routledge Classics, 2001), 87, 68.

449 Julius Evola, *Teoria dell'Individuo Assoluto*, (Roma: Edizioni Mediterranee, 1988), 181.

450 *Digha Nikāya* 1 (*Brahmajāla Sutta*).

a fire not returning to ground it has burned, / live alone like a horned rhino."[451]

In the final analysis, we can say that solipsism is one of the main principles of Tradition, a principle which cannot be ignored. The idea — interpreted in the language of philosophy — is always there in the background. Whichever sacred text one is reading, it will be there implicitly; in the *Bhagavad-Gītā*, for instance, I am *Kṛṣṇa* and I am *Arjuna*, I am his bow and I am his arrows, I am the chariot and the battlefield, I am all the characters, animals and things mentioned. It must be underscored again that without solipsism, Tradition or spiritual realisation makes no sense: so, regarding solipsism, to make a tiny concession would mean to give up the whole idea.

---

451 *Sutta Nipāta*, I. 3. 62, trans. Bhikkhu Sujato, *suttacentral.net* (https://suttacentral.net/snp1.3/en/sujato?lang=en&layout=plain&reference=none&notes=asterisk&highlight=false&script=latin).

A TRADITIONALIST INQUIRY INTO NATURE

Eduardo Zarelli

What is nature?

The word "nature" comes from the Latin *natura*, which originated as a future participle of the verb *nascor, nasci*, "to be born": thus, it means what "is going to be born," "is about to be born." Therefore, the word does not express the concept of a static reality, but rather a dynamic one, a reality that is not merely actual, but potential and future. The word is also employed in this way by the great Epicurean poet-philosopher Lucretius in his masterwork *De rerum natura*. In turn, *natura* is the Latin translation of the Greek word *physis*, which derives from the root of the verb *phyo*, which means "to beget" or "to grow": according to the Greeks, therefore, nature is the ensemble of all things which are born, live, grow and die (even without distinguishing between those things which properly "live" and those which simply "exist").

"Physicists" or "physiologists" is what Aristotle called the early investigators of nature, i.e., the exponents of the school of Miletus in Asia Minor: Thales, Anaximander, and Anaximenes. Aristotle himself later distinguished "first philosophy," that is metaphysics, from other "second philosophies," among which he placed the study of nature or "natural philosophy." This means that, in Western culture, philosophy was born together with the study of nature, or better still, it was born as an investigation into the world of nature, its movement, and its becoming. According to our way of thinking, the first Greek philosophers were also the first scientists; on the one hand, they see the world as "full of gods" (Thales' hylozoism), and on the other hand, they are well determined to analyse the causes of the phenomena according to a rigorously rational approach.

Not even Plato operated with a true distinction between metaphysics and the philosophy of nature; in the *Timaeus*, he outlined a magnificent fresco of the origin of the world, which is at once a search for the first causes (the work of the divine creator, the Demiurge) and a description of the states of matter out of which all living beings are shapen (the five regular polyhedrons as the fundamental structure of everything that exists, in the forms of fire, air, water, earth, and aether). The distinction is present, as we have seen, in Aristotle, and even more so in his disciples, but not in the wholly modern sense of a distinction between philosophy and science. According to Aristotle, metaphysics is the first philosophy and also, at the same time, absolute science.

Gradually, as first philosophy began to lose the consensus of thinkers, natural philosophy detached itself from the tree of philosophy and became an autonomous science, especially with the Renaissance naturalism of Telesio, Bruno, and Campanella, and then, above all, with the so-called revolution carried out by Francis Bacon, Galileo, Descartes, and Newton; eventually, with Kant, metaphysics was finally unseated from its throne and relegated to the attic, while natural science, having severed the last link with what had generated it, gave to itself a completely independent structure, claiming the "truth" of knowledge for itself alone.

Today we almost take for granted that scientific knowledge, understood in Galileo and Descartes' sense, is the fundamental modality of knowing, the only one which, finding objective confirmation in the reality of things, through experimentation and the formulation of laws, can aspire to the status of realistic and «true» knowledge (these two now appear interchangeable), whilst all other forms of knowledge, including philosophical knowledge (maybe even reduced to logical analysis of language), appear to be nothing else than more or less relative, more or less imaginative speculation.

As a consequence, we even assume that "nature" is the ensemble of the forces, phenomena, and qualities of the visible world, considering the latter as a synonym of "reality"; *sic et simpliciter*: the world that we see is reality, and reality is the world that we see. According to modern culture, a supernatural plane of reality does not exist, just as there is no preternatural plane of reality: materialism is no longer a philosophical school among the many, but the universally admitted implication of whatever discourse on reality.

However, at this point we might ask ourselves: are we really sure that such a setting, which identifies visible reality as experienceable with senses and investigable with the tools of materialist science, is reality itself *tout court*, reality as such? Are we sure that a large chunk of reality is not left out of such an outlook? That is to say, that part of reality that cannot be seen, that cannot be experienced with the senses, that can neither be subjected to experimental verification nor even formalised into mathematical laws and hypotheses; that part which, nonetheless, the ancients, as well as the medievals, considered the living and throbbing heart of reality, from which everything that exists and falls under our senses is begotten.

Perhaps the time has come to reconsider the vicissitude of the concept of "nature," to free it from the Enlightenment and positivist encrustations which have had their day and which belong to a very precise phase in the history of Western thought. It is time to go back to thinking of nature in the way Plato, Aristotle, Augustine, and Thomas Aquinas thought of it, but also Leibniz, Pascal, Berkeley, Kierkegaard, and all the rest of that minority — yet by no means insignificant — stream of modern thought which has not repudiated and cancelled the spiritual dimension. This stream of thought, moreover, seems to find increasingly significant corroboration precisely in the most recent achievements of contemporary science, starting with the physics of sub-atomic particles.

To the question "What is nature?", we should thus not be in a hurry to answer "the ensemble of phenomena and forces which exist and are observable on the physical level," but instead we should ponder an answer which takes into account that whole portion of reality that cannot be directly observed and not even hypothesised or deduced in a materialistic sense, but which acts as a substrate, support and, at the same time, as the efficient and final cause of the world of physical phenomena, physical entities, and of everything we can see, touch, measure and experience.

Therefore, nature is much more than the sum of individual material entities, of their reciprocal action and of the relationships which link them to each other; nature is not merely the succession of minerals, plants, animals, planets, stars, and nebulae, but is the manifestation of a deep, invisible, luminous reality. Indeed, according to Heidegger, *physis* is related to *phàos*, "light," light being an attribute of what lives.

Domenico Tricerri summarised this point as follows: "The definitions that scientists give of Nature are varied and conflicting, but everyone agrees that it is something finite."[452]

William Wollaston asks himself: "What is nature, to attribute such wonderful works to it?" And he answers: "It is nothing but an abstraction thrown as dust into our eyes for hindering us from seeing the works of an intelligent First Cause."[453]

Georges-Louis Leclerc de Buffon in turn writes:

Nature is the system of laws established by the Creator for the existence of things and the succession of beings. Nature is not

---

[452] Domenico Tricerri, *Meraviglie della natura* (Vicenza: Edizioni Paoline, 1967), 9-11.

[453] Luigi Maria Torcoletti, *Alla ricerca di Dio* (Milan: Santa Lega Eucaristica, 1925), 17.

a thing..., it is not a being, but it may be regarded as a power which embraces everything. This power is the part of divine potency that manifests itself; it is an ever-living work, an artificer who works without interruption, an agent who knows how to employ everything for the achievement of its goal. Time, space and matter are its means; the universe is its subject; motion and life are its purpose; the phenomena of the world are its effects; the forces of attraction and repulsion are its main tools; heat and active organic molecules are its main principles of action for the formation and development of beings.[454]

Lamarck, by saying that nature "is the wonderful product of the divine will" and that we should conceive it "as a whole formed by its parts towards a goal known to its Doer,"[455] already approaches the realistic and objective definition of P. Secchi, who says: "What we call Nature is nothing else than the work of art of the Utmost Maker," that is to say, the whole of creation.

Nature, in short, Premoli says, is "all that is in the universe,"[456] divided into kingdoms and provided with the power to generate laws. The three kingdoms into which the universe is divided are called the "kingdoms of nature"; the forces that yield all the changes which happen within them, by destroying or altering given beings and begetting other ones, are called the "forces of nature"; the fixed and immutable laws according to which beings are constituted, operated and destroyed, are called the "laws of nature"; the continuous succession of generations and alterations, for which in the twilight of given things we see the rise of other things which replace them, is called the "course of nature," in the likeness of the course of a river which, always in motion, exchanges the waters which go to the sea with the waters which come down from the mountains.

---

454 G.-L. Leclerc de Buffon, *Histoire universelle*, vol. X, 2.

455 J.-B. Monet de Lamarck, *Histoire naturelle des animaux sans vertèbres*, vol. I, 2nd ed. (Paris: Balliére, 1835), 178.

456 Palmiro Premoli, *Nomenclatore scolastico*, entry "Natura".

Nature, therefore, is not a sheer abstraction, is not a simple system of laws, is not only an order of things or an all-embracing power, but is "the complex of all beings that are in the world, endowed with forces and laws to preserve and renew itself." It may nonetheless be defined as an abstraction and a personification in the sense that we are led to conceive Nature as a being that thinks and acts, in the manner of those poets who give soul and life to things that do not have them. Indeed, in rather common speech we say: "nature is beautiful, nature works, nature renews itself, nature speaks, nature ongoingly destroys the beings to which it itself had given life." We oppose nature to God and we say "God and Nature"; we oppose it to mankind and we say "Nature and mankind"; we oppose it to art and we say "Art imitates Nature"; we even oppose nature to itself and say "nature and its forces, nature and its laws, nature, and its effects"; we thus conceive of Nature as a great living and acting whole.

The wonderful token of this is the sonnet "Nature and Art" by Giacomo Zanella:

Thus said Nature to Art:	Disse Natura all'Arte: "Io tutto quanto
"Everything that in the world forthcometh,	nel mondo appare, dall'atomo alla stella,
from atom to aster, from the elephant to the floweret	dall'elefante al fiorellin che abbella
which the cloak of smiling Spring bedecketh,	della ridente primavera il manto,
wholly I create, wholly I enliven. And thou	tutto creo, tutto avvivo. E tu col canto
with the harrowing song and silent speech	angustio e con la tacita favella
of thy hues, oh daring handmaid,	de' tuoi colori, temeraria ancella,
of vying with me thou braggest the pride?"	di meco gareggiar t'arroghi il vanto?"
Thus answered Art: "Although thou createst, thou not curest	L'Arte rispose: "Se tu crei, non curi
thy works: of blooms the field thou cloakest,	L'opere tue: di fiori ammanti il campo,
then with swift change from us thou them thievest,	poi con rapida vece a noi li furi,
as if thy pacts thou thyself hadst in despise;	qual se i tuoi patti abbia tu stessa a scherno;
I seize on the fly any fleeing flash of thine,	io colgo a volo un tuo fuggiasco lampo,
and with rhyme and brush it I eternalise."	e con la rima e col pennel lo eterno."

A Traditionalist Inquiry into Nature

Indeed, this is Giacomo Zanella, a great philologist, a great poet, yet an almost forgotten voice, whom many high school and even university students have never had the occasion to meet along their study routes, despite having faced, or having believed to face, everything that has had a major literary and cultural relevance over the course of our nineteenth century. Zanella, while reflecting with a sort of awe on the mystery of the cosmos, for example in front of a fossil shell lain on his table, knew and felt that nature is only the visible manifestation of the bright power of Being, and that limiting oneself to its quantitative and descriptive analysis, as if this exhausted the field of reality, means excluding the uttermost essence of the world.

Will beauty save the world? This question that a character from *The Idiot* poses to Prince Myshkin, the protagonist of Dostoyevsky's novel, contains a challenge: to measure oneself against Beauty in the age of nihilism. Does the metaphysical dimension of Beauty still have a possible role in the critique of the disenchantment of modernity?

One of the peculiar characteristics of current Western society — whose model overflows beyond its geographic bed and imposes itself across the whole planet — is the domination of the titanic, which is characterised by formlessness, the redundancy of means in the absence of ends, consumerism, the incurable conflict with nature, the inexhaustible squandering of resources in direct proportion to the production of waste, the automatism of technological development, and the primacy of economy over all other aspects of life and culture. The critique of the outcome of development, understood as quantitative cumulation, passes through the objection to unlimited growth even on the qualitative, symbolical and imaginative plane of art. The aspects of hedonistic society which have plagiarised contemporary art are decisive: the myth of the "new" as an end in itself; exaggerated individualism; the destruction of memory, and therefore of tradition; the separation, in creative doing, from the continuity which linked art to craftsmanship; the removal of beauty as an aesthetic canon with the reduction of artistic action to conceptual modalities unfolding themselves as fleeting, eccentric, ephemeral, obsolescent objects or installations. Such art belongs to a mercantile regime, massifying as never before, because in economic systems aimed at growth this is the officially recognised art, financially supported and imposed by powers-that-be.

Etymologically, the adjective "modern" comes from the Latin adverb *modo*, which means "now"; the meaning of the adjective "modern" is therefore analogous to that of the adjective "hodiernal" (Latinate term meaning "of today," "of nowadays"). "Modern" is what is happening now. We know that, in historiography, the "modern" epoch (1492-1815) is not the current one, and it will be less and less so in the future, but in today's dominant common usage the adjective "modern" is not limited to denoting what is happening now; rather, it hints to an advancement towards the "better." The vectorial conception of history as progress, secularised with the Enlightenment and strengthened in the nineteenth century, both with idealistic finalism and with positivistic determinism, takes shape within the current techno-scientific "common sense," a reason for which what is happening now is as such in itself better than what happened in the past, and what will happen in the future will be better than what is happening now. In short, the future will be better because it is innovative: if it were limited to repeating what has already happened, it would not warrant the induced improvement.

On the other hand, what is the mechanism of consumer society? If the aim of an economic system is the growth of the production of goods, it does not matter whether the produced things are good (and "beautiful") or bad (and "ugly"); the fundamental point is that there are more and more of them and, as a consequence, they can be bought without limits. The human being is reduced to an entity of induced needs, which are satisfied by endlessly multiplying useless and harmful things, which, however, guarantee "development" intended as material accumulation.

This unusual growth is not given in nature, and in living organisms it produces tumours. Cancer is an illness caused by an uncontrolled proliferation of cells: these cells, no longer recognising themselves within the general coherence of the organism, lose the ability to interpret the indications of the genetic code which guides them, are unable to limit themselves in functional completeness, and reproduce themselves pathologically. Oncogenesis is therefore due to cloning (multiplication of one cell alone), anomy (growth independent of physiological organic factors), anaplasia (lack of coordinated cell differentiation), metastasis (reproduction far from and in areas other than the area of origin); in other terms, cancer is a manifestation of the preterminal phase of various disharmonies and imbalances, which determines or accelerates the death of the organism. This is the entropy of the existential meaning of the living being. If more and more things are produced, more and more things have to be bought and, in order to induce people to buy an increasing amount of them, one cannot continue to produce the same things. To keep the demand for goods alive, the system has to continuously produce something new. In this way, "buying" becomes a value in and of itself, one that is indispensable to prevent the collapse of the economic system whose aim is the growth of the production of goods. Within an economic system founded upon the exponential growth of the production of goods, it is the "worthening" ("valorisation") of what is new, as opposed to what is traditional, that has to become the founding element of the shared value system. Therefore, newness must be identified with progress and improvement and must be wished for independently from any evaluation of goal and sense. Contemporary art and its mingling with the spread of advertising in a society reduced to a "spectacle" —

in Guy Debord's words — contributes decisively to shaping the collective imagination of Western countries and to offering a mass consensus to the process which replaces subsistence community economies with those of market exchange and consumeristic growth. Creative destruction, theorised by Joseph Schumpeter as the engine of progress and the founding connotation of the industrial mode of production, is in fact the identity card of modernity.

Critics of "limitless" growth, its destructive effects on ecosystems and its shaping of civilisation itself, cannot but be against the worthening of innovation in itself, because the level reached by the growth of production and consumption requires an unsustainable amount of renewable resources. Likewise, critics of contemporary art cannot fail to ascertain its cultural clinging to the consumer economy. That is, one cannot ignore the syntony which exists between the sacrifice of beauty and the self-referential quest for innovation and evenemential evanescence. This means the destruction of the beauty of the world by the technological innovation of process and product, inscribed within reductionistic mechanicism and aimed at the growth of production and consumption of goods.

The artist does not create from nothing; he appeals to the invisible, brings to the mind a symbolic reference or, still better, he remembers, discerns, and evokes with the heart models, archetypes, ideas, suggestions, empathies, feelings, and emotions which gravitate in a sphere of relationships and connect him, by original ways, to the otherness of spirit, nature, history, culture, the mankind of bygone generations. A work of art is successful when it reveals a holistic completeness, in which the whole results as being something greater than the causal summation of its parts. Fine art is spontaneous like the beauty of nature, but the artwork is neither a mechanical imitation of nature nor an interpretation of reality. It does not come from the intellect; rather, it is the result of sentiment, which, within the work of art, outspeaks the universal in the particular, the intelligible in the sensible, the infinite in the finite.

In archaic Greek culture, the term *kalós*, which we usually translate as "beautiful," did not have an "aesthetic" meaning; when the poetess Sappho speaks of *kalé seléne*, she does not allude to the "beautiful moon" as we would be led to believe, but to the *full moon*. The moon is *kalé*, "beautiful," because it is full, that is to say whole, accomplished, lacking nothing. In short, according to classical culture and mentality, what is beautiful is anything that presents itself with the characteristics of a complete form. What springs out from these assumptions is the conviction, widespread throughout Greco-Latin antiquity, that perfection, and therefore also beauty, coincides with finiteness. If something that is integral, something that lacks nothing, is to be considered beautiful, then it is evident that such a thing, in order to be beautiful, has not to be in-finite, i.e., without *fines*, without con-fines, borders; on the contrary, it ought to have complete edges. Indeed, beauty, indeed, as a carrier of harmony, symmetry, and eurhythmy, proposed itself as the measure and order of being and of the world, as a measure and an order which warranted — in a broad, ecological sense — the habitability of the Cosmos and therefore, ultimately, made the latter the compendium of cosmic lawfulness. As a consequence, this shows a conception of the Beautiful as an ideal image of the Good, and therefore as something that may be counted among the first principles of Being.

Economism, environmental devastation, egotistical behaviours, gigantism, the anonymity of the metropolis with the insignificance of its (non)places, and unaesthetic rationalist furniture are some of the symptoms of the repression of beauty implemented by pragmatism; they are derivative of the loss of that feeling of measure, cosmic harmony, modesty and grace which reveals the essence and ignites eros, the love for the soul in all of its manifestations. The Self — to use James

Hillman's words — can manifest itself only, on the one hand, as an "interiorisation of the community," and, on the other hand, as a continuity with the Cosmos. What distances us from ourselves and makes us strangers to ourselves is the loss of contact with what we are and above all what we feel — it is a sort of anaesthesia. Comparably, what distances us from the soul of a place is the anaesthesia itself, the state of being devoid of that sensitivity that makes us aware of what defaces, uglifies, buries, and cements it. Only love for the ineffable may venture "beyond the line" of the already experienced, of the banal, the taken for granted and the serial, as well as its false opposite, the novelty of progress, precisely because there are only opposites of the same kind, as Aristotle says.

"Degrowth" is first of all a call to offbeat, nonconformist thinking. According to the words of Jean Baudrillard, it is a palinody, literally an ode, or in general a composition, which reverses and subverts a previous one. It is a healthy turnaround that is necessary for the simple reason that the current development model is unsustainable. It would be more appropriate to call it non-growth, given that it has nothing of the utopian abstraction, but expresses a realistic and responsible counter-trend signal, a concrete pathmark for embarking on a different track along which to address and weather postmodernity, to estrange oneself from the conditionings of the consumer society in order to remould science, technology, and society in a way that culturally adheres to nature, which is made up of virtuous cycles and not of unlimited linearities. Industrial civilisation is made possible by the utilitarian artifice of a dissipative, titanic growth. Contrariwise, the civilisation of being expresses itself in the sense of the limit, of the shaping of the flow of becoming and of cultural evolution — rather than in evolutionistic materialism —, in the tragic sense of the eternal provisionality of the human condition as part of a cosmic breathing whereby the Living One reveals itself in the presence of its absence.

A Traditionalist Inquiry into Nature

Martin Heidegger speaks of an ongoing opposition between World and Earth, as a real struggle in which the contenders elevate themselves — one another — in the self-affirmation of their own essence. In this struggle, each one brings the other to be above what it is. World and Earth are always in contrast and conflict with one another, for only thusly do they find their place in the strife for illumination and concealment. Earth and World cling to the primordial forces represented by the Taoist trigrams of *Yin* and *Yang*, that is to say, respectively, *kun* (receptivity) is associated with the darkness of Earth, and *qian* (creativity) is associated with the openness of Heaven. Earth, therefore, is like *Yin*, the assiduous, unweary, unconstrained, covering and preserving principle, which dooms to failure any attempt to penetrate it. *Yin* originally means "cloudy," "dark." In contrast, Heidegger describes the World as open. The World, therefore, is like *Yang*, the self-unfolding principle. *Yang* originally means "banner flying in the sunlight," and it, therefore, betokens things that are illuminated and clear. Just as happens between Earth and World, between *Yin* and *Yang* there arises that type of conflict which, according to Heraclitus, is the "the father of all things, king of them all." The struggle considered here is a generative conflict, in which the fighters are indispensable to one another; in fact, it outlines what has neither been said nor thought of until that moment, and this always springs out as a beginning, an origin, a myth. This struggle, which leads to a continuous overturning, is not without meaning, since it is subject to the law that permeates everything — the Tao, the "Way", the Style —, which is why, regardless of the outcome, what is essential in it is the way of living, not dying, not crystallising. When preference is given to just one aspect, that is, rationality, then inwardness, empathy, intuition, and Being itself are not listened to, and we forget that the World calls upon and asks for the Earth, and the other way around. Microcosm and macrocosm interweave the way of Beauty, the measure of appropriateness, since, as Heraclitus affirms, "the concealed harmony is more powerful than that which manifests itself." Ultimately, the path beyond modernity unequivocally passes through an aesthetic, imaginal, and symbolical ridge, one that is furthest from any reductionism: rebelling against the present state of things is right, but it ought to be done because it is beautiful.

Translated by U.X.A.

HEIDEGGER AGAINST THE TRADITIONALISTS

Collin Cleary

Introduction

Many of those who adhere to Traditionalism[457] also profess an interest in the philosophy of Martin Heidegger. My own work has been heavily influenced by both Traditionalism and Heidegger. Indeed, my first published essay ("Knowing the Gods") was strongly Heideggerian, and appeared in the flagship issue of *Tyr*, a journal which describes itself as "radical traditionalist," and which I co-founded. This is just one example; many of my essays have been influenced by both schools of thought.

In my work, I have often made the assumption that Heidegger's philosophy is compatible with Traditionalism. This assumption is shared by many others to the point that it is sometimes tacitly believed that Heidegger was some kind of Traditionalist, or that Heidegger and the Traditionalists had common values and, perhaps, a common project. These assumptions have never really been challenged, and it is high time to do so. The present essay puts into question the Heidegger-Traditionalism relationship. Doing so will allow us to accomplish three things, at least:

---

[457] I will capitalize the "t" in Traditionalism to indicate the school of Guénon, Evola, et al., as opposed to "traditionalism" in the looser, broader sense of the term. This device is necessary, as I will be using the term in both senses. I should also note that it is primarily the Traditionalism of Guénon and Evola that I am concerned with here. I am comparatively less interested in the "softer" Traditionalism of figures like Coomaraswamy, Schuon, Huston Smith, etc. Most of the objections raised against Guénon and Evola herein would apply to these authors as well.

(a) *Arriving at a better understanding of Heidegger.* This is vital, for my own study of Heidegger (in which I have been engaged, off and on, for over thirty years) has convinced me that he is the only great philosopher of the last hundred years – and quite possibly the greatest philosopher who ever lived. I don't make such claims lightly, and feel that I have only recently come to truly appreciate how much we need Heidegger. Yet reading Heidegger is extremely difficult. The present essay will help to clarify his thought by putting it into dialogue with the Traditionalists, whose writings are much more accessible, and probably more familiar to my readers.

(b) *Arriving at a better understanding of Traditionalism.* We will find that in important ways Heidegger's thought is *not* compatible with Traditionalism. The reason for this is that from a Heideggerian perspective Traditionalism is fundamentally flawed: it is thoroughly (and unreflectively) invested in the Western metaphysical tradition which, according to Heidegger, set the stage for modernity. In other words, because Traditionalism uncritically accepts the validity of Western metaphysical categories, it buys into some of the foundational assumptions of modernity. In the end, Traditionalism has to be judged a thoroughly modern movement, an outgrowth of the very epoch reviled by the Traditionalists themselves. All this, again, becomes clear only if we view Traditionalism, and Western intellectual history, from a Heideggerian perspective. I believe that that perspective is correct. Thus, part of the purpose of this essay is to argue that we need to adopt a more critical approach to Traditionalism.

(c) *Arriving at a new philosophical approach.* Although I will argue that Heidegger and Traditionalism are not compatible, the case can nonetheless be made that Heidegger is a traditionalist *of sorts*, and that, for Heidegger, something like a "primordial tradition" does indeed exist (though it is markedly different from the conceptions of Guénon and Evola). In short, through an engagement with Heidegger's thought, and how it would respond to Traditionalism, we can arrive at a more adequate traditionalist perspective – one which shares a great many of the values and beliefs of Guénon and Evola, while placing these on a surer philosophical footing. I believe that there are limits to Heidegger's approach, and that it is flawed in certain ways. Here we achieve a perfect symmetry, for these flaws are perceptible from a traditionalist perspective, broadly speaking. This is a topic I cannot cover in the present essay, but I will write about it in the future, and what I have to say will be of interest to anyone influenced by neo-paganism, especially Ásatrú, or the Germanic pagan revivalist movement.

In the end, we will not arrive simply at a fusion of Heidegger and Traditionalism, since both are transformed through the dialogue into which I put them. We will arrive instead at a new philosophical perspective, a new beginning for Western philosophy, one that has rejected Western metaphysics and that seeks to prepare the way for something yet to come, something beyond the modern and the "post-modern."[458] This new beginning is possible because the groundwork was laid by Heidegger, Guénon, and Evola (to name only three).

The project described above is ambitious, and it cannot be carried out in a single essay. Thus, the present essay is merely an introduction to this project, which will have to be worked out in a number of essays (some of which have already been published at *counter-currents.com*). Here, I will limit myself mainly to a basic discussion of Heidegger in relation to Traditionalism, his knowledge of Traditionalist writings, and the criticisms he would likely have leveled against this school of thought.

Anti-Modernism in Heidegger and the Traditionalists

The primary reason Heidegger gets associated with Guénon and Evola is that all three were trenchant critics

---

[458] In suggesting that a "new beginning" is possible for philosophy, I am not being grandiose. I am simply following Heidegger, who suggested that his philosophy represented "another beginning" (*andere Anfang*).

of modernity. Heidegger and the Traditionalists hold that modernity is a period of decline, that it is a falling away from a primordial, "originary"[459] position that was qualitatively different, and immeasurably superior. Further, the terms in which these authors critique modernity are often remarkably similar, as I shall demonstrate.

Consider these lines from Heidegger's *Introduction to Metaphysics*, worth quoting at length because they sound like they could have come straight out of Guénon's *The Reign of Quantity and Signs of the Times*:

> When the farthest corner of the globe has been conquered technologically and can be exploited economically; when any incident you like, at any time you like, becomes accessible as fast as you like; when you can simultaneously "experience" an assassination attempt against a king in France and a symphony concert in Tokyo; when time is nothing but speed, instantaneity, and simultaneity, and time as history has vanished from all Dasein of all peoples; when a boxer counts as the great man of a people; when the tallies of millions at mass meetings are a triumph; then, yes then, there still looms like a specter over all this uproar the question: what for? – where to? – and what then? The spiritual decline of the earth has progressed so far that peoples are in danger of losing their last spiritual strength, the strength that makes it possible even to see the decline [which is meant in relation to the fate of "Being"] and to appraise it as such. This simple observation has nothing to do with cultural pessimism – nor with any optimism either, of course; for the darkening of the world, the flight of the gods, the destruction of the earth, the reduction of human beings to a mass, the hatred and mistrust of everything creative and free has already reached such proportions throughout the whole earth that such childish categories as pessimism and optimism have long become laughable.[460]

---

459 "Originary" (*ursprünglich*) is a term frequently used by Heidegger.

460 Martin Heidegger, *Introduction to Metaphysics*, trans. Gregory Fried and Richard Polt (New Haven, CT: Yale University Press, 2000), 40-41. This was originally a lecture course given by Heidegger in 1935. It was published for the first time in German in 1953. The material in square brackets was added by Heidegger when the lecture course was published in 1953.

In a later passage, Heidegger emphatically reiterates much of this: "We said: on the earth, all over it, a darkening of the world is happening. The essential happenings in this darkening are: the flight of the gods, the destruction of the earth, the reduction of human beings to a mass, the preeminence of the mediocre."[461] Consider also this passage:

> All things sank to the same level, to a surface resembling a blind mirror that no longer mirrors, that casts nothing back. The prevailing dimension became that of extension and number. *To be able* – this no longer means to spend and to lavish, thanks to lofty overabundance and the mastery of energies; instead, it means only practicing a routine in which anyone can be trained, always combined with a certain amount of sweat and display. In America and Russia, then, this all intensified until it turned into the measureless so-on and so-forth of the ever-identical and the indifferent, until finally this quantitative temper became a quality of its own. By now in those countries the predominance of a cross-section of the indifference is no longer something inconsequential and merely barren but is the onslaught of that which aggressively destroys all rank and all that is world-spiritual, and portrays these as a lie. This is the onslaught of what we call the demonic [in the sense of the destructively evil].[462]

Finally, let us consider a passage from a later text, *What is Called Thinking?* (1953):

> The African Sahara is only one kind of wasteland. The devastation of the earth can easily go hand in hand with a guaranteed supreme living standard for man, and just as easily with the organized establishment of a uniform state of happiness for all men. Devastation can be the same as both, and can haunt us everywhere in the most unearthly way – by keeping itself hidden. Devastation does not just mean a slow sinking into the sands. Devastation is the high-velocity expulsion of Mnemosyne [N.B.: The goddess of memory – C.C.]. The words, "the wasteland grows," come from another realm than the current appraisals of our age. Nietzsche said, "the wasteland grows" nearly three quarters of a century ago. And he added, "Woe to him who hides wastelands within."[463]

---

461 Ibid., 47.

462 Ibid., 48-49. Bracketed phrase added by Heidegger for the 1953 edition.

463 Martin Heidegger, *What is Called Thinking?*, trans. J. Glenn Gray (New York: Harper Perennial, 1968), 30.

These passages give a fairly good summation of the essentials of Heidegger's critique of modernity, which is worked out in much greater detail in his entire oeuvre. (Arguably, Heidegger's confrontation with modernity is the central feature of his philosophy.) We may note here, especially, four major points.[464] I will set these out below, along with quotations from Guénon's *Reign of Quantity*, for comparison:

(a) The predominance of the "quantitative" in modernity; the triumph of the quantitative over the qualitative:

Guénon: "The descending movement of manifestation, and consequently that of the cycle of which it is an expression, takes place away from the positive or essential pole of existence toward its negative or substantial pole, and the result is that all things must progressively take on a decreasingly qualitative and an increasingly quantitative aspect; and that is why the last period of the cycle must show a very special tendency toward the establishment of a 'reign of quantity.'"[465]

(b) The cancellation of distance in the modern period; the increasing "speed" of modernity:

Guénon: "[Events] are being unfolded nowadays with a speed unexampled in the earlier ages, and this speed goes on increasing and will continue to increase up to the end of the cycle; there is thus something like a progressive 'contraction' of duration, the limit of which corresponds to the 'stopping-point' previously alluded to; it will be necessary to return to a special consideration of these matters later on, and to explain them more fully."[466]

---

[464] One point is omitted from the discussion below, one which my readers might expect me to discuss: "the flight of the gods." What Heidegger means by this, however, is complicated, and far from obvious. I will discuss this issue in a future essay.

[465] René Guénon, *The Reign of Quantity and the Signs of the Times*, trans. Lord Northbourne (Hillsdale, NY: Sophia Perennis, 2001), 43.

[466] Ibid., 42.

And furthermore: "The increase in the speed of events, as the end of the cycle draws near, can be compared to the acceleration that takes place in the fall of heavy bodies: the course of the development of the present humanity closely resembles the movement of a mobile body running down a slope and going faster as it approaches the bottom..."[467]

(c) Modernity's leveling effect; the destruction of an order of rank:

Guénon: "It is no less obvious that differences of aptitude cannot in spite of everything be entirely suppressed, so that a uniform education will not give exactly the same results for all; but it is all too true that, although it cannot confer on anyone qualities that he does not possess, it is on the contrary very well fitted to suppress in everyone all possibilities above the common level; thus the 'leveling' always works downward: indeed, it could not work in any other way, being itself only an expression of the tendency toward the lowest, that is, toward pure quantity..."[468]

(d) Modernity's reduction of everything to uniformity:

Guénon: "A mere glance at things as they are is enough to make it clear that the aim is everywhere to reduce everything to uniformity, whether it be human beings themselves or the things among which they live, and it is obvious that such a result can only be obtained by suppressing as far as possible every qualitative distinction..."[469]

In later works, Heidegger explicitly ties modernity's will towards uniformity to the "mechanization" of human beings. The spirit of technology becomes so totalizing that finally human beings themselves are "requisitioned" (to use a Heideggerian expression) and integrated as subsidiary mechanisms within the vast machine of modernity. In this

---

[467] Ibid., 43. For similar remarks see Julius Evola, *Meditations on the Peaks*, trans. Guido Stucco (Rochester, Vermont: Inner Traditions, 1998), 45-46.

[468] Guénon, *Reign*, 51-52.

[469] Ibid., 48.

connection, consider this passage from Guénon, worth quoting at length:

> Servant of the machine, the man must become a machine himself, and thenceforth his work has nothing really human in it, for it no longer implies the putting to work of any of the qualities that really constitute human nature. The end of all this is what is called in present-day jargon 'mass-production,' the purpose of which is only to produce the greatest possible quantity of objects, and of objects as exactly alike as possible, intended for the use of men who are supposed to be no less alike; that is indeed the triumph of quantity, as was pointed out earlier, and it is by the same token the triumph of uniformity. These men who are reduced to mere numerical 'units' are expected to live in what can scarcely be called houses, for that would be to misuse the word, but in 'hives' of which the compartments will all be planned on the same model, and furnished with objects made by 'mass production,' in such a way as to cause to disappear from the environment in which the people live every qualitative difference.[470]

One last quotation from Guénon: "Man 'mechanized' everything and ended at last by mechanizing himself, falling little by little into the condition of numerical units, parodying unity, yet lost in the uniformity and indistinction of the 'masses,' that is, in pure multiplicity and nothing else. Surely that is the most complete triumph of quantity over quality that can be imagined."[471]

It would be pointless to amass further such quotations from Guénon since his work is replete with them. It would be equally pointless to quote the many virtually identical observations from Evola. A substantial amount of Evola's work is occupied with elaborating and extending Guénon's critique of modernity, to which Evola devoted entire volumes

---

[470] Ibid., 60-61. Compare this to some remarks by Alexandre Kojève: "Hence it would have to be admitted that after the end of history men would construct their edifices and works of art as birds build their nests and spiders spin their webs, would perform their musical concerts after the fashion of frogs and cicadas, would play like young animals and would indulge in love like adult beasts." See *Introduction to the Reading of Hegel*, ed. Raymond Queneau and Allan Bloom, trans. James H. Nichols, Jr. (Ithaca, NY: Cornell University Press, 1969), 159 (footnote).

[471] Guénon, *Reign*, 194.

(e.g., *Revolt Against the Modern World*, *Ride the Tiger*, *Men Among the Ruins*, etc.). However, their positions diverge when Evola advocates that the superior man respond to modernity by "riding the tiger" (i.e., utilizing certain negative elements of the modern world, which might destroy lesser men, for the positive purpose of self-realization).

The Evola Quotation in Heidegger's *Nachlass*

The foregoing has hopefully demonstrated to the reader that Heidegger and Guénon held strikingly similar views on modernity. Although Heidegger knew individuals who respected Guénon (e.g., Carl Schmitt and Ernst Jünger), no evidence has emerged that Heidegger actually read Guénon's work. Recently, however, evidence *has* emerged that Heidegger read Evola. However, far from supporting the idea that Heidegger was influenced by Evola or sympathetic to him, an examination of this evidence will demonstrate exactly where Heidegger parts company with Traditionalism.[472]

Amongst Heidegger's *Nachlass* (the papers left behind after his death) a handwritten note has been found in which the philosopher quotes a passage from Friedrich Bauer's 1935 German translation of *Revolt Against the Modern World* (*Erhebung wider die moderne Welt*). Here is the passage as Heidegger copied it out:

> Wenn eine Rasse die Berührung mit dem, was allein Beständigkeit hat und geben kann — mit der Welt des Seyns — verloren hat, dann sinken die von ihr gebildeten kollektiven Organismen, welches immer ihre Größe und Macht sei, schicksalhaft in die Welt der Zufälligkeit herab.

---

472 The discovery of the note in 2015 received some attention in the German press. Writing in the *Frankfurter allgemeine Zeitung*, Thomas Vasek claims that "textual comparisons suggest that Heidegger had not only read Evola, as this note indicates, but was also influenced by his ideas from the mid-thirties on, from his critique of science and technology, his anti-humanism and rejection of Christianity, to his 'spiritual' racism." This is a completely baseless, and, indeed, ludicrous assertion, as I will shortly demonstrate. See Greg Johnson's analysis of the Heidegger note and Vasek's article here:
https://counter-currents.com/2016/02/notes-on-heidegger-and-evola/

And here is a translation:

> When a race has lost contact with what alone has and can give it permanence [or "stability"; *Beständigkeit*] – with the world of Beying [*Seyns*], then the collective organisms formed by it, whatever be their greatness and power, are destined to sink down into the world of contingency.[473]

For comparison, here is the *entire* passage from Bauer's text:

> Wenn eine Rasse die Berührung mit dem, was allein Beständigkeit hat und geben kann – mit der Welt des "Seins" – verloren hat, dann sinken die von ihr gebildeten kollektiven Organismen, welches immer ihre Größe und Macht sei, schicksalhaft in die Welt der Zufälligkeit herab: werden Beute des Irrationalen, des Veränderlichen, des "Geschichtlichen," dessen, was von unten und von außen her bedingt ist.[474]

We immediately notice two things when Heidegger's handwritten version is compared to the original. First, Heidegger has rendered *Sein* as *Seyn*. Second, Heidegger replaces a colon with a period and omits the last part of the sentence entirely. The part after the colon can be translated as follows: "[to] become prey to the irrational, the changeable, the 'historical,' of what is conditioned from below and from the outside." Why did Heidegger make these changes? Fully answering this question will allow us to see that Heidegger actually rejects Evola's Traditionalism in the most fundamental terms possible.

First of all, it is likely that this undated note comes from sometime in the 1930s. During this time, Heidegger began utilizing *Seyn*, an archaic German spelling of *Sein* (being). But why? What did this signify? It was not simply eccentricity on

---

473 Anglophone translators of Heidegger have adopted the convention of rendering *Seyn* as "Beyng." The "s" at the end of *Seins/Seyns* in the passage simply indicates the genitive case. The nominative is *Sein/Seyn*.

474 Julius Evola, *Erhebung wider die moderne Welt*, trans. Friedrich Bauer (Stuttgart: Deutsche Verlags-Anstalt, 1935), 65. The translator actually leaves out portions of Evola's text, but since Heidegger only read the translation and not the original, these omissions do not concern us here. For the full passage in English translation, see Julius Evola, *Revolt Against the Modern World*, trans. Guido Stucco (Rochester, VT: Inner Traditions, 1995), 56-57.

Heidegger's part. By *Seyn*, Heidegger meant something distinct from *Sein*, which refers to the being that beings have ("being as such"). *Seyn* instead refers to what Heidegger calls elsewhere "the clearing" (*die Lichtung*). This metaphorical expression refers to a clearing in a forest, which allows light to enter in and illuminate what stands within the clearing. Thomas Sheehan describes Heidegger's clearing as "the always already opened-up 'space' that makes the being of things (phenomenologically: the intelligibility of things) possible and necessary."[475] The clearing is what "gives" being. Heidegger writes in "The End of Philosophy and the Task of Thinking" (1964):

> The forest clearing is experienced in contrast to dense forest, called *Dickung* in our older language. The substantive "opening" [*Lichtung*] goes back to the verb "open" [*lichten*]. The adjective *licht* "open" is the same word as "light." To open something means: to make something light, free and open, e.g., to make the forest free of trees at one place. The openness thus originating is the clearing... Light can stream into the clearing, into its openness, and let brightness play with darkness in it. But light never first creates openness. Rather, light presupposes openness. However, the clearing, the opening, is not only free for brightness and darkness, but also for resonance and echo, for sounding and the diminishing of sound. *The clearing is the open region for everything that becomes present and absent.* . . . What the word [opening] designates in the connection we are now thinking, free openness, is a "primal phenomenon" [*Urphänomenon*], to use a word of Goethe's.[476]

Consider a simple example. I approach an unfamiliar object sitting on my doorstep. From a distance I cannot place it; try as I might, it remains a mystery. But as I approach closer still, all is revealed: I see now that it is an Amazon box. In this moment, what has occurred is that the being of the object – what it *is*, what its meaning is – becomes present to me.[477] In order for this to be possible at all, I must bear within me

---

[475] Thomas Sheehan, *Making Sense of Heidegger: A Paradigm Shift* (Lanham, MD: Rowman and Littlefield, 2015), 20.

[476] Martin Heidegger, *Basic Writings*, ed. David Farrell Krell (New York: Harper and Row, 1977), 384-385. This essay was translated by Joan Stambaugh; italics added.

[477] Sheehan argues at length that, for Heidegger, being and meaning are identical.

a certain special sort of "openness," within which the being of something makes itself known, or makes itself present.[478]

Contrary to how empiricists tend to conceive things, I don't actually *experience* myself as hanging a label onto the object, or slotting it within a mental category. This is an analysis *after the fact* of experience, not what I actually experience. If we are truer to the phenomenon than the empiricists (i.e., if we are good phenomenologists), we have to report that the experience is actually one in which the being of the thing seems to "come forth," or to display itself as we explore the object. But, again, this is only possible because of the "openness" referred to earlier. In this openness, being displays itself; it "lit up" within the "space" of the metaphorical "clearing."

Thus, for Heidegger it is possible to speak of something deeper or more ultimate than being itself (hence, an *Urphänomenon*): that which *allows* our encounter with the being of beings in the first place; the open clearing. When Heidegger famously refers to "the forgottenness of being" (*Vergessenheit des Seins*) he is actually referring to the forgottenness of the clearing.[479] The clearing is forgotten in the sense that we have forgotten *that in virtue of which* being is given to us. As I will discuss later, Heidegger holds that the Western metaphysical tradition, beginning with the Pre-Socratics, systematically forgets the clearing. He writes: "In fact, the history of Western

---

478 This way of expressing things should be understood as figurative, and preliminary. Actually, Heidegger wants to entirely avoid a "subjective" treatment of the clearing as some sort of "faculty" or Kantian *a priori* structure that I "bear within me." The reason, at root, is that this treatment of the clearing is phenomenologically untrue. I do not, in fact, experience the clearing as something "in me" that is "mine." Still less do I experience it as something over which I have any kind of influence or control. There is thus no real basis for "subjectivizing" the clearing, for locating it "within the subject." Indeed, Heidegger critiques the subject/object distinction prevailing in philosophy since Descartes, which locates certain "properties" as "within" a subject, as if this subject is a kind of cabinet in which we dwell, removed from an "external world." See Heidegger, *Being and Time*, trans. Joan Stambaugh, rev. Dennis J. Schmidt (Albany, NY: State University of New York Press, 2010), 60-61.

479 Generally speaking, this is correct. Unfortunately, Heidegger is inconsistent with his use of *Sein/Seyn*, sometimes referring to being, sometimes to the clearing that gives being.

thought begins, not by thinking what is most thought-provoking, but by letting it remain forgotten."[480]

Now, by contrast, when Evola speaks of "the world of being" (*Welt des Seins*; *mondo dell'essere*) in this passage and elsewhere, he is referring to a Platonic realm of timeless essences that are the *true* beings, in contrast to the changeful, impermanent terrestrial beings we encounter with the five senses.[481] Traditionalism is heavily dependent on this Platonic metaphysics. Consider, for example, Evola's words from the very beginning of *Revolt*:

> In order to understand both the spirit of Tradition and its antithesis, modern civilization, it is necessary to begin with the fundamental doctrine of the two natures. According to this doctrine there is a physical order of things and a metaphysical one; there is a mortal nature and an immortal one; there is the superior realm of "being" and the inferior realm of "becoming." Generally speaking, there is a visible and tangible dimension and, prior to and beyond it, an invisible and intangible dimension that is the support, the source, and the true life of the former.[482]

Not only does Heidegger reject this Platonic metaphysics, he sees it as the first major stage in the decline of the West. Its inception is essentially identical with the "forgottenness" of the clearing spoken of a moment ago. The reasons Heidegger sees Platonic metaphysics as decadent are complex, but I will briefly summarize them.

Heidegger tells us that the early Greek response to being was "wonder" (θαῦμα): "wonder that beings are and that humans themselves are and are in the midst of that which they are not."[483] But the Greeks wondered not just at the fact

---

480 Heidegger, *What is Called Thinking?*, 152.

481 This same point, contrasting what Evola and Heidegger mean by "Being," is made by Greg Johnson in his analysis of Heidegger's usage of the Evola quotation. I am indebted to Greg Johnson for bringing this entire subject to my attention in the first place. See his treatment of the subject here: https://counter-currents.com/2016/02/notes-on-heidegger-and-evola/

482 Evola, *Revolt*, 3.

483 Heidegger, *Contributions to Philosophy (Of the Event)*, trans. Richard Rojcewicz and Daniela Vallega-Neu (Bloomington, IN: Indiana University Press, 2012), 37.

that beings present their being to mankind, but that this presentation comes forth out of concealment, and returns to concealment. Something may present itself to us in its being, but it never presents the entirety of its being. Much remains hidden. For every partial display, there is a withdrawal, a concealing. Early Greek thinking affirms this play of presence and absence. It recognizes that there is an ineluctable element of absence or concealment to being (as Heraclitus said, *phusis kruptesthai philei*, "*phusis* ["nature," or, Heidegger argues, being] loves to hide"[484]). Not all is revealed to us. What does get revealed always emerges out of hiddenness, and then returns into hiddenness again. In other words, early Greek thinking affirms *mystery*. In so doing, it affirms that there are limits to our knowing; to our ability to make *what is* fully present and intelligible. To attempt to overcome those limits is hubris; it is the attitude of the Titans, who would like nothing better than to overcome the gods.

Starting with some of the Pre-Socratic thinkers, however, an intellectual shift begins to take place that is only fully realized with Platonism. This shift is referred to in Heidegger studies as a movement toward "the metaphysics of presence" (a term actually coined by Jacques Derrida). Thinkers begin to demand, implicitly (it is not made explicit until the modern period) that *what is* be constantly present, in the sense of fully available and intelligible. This means that absence or concealment, as inherent in the nature of being, comes to be denied, discounted, or, to speak more like Heidegger, "forgotten."[485]

On a more fundamental level, forgotten too is the clearing in which beings display their being. The clearing is itself

---

[484] Heidegger argues at length that for the Greeks *phusis* = being. See Heidegger, *Introduction to Metaphysics*, 15-16.

[485] Forgotten too is the clearing, which Heidegger says is "self-concealing." Recall that the clearing is that in virtue of which things display themselves to us in their being: this "happens" within the clearing. But the clearing does not display itself. In a sense, it "*absents*itself" so that beings can *presence* themselves. But this new mindset in Greek thought to which I am referring denies absence and mystery, thus it cannot come to the realization that the clearing even exists.

a kind of absence, and Heidegger explicitly refers to it as a "mystery" (*Geheimnis*).[486] The clearing itself does not (and cannot) appear to us as a being might. Since the clearing is the open "space" in which things appear to us in their meaningful presence, in order for it to appear to us the clearing would have to appear *in the clearing*, in itself, which is absurd. The clearing is a certain sort of "nothing," an absence, an "open space" in which we encounter the being of things. Thus, Heidegger understands the clearing as "withdrawing itself" so that beings may presence themselves to us within it. The clearing is thus "intrinsically hidden." However, it is possible to *infer* the existence of the clearing (as the transcendental condition of being), as Heidegger does. The clearing was glimpsed, he believes, by the early Greeks (for example, the pre-Socratic thinkers Heraclitus and Parmenides), then forgotten again.

The metaphysics of presence overlooks the clearing entirely, then attempts to accommodate the being of beings to that aspect of human nature that is deeply uncomfortable with mystery, and believes that it can cancel absence and mystery altogether and bring everything into the light. It is this hubris that asserts itself in the Western metaphysical tradition from Platonism (in which it first truly becomes clear) to Nietzsche. But how exactly is poor old Plato to blame?

In Platonism, we find the insistence that being, *true* being, is identical with "the forms." What are forms? The Greek word translated as "form" is *eidos* (εἶδος) which meant the "look" of a thing, in the sense of its appearance, its *phainomenon*. So, in actual fact, being is defined here as presence to a human knower. "Idea" (ἰδέα) has a similar etymology. Heidegger writes that "An ἰδέα is what-is-sighted. What-is-sighted is sighted only in and for an act of seeing. . . . We finally have to get serious about the fact that Plato gave the name 'ideas' to being [*das Sein*]."[487] Unlike the being wondered at by the early Greeks, however, the presence of the form comes without

---
486 See Sheehan, *Making Sense of Heidegger*, 75-76, 226.

487 Ibid., 84 fn. 85.

any concomitant absence, for the *eidos* presents itself to the intellect of man, and is fully intelligible by intellect.

The form has no "dark side" – no side that conceals itself from us, no mystery. It is fully intelligible because it is fully present; it hides nothing. Moreover, it remains always available to intellect, for it is eternal and unchanging. When I encounter some object in nature, the "look"/form of the thing announces itself. The thing is intelligible insofar as my intellect "sees" the form that it "partakes of" (to use the Platonic language). Unlike the thing, however, this form never changes nor can it cease to exist. The thing resists the intellect's efforts to understand it. Its form, by contrast, presents itself as firm and constant; it is fully knowable and fully available.

Thus, Platonism declares that the form is what truly is, precisely because it reveals itself to intellect as permanent, unchanging, and fully intelligible. The sensible particulars that partake of forms either *are not*, or they have, at best, a kind of derived being. Thus, Platonism rejects the physical, sensible world as fundamentally "unreal," and declares the intelligible world, the world of forms only accessible to human intellect, as true reality, the "world of being," to borrow Evola's expression, discussed earlier. It is crucial to see that what has actually occurred in Platonism is that the understanding of being has been narrowed down to what satisfies human needs and preferences – specifically the preference for the knowable over the unknowable, the present over the absent, the predictable over the unpredictable. Voila! A world of forms is discovered; a world of objects that are knowable, forever present, and predictable. A world of true being. The other world, the physical world that frustrates and disappoints, is but a dream.

We also happen to prefer the manipulable to that which frustrates our desires. And it is likewise crucial to see that, for Heidegger, this shift to "the metaphysics of presence," to insisting that being must be what makes itself fully available to human knowers, is simultaneously an insistence that *what is* be fully manipulable. Understanding and manipulation, intellect and will, are coupled in Platonism in the following way. The forms satisfy the intellect's desire that *what is* be fully intelligible. They also provide "models" or standards against which the sensible world is to be judged. The lesser beings of sense and physicality are seen in the light of the higher, truer beings of intelligibility – and inevitably found wanting. The urge to try and transform sensible being to bring it closer to the ideal, to intelligible being, becomes almost impossible to resist.

Heidegger has adopted an interpretation of Platonism that could accurately be described as Nietzschean: Platonism stems from a "world denying" or "life denying" impulse; it damns this world in favor of an invented world that never disappoints. Then the spiritual descendants of Platonism proceed, disastrously, to tinker with this world to try to remake it in the image of the ideal. Here we see the seeds of modernity's will to mastery over nature, as well as the seeds of modern political "idealism," as exemplified by the Jacobins and the Communists, among others. *All* the aspects of modernity Heidegger was quoted earlier as deploring are ultimately traceable, he believes, to Platonic metaphysics.[488]

How Platonism's "metaphysics of presence" is taken up and transformed by later philosophers cannot occupy us here. Suffice it to say that Heidegger completely rejects Evola's idea that a "race" declines when it has "lost contact" with being, because, as already noted, the sense of "being" meant by Evola is Platonic. Quite the reverse: Heidegger believes that our

---

488 The reader will have noted that in the foregoing I have usually referred to "Platonism" rather than to Plato. The reason for this is that while the above accurately describes what the philosophical tradition takes to be "Platonism," careful study of the dialogues suggests that Plato was not necessarily a Platonist. There are suggestions in the dialogues that Plato recognizes that the forms may not be entirely intelligible, or may not even be knowable at all. Heidegger is aware of this problem. However, in his history of metaphysics Heidegger is primarily concerned with what the philosophical tradition *took* to be Plato's positions, because it was this interpretation that shaped the history of Western thought, not what Plato might "really" have meant.

race has declined *precisely* through its turn toward Platonic metaphysics, and its turn away from the affirmation of the primal mystery of the clearing. Thus, when Heidegger swaps *Sein* for *Seyn* in the passage at issue, he is *entirely* changing the meaning of what Evola is saying. He is rewriting the passage so that it agrees with his own position: the decline of the West stems from its forgottenness of *Seyn* (the clearing) and its embrace of the Platonic *Sein* (being) of the Western metaphysical tradition.

Heidegger omits the last part of Evola's sentence for similar reasons. Let us look again at those words. Evola tells us that when a race has lost contact with "the world of being" it will "become prey to the irrational, the changeable, the 'historical,' of what is conditioned from below and from the outside." Heidegger omits these words because he rejects Evola's dichotomy between "being" and "the historical." Heidegger argues, in fact, that *Seyn*/the clearing is inherently historical (*geschichtlich*), and changeable (*veränderlich*). The being of things actually changes as culture changes. This is the same thing, fundamentally, as saying that the meaning of things changes over time.

But could the being/meaning of the Amazon box on my doorstep ever change? Of course. Imagine a future world without Amazon, or one in which Amazon has been declared a monopoly and broken up into a number of different, competing entities. No more Amazon boxes on doorsteps. When you do see them, you see them in museums and you no longer see them simply as utilitarian objects. You no longer think, on glimpsing one, "Oh, my copy of *Being and Time* has arrived." Instead, the Amazon box takes on a new meaning: as symbol of a dark time we are, happily, well beyond; a time in which we allowed companies like Amazon not only to corner the market and put all smaller competitors out of business, but to shape the information we have access to through censorship and the banning of books.

Thus, if the being/meaning that things have for us changes over the course of history, as culture and circumstances change, then, contra Evola, being is inescapably "changeable" and "historical." Evola also says that a race which loses contact with his idea of being falls prey to "the irrational" (*das Irrational*, in the German translation). Would Heidegger endorse this as well? Is his idea of being "irrational"? Well, Heidegger *does* argue that historical-cultural shifts in being/meaning are not fully intelligible to human beings. The reason for this is that it is always *within Seyn*/the clearing that things are meaningful or intelligible to us. It therefore follows that *Seyn*/the clearing itself is *not* ultimately intelligible. In a highly qualified sense, we could thus describe it as "irrational." That Evola implicitly endorses the equation of being with "the rational" in this passage is extremely ironic. The modern inflection of the Western metaphysical tradition constructs this notion of the "irrational" as a kind of bugaboo: it is the inversion of everything modernity takes to be "rational" (it is the supposedly *un*measurable, *un*quantifiable, *un*observable, *un*testable, etc.). It is in its conception of "the rational" that we find the essence of modernity.

Conclusion

Heidegger would have regarded Guénon and Evola as philosophically naïve – for several reasons. First, they uncritically appropriate the Western metaphysical tradition in the name of combating modernity. Yet, as I have already discussed, Heidegger argues that that tradition is implicated in the decline of the West. Second, the Traditionalists assert that this metaphysical tradition is "perennial" or timeless. They take Platonism as preserving elements of a primordial tradition that antedates Plato by millennia. They hold that the time of Plato belongs to the *Kali-Yuga* (the fourth age, the decadent "Iron Age"), but they take Plato (and other ancient philosophers) to be preserving an older, indeed timeless wisdom. However, this is pure speculation, for which there is no solid scholarly evidence.[489]

A further Heideggerian objection to Traditionalism may be considered at this point, and it is an extremely serious one. Both Heidegger and the Traditionalists decry rootless modern individualism. However, Heidegger's critique goes much further. Recall that for the philosopher being is inherently historical and changeable. What things *are* for us, or what they mean, is determined in part by our historical situation. Human beings are always embedded in a set of concrete historical, cultural circumstances. Heidegger writes: "Only insofar as the human being *exists* in a definite *history* are beings given, is truth given. There is no truth given in itself; rather, truth is *decision* and *fate* for human beings; it is something *human*."[490] This does not, however, mean that truth, as human, is something "subjective":

> We are not humanizing the essence of truth: to the contrary, we are *determining the essence of human beings on the basis of truth*. Man is transposed into the various gradations of truth. Truth is not above or in man, but *man* is in *truth*. Man is in truth inasmuch as truth is this happening of the unconcealment of things on the basis of creative projection. Each individual does not consciously carry out this creative projection; instead, he is already born into a *community*; he already grows up within a quite *definite* truth, which he confronts to a greater or lesser degree. Man is the one whose *history* displays the *happening of truth*.[491]

As a result of this stance, Heidegger rejects both the Enlightenment ideal of a "view from nowhere," as well as rootless, modern cosmopolitanism.

---

[489] The Traditionalists are in much the same position as the Renaissance "Hermeticists" who falsely believed that the *Corpus Hermeticum* contained an Egyptian wisdom that far antedated Plato and the Greeks, and from which those philosophers had taken their basic doctrines. In reality, the *Corpus Hermeticum* was no older than the first century BC, and it derived its doctrines, in large measure, from Plato and his school.

[490] Martin Heidegger, *Being and Truth,* trans. Gregory Fried and Richard Polt (Bloomington, IN: Indiana University Press, 210), 134. Italics in original.

[491] Ibid., 136. Italics in original.

Consider, however, the following lines from *The Reign of Quantity*. Guénon writes disapprovingly of "those among the moderns who consider themselves to be outside all religion" – i.e., freethinking individualists. He asserts that such men are "at the extreme opposite point from those who, having penetrated to the principial unity of all the traditions, are no longer tied to any particular form." This latter position, of course, is that of Guénonian Traditionalism itself. In a footnote, he then approvingly quotes Ibn 'Arabî: "My heart has become capable of all forms: it is a pasture for gazelles and a monastery for Christian monks, and a temple for idols, and the *Kaabah* of the pilgrim, and the table of the *Thorah* and the book of the *Quran*. I am the religion of Love, whatever road his camels may take; my religion and my faith are the true religion."[492]

Though Guénon contrasts the position of the modern freethinker to the Traditionalist, Heidegger would doubtless argue that there is a fundamental identity between them. The freethinker imagines that he has freed himself from any cultural-religious context and become a kind of intellectual or spiritual cosmopolitan. *Yet the Traditionalist thinks the exact same thing.* The only difference is that the freethinker believes he has cast off religion or "spirituality" itself, whereas the Traditionalist imagines that he adheres to a decontextualized, ahistorical, and universal spiritual construct called "Tradition." This standpoint too is fundamentally modern.

One might object, however, that Guénon's decision to convert to Islam and "go native" in Cairo, where he spent the last 20 years of his life, indicates that he was aware that tradition could not be a free-floating abstraction, and that to be a true Traditionalist one has to choose a living tradition and immerse oneself in it. This is true, as a statement of Guénon's views. But the very idea that one can *choose* a tradition buys into the modern conception of the autonomous self who may, from a standpoint of detachment from any cultural or historical context, survey the different traditions and select one. It is

---
492 Guénon, *Reign*, 62-63.

no use here to point out that all Muslims must, in a sense, "choose" Islam, as it is not an ethnic religion but a creedal one, whose faith all adherents must profess, and to which anyone may convert. This is a valid point, but a superficial one. Islam emerged from a cultural and historical context quite alien to the West, into which no Westerner may ever *truly* enter.

Finally, let us now consider a couple of objections to this Heideggerian critique of Traditionalism. First, defenders of Traditionalism might respond that Guénon and Evola are primarily grounded in the Indian tradition, and not in Western metaphysics at all. There are essentially two pieces of evidence for this claim. The first is Guénon and Evola's endorsement of the Hindu cyclical account of time, of the *yugas*, which is indeed quite ancient. Both seem to accept this teaching in rather literal terms, right down to the traditional Hindu calculations of the time span of each *yuga* (which strike most modern readers as arbitrary inventions). Second is the primacy granted by both thinkers to Vedanta. Both Guénon and Evola regard the teachings of the Upanishads as an expression of a very ancient ur-metaphysics, which constitutes a "perennial philosophy."

The dependence of the Traditionalists on the Indian tradition is very real. The trouble, however, is that they interpret the Indian materials in terms of the categories and terminology of Western metaphysics. Indeed, this is especially true of Guénon, who shows no signs of recognizing that there is anything problematic about understanding the Upanishads in terms derived from Platonic and Aristotelian philosophy. For example, right at the beginning of *The Reign of Quantity*, Guénon discusses the duality of *Purusha* and *Prakriti* using the categories of "essence and substance" – then, a page later, he appeals to "form and matter," then to "act and potency."[493] This is all Aristotelian terminology. Moreover, there is no attempt on Guénon's part to recover the "originary" sense of these terms in Aristotle (as Heidegger attempted in his lecture courses

---

493 Ibid., 11-12.

on Greek philosophy). Instead, he unhesitatingly adopts the medieval scholastic understanding of these distinctions.

It may be that Guénon thought it was valid to discuss Vedanta in Platonic-Aristotelean terms because he regarded the Platonic tradition as itself an expression of the perennial philosophy. Thus, he simply decided *a priori* that Vedanta and Platonism are two streams flowing from the same source: primordial Tradition. But, again, this is pure speculation. The bottom line is that Guénon and Evola *do* accord special primacy to the Indian tradition over Western metaphysics – but they see the former through the lens of the latter. Thus, despite their interest in Indian thought, they are still thoroughly beholden to Western metaphysics.

What did Heidegger have to say about tradition (tradition in general, not "Tradition")? In "The Age of the World Picture" (1938), he warns us against "merely negating the age" and writes that "The flight into tradition, out of a combination of humility and presumption, achieves, in itself, nothing, is merely a closing the eyes and blindness towards the historical moment."[494] But Heidegger also argues that the turn toward metaphysics is a *turn away* from a more authentic way of encountering being. It is in this latter conception that we find what may be the equivalent of "primordial tradition" in Heidegger's thought. It is quite possible, indeed, to argue that while Heidegger is not a Guénonian or Evolian Traditionalist, he is actually *more traditionalist* than the Traditionalists, if he is correct in seeing Platonic metaphysics as decadent. To defend this provocative claim, however, will require another essay.[495]

---

494 Martin Heidegger, *Off the Beaten Track*, trans. Julian Young and Kenneth Haynes (Cambridge: Cambridge University Press, 2002), 72.

495 This essay is an edited and expanded version of a text that originally appeared at *Counter-Currents*: https://counter-currents.com/2020/12/heidegger-against-the-traditionalists-part-one/

TRADITIONALISM AND (MIS-)UNDERSTANDING HEIDEGGER

Askr Svarte (Evgeny Nechkasov)

One significant attempt at understanding and evaluating the thought of Martin Heidegger belongs to the pen of one of the key "founding fathers" of Traditionalism, Julius Evola, in his book *Ride the Tiger*.[496] This work itself was a milestone and turning point for all of Traditionalism. Released in 1961, it contained a series of qualitative reflections on Evola's attempts at exerting a Traditionalist influence and implementing the Traditionalist project in the world by way of directly participating in Third Way politics in the period up to and during the Second World War. Evola acknowledged the impossibility of turning off the track of history, for the latter has been laid down as the due, that is to say as metaphysical and Dharmic predestination. Evola saw the Traditionalist's task as maintaining the inner vertical of the spirit and seeking out other ways and interpretations of the sacred in a dying world which awaits only further deterioration and decay.[497]

Thus, on the one hand, Evola's turn to deal with Heidegger's thought, which in those years had already been developing along the pathways of the "Turn" (*Kehre*), would be very logical and timely. On the other hand, however, it bears recognizing that Evola's attempt at understanding and interpreting the Black Forest master turned out to be extraneous and an utter failure.

---

[496] Julius Evola, *Ride the Tiger: A Survival Manual for Aristocrats of the Soul*, trans. Joscelyn Godwin and Constance Fontana (Rochester: Inner Traditions, 2003).

[497] I take up this pursuit of other ways and interpretations of the sacred in the contemporary technological world in my recent book *Tradition and Future Shock: Visions of a Future that Isn't Ours* (PRAV Publishing, 2023).

Sixteen years after the end of the Second World War, Evola turned to the early, prewar Heidegger of the period of *Being and Time*. Evola's task was to criticize the "dead end of existentialism," and one can agree with a number of aspects of his harsh judgments. Evola taught the doctrine of the "differentiated man" who remains faithful to the ideals and spiritual vertical of Tradition in the era of maximal apostasy and nihilism, and he carved out this human type in polemic with the characteristic signs and teachings of modern nihilism. But, in the case of his references to Heidegger, we encounter a whole heap of problems pertaining to a lack of understanding of Heidegger's ideas and an ignorance of the broader contexts, details, and current state of development of these ideas outlined by Heidegger himself in the early 1960s. Evola blindly rushed into criticism, which *post-factum* renders his perspective weak and at a loss in a number of instances.

Evola noted that the roots of existentialism go back to the "lost generation" that was deeply traumatized by the most recent crisis of the modern world, i.e., the war. He imputed to armchair philosophers a petty-bourgeois way of life as well as, alongside the more active public non-conformists, an overall profanism and engagement to abstractions intrinsic to Western European thinking and cut off from their metaphysical roots. For Evola, existentialism is largely reducible to a form of nihilism, as it appeals to the theme of the "nothing" discovered after the death of the Christian God and the re-posed problem of existing in such a world. For Evola, existentialism in many respects continues the line of Friedrich Nietzsche and Søren Kierkegaard, that is to say a phenomenon of modernity cut off from the metaphysical spirit of Tradition. The ideologist of Traditionalism thus turned to attack what were, in his opinion, the key figures of existentialism: Jean-Paul Sartre, Karl Jaspers, and Martin Heidegger.

In the case of Sartre, Evola addressed the latter's classic theme, the "burden of freedom," that is the thrownness of the individual, lacking any roots in formerly traditional culture, into lonely confrontation with themself, "sentenced to be free." Evola highlights the practically fatalistic and pessimistic tones of freedom in Sartre; for this left-wing French intellectual, freedom is what one is coerced to endure in a world without God. Our Italian thinker contrasts this to accepting freedom as a space of will, in which pain, tragedy, and death can be fully endured and transposed in terms of something greater.

Jaspers is the only one whom Evola mentions on a positive note as being "perhaps the only one among the existentialists to make a few superficial references to 'metaphysics,' confused by him with mysticism."[498] Throughout his numerous articles, Evola on more than one occasion harshly critiqued the relatively popular psychoanalysis and Freudianism of his time, which he called the "psychoanalytical infection" and deemed to be a force destroying European man and his connection with the sacred. Likewise, since his early years, Evola was critical of Christianity overall. Hence the inexplicable, self-contradictory nature of his minimal sympathy for Sartre's very same psychoanalytical existentialism and soft Christian theology

The problem with Evola's (mis)understanding of Martin Heidegger's ideas lies precisely in that he reads Heidegger's views from the period of *Being and Time* entirely through the prism of the extremely popular existentialism of Jean-Paul Sartre and Karl Jaspers. For Evola, Heidegger is of equal value to the latter two, and at times he appears to simply be their epigone. In other words, Evola refers to the Schwarzwaldian thinker as if to a "comma" appended to one of his German friends and one French intellectual, as if together they constituted some common field of ideas and were in solidarity with each other on the whole. In fact, however, the case is utterly the opposite.

Back in 1946-47, Heidegger wrote and then published his iconic "Letter on Humanism" as a response to Sartre's theses. In this text, Heidegger radically demarcates his ideas from

---

498 Evola, *Ride the Tiger*, 79.

Sartre's and from the philosophy of existentialism as a whole. Without a doubt, Heidegger exerted a strong and even decisive influence on Sartre and Jaspers, but their ensuing, independent development of their own ideas led them in directions altogether opposite to the pursuits of Heidegger's project. Consequently, Heidegger considered it necessary to publicly, immediately after the war, distinguish how he did not belong to this fashionable philosophical current. For Heidegger, existentialism remains a kind of metaphysics, and, judging in line with his own philosophy, can in many respects be attributed to one of the intellectual strategies of *das Man*, which means that such leads us astray from understanding the Truth of Being.

More detailed critique and even invective against Jaspers were presented by Heidegger in his later works and in his *Black Notebooks*, which were published long after his death and Evola's. Thus, Evola simply could not have known Heidegger's more detailed issues with Jasper's existentialism. Nevertheless, the substantial divergence between these two Germans' ideas was already widely known throughout closely intertwined intellectual circles in Europe in Evola's time.

Even more erroneous is how Evola attributes to Heidegger, by way of identifying his thought with Sartre's, a perspective that is closed-off to the vertical dimension, and his allegation of Heidegger's "phenomenological agnosticism." The roots of this most crude error lie, once again, in reading Heidegger through Sartre, and in the fact that Evola was fundamentally unfamiliar with Heidegger's detailed and complex theological project as well as Heidegger's views on the role of *mythos* and the sacred in the being of man. In the very same postwar period, however, Heidegger was already publicly professing such perspectives, and he recognized the early experience and exposition of his *Being and Time* to have been unsuccessful and "too phenomenological," even too loaded with "existentiality."

Evola did not grasp the point that is of principal importance to understanding Heidegger's ideas on Being and here-being (*Dasein*), namely, the differentiation between Being (*Sein/Seyn*) and beings (*Seiende*). Evola passes over the most interesting and productive points in the critique of existentialism from theological perspectives. He remarks that "a certain type of existentialism could also lead to another point already established here: that of a positive antitheism, an existential overcoming of the God-figure, the object of faith or doubt."[499] Here, Evola himself figures as an apologist for merging the I, Being, and God (which for him is transcendence) in an apophatic "invisible preference." The difference is that, for Evola, as a radically positioned Traditionalist, what is of principal importance is transcendence, transcending the earthly level and the ordinary through the figure of the Divine and theosis, whereas existentialism and phenomenology are oriented towards the "middle world," to speak in mythological language. An academic phenomenological approach to studying traditions and myths would come to be developed by Mircea Eliade who, like Evola, considered himself a student of the ideas of René Guénon.

We can find similar affirmations of a merging of the self present in the world with the Divine and Being in Christian mysticism, yet elsewhere Evola rightly notes the obvious Advaitist, Eastern, and Neoplatonic correspondences of some of the necessary preconditions for such an "existential project." Namely, this is the need for a primordial principle that sets destiny and the need to remain true to this principle as one's own I. The "unfavorable soil" of existentialism produces a rift in consciousness and the human being between Sartrean existentialism and this need which permeates the whole vertical. For Evola, such a rift is a sign of decline.

Unfortunately, Evola's whole analysis and critique of existentialism has nothing to do with Heidegger and his mature project, which is otherwise rich in all the necessary questions for Traditionalism. It may be affirmed that Evola was not familiar with this project at all and that he did

---
499 Evola, *Ride the Tiger*, 81.

not understand the key methods of the German master's philosophizing. When Evola writes about Heidegger, he is only expressing illusions, emotions, and issues which, while in some instances being genuinely right from a Traditionalist standpoint, pertain to the "populism" of the thundering, left-wing, unmistakably anti-sacred Sartre and his epigones, whose relation to our German thinker is extremely indirect and far-fetched.

At the same time, there is the fact that both Julius Evola and Martin Heidegger belonged to two very tightly interconnected ideological currents which some scholars and adherents consider to have been a single European intellectual field and cauldron in the early 20th century, namely Traditionalism and the Conservative Revolution. Evola and Heidegger also shared a common circle of friends, including Carl Schmitt, Ernst Jünger, etc.

Furthermore, long after Heidegger's death, a handwritten note was discovered among his remaining estate (*Nachlass*) with a quote from the 1935 German edition of Evola's *Revolt Against the Modern World*.[500] This discovery allows us to claim that Heidegger was indeed familiar with one of the most representative books of the philosophy of Traditionalism. Moreover, not only did Heidegger extract a passage from Evola's programmatic book, but he immediately appropriated it for his own interpretation in a way which substantially illuminates the perspectives of these two philosophies in relation to one another. Heidegger excerpted the following thought[501]:

> Wenn eine Rasse die Berührung mit dem, was allein Beständigkeit hat und geben kann — mit der Welt des Seyns — verloren hat, dann sinken die von ihr gebildeten kollektiven Organismen, welches immer ihre Größe und Macht sei, schicksalhaft in die Welt der Zufälligkeit herab.

---

500 See Julius Evola, *Revolt Against the Modern World*, trans. Guido Stucco (Rochester: Inner Traditions, 1995).

501 For the translation and discussion of this fragment, see Collin Cleary, "Heidegger against the Traditionalists" in this volume.

When a race has lost connection with what alone has and can give it constancy – with the world of Beyng, — then the collective organisms formed by it, whatever be their greatness and power, are doomed to sink down into the world of contingency.

This rendition differs substantially from the original passage in Evola's book:

> Wenn eine Rasse die Berührung mit dem, was allein Beständigkeit hat und geben kann — mit der Welt des *"Seins"* — verloren hat, dann sinken die von ihr gebildeten kollektiven Organismen, welches immer ihre Größe und Macht sei, schicksalhaft in die Welt der Zufälligkeit herab: *werden Beute des Irrationalen, des Veränderlichen, des "Geschichtichen," dessen, was von unten und von außen her bedingt ist.*
>
> When a race has lost connection with what alone has and can give it constancy — with the world of *"Being"* — then the collective organisms formed by it, whatever their greatness and power, are doomed to sink down into the world of contingency: *to become prey to the irrational, the changeable, the 'historical,' of what is conditioned from below and from the outside.*[502]

What is immediately striking is Heidegger's change of the word *Sein* to *Seyn*. What gives a race[503] its constancy and stability is not simply being-as-beings or a super-beingful source of the world, but rather, as Heidegger articulates here, the apophatic instance of Beyng-as-nothing. As a classical Traditionalist, Evola upholds Being as the highest form of all being(s), as the transcendent, as the Platonic world of Ideas. Evola advocates the fundamental doctrine of two natures, higher being and the sublunar world of becoming, which constitutes the classical two-level structure of metaphysics. For Heidegger, however, metaphysics and Plato in particular are a principal milestone in the oblivion of Being and the decline of the whole Western world. Already in this point, we can see that Heidegger fundamentally rejects Evola's metaphysical approach on the

---

502 The italics designate the parts which Heidegger edited or omitted.

503 Here it bears clarifying that Evola did not see race in the biological terms of vulgar racism; his works most often treat race as "race of the spirit," equivalent to the classical estates, castes, Varna, or Plato's metallic souls.

one hand, while on the other he immediately adjusts the proportions of this quote in tune with his own train of thought.

Hence also follows the reason why Heidegger omitted the final sentence following the colon: "to become prey to the irrational, the changeable, the 'historical,' of what is conditioned from below and from the outside." For Heidegger, Beyng principally presences historically, especially in the spheres of philosophy and poetry, where the most important words ripen and speak forth, forming the world (*Welt*) in their circles and echoes. Moreover, the being of things is just as fundamentally mutable as culture. The definition of "what is a thing" and "being" can radically differ from culture to culture. Only in the early 21st century has Traditionalism matured to assimilate and begin to operate with the paradigm of ontological pluralism (the plurality of cultures + the plurality of natures) and the linguistic understanding of Tradition, thereby correcting and overcoming some of the implicit Eurocentric ontological and gnoseological premises of classical Traditionalism itself.[504] Besides the "horizontal" plurality of the noetic worlds of different peoples and their traditions, the question can be raised as to the temporal mutability of things and beings, their movement and degeneration, decline, dissolution, and oblivion, as well as the shift from authentic thing to utilitarian simulacrum divorced from any sacred source. In such a case, "mutability" is prefigured into the world as the eschatological due. With respect to the "irrational," which Evola imputes as a negative principle, and into which the sublunar world falls in its divorce from Beyng, here it bears only recalling that Heidegger placed irrationalism on an even lower rung than the dry rationality responsible for the oblivion of Beyng and the *Zeitgeist* of modern thinking.

Striving to hold on to the unchanging without fail, to keep oneself at the point of the immovable principle, in the centre

---

[504] See Askr Svarte, *Tradition and Future Shock: Visions of a Future that Isn't Ours*; idem., *Polemos: The Dawn of Pagan Traditionalism*, trans. Jafe Arnold (PRAV Publishing, 2020). See also Alexander Dugin, "René Guénon: Traditionalism as a Language" in this volume.

within the circle, is, on the whole, quite characteristic of Evola's "personal equation."[505] But Heidegger's structure does not entail a fundamental mutability or mere mutability ("plurality without unity"). In Heidegger's optic, the "immovable" source must be founded in an apophatic instance and be shepherded or guarded by, to use Evola's language, a kind of "elite." One has the impression that, while unmistakably understanding and even directly proclaiming the intention to transcend a personal God towards the apophatic "invisible presence," Evola still regularly slips from the apophatic heights into the cataphatic valley and struggle of values and politics. In this lies one of the qualitative differences between his inner metaphysical orientation, the nature of his soul, and René Guénon's inherent "Brahminical" stake on apophaticism. Of course, neither Guénon nor Evola were integrated into Hinduism or practicing adepts of Vedanta and Tantra. Instead, in this case we are talking about the principles, style, and orientations that were characteristic of their standpoints and thinking.

The American thinker Collin Cleary, an expert on Tantrism and Hegel, points to the naïveté of Traditionalists' notion of the "eternal" or timeless nature of metaphysical tradition. For example, Traditionalists take Plato and Platonism to be the highest, constant form of expressing the ideal order and describing the world of ideas, ignoring the fact that Platonism appeared in an era when the Greek tradition was already in deep decline, and that before Plato there was the thought of the outstanding Presocratics as well as earlier mysteries and cults. Plato is already the Iron Age, but he is voluntaristically exalted as the Sophia Perennis (the Eternal Wisdom). Moreover, across diversely ranging interpretations, especially in Aristotelianism, Plato's philosophy underlies all of the classical and modern socio-political ideologies and doctrines.

Besides their obvious contradictions and mutual critiques, Cleary points out how Guénonian Traditionalism and

---

505 See Julius Evola, *The Path of Cinnabar: An Intellectual Autobiography*, trans. Sergio Knipe (United Kingdom: Integral Tradition Publishing, 2009).

Heideggerian philosophy coincide in many of their assessments of modernity, as both reject the ideas of the Enlightenment, the "reign of quantity" or calculative thinking, uprooted modern cosmopolitanism, the acceleration of time and history in their dissolution, the destruction of hierarchies and the reduction of beings to singular, universal standards, templates, and mechanisation, Cartesian subject-object dualism and the speculative view of the world from the standpoint of absolute objectivity, etc. We can also directly link the cultural crisis of Western-centric civilisation to Heidegger's bored mass of *das Man*[506] and the culture that the latter produce so as to hide from death (in more Traditionalistic language, from their personal and universal eschatology). In the incessant whirl of simulacra and sensations, religions and traditions themselves — even if ultimately credible and authentic in their forms and reconstructions — come to be divorced from Beyng and from authentic Dasein which might speak their myths, and become merely other projections of simulacra and signs onto screens, completely empty, superficial actions and imitations which do not bind anything and which lead nowhere.

Finally, upon attentively and delicately heeding the nuances of Heidegger's view on the nature of the Divinities, their reasons for abandoning the world, and on the question of the relations between the axes of Heaven-Earth, Divinities-Mortals, and Beyng-Sacred-Myth, we can see that Heidegger in many respects had insight into and thought through similar questions to those concerning Traditionalists, but he arrived at them along a different trajectory and likewise offers a different way out.

Cleary puts forth an even more succinct and rich summation of the comparability of Traditionalism and Martin

---

506 The German *das Man* is the impersonal pronoun "anyone" or "they." In Heidegger's works, *das Man* refers to Dasein's inauthentic mode of being-in-the-world, which gives rise to correspondingly inauthentic culture. See Askr Svarte, *Gods in the Abyss: Essays on Heidegger, the Germanic Logos, and the Germanic Myth*, trans. Iliya Koptilin and Daniil Granovskiy (London: Arktos, 2020); idem., *Tradition and Future Shock: Visions of a Future that Isn't Ours*.

Heidegger's philosophy: "while Heidegger is not a Guénonian or Evolian Traditionalist, he is actually *more traditionalist* than the Traditionalists."[507] On the whole, we agree with such an intermediate determination of Heidegger's relation to Traditionalism; furthermore, we seek to bring this "more radically Traditionalist" to its glaring extremes.

In the Russian-speaking space, the largest-scale Traditionalist approach to Martin Heidegger's philosophy has been carried out in the works of Alexander Dugin. Dugin's books on Heidegger are some of the best introductions to the major questions of his philosophy, with all the necessary considerations given for linguistic differences and the problems with translating philosophical terms amidst inevitable semantic shifts.[508] However, beyond his completely correct and unbiased presentation of the Black Forest thinker's main ideas and the trajectories of his forest paths of thinking, Heidegger's fundamental-ontology is important to Dugin for constructing a number of philosophical concepts as well as for his own independent attempt at bringing about a convergence between Heidegger and Traditionalism.

Dugin's most important contribution to developing Heidegger's ideas is his substantiation of the thesis of a plurality of Dasein(s). Heidegger himself habitually reduced Dasein to European man and European structures, which he implied by default while periodically emphasising the special role to be played by the Germans as a people in the "end of one and the beginning of another Western thinking." Dugin moves to recover what otherwise seems to lie waiting on the surface and draws attention to the fundamental and qualitative differences in the forms of life worlds and cultural modes, i.e., the being-in-the-world(s) of different peoples, including

---

507 Cleary, "Heidegger against the Traditionalists".

508 See Alexander Dugin, *Martin Heidegger: The Philosophy of Another Beginning*, trans. Nina Kouprianova (Arlington: Radix / Washington Summit Publishers, 2014). Idem., *Martin Heidegger. Poslednii bog* [Martin Heidegger: The Last God] (Moscow: Department of Sociology of International Relations of Moscow State University / Academic Project, 2014).

those exotic as well as those similar to one another. That is, in different corners of the middle world, in accordance with the differing grammars and semantics of different languages and differences in the deep structures of thinking, *mythoi*, and *logoi*, Dasein exists in different ways which at times are altogether dissimilar. If we take the thesis that "the fate of Europe is the fate of the world" to be true, then the whole diversity of cultures and civilisations should, in the spirit of the modern idea of progress, be reducible to and gravitate towards the Western European path of development and its anthropo-cultural, ontological, and gnoseological paradigm. Rejecting the very idea of a universalism of fate has a long and, without a doubt, truthful and convincing history in European thought itself, one which cannot discount the influence of Heidegger's own critique and relativization of the European Logos' claim to absoluteness.[509] In turn, Dugin strives to demonstrate, and at times does so altogether convincingly, that within the world we are dealing not with one Dasein, but with a multiplicity of Dasein's which approximately correspond to or correlate with the nomenclature of extant peoples and civilizations.[510] There exist different Dasein's— regardless of their degree of "primitiveness" or "development," "barbarism" or "civilizedness." This approach overcomes Heidegger's own implicit universalism or Eurocentrism.

When it comes to the eschatology of Beyng, as in the trajectory outlined by Heidegger throughout his works, we can immediately draw the conclusion that such is a specific trait or erroneous result of Western thinking that is Greek at its core. It cannot be ruled out that there are structural errors

---

509 See Askr Svarte, *Tradition and Future Shock: Visions of a Future that Isn't Ours*.

510 See Dugin's *Noomakhia* series, an outline and excerpts of which are available in English at *Eurasianist Internet Archive* [https://eurasianist-archive.com/item/noomakhia/]. See in particular "The Horizons of Cultures: The Geography of Logoi" [https://eurasianist-archive.com/2019/06/20/noomakhia-geosophy-the-horizons-of-cultures-the-geography-of-logoi/]. See also Alexander Dugin, "Plural Anthropology — The Fundamental-Ontological Analysis of Peoples," trans. Michael Millerman, in Jeff Love (ed.), *Heidegger in Russia and Eastern Europe* (London: Rowman & Littlefield, 2017).

present in other theologies, predetermined by the very vector of Beyng's concealment, which also lead to collapse; but, being Europeans, we must first and foremost figure out ourselves, our destiny, and our position in the world. In this case, the "planetary" decline affecting other, non-European and even non-Indo-European peoples and tribes would be a product of the imposition of a single fate and eschatology through Abrahamic missionarianism, colonialism, and globalism. Insofar as, in one way or another, all "high" mythologies and theologies bear a universal character, and given that traces of eschatological motifs can be found in all tales and myths, we can speak of an antinomian coincidence and paradox of eschatology. Western civilization spreads its oncological ontology and expands its sphere of influence, with its intrinsic alienation and rapid flight into the structures of the *Gestell*[511] and *das Man*, and thereby denies and liquidates the original, unique trajectories of the eschatologies indicated in the myths of different peoples, replacing them and imposing upon all the West's own being-towards-death. At the same time, however, in denying other cultures their own authentic end to existence can by all means be read as a normative variation of a quite harsh and rapid break of eschatology as such. Moreover, insofar as everything in the middle world is condemned to finite and death, this means that the global sunset and decline is still, at any rate, a fulfillment of the due — in one way or another, the due decline comes about. Therefore, the fate of the West is the downgoing (*Untergang*) and dragging of the whole world into the abyss with it. Understanding such a fate, Evola maintained the hope that if Europe is condemned to enter the darkness first, then it has the change of being the first to come out on the other side. In the Traditionalist optic, this corresponds to the renewal of the cycle or the metaphor

---

[511] Heidegger's term *Gestell*, or "Enframing," refers to the particular order and mode of calculating and mechanically producing metaphysical truth that corresponds to the thinking of Modernity, the industrial and post-industrial types of society, and the unbridled flourishing of technology which comes to penetrate the social and human body. See Askr Svarte, *Tradition and Future Shock: Visions of a Future That Isn't Ours*.

of worldwide initiation — after all, passing through death and rebirth is always at the core of initiation.[512] This intention is complementary to and resonant with Heidegger's ideas on history and Another Beginning.

Similarly, for Dugin, the plurality of Dasein(s) and the possibility of Another Beginning are needed to substantiate the fundamental possibility of an independent, original (or "originary"), unique Russian philosophy, one which will not simply be a continuation of or commentary on Western or Eastern philosophy.[513]

In his endeavor to reconcile Heidegger and Traditionalist metaphysics, Dugin places special import on differentiating between two approaches to the ontology and gnoseology of Neoplatonism.[514] He distinguishes one approach which draws on the *Timaeus* and yields a "closed Platonism," i.e., a world of extant idea-beings and extant copy-beings, between which is situated the extant Demiurge-Creator-Being. Such a "closed-off" Platonism deals only with extant beings, albeit very different in their essential qualities, and is therefore "hermetically" sealed off from Nothing and Non-Being. This line is most clearly of all continued in Aristotle's logic, Thomism, ensuing Christian theology (to which the fundamental rift between the Creator and the created world is intrinsic), and post-Christian ontology and gnoseology (where "God is dead").

On the other hand, drawing on Neoplatonism as an original reading of Plato from the standpoint of the *Parmenides*, Dugin points to the Neoplatonists' and especially Plotinus' paradoxical reinterpretation of the key instance of the One. Contrary to Parmenides' thesis that "Being is, Non-Being is not," Plotinus

---

[512] For our part, we insist on an extremely literal reading of this structure: the only chance for "salvation" or "another way" for Europe and the world is through completely, literally dismantling and liquidating the modern, science-centric, industrial, digital civilization along with its culture and anthropological types.

[513] See Alexander Dugin, *Martin Heidegger: Vozmozhnost' russkoi filosofii* [*Martin Heidegger: the Possibility of Russian Philosophy*] (Moscow: Academic Project, 2011).

[514] Dugin, *Martin Heidegger. Poslednii bog.*

and the Neoplatonists rescue the One from the circle of any categories and from any criteria pertaining to beings, which is to say that they understand the One strictly apophatically: the One is the simplest that is not, i.e., it "is" No-thing. This Platonic topography is therefore open on top, constituting an "open Platonism" which maintains the "primordial instance" of the semantic axis of One-Being-Nothing, access to which is possible ecstatically, but not gnoseologically (since any attempt to know the One-as-Nothing rationally leads only to the opposite of knowing the One). The One-Nothing is not divorced from the Intellect and the world of the many (ἕν πολλά), but is immanently co-inherent within.

This Neoplatonism largely inspired the Rhineland mystics, especially Meister Eckhart, whom Heidegger rather reverently references in his works. But Heidegger understood Neoplatonism itself to be a form of ancient mysticism, probably not least because of the late Neoplatonists' emphasis on theurgy, astrology, and magic and their incorporation into a single corpus of emanations. Nevertheless, it is on the basis of such an "open Platonism," to which Heidegger did not pay any attention, that Dugin sees the rightful possibility of a convergence and the possibility of a space for two-directional translation between Heideggerian and Traditionalist philosophy.

For Dugin, Neoplatonism also offers a way for synthesizing Heidegger's philosophy and Orthodox Christian doctrine. Since the Orthodox foundation of the Russian Logos is axiomatic for Dugin, he distinguishes therein a Greek Neoplatonic ground that spans all the way to the Christian mysticism and Sophiology of the Russian Silver Age in Vladimir Solovyov and Frs. Sergei Bulgakov and Pavel Florensky. In addition, Dugin argues that it was none other than the Aristotelian-Thomistic, Catholic branch of Christianity, and not Byzantine-Russian Orthodoxy, that was the focus of Heidegger's critique. Accordingly, Russian Heideggerian philosophy — the Russian Logos as such —

is inevitably reduced to Sophiology, Orthodox theology, and the teachings of the Holy Church Fathers.

The problem with Orthodox Neoplatonism being a bridge and "key" to Heidegger lies at once in three aspects. The first is that Heidegger critiqued not mere individual or strictly Catholic aspects of Christianity, but Christianity's fundamental metaphysical principle of determining God as a being and the principle of the *ens creatum* ("createdness" -> "ready-to-handness") of the world. This dogmatic premise does not depend on any selected branch or on any ensuing development of Christianity, but lies at the core of Christian (and, more broadly, Abrahamic) metaphysics and ontology (or ontotheology) as such.[515] The second lies in that the mystical branch in Orthodox Christianity was not originally intrinsic to the latter, but was constructed and construed as normative (although remaining disputed to this day[516]) only at a much later time. In addition, it is the position of the Church itself that there is no secret, mystical, initiatic, esoteric doctrine within Christianity, whose very distinctive character is its openness to all people and its universal revelation. This allowed the classical Traditionalists to doubt the initiatic component of Christian doctrine and to prefer apocryphal currents or altogether modern Hermitic-occult esoteric traditions from the Renaissance to our days.[517]

Moreover, such "Christian esotericism" stressed by Dugin largely retains and harbors the intellectual and linguistic structures of pre-Christian mysteries and cults, particularly those pertaining to Platonism and Neoplatonism. The very existence of Christian theology's intimate reliance upon and tight boundedness to Platonism and Neoplatonism exposes

---

515 See Askr Svarte, *Polemos*; idem., *Polemos II: Pagan Perspectives*, trans. Jafe Arnold (PRAV Publishing, 2021).

516 It is worth noting that a number of Orthodox Christian theologians and experts have gone so far as to define Dugin's whole philosophy and theological constructions as "marginal" or altogether "heretical."

517 See Askr Svarte, *Polemos*; idem., *Polemos II*.

and divests Christianity itself — and, once again, it is this intertwined ontotheological construction that Heidegger recognized as being that most erroneous foundation underlying Western thinking.

This situation is manifoldly complicated by the fact that already at the Synod of Constantinople in 543, on the orders of Emperor Justinian, the Fifteen Anathemas denounced Platonism in the guise of Origen and his teachings. Even before then, Justinian had already closed down the Platonic Academy in Athens once and for all in 529. In the 11th century, "Hellenic wisdom" was once again anathematized in the guise of the Neoplatonist John Italus. The anathema against Italus, a student of the Neoplatonist Psellus, came in the same century as the Great Schism of 1054, which divided Christianity into the Catholic and Byzantine branches. Despite this divergence, the key anathemas against Platonism and Neoplatonism remain common to all denominations. Disputes over Neoplatonic influence reemerged in judgements on the orthodoxy of the teachings of Meister Eckhart and the Rhineland mystics, the mystical Hesychastic teachings of Gregory Palamas, and among the Catholics Platonism was once again anathematized in the guise of John Scotus Eriugena.

Dugin himself altogether honestly admits both the "smuggled" and partly heretical character of this (Neo-)Platonic line within Christianity, he acknowledges the negative role of creationism as a gateway and "founding father" of Modernity, which in many respects developed as the secular or inverted continuation of creationism's structures, and he also recognizes the definite proximity between Heidegger's numerical structures and pre-Christian archetypes.[518]

---

[518] See Alexander Dugin, *Postfilosofiia: tri paradigmy v istorii mysli* [*Post-Philosophy: Three Paradigms in the History of Thought*] (Moscow: Eurasian Movement, 2009); Idem., *V poiskakh temnogo Logosa: filosofsko-bogoslovskie ocherki* [*In Search of the Dark Logos: Philosophico-Theological Essays*] (Moscow: Academic Project, 2013). See also the footnotes in Dugin, *Martin Heidegger. Poslednii Bog.*

In his fundamental work *Martin Heidegger: The Last God*, Dugin distinguishes four possibilities for the human being to assimilate and take up a relation to the philosophy of the Swabian master. In broad strokes, these options constitute four different "humanities" in the spirit of "race" evoked in the passage that brought together Evola and Heidegger:

> 1. The possibility of being grounded as *Da-sein*, of becoming *Da-sein*'s "grounding founders." Such a person belongs to the "future ones," the *Zu-Künftigen*. Only the "rare" and "few" — philosophers, thinkers, poets, heroes — can be such.
>
> 2. The possibility of being part of a people, i.e., serving as Dasein's surrounding world through directly yet delicately treating beings and the beingful world as natural, near and kin to the people (*prirodnoe*), as that which "sprouts" and "cultivates." Such is the peasant's relation to *Da-sein* and to the world, which holds the keys to the ancient agrarian metaphors that predetermined the structure of the First Beginning of philosophy among the Presocratics (φύσειν-λέγειν, whence originate "physics" and *Logos*).
>
> 3. The possibility of insisting on the old Logos, conservatively upholding previous phases of its movement before its collapse in the face of onsetting nihilism. (This position is doomed, because it is based on fear before the *Untergang* and the knowledge that comes with nihilism).
>
> 4. The possibility of submitting to the energies of nihilism, optimistically rejoicing in a dayless and nightless world, refusing to pay any attention to any of the catastrophic phenomena around us, and resting content with the last crumbs of the disintegrated Logos in the form of improving technologies and primitive corporeal care for oneself (liberalism, globalism, the consumer society, progress).

Until approximately 2013-14, Dugin's philosophical positioning dwelled in the sphere of the first and second anthropological and existential possibilities, but nowadays we are witnessing a conscious retreat or even lapse into apologetics for the third position. In other words, Dugin has moved away from Heideggerian positions and the Traditionalism of Evola's *Ride the Tiger* towards reactionary Modernity, towards mainstream Russian conservatism and political Orthodoxy, and philosophically towards classical metaphysics in its most problematic form, namely, apologetics for Plato and Aristotle against Nietzsche and Heidegger.[519]

We can summate Alexander Dugin's endeavor to work out a convergence between Traditionalism and Heideggerianism thusly: in its premises, it is well-developed, extensive, detailed, and promising, but in its finished, current form, it runs quite contrary to the direct warnings of Heidegger himself as well as to Christian dogma. In the end, this attempt has been thrown and left at an impasse.

In general, appealing to Martin Heidegger's philosophy is a quite commonplace and normative phenomenon among Traditionalists today. Much productive work and preliminary, albeit often superficial, comparisons have been put forth. It can be said that there is an ongoing aspiration or even "longing" to merge or synthesize these two philosophies. This is not without reason: mastering and appropriating Heidegger's philosophy allows for a deeper and broader grounding of the critique of Modernity, even while Traditionalists leave Modernity's metaphysical core in ancient forms of traditional metaphysics untouched.

In the sphere of socio-political and cultural critique, Heidegger's arguments and original methods are employed and draw interest as instruments for political agitation, such as in the discourse of the European New Right. Many different right-wing conservative forces want to incorporate Heidegger into the ranks of their like-minded thinkers, at times without knowing or even delving into his thoughts on the matter of modern political agitation and other such machinations which lead astray from the foremost guiding question of Being.

In the sphere of postwar theology (predominantly Christian — Catholic and Protestant), Heidegger's ideas have also exerted a rather existential-humanistic influence.

---

[519] See Dugin's most recent books: *Internal'nye ontologii. Sakral'naia fizika i oprokinutyi mir* [Internal Ontologies: Sacred Physics and the Overturned World] (Moscow: Direktmedia, 2022); *V prostranstve velikikh snov* [*In the Space of Great Dreams*] (Moscow: Academic Project, 2022).

Contrary to this philosopher's own direct objections, some of his theses on *Dasein*, being-in-the-world, and alienation have been incorporated into Christian theological doctrines. But such attempts exhibit a rather extravagant and voluntaristic character in the spirit of "soft" or "minimal" theology.

Yet, as we can see, despite the indisputable congruence between some of their key evaluations, Heidegger and Traditionalism differ so substantially in their reconstructions of the genesis of the crisis of the modern world and their proposed ways out of it, that the situation in many ways resembles a sharp existential bifurcation of "either-or." As the aspiration to synthesize and reconcile Traditionalist philosophy and Heidegger's fundamental-ontology continues to be discussed among international Traditionalist milieux, it is necessary to raise a bridge between the two. But the uneasy question remains open: Will this bridge connect these two shores of thought, or will it finally transport suffering wayfarers from one shore to the other?[520]

Translated by Jafe Arnold

---

[520] The present text was originally a partial excerpt and condensed summary of a section of my forthcoming book *K Drugomu Mifu* [*Towards Another Myth*] (Russia: Totenburg, 2023). It has been edited and equipped with broader citations especially for this volume.

YURI MAMLEEV'S *FATE OF BEING* AS A RESPONSE TO GUÉNON'S METAPHYSICS

Charlie Smith

Yuri Mamleev (1931–2015) – founding member of the notorious congregation of Moscow metaphysicians known as the "Yuzhinskii Circle" and inimitable sage of the 1960s Soviet underground – posed the following question in his premier metaphysical tract, *The Fate of Being*:

> [C]ould there be something on the Periphery [...] which is "absent" at the Center? Put more aptly, is there something there which is metaphysically valuable and which the Center lacks? Perhaps some exclusive metaphysical possibility which cannot be found in the blinding rays of the Center's light (for Light can blind)?[521]

In a strictly conditional sense – if by "Center" we understand the supreme divine reality and by "Periphery" we understand the illusory manifestations of that reality – one could call Mamleev a metaphysical "nihilist." But he may only be described as such insofar as he calls for an orientation toward radical nothingness: a meta-metaphysics (or a 'pataphysics[522] by other means). One might call him a "positive nihilist" who does not reject the hierarchy of divine principles anarchically, but

---

521 Yuri Mamleev, *Sud'ba bytiia: za predelami induizma i buddizma* (Moscow: Enneagon, 2006), 86.

522 A term coined by Alfred Jarry in his novel *Exploits and Opinions of Dr. Faustroll, Pataphysician*, 'pataphysics is "the science of that which is superinduced upon metaphysics, whether within or beyond the latter's limitations, extending as far beyond metaphysics as the latter extends beyond physics. ... 'Pataphysics will be, above all, the science of the particular, despite the common opinion that the only science is that of the general. 'Pataphysics will examine the laws governing exceptions, and will explain the universe supplementary to this one." Alfred Jarry,, *Exploits & Opinions of Dr. Faustroll, Pataphysician: A Neo-Scientific Novel* (Exact Change, 1996), 21.

rather ascends them to reach his most authentic metaphysical habitation before then turning back to regard the grossest, most irrational reaches of the metaphysical Periphery, beyond which the antithesis to the "Supreme Center" beckons him to the unknown and unknowable "outside."

I argue that we can discern the following features in Mamleev's metaphysical doctrine and practice: (1) a simultaneous systematicity and idiosyncrasy conditioned by the inherent alienation of Russian metaphysical thinkers within the Soviet Union, in addition to the conditions of modernity as a whole; (2) an adherence to the precepts of the twentieth-century metaphysical school known as Traditionalism, founded by René Guénon (1886–1951), which holds the Hindu doctrine of *Advaita Vedānta* to be the chief structural authority of metaphysics; (3) an emphasis on total identity between the highest vedic metaphysical principle (Supreme Oneness) and the Self (the Supreme I), which is expressed in the non-dualist form of *Vedānta* as "*Ātmā is Brahma*" and by Mamleev as "I = I"; (4) a subsequent emphasis on directing the supreme Self back toward the uttermost Periphery of the manifest worlds where, through contemplation of the negative moments of death and suffering, one may gain passage through "tears" in the screen of the physical world into something absolutely alien to the Supreme I – the object of what then becomes a meta-metaphysical gnosis; and, finally, (5) active realization of this process through the literary method which Mamleev has coined "metaphysical realism."

In elucidating these moments of Mamleev's sur-apocryphon, *The Fate of Being* (composed between the late 1960s and 1997), I will also consider the possible connections this text bears to the theogonic notion of *Ungrund* as formulated by Jacob Boehme (1575–1624) and subsequently interpreted by Nikolai Berdiaev (1874–1948), whom Mamleev numbers among the most important Russian philosophers in questions of metaphysical reality, and who may quite possibly have served as a vital inspiration for the most unique component of Mamleev's metaphysics: his so-called "Final Doctrine."[523]

In the opening section of *Fate of Being*, Mamleev stresses that the "spiritual situation" of unofficial Soviet culture in the 1960s and 1970s is the origin from which his entire metaphysics proceeds:

> Everyone sought paradoxical solutions. Even the modern situation of humanity was perceived as a paradox thanks to its absurdity. And one could only find an exit from absurdity (for even the everyday is absurd – it is almost as though nothing avoided absurdity in the twentieth century) in the extremities of paradox and marginality.[524]

The impetus for any metaphysical search, he claims, was not only a recognition of the absurdity of Soviet (and, more importantly, "modern") life, but also the possible importance and value that this absurdity might hold. It was in search of marginal realities that Mamleev and his cohorts in the Yuzhinskii Circle first began to discover mystical tracts at the Lenin Library in Moscow, where they encountered certain texts regarding eastern metaphysics and western esotericism.[525] Mamleev relates how, at the very peak of the Thaw, the Soviet authorities were so assured of their triumph over "obscurantist" ideas that they had ultimately decided to make these previously forbidden collections available to the public.

In addition to these discoveries, Mamleev claims that his milieu had already more or less established their own idiosyncratic form of metaphysics which they then referred to as the "I Religion." As he explains, the main source of this "faith" was intuitively "derived from a primal inner reality (within me)" and that "the 'personal' principle of this faith" was provided to them in an "*a priori*" manner:

> It was given to me at birth. And only afterward, in recognizing this reality, have I discovered the being of faith. As a result, this is

---

523 Mamleev, *Sud'ba*, 20.

524 Mamleev, *Sud'ba*, 26.

525 Yuri Mamleev, *Vospominaniia* (Moscow: Traditsiia, 2017), 48.

not a religion of Revelation. If one likes, it is a religion of Internal Reality.[526]

The object of veneration, as one might gather, is the "I" itself; this "I," however, is not the immediate "ego" of a given person, but rather the inherent selfhood that subtends it in the causal order. This is the "Supreme I," which:

> contains the absolute fullness of reality and transcendence; at the same time, it is the personal I of the believer, his own self-arriving [*samogriadushchee*]; and this moment is the key to the mystical secret of I-ness. This understanding of one's personal I as the sole reality renders the concept of God as separate from the I of reality meaningless.[527]

Ultimately, Mamleev discards the label of "religion" as a description of this metaphysical approach. He instead describes his variety of what may be called a meta-metaphysics as a third path – beyond religion and metaphysics – which allows one to "'[enter]' the transcendent sphere, which rests on an internal, metaphysical, [...] given (reality), inherent to a particular person or group of people."[528]

In its final compositional form, the *Fate of Being* is intertextually bound up with René Guénon's central 1925 treatise on metaphysics, *Man & His Becoming According to the Vedānta*. While Guénon's explication of the Hindu doctrine of *Advaita Vedānta* – absolute identity between the supreme Self of man (*Ātmā*) and the supreme metaphysical Oneness (*Brahma*)[529] – is a crucial component of Mamleev's text, the concepts of the *Vedānta* neither exhaust nor enclose those of the latter doctrine. Mamleev acknowledges Guénon's Traditionalist position, which holds that *Advaita Vedānta* is the most purely metaphysical doctrine and, therefore, the

---

526 Mamleev, *Sud'ba*, 31.

527 Mamleev, *Sud'ba*, 33.

528 Ibid., 42.

529 René Guénon, *Man and His Becoming According to the Vedanta*, trans. Richard C. Nicholson (Hillsdale: Sophia Perennis, 2001), 74; 143.

authority in all metaphysical questions[530], but does not see "metaphysics" as the ultimate horizon of knowledge; rather, the supreme metaphysical identity must first be acquired through "God-realization" or identification with *Ātmā* as the first step toward an encounter with something beyond metaphysics. Therefore, Mamleev takes great pains to solidify his position with regard to Traditionalism:

> [T]hat which I have explained can hardly be said to 'contradict' Tradition. On the other hand, my doctrine represents an original point of departure which allows me to 'gaze' at the Absolute from the perspective of 'my own' self-being.[531]

The Fate of Being is a "metaphysical" doctrine in contrast with religion, which maintains the duality between God and humanity. Mamleev rejects the religious notion of a "Creator," conceived as separate from creation, writing:

> Metaphysics is much broader than any theological conceit. The insufficiency of such theological doctrines (despite their relative value) is the result of their rationality and, sometimes, their anthropomorphism. They often even propose some kind of 'goal' or even 'plan' of creation, while on a deeper level of understanding the creation is above any conception of a 'goal' (at least in our understanding of the word). Moreover, Divinity is higher than Reason and has the unimpeachable "right" to exercise its metaphysical 'arbitrariness.'[532]

However, the operative distinction between Mamleev's meta-metaphysics and Guénon's metaphysics is that the Guénon treats identification with the metaphysical Center as the end of all knowledge, whereas Mamleev sees it only as a means of returning to a Periphery that has been fundamentally transformed through the perspective of that Center.

If, as Guénon holds, "supreme Knowledge is in its essence incommunicable so that none can attain to it save by himself

---

530 Ibid., 1.

531 Mamleev, *Sud'ba*, 81.

532 Mamleev, *Sud'ba*, 84.

alone,"[533] this gives Mamleev his sanction for autarchic metaphysical exploration; the non-dualistic *Vedānta* is by its very nature autarchic since it holds that there is no gulf between God and he who bears His divine "image." "*Ātmā*," or the Supreme Self, is that by which "all things are manifested, and which is not itself manifested by anything [...]"[534] – that which is beyond determination while determining that which it manifests. The order of manifestation (to be understood not in temporal sequence, but rather as a causal chain) begins with *Ātmā* itself, which is entirely unmanifested while enclosing all possibilities of manifestation; the movement from non-manifestation to manifestation is constituted by a "ray" projected from *Ātmā*, which is Pure Consciousness itself (or *"Chit"*); the first manifestation is formless – this is the substantial matrix or ground upon which forms take shape, known as *"Prakṛti"*; the determination or essential cause which *Prakṛti* receives from *Ātmā* is called *"Puruṣa"*; it is from the operation of *Puruṣa* on *Prakṛti* that the formal manifestations emerge; within formal manifestation, the first to arise is of a subtle nature – the "living soul" or *"Jīvātmā"*; from the soul then comes the crudest of all manifestations – the physical body.[535] This model describes an arrangement of manifested "envelopes" which all depend on the Supreme Self, but which, in relation to it, have no reality. *Ātmā* (*qua Brahma*) is:

> 'without duality,' and [outside of it] is nothing, either manifested or unmanifested. [A]nything which leaves something outside of itself cannot be infinite, being limited by that very thing which it excludes; and thus the World, taking this expression as meaning the whole of universal manifestation, is only distinguishable from *Brahma* in an illusory manner, while on the contrary *Brahma* is absolutely 'distinct from that which It pervades,' [...] and [...] universal manifestation in its entirety is rigorously nil in relation to [*Brahma's*] Infinity.[536]

---

533 Guénon, *Man and His Becoming*, 17.

534 Ibid., 51.

535 Guénon, *Man and His Becoming*, 54.

536 Ibid., 72-3.

As Mamleev assures us, he does not contradict this principle; but it is this nil – this absurdity of metaphysics – which nonetheless becomes his object.

The majority of *The Fate of Being* – in elaborating both the "I Religion" of the Yuzhinskii Circle and the doctrine of *Advaita Vedānta* – turns out to be the basis for Mamleev's explicit metaphysical doctrine – "The Final Doctrine." It should be noted that this "doctrine" is necessarily speculative; it has not "arrived" at its conclusion, which is to say that it is constantly approaching its object, which is ultimately unknowable and, by definition, obscure. In a gesture of what could almost be called "reverse sublimation," Mamleev sets this final movement in the outermost reaches of manifestation, at the level of the crudely embodied human being:

> The idea of the truly transcendental (as opposed to the falsely transcendental, based on non-knowledge) is some kind of strange, faceted stone of human being. One may truly say that man is always striving to push past the edges of what he has achieved, beyond the boundaries of that which he has realized… But can one go beyond God, beyond the Absolute (especially when, through God-realization, he identifies himself with God)?[537]

For Mamleev, it is as though transcendence itself supersedes God (or, in other words, as though transcendence is the ground for God). But, in this sense, transcendence is never a *fait accompli*. On the contrary, what Mamleev calls "true transcendence" is dynamic and ever active, while remaining an eternal principle. As he writes, "[the eternally transcendent] must [...] lie beyond God as One, and beyond all that comprises Reality, as well as that upon which Reality rests."[538] Whereas the metaphysical "Center" constitutes absolute Reality, the Periphery constitutes an extreme boundary – a pale reflection – of that Reality, beyond which "nothing can exist." But, on the very strength of the negative power of words to allude to things that are not, Mamleev finds an

---

537 Mamleev, *Sud'ba*, 89.

538 Ibid., 90.

exit into something which is the other of Reality. He refers to this Other as the "Abyss," and describes his Final Doctrine as a means of making contact with it:

> [O]ne must tear himself away from his absolute, eternal, and primordial foundation after having realized it. The first stage of this separation involves a return from the sphere of the realized Absolute into the world which lies on the Periphery of Being, for it is precisely there (and not in the triumphant fullness of the Absolute) where one will find "holes" leading into true Darkness – the Abyss beyond the Absolute. It is in this act that we learn the supreme meaning of our limited world's being and creation: for it is not in the blinding light of the Absolute, but precisely in the world of suffering and negation that this breakthrough into the Abyss becomes possible.[539]

In this scheme, all of the apparent negatives of manifested life are inverted into positives: suffering, death, and privation are no longer foreclosures on existence, for they have become howling doorways into that which the Absolute excludes. If the Absolute excludes nothing due to its status as the central locus of Reality, then it is nothing – the absolute other of the Supreme One – which these carnal catastrophes allow one to enter.

If the main premise of *Advaita Vedānta* can be condensed into the formula "*Ātmā* is *Brahma*" (or, in Mamleev's notation I = I), then the Final Doctrine disrupts the circle of identity as a means of transcending it:

> [I]n the Abyss – the trans-darkness – there can be no principle of self-correspondence (which is the principle of being). It is as if everything becomes the beyond of itself. This utter beyond-ness in relation to the Self (the absolute absence of immanence) suggests, among other things, the absence of being. And it is "beyond-ness [*potustoronnost'*]" which defines a new principle – that of Night. If the highest form of self-correspondence and being can be expressed in the formula I = I then, in the Abyss, one could imagine the formula I = I ≠ I. This means that, even though the eternal I is preserved (the first part of the formula), this identity is undone in the Abyss. The formula I ≠ I refers to a false identification (as

---

539 Ibid., 92

when one falsely identifies with one's body); but, more than this, it alludes to the fact that the principle of self-identification is violated in general and that that which lies on the other side of the I is not the I itself (as in the usual form of self-identification), but is that which is not.[540]

If, at an earlier stage, Mamleev has asked whether the Periphery possesses something which the Center lacks, then here he has provided an answer of sorts. Because the Center possesses absolute being ($I = I$), it does not lack being; one may invert this idea as follows: because the Center does not possess absolute non-being ($I \neq I$), it lacks the opposite of being. And yet one cannot approach the Abyss as something paradoxically positive without first achieving God-realization; only after having achieved absolute being can the Supreme I recognize its lack of absolute non-being, hence $I = I \neq I$.

This picture of meta-metaphysics, if one may indeed use such an expression, is in many ways reminiscent of the concept of *Ungrund*, expounded by Jacob Boehme in his later corpus – especially in his exegetical magnum opus concerning the Mosaic Genesis, *Mysterium Magnum* (1623). Such a comparison would not be arbitrary, as it is precisely to this concept that Nikolai Berdiaev devoted an essay[541], seeing it as a category of metaphysical freedom; and throughout his doctrinal texts – *The Fate of Being*[542] and *Russia Eternal*[543] – Mamleev names Berdiaev as one of the few essentially Russian philosophers.

As Boehme writes in the opening pages of *Mysterium Magnum*, "When I consider what God is [...] He is the will of the abyss."[544] It is that core principle of God to which Boehme refers as the "Great Mystery." Further, in a Johannine key, he

---

540 Mamleev, *Sud'ba*, 94-5.

541 Nikolai Berdiaev, "Iz etiudov o Ia. Beme. Etiud I. Ucheniie ob Ungrund", *Put'* 20 (1930), 47-79.

542 Mamleev, *Sud'ba*, 20.

543 Yuri Mamleev, *Rossiia vechnaya* (Moscow: Eksmo, 2011), 100-16, passim.

544 Jacob Boehme, *Mysterium Magnum* (Hermetica, 2007), 1.

goes on to say that "the Word is the will of the abyss [...] wherein the origin of eternal life is."[545] And when Berdiaev applies an interpretation to these initially cryptic phrases, he qualifies that this abyss – an integral part of God's nature – is fundamentally "irrational."[546] The term *"Ungrund"* can be directly translated into English as "Unground" or "Groundless Ground." Already, this word seems to contain a rational contradiction since, like the famous Freudian discussion of the notions *"Heimlich"* and *"Unheimlich,"* both a thesis and an antithesis are present within it. As Berdiaev claims:

> Boehme was the first, in the history of thought belonging to the new age, to make a discovery which would later play a massive role in German idealism - that one can only uncover the true nature of things by means of the other which opposes them. Light cannot be understood without darkness, nor can good without evil or the spirit without the resistance of matter.[547]

Boehme very clearly evokes the abyss of *Ungrund* in terms of a kind of "will," and Berdiaev sees this will as the very precondition for being itself, to include the being of God – and so *Ungrund* is construed not only as the basis of cosmogony, but also of theogony. This freedom, Berdiaev suggests, is neither a psychological nor an ethical category, but rather "a metaphysical doctrine concerning the original basis of being":

> For [Boehme], freedom is not the foundation of man's moral responsibility or a regulation of man's relationship with God and with his fellows, but an explanation of the genesis of being and, moreover, the genesis of evil as both an ontological and cosmological problem.[548]

In this light, we might also say that Mamleev's interest in the "Abyss" beyond absolute Being is equally provoked by the question of freedom and of the evils of manifest existence.

---

545 Ibid., 3.

546 Berdiaev, "Iz etiudov", 52.

547 Ibid., 53.

548 Berdiaev, "Iz etiudov", 67.

Whereas Boehme regards this metaphysical freedom as the precedent of creation, however, Mamleev approaches the abyss from the other direction, pushing out against the farthest boundaries of this illusory creation in an attempt to reach the primordial ground outside of being.

It is at this juncture that we move from the doctrinal aspects of Mamleev's meta-metaphyics to the practical side. After all, a theoretical discourse on matters such as these can only go so far in actually approaching the Abyss. More important than explicitly formulated ideas in this regard are images themselves which, as Mamleev tells us, possess "many planes and [are] more paradoxical than a simple thought. Therefore, the literary text is often more profound, metaphysically and philosophically, than a strictly philosophical text (or the two are at least equal in value)."[549] The emblematic image of the Final Doctrine is "the night with a bolt of lightning flashing in it (lightning being the symbol of the immortal 'I')."[550] This Mamleev calls his "Eye into the Abyss," a novel "organ" which, though only possible after one has achieved God-realization, can only be grown at the Periphery, where it is conditioned by its inevitable corruption – its immediate contact with a negation that "annihilates all common notions of sight."[551] Guénon, in tracing the Sanskrit root "*vid*," from which both "knowledge [*vidyā*]" and "*Vedānta*" derive, also notes that it is the basis for the word "lightning [*vidyut*]," which is the result of the relationship between light and sight. As he writes, "the flash of lightning illumines the darkness; the latter is the symbol of "ignorance [*avidyā*]" while knowledge is an inner illumination."[552] In a similarly imagistic fashion, Boehme writes in his *Six Theological Points* (1620) that:

> the eternal Unground out of nature is a will, like an eye wherein nature is hidden; like a hidden fire that burns not, which exists

---

549 Mamleev, *Sud'ba*, 100.

550 Ibid., 95.

551 Ibid.

552 Guénon, *Man and His Becoming*, 143.

and also exists not. It is not a spirit, but a form of spirit, like the reflection in the mirror. For all the form of a spirit is seen in the reflection or in the mirror, and yet there is nothing which the eye or mirror sees; but its seeing is in itself, for there is nothing before it that were deeper there.[553]

And so, just as God's existence is due to his freedom to exist, our knowledge is unlimited as a result of our untrammeled freedom to see by means of the multifaceted and unlimited image. Mamleev calls this specific orientation toward artistic (and, more specifically, literary) activity "Metaphysical Realism." One may call this not a literary method, but a metaphysico-literary doctrine, as to compose a metaphysical-realist text is to do no less than to draw near to the Abyss beyond being. Mamleev describes the task of the metaphysical realist as follows:

> [T]he metaphysical realist must strive to be anything but a romantic; he must be a super-realist [*sverkhrealist*], who takes as his point of departure a deep knowledge of visible life (a knowledge far deeper than that required of the average realist of the nineteenth century). However, this knowledge of visible life must only serve the metaphysical realist as the initiating moment, after which his penetration into a more harrowing reality must develop. The chief tendency of creativity, therefore, announces its demands even in the depiction of everyday situations in life: there is no place here for the minutiae of human existence, as these details do not provide 'windows' into the deeper reality; essentially, for the metaphysical realist, visible life should become a symbol or analogue of the highest (or alternatively, the most infernal) realities; yet these realities (given that the author is, after a fashion, a 'realist'), are not received only through allusions, in semi-shades as with the symbolists of the *fin-de-siècle*, but rather must present themselves nakedly, visibly, and overwhelmingly while pushing the depiction of lower reality to the background and presenting the reader with a vision of abysses laid bare...[554]

In a manner both literal and confoundingly obscure, Mamleev demonstrates this premise in his fictional counterpart to

---

553 Jacob Boehme, *Six Theosophical Points* (Ann Arbor: University of Michigan Press, 1965), 12.

554 Mamleev, *Sud'ba*, 101-2.

Yuri Mamleev's Fate of Being as a Response to Guénon's Metaphysics

The Fate of Being – a 1992 text entitled *The Final Comedy*. In a preamble to a series of increasingly putrid vignettes, a character whose name translates into English as "Worldeater [*Miroedov*]," having sequestered his corpse in its inhumed coffin, becomes enamored with its inert, decaying rump which "[blocks out] God with its mass."[555] At another moment, as he looks upon his corpse, it appears to "[crack] open its eye and, with this black eye that [seems] to have collapsed into an abyss, [looks] upon that which is absolutely incomprehensible."[556] Finally, spreading out above this paradoxical scene which is only visible to the deceased is the "sky – the black, bottomless sky of hell with its gaps opening up to the zenith, gaps which [extend] into the supreme darkness and [pull] even the gods in after them."[557]

---

[555] Yuri Mamleev. *Posledniaia komediia: Sobraniie sochinenii*, vol. 2 (Moscow: Eksmo, 2017), 12.

[556] Ibid., 13.

[557] Ibid.

TRADITION AND TRADITIONALISM IN CONTEMPORARY SLAVIC NATIVE FAITH: MY SUBJECTIVE VIEW

Veleslav Cherkasov

I.

Tradition (from the Latin *trādō* — "transmit"), in the literal etymological sense of the word, means that which is "handed along," "passed down," or "transmitted" — from generation to generation, from ancestors to descendants, from antiquity to the present.

In the modern world, however, Tradition (precisely with a capital "T") is more like that which could have been transmitted, but which, as a consequence of a number of objective and subjective reasons, has instead ended up being either partially lost or not received or heard by its heirs and descendants.

In this sense, the emergence of such a phenomenon as Traditionalism, predominantly philosophical in nature, was the consequence of individuals and cultures recognizing the tragic rift between Tradition and traditions on the one hand, and between the world of Tradition and the modern world which has evermore rapidly been "burning bridges" with the traditional past.

II.

In contemporary Russia, "classical" Traditionalism, based on the works of René Guénon, Julius Evola, Mircea Eliade, Frithjof Schuon, Ananda Coomaraswamy, and other 19th-20th-century thinkers, became relatively widely-known (outside of specialist circles) only in the 1990s, primarily thanks to the works of the prominent Russian philosopher and public figure Alexander Dugin. Dugin is, by all accounts, the first Russian Traditionalist philosopher, and his historic significance lies above all in that he has paradoxically gone beyond philosophy as well as Traditionalism (which happens to be the norm in Russia, by the way). Dugin has convincingly articulated that the mainstay of the true philosopher in the modern, de-sacralized world is the "radical self" within, not external clerical vestments.[558] Dugin's philosophy has brilliantly substantiated this idea, all the while as his personal religious leanings have shown just how pitiful a sight a philosopher becomes when the church *fofudya*[559] turns into a straitjacket for his freedom-loving spirit. I first met Dugin in the mid-1990s, when this philosopher, still beardless and without an Old Believer's tunic, delivered brilliant lectures at the Mayakovsky Museum in Moscow, not far from Lubyanka. The writer Yuri Mamleev and the philosopher Geydar Dzhemal could be seen there, as could representatives of right-wing ideology not yet banned in Russia. Ever since then, I have unwaveringly respected Dugin as a Traditionalist thinker despite the fact that our ideological and life paths have long since diverged.

Besides Dugin, among the other Russian Traditionalists I've happened to meet in my time, there is Vadim Shtepa, the author of the book *Inversion*, which in the late 1990s seemed

---

[558] Assessing Dugin's activism, especially on the political stage in recent years, goes beyond the scope of this small article.

[559] The term *"fofudya"* refers to a type of Eastern Orthodox Christian clerical clothing. In the present usage, the term bears the pejorative meaning of "Orthodox straightjacket" and refers to disingenuous Christian fanaticism. The term can be seen as a counterpart to the pejorative slang *"dolboslavie"* used to refer to marginal, New Ageist simulacra of Slavic Native Faith.

to many to represent a possible alternative to the then rising "Orthodox Christian Duginism," but which ultimately ended up being practically forgotten by the adherents of "Russian" clerical pseudo-traditionalism inverted by the peculiarities of national religious demagogy.

Perhaps it is also worth mentioning here the Traditionalist *skomorokh*[560] Oleg Fomin, who passed away young, and his journal *Bronze Age*, which brought together a passion for marginal poetry, the conspirological works of Vladimir Karpets, a genius close to insanity, and medieval Western European alchemy in the interpretation of Fulcanelli. Fomin called himself an "Orthodox Christian fascist," yet he gladly printed my pagan-themed verses in his journal. He considered Dugin to be a latent pagan, Geydar Dzhemal to be a scumbag, Russian culture to be a form of dual-faith, and myself to be at once a secret Khlystian "prophet" and a Bespopovets Old Believer, which he said with a certain malevolent salacity that I didn't understand at the time.

In 1995, Anton Platov, a runologist and scholar of the Northern (Nordic) tradition, began publishing the almanac *Myths and Magic of the Indo-Europeans*, which included articles by various authors on the sacred traditions of the ancient Celts, Germanics, and Slavs. The 9th and 10th issues of the almanac that came out in 2000 and 2002 featured some of my own works on the reborn Slavic tradition (an article on the name of the Rodoliubie community) and on the ancient Scandinavian tradition (the article "Viking Treasures and Nordic Fortune"). Although Platov called himself a "Traditionalist," he imparted this term with a different meaning than the Guénonian or Duginian one, and he treated the bearded Orthodox Christians of Dugin's milieu with undisguised irony. Unlike the writings of Dugin, Shtepa, and Fomin, Anton Platov's works went on to influence the emergence and development of contemporary Slavic Native Faith (*Rodnoverie*).

---

560 The *skomorokhi* were medieval Slavic "jesters," musicians, and actors.

III.

In 1999, one of my early books, entitled *Tradition*, saw the light of day and was the first in Russia to shed light on "classical" Traditionalism from the perspective of Slavic paganism. The book was a resounding slap in the face not only to the Orthodox *fofudya*-wearers and lumpen-traditionalists on church parvises, but also to the post-Soviet space's crafty, turban-wearing predators who were then beginning to sink their teeth into the decrepit flesh and bones of Tradition with the aim of grabbing fatter pieces for their own benefit, tearing them out of the teething snouts of the watchdogs of agonizing KGB-ish Orthodoxy. The programmatic article that opened *Tradition*, "We, Pagans…", which I wrote in 1998, had the following to say in particular:

In presenting to readers this compilation devoted to Paganism, we should first and foremost make sure that both the authors and the readers understand the term "Paganism" in more or less the same way. It is natural for different people to have different opinions on such complex (or such simple…?) subjects as Religion, Spirituality, etc. (It suffices to recall just how different are the interpretations of the notion of "God" in different people's words). But in order for an idea to be received as adequately as is possible for its exposition, it is necessary to have a clear-cut representation of precisely what meaning the authors impart to the term they use. We will not delve into speculations on the conditions of cognizing the world as such, the capacity to understand one another (and not one's own interpretation of another), etc. etc. — we will immediately proceed to the point.

And so, Paganism. Before giving a positive definition of this term, let us consider a negative definition, i.e., we will point out what, in our opinion, Paganism is not (or, in the very least, what it is not limited to).

(1). First of all, Paganism is not a "return to the past," it is not a chronological return backwards, but rather the restoration of the

mystical (and mythological) connection with the sacred Principle (proceeding from the cyclical conception of history), the Eternal Return to the supra-temporal Source of Tradition, a rupture in the "sick infinity" of profane time and the reunification of the human being with supra-individual, sacred, Mythological reality (merging with the Archetype of the Principle). In other words, Paganism is not a return to the human past, but reunion with the Divine Eternal Present which, in fact, is not originally divorced from each of us, but which we have "forgotten" —, i.e., we have "forgotten" our indissoluble connection with it (in this, in essence, lies what Advaita-Vedanta calls avidya or "ignorance"). We are all primordially Pagans, people of Tradition, God is in all of us, and we are primordially He Himself ("Atman is Brahman"), but we have "forgotten" this in the meanwhile...

(2). Nor should Paganism, the primordial, integral Tradition that arises out of the very nature of things (being the SELF-revelation of the Divine through the nature of everything that exists, which is ultimately the manifestation of the Divine Itself), be equated with one or another array of folk superstitions generated by ignorance and the limitations of the human mind (as well as ontological ignorance, avidya, or the lack of direct knowledge of one's own true — Divine — nature and the nature of everything that exists). It could be said that Tradition manifests itself in the world in correspondence with the level of consciousness of its bearers. Therefore, whoever equates the integral Tradition with primitive folk superstitions is only affirming the fact of their consciousness' "enslavement" on the corresponding level of development. In truth, whoever blasphemes God does not blaspheme Him, but their own limited notions about Him...

(3). It is also impossible to agree with the argument that Paganism is a product of primitive consciousness. In our Iron (Black) Age, in the epoch of maximal remove from the Golden Age of the celebration of the Spirit, in this age in which all sacred (Spiritual) values have been subjected to monstrous profanation, inversion, and degradation, everything genuinely Traditional is declared to be "primitive" while the total degeneration around us is held to be evolution and development. Is it any wonder, then, that sacred Antiquity is presented by modern "philosophers" (in love with the "wisdom of this age") as a state of the deepest barbarism and savagery, while modern "civilized savagery" is presented as the pinnacle of development? Despite this, Tradition cannot disappear and degrade completely, for it comes to us not along the horizontal plane of matter, but by the vertical of the Spirit. In other words, Tradition is primordially above human delusions, and therefore cannot be finally absorbed by them. One can always be a Pagan, a person of Tradition, in any era and in any historical (or any other) conditions, because the connection with tradition is determined by inner factors (i.e., degree of SELF-consciousness), not external ones.

(4). Paganism does not divide the ONE reality into self-contained opposites. Certainly, it knows the division into the "sacred" and the "profane," but this division is not ontological, not essential, but pertains to the sphere of limited human perception. The world in and of itself is not divided into "right" and "left," "good" and "evil," "above" and "below." These divisions are the products of a perception that is clouded by ignorance and separates itself from the world, separates the world from God, and separates God from the true nature of man and everything that exists, i.e., such a perception evaluates the world exclusively from the position of its own conditioned "I" ("ego"). At the heart of the world, there are not two opposite principles, but ONE DIVINE PRINCIPLE of which these other elements are manifestations...

(5). Paganism's manifestations in the world are always national, although Paganism as such (as the Principle) cannot be reduced to any national idea. Paganism, being the natural, primordial, foundational religiosity of man, can never be completely absorbed by the unique national selfhood and singularity of any people. Of course, different peoples (not to mention races) embody the principles of the integral Tradition in their national cultures in different ways, but despite this, Pagans of different nationalities will more easily find a common language with each other than with the followers of the various "world religions" (which are founded not on the Primordial One Tradition, but on the individual opinions of their founders). It is therefore no coincidence that the Pagan world knew no "religious wars" in the form that they have always and are still being waged by the adherents of the "world religions"...

(6). Paganism does not separate the Creator and creation with an insurmountable abyss; it does take the world to be "created out of nothing." Instead, it understands the world to be a manifestation of the Divine. (However, the Divine, being indefinable in Essence, might be correlated not only with the ABSOLUTE FULLNESS of EVERYTHING, for everything originates in IT, but also with the ABSOLUTE EMPTINESS of NOTHING, for the DIVINE is not some-thing). In other words, Paganism postulates the idea of manifestationism, not creationism — i.e., not the creation of the world by God, but the manifestation of God through the world (whereby God is not identical to the world and is not exhausted by it, although the nature of everything that exists, including the human being, is, without a doubt, recognized to be Divine). In Paganism, thus, man is not a "servant of God" (which would be possible only upon completely equating man with his corporeal form, which, unlike the immortal Spirit, is His instrument that occupies a subordinate position; whereas from the point of view of Paganism, man can in no way be reduced to his corporeal, energetic, sensual and thinking shells, which are the four "machines" governed by the Spirit, that is by man HIMSELF). Man is a part of God Himself and is identical to the Whole in potentiality ("TAT TVAM ASI" — "THAT [BRAHMAN] ART THOU THYSELF [ATMAN]")...

(7). Paganism annuls any contradiction between monotheism and polytheism, for it postulates the idea of the ONE PRINCIPLE manifest through multiplicity. Thus, all the Gods of Paganism are in essence personifications of various aspects of the ONE PRINCIPLE, that WHICH keeps the world from returning to the state of primordial Chaos, which would be irreversible if the world was ruled by a multiplicity of separate, personal Gods.

One could truly endlessly write about various aspects of the integral Tradition (which covers all spheres of being without exception) which have mistakenly been identified by some thinkers (who have lost connection with Tradition) with the Whole in all of its fullness, whereby one or another individual aspect of Tradition is absolutized. All of these enumerations are not alien to Tradition, but are merely incomplete "lists" of the constituent parts of the That Which qualitatively Is more complex than all individual opinions that simplify (and thereby paradoxically complicate) the actual, Divinely simple state of things. In this, in fact, is rooted Paganism's deep tolerance towards its critics, for their opinions do not contradict Tradition, but are only separate parts seen from the position of one or another observer. Any position, as is well known, is limited by definition, for it reflects not so much the Whole Itself, but rather an individual view of It from the standpoint of the beholder. Pure Tradition embraces everything...

So, the time has come to finally give a positive definition of Paganism.

Paganism is the foundational, supra-confessional form of any religious experience that originates not in the limited consciousness of any single person, but stems from the very nature of reality, from the natural capacity of the GOD-experience that is characteristic of all existence. Therefore, any religious and mystical tradition is not something isolated and self-extant, but one form of manifestation of the One Eternal Tradition (in Sanskrit: Satya Sanatana Dharma — "True Eternal Religion-Law").

Being a manifestation of natural, primordial religiosity, Paganism cannot have the same dogmas and take on the same forms for all, which Pagans would then be compelled to follow without exception and in spite of the obvious differences between levels of consciousness.

Paganism, being the One Eternal Tradition, manifests itself in different historical, racial, ethnic, geographical, and other conditions and forms, while remaining one and immutable in Essence, for although it spreads along the "horizontal" of conditioned human consciousness, it originates in the "vertical" of the SELF-revelation of the Spirit.⁵⁶¹

Now, of course, I would express much of the above in different terms, yet the general message of the article seems to me to remain truthful and meaningful.

IV.

Among contemporary Russian pagan philosophers who are Traditionalists in the Guénonian sense of the term, it bears singling out Evgeny Nechkasov (Askr Svarte), whose works combine Heidegger's philosophy, Dugin's Traditionalism (cleansed of its *fofudya*), and high pagan theology. It is telling that the title of one of Nechkasov's key books bears in its subtitle the term *Pagan Traditionalism*. The latter work represents a fundamental study of the problems confronting the rebirth of pagan traditions in the modern world, and it has no comparison in terms of the scope of its coverage and the depth of its working through the religio-philosophical and historical material presented therein.⁵⁶²

Nechkasov himself is a follower of the Germanic-Scandinavian tradition, so his influence on contemporary Slavic Native Faith is, in a certain sense, indirect. On the other hand, Nechkasov's close, friendly (as well as harshly polemical) and creative ties with many representatives of Slavic Native Faith cannot help but contribute to the ideas of "classical" Traditionalism penetrating the Native Faith milieux, in which questions of Slavic history, native culture, and current ethnography seem at present to take priority over abstract philosophical discourse pertaining to the key questions of Traditionalism.

---

561 I. Cherkasov (ed.), *Traditsiia: Sbornik statei* (Moscow: Institut Obshchegumanitarnykh Issledovanii, 1999), 11-18.

562 Askr Svarte, *Polemos: The Dawn of Pagan Traditionalism*, trans. Jafe Arnold (PRAV Publishing, 2020); idem., *Polemos II: Pagan Perspectives*, trans. Jafe Arnold (PRAV Publishing, 2021).

Also worthy of note is the Traditionalist almanac *Warha*, published by Nechkasov from 2015 to 2020 (totaling seven issues in Russian and two in English), as well as the succeeding almanac *Alföðr*, in publication since 2021, both of which have set a high bar for philosophical discourse in the Germanic-Scandinavian tradition as well as Slavic Native Faith, whose followers' works (including my own) are well attested in both almanacs.

V.

On the whole, to sum up the above, the conclusion may be drawn that contemporary Slavic Native Faith, taking into consideration all of its diversity, cannot be reduced to "classical Traditionalism," just as the latter cannot be reduced to Slavic Native Faith. I think time will tell whether this is a merit or a shortcoming of contemporary Native Faith, and whether it will be eliminated over time or, perhaps, will be cause for the development of new forms of Slavic tradition. Yet, nevertheless, it is difficult to imagine and fully understand Slavic Native Faith as we know it today outside of Traditionalist discourse.

Translated by Jafe Arnold

THE POLITICAL DIMENSION OF TRADITIONALISM IN RENÉ GUÉNON AND JULIUS EVOLA: DEFINING THE IDEAL PRINCIPLES OF SOCIAL ORGANIZATION

Dmitry Moiseev

The key feature of the strain of thought known as Traditionalism which emerged from the works of René Guénon (1886-1951), Julius Evola (1898-1974), Ananda Kentish Coomaraswamy (1877-1947), and Frithjof Schuon (1907-1998), is the affirmation of the existence of a "primordial wisdom" (*Sophia Perennis*) that is the source of all of the world's religions and major spiritual doctrines. Methodologically, Traditionalism appeals to a hermeneutic perception of mythology, folklore, and esoteric aspects of religious doctrines, by means of which, and with the aid of intellectual intuition, one can come to grasp the metaphysical character of the content stored up in the abovementioned objects of spiritual culture.

The present essay endeavors to distinguish the politically-minded content that may be found in the works of the two most important Traditionalists, René Guénon and Julius Evola. This is no trivial task when one takes into consideration the peculiarity that the Traditionalist corpus does not contain any positive social theory, all the while as it presents a systematic critique of modern socio-political phenomena. At the same time, however, this critique was solidified in the classic works of Traditionalism on the basis of a clear vision of a normative ideal for societal structure which can be reconstructed from the primary texts of Guénon and Evola. The ideal they imply is that of the organic and differentiated traditional state. This political vision is inextricably bound up with Traditionalism's idealistic ontology and its distinctive anthropology and ethics. In what follows, we will examine the key political allusions to be found in the crucial works of these two authors.

The Ideal Societal Structure in the Works of René Guénon

René Guénon's works laid the groundwork of Traditionalism. Throughout his works, this French thinker argued that all traditional civilizations in all parts of the world were founded on a series of fundamental principles, and that a gradual departure from these principles conditioned the crisis state of the modern world and the modern remove from the "metaphysical layer of being."

In his work *The Reign of Quantity and the Signs of the Times* (1945), Guénon speaks of the gradual "hardening of the world," the ineluctable shift from the dominance of "metaphysical" principles to material and secular values. In the Traditionalist view, this declining process constitutes "a gradual movement away from the principle, and thus away from the primal spirituality."[563] One should note that, for Guénon, "metaphysics" was not a field of philosophy, but rather a certain unchanging super-world, comparable to Plato's world of Ideas. Man, embarking on the path of ascesis – of intellectual and spiritual self-realization – can come into contact with this word, find within it a firm support for his own being, and thereby transform his life into something more than life.

---

563 René Guénon, *Tsarstvo kolichestvo i znameniia vremeni* (Moscow: Belovod'e, 2011), 121. [René Guénon, *The Reign of Quantity and the Signs of the Times*, trans. Lord Northbourne (Hillsdale: Sophia Perennis, 2004), 113].

In *The Crisis of the Modern World* (1927), Guénon writes that "in civilizations of a traditional nature...it is the pure metaphysical doctrine that constitutes the essential, everything else being linked to it, either in the form of consequences or applications to the various orders of contingent reality."[564] In this case, the sciences as well as social institutions are structured and arranged hierarchically, with the strictest primacy given to the "metaphysical."

According to Guénon's vision, it is precisely the "metaphysical world" which stands as the real world – the world of pure knowledge. The principal distinction between Guénon's model and the presumptions known to us from the history of Western European idealism consists in the fact that, for the former, this is not a world of transcendent principles and abstractions, but a world of active forces which are invisible but intelligible. We can locate the manifestations of this world in the symbols, myths, and series of historical patterns which Guénon analyzes. He thinks about this "primordial" Tradition as the sole, original ground of sacred knowledge from which all religious currents gradually emerged.

Guénon thus prepared the way for a socio-political interpretation of Traditionalism. He was certain that the sages of the past, bearers of traditional wisdom and partakers in mystical union with the world of the sacred, brought into relief a number of principles upon which society ought to be based. These principles are supposed to endow life with higher meaning. One key principle which, according to Guénon, is characteristic of any traditional society, is that of hierarchy expressed in castes. In his work *Spiritual Authority and Temporal Power* (1929), this French thinker elaborated:

> the distinction between castes in the human species constitutes a veritable natural classification to which the distribution of social functions necessarily corresponds. In effect, each man, by reason of his proper nature, is suited to carry out certain definite functions to

---

564 René Guénon, *Krizis sovremennogo mira* (Moscow: Eksmo, 2008), 51. [René Guénon, *The Crisis of the Modern World*, trans. Marco Pallis, Arthur Osborne, Richard C. Nicholson (Hillsdale: Sophia Perennis, 2004), 42].

the exclusion of all others; and in a society established on a regular traditional basis, these aptitudes must be determined according to precise rules, so that, by the correspondence of the various functions with the principal categories in the classification of 'individual natures', each finds his proper place (barring exceptions due to errors of application which, although possible are reduced to a minimum, and thus the social order exactly expresses the hierarchical relationships that result from the nature of the beings themselves.[565]

Guénon's optimal society is therefore a hierarchical one. Only such a society can be truly organic, since, in agreement with the Traditionalist approach, every person possesses definite capabilities, functions, talents, as well as their own spiritual level, which is of critical importance. An organic society in which each member occupies a necessary and appropriate place is harmonious, since it minimalizes the possibilities for individual, existential incongruities which yield internal conflict.

For Guénon, it is of utmost importance that such a society politically expresses the dominance of the transcendent foundations whose social expression is just hierarchy. He elucidates the fundamental meaning of this principle as follows:

> All that is, in whatever mode it may be, necessarily participants in universal principles, and nothing exists except by participation in these principles, which are the eternal and immutable essences contained in the permanent actuality of the divine Intellect; consequently, one can say that all things, however contingent they may be in themselves, express of represent these principles in their own manner and according to their own order of existence, for otherwise they would only be a pure nothingness. All things, in every order of existence, are connected and correspond to one another so as to contribute to universal and total harmony; for harmony, as we have already said, is nothing other than the reflection of principial unity in the multiplicity of the manifested world...[566]

---

565 René Guénon, *Dukhovnoe vladychestvo I mirskaya vlast'* (Moscow: Belovod'e, 2012), 17. [René Guénon, *Spiritual Authority and Temporal Power*, trans. Henry D. Fohr (Ghent: Sophia Perennis, 2001), 9].

566 Ibid., 21 [Ibid., 12].

This unified, harmonious order degrades the further one "descends" down the spiral of time, the historical expression of which is the emergence of conflict between the two powers: "The opposition between the spiritual and temporal powers is found in one form or another among almost all peoples... Among almost all peoples and throughout diverse epochs - and with mounting frequency as we approach our own times - the wielders of temporal power have tried, as we have said, to free themselves of all spiritual authority..."[567] Guénon clarifies:

> in the final analysis, the dispute usually bears on the question of the hierarchical relationships that should exist between them. It is a question of a struggle for supremacy, a struggle invariably arising in the same manner: having first been subject to the spiritual authority, warriors, the holders of the temporal power, revolt against this authority and declare themselves independent of all superior power, even trying to subordinate to themselves the spiritual authority that they had originally recognized as the source of their own power, and finally seeking to turn the spiritual authority to the service of their own domination.[568]

The French thinker then explains the particularities of these two types of power:

> royal power is indeed synonymous with temporal power, even when this latter is taken in its broadest sense... As for the priesthood, its essential function is the conservation and transmission of the traditional doctrine, in which every regular social organization finds its fundamental principles. This function is, moreover, obviously independent of all the special forms the doctrine may take in adapting to the particular conditions of any given era, for these forms do not in any way affect the substance of that doctrine, which remains everywhere and at all times identical and immutable, provided the traditions involved are authentically orthodox.[569]

Thus, for Guénon, both spiritual and temporal power are indispensable components of traditional order; certain people are predestined to occupy positions in either one or the other of these elite social strata in accordance with their

---
567 Ibid., 15 [Ibid., 15, 49].

568 Ibid., 25 [Ibid., 16].

569 Ibid., 27-8 [Ibid., 17-18].

spiritual predispositions and by means of traditional, initiatic procedures.

The crisis into which the modern world has been plunged - and a theme which runs like a thread throughout Guénon's intellectual works - has in many respects been conditioned not only by spiritual causes (such as the "hardening of the world" mentioned above), but also by the political causes associated with them, particularly the loss of the traditional view of authentic power, which has become a "consequence of the encroachment of the temporal upon the spiritual,"[570] and the separation of the West from its own tradition.

The most correct expression of spiritual authority and temporal power given as an example by Guénon is furnished by the ancient Indian tradition:

> To the Kshatriyas normally belongs outward power since the field of action, which concerns them directly, is the external and perceptible world; but this power is nothing without an interior principle, a purely spiritual one, that incarnates the authority of the Brahmins and in which it finds its only real guarantee. We see here that the relationship between the two powers could still be represented by that between the 'interior' and the 'exterior', a relationship that in fact symbolizes well that between knowledge and action or, to put it differently, between the 'mover' and the 'moved'... It is from the harmony between this 'interior' and 'exterior' - a harmony moreover that must not be conceived as a kind of 'parallelism', which would imply an ignorance of the essential differences of the two domains - that there results the normal life of what can be called the social entity.[571]

According to this French thinker, in their normal traditional state, spiritual and temporal power find themselves in an arrangement of strict, mutual dependency:

> In exchange for the guarantee of their power by the spiritual authority, the Kshatriyas must use this power to ensure that the Brahmins will have the means to peacefully accomplish their proper function of knowledge and teaching, sheltered from trouble

---

570 Ibid., 35 [Ibid., 24].

571 Ibid., 55 [Ibid., 41].

and agitation. This is what is represented in Hindu symbolism by the image of Skanda, lord of war, protecting the meditation of Ganesha, lord of knowledge.[572]

Any departure from this mutual dependency or any usurpation of total power by the warrior caste leads to a mixture of roles and, consequently, to both social and spiritual degradation.

All the risks of the destruction of harmonious order which Guénon laid out were embodied in the life of the West a century ago. One of the most important stages of socio-political degradation was the formation of the modern idea of the nation and, by extension, nation-states. Guénon dwells on this point:

> the establishment of 'nations' made possible actual attempts to subjugate the spiritual to the temporal, implying a complete reversal of the hierarchical relations between the two powers. This subjugation found its most definitive expression in the notion of a 'national' church, that is, one subordinated to the State and confined within its limits. The very phrase 'state religion' is a deliberate equivocation signifying fundamentally nothing else than that religion is used by the temporal government to ensure its own domination; it is religion reduced to no more than a mere factor of the social order.[573]

The further progress of historical time, as we see in the events of both the 20th and 21st centuries, only confirms the phenomena of the crisis described by Guénon. Through the efforts of Marxism – first political, then "cultural" – the transcendent as such has been systematically worked out of the existential fabric of modern man, which is inevitably reflected in the advanced degradation of the political sphere. The chimera of egalitarianism, which revealed itself to the West in full in the course of the French Revolution and then in the rivers of bloodshed in the 20th century, is (if we adopt Guénon's model) the most demonic of all socio-political distortions.

---

572 Ibid., 56 [Ibid., 42].
573 Ibid., 79 [Ibid., 61].

In concluding his *Spiritual Authority and Temporal Power*, Guénon poses two open questions:

> Among those who understand that it is necessary above all to denounce the vanity of 'democratic' and 'egalitarian' illusions in order to escape the social chaos in which the Western world is foundering, how many have a notion of true hierarchy based essentially on the differences inherent in the very nature of human beings and on the degrees of knowledge to which they have effectively attained? Among those who declare themselves adversaries of 'individualism', how many are conscious of a reality that transcends the individual?[574]

These questions must naturally go unanswered. If, in traditional society, just hierarchy was supported by social institutions, then in this respect the modern world is chaotic in its structure and cannot be described as valid in Guénonian terms; in this case, the analytical apparatus which would be more adequate than the Traditionalist vision – inclined as it is toward the affirmation of a normative ideal, i.e., that which is duty-bound and proper – is to be found in the scientific discoveries of the 20th-century sociology of elites. We may examine the further development of the Traditionalist conception of the socio-political ideal as invariably rooted in a spiritual worldview in the works of the Italian thinker Julius Evola.

The Political Aspects of Julius Evola's "World of Tradition"

Julius Evola may be credited with developing both the ontological and political aspects of Traditionalism. He proposed his own idealist and ontological system ("magical idealism") which, besides aspects of Western European idealist philosophy, reflects a number of positions common to the Buddhist and Taoist worldviews.

The developments of Evola's early "philosophical period" (1921-27) were later integrated into his mature Traditionalist worldview, elaborated most completely in his book *Revolt*

---

574 Ibid., 104 [Ibid., 83].

Against the Modern World (1934). Here, Evola conceives and meticulously grounds the Traditionalist point of view, in accordance with which the historical process turns out to be an absurdity, and in reality has no legitimacy, other than as a gradual and incessant degradation of spiritual, social, and political forms. As in Guénon's perspective considered above, Evola's understanding of the political is inextricably connected to the "metaphysical," which he illustrates through the traditional "doctrine of two natures" – the cornerstone of the ontology of *Revolt*. Evola writes:

> there is a physical order of things and a metaphysical one; there is a mortal nature and an immortal one; there is the superior realm of "being" and the inferior realm of "becoming." Generally speaking, there is a visible and tangible dimension and, prior to and beyond it, an invisible and intangible dimension that is the support, the source, and true life of the former.[575]

Herein lies the primary, radical distinction between the "world of Tradition" and the "modern world." The latter is essentially secular and materialistic; it rejects the fundamental causality that lies behind the tangible. For the person belonging to the "world of Tradition," on the contrary, the "invisible" is "as real, if not *more* real, than the data provided by the physical senses."[576] He perceives the "other" world no less vividly than the "given extant world," and these "two natures" are interconnected. As Evola claims, the "man of Tradition" knows the way from one world to the other – he knows the way to "fall" as well as the way to "liberation."

Proceeding from the "doctrine of two natures" is a view of the political as an indispensable part of the sacred order:

> The traditional world knew divine kingship. It knew the bridge between the two worlds, namely, initiation; it knew the two great ways of approach to the transcendent, namely, heroic action and contemplation; it knew the mediation, namely, rites and

---

575 Julius Evola, *Vosstanie protiv sovremennogo mira* (Moscow: Prometei, 2016), 21. [Julius Evola, *Revolt Against the Modern World*, trans. Guido Stucco (Rochester: Inner Traditions, 1995), 3].

576 Ibid., 22. [Ibid., 4].

faithfulness; it knew the social foundation, namely, the traditional law and the caste system; and it knew the political earthly symbol, namely, the empire.[577]

In light of such ideas, the sacral legitimization of secular power appears to be a necessity which, according to traditional doctrines, is but a consequence of the supremacy of the "beyond."

Evola explains the sacred symbolism of the emperor's rank in terms of the qualitative, existential distinction of those who have held it:

> In the world of Tradition the most important foundation of the authority and of the right (*ius*) of kings and chiefs, and the reason why they were obeyed, feared, and venerated, was essentially their transcendent and nonhuman quality. This quality was not artificial, but a powerful reality to be feared. The more people acknowledged the ontological rank of what was prior and superior to the visible and temporal dimension, the more such beings were invested with a natural and absolute sovereign power.[578]

In the "world of Tradition," the ruler is only legitimate in light of his own existential supremacy; this legitimacy does not result from his authority, unusual strength, or his mind, to say nothing of the idea that a certain secular body (the conventional "people") has entrusted him with his power. According to Evola, the legendary rulers of the ancient era, themselves beyond the boundaries of historical time, synthesized both an imperial and a clerical function – worldly power and great wisdom – and were the prime intermediaries between their subject peoples and the "transcendent super-world," showing the way to liberation. The later separation of the political and the clerical, in the process of which the function of the emperor came to be seen exclusively in terms of worldly dominion, was in itself a phenomenon of decline and degradation.

---

577 Ibid., 24. [Ibid., 6].

578 Ibid., 25. [Ibid., 7].

Another crucial expression of the "doctrine of two natures" in the "world of Tradition" evinces itself in the sphere of legislation. Evola points out that:

> traditional man either ignored or considered absurd the idea that one could talk about laws and the obedience due them if the laws in question had a mere human origin - whether individual or collective. Every law, in order to be regarded as an objective law, had to have a "divine" character. Once the "divine" character of a law was sanctioned and its origin traced back to a nonhuman tradition, then its authority became absolute: this law became then something ineffable, inflexible, immutable, and beyond criticism.[579]

For this reason, primordial legitimacy also lay beyond the bounds of the material and the "human," and only the remotest consequences of this sacred law could be applied to the spheres of social routine. It would be difficult for a "man of Tradition" to imagine a law that was solely the product of human will, with all its inconstancy and ephemerality.

We can observe an even greater distinction between the "world of Tradition" and the "modern world" in the aims and principles of the state apparatus. If, as is commonly believed today, modern governments exist first and foremost to provide a comfortable and secure life for their citizens, then the state found in the "world of Tradition" is, above all else, a bridge between the worlds of the "two natures" – the physical world and the "transcendent" world. As Evola puts it, "Traditionally the state had a transcendent meaning and purpose... [it was] a manifestation of, and a path to, the 'world above.'"[580] In other words, the state fulfilled a universal, sacred mission; it possessed a teleology proper only to itself which was expressed in, among other things, the social realm. All governmental institutions, regulated by sacred law, together with the administrating ruler, in whom the functions of king and priest were synthesized, showed the governed a path toward great liberation beyond space and time. This explanation of

---

579 Ibid., 45. [Ibid., 21]

580 Ibid., 47. [Ibid., 22].

Evola's provides a teleological answer to the question of the significance of the state – the political form is only justified when it represents the "eternal path," the institutional expression of the bridge between the worlds of the human and the divine.

This line of thought connects the ideas of power, legality, and the state with the symbolism of empire, which stands as the bastion of cosmic order. Baron Evola notes:

> The relationship between *aeternitas* and *imperium* is also found in the Roman tradition; hence the transcendent, nonhuman character with which the notion of *regere* is associated; this is why the pagan world credited the gods for the greatness of Rome, the city of the eagle and of the axe. According to another view endowed with a deeper meaning, the "world" will not end as long as the Roman Empire existed. This idea is connected to the function of mystical salvation attributed to the empire, provided that the "world" is not understood in physical or political terms but rather in terms of "cosmos" and of a dam of order and stability containing the disruptive forces of chaos.[581]

Empire is the ideal of the god-man; it is universal and holds dominion over all things, both worldly and spiritual. It was only relatively recently (compared to the other abovementioned ideals) that this ideal degenerated – one could still hear echoes of it in the European Middle Ages of the Ghibellines.[582]

In the "world of Tradition," which Evola sees as the harmonious ideal of a legitimate order, all that is political possesses a sacred, "transcendent" legitimacy, which provides it with its fundamental and principle distinction from the modern world.

---

581 Ibid., 52 [Ibid., 27].

582 Here it is important to note that Evola does not consider the European empires extant during the period of imperialism to have been properly traditional empires. He holds that the last governmental formation that carried an authentically imperial substance was the Holy Roman Empire of the Hohenstaufen dynasty, which subsided in 1268: "With the Hohenstaufen dynasty Tradition had a last bright flicker; eventually the empires would be replaced by 'imperialisms' and the state would be understood only as a temporal, national, particularistic, social, and plebeian organization." - Ibid., 54 [Ibid., 28].

In the context of discussing the political dimension in Evola's Traditionalism, the question of inequality requires special attention. The "world of Tradition" is a world of natural inequality which is postulated as normative. The presence of a strict, unquestionable hierarchy among the estates and the people belonging to them was an inextricable feature of any authentically traditional civilization. Once more, the "doctrine of two natures" lies at the core of caste distinctions: "the supernatural element was the foundation of the idea of a traditional patriciate and of legitimate royalty: what constituted an ancient aristocrat was not merely a biological legacy or a racial selection, but rather a sacred tradition."[583] Priests occupied the highest social tier (such as the Brahmins of traditional India) by virtue of being the closest to divine power and bearing witness to the affairs of the sacred order.[584] The highest castes oftentimes traced their lineage from divine ancestors (*divi parentes*) whose strength was transmitted to them as a birthright and through the strict observance of tradition and rites. As with divine kings, the nature of the traditional priesthood and aristocracy in the "world of Tradition" is rooted in the fundamental ontological distinction between them and the plebeians; this distinction was emphasized through rituals of "second birth," a birth "in the spirit" resulting from the realization of initiatic ritual. Evola tells us:

> The caste system is one of the main expressions of the traditional sociopolitical order, a "form" victorious over chaos and the embodiment of the metaphysical ideas of stability and justice.

---

583 Ibid., p. 64 [Ibid., 36].

584 It should be noted that, in their evaluations of the supreme role of the priesthood, Evola and Guénon significantly depart from one another. According to Guénon, the primacy of the priestly caste is rooted in the primordial order of Tradition and is not subject to doubt. Against this view, Evola proposes the idea that, in the primordial order of the "Golden Age," the figures of the king (the head of the Kshatriyas) and the priest were united in the singular figure of the king-priest (the "symbolism of Melchizedek"); moreover, he states that the separation of the clergy into a distinct caste and their dominion over the warrior caste should be regarded as the first evidence of decline. See the chapter "On the Hierarchical Relationship Between Royalty and Priesthood" in *Revolt*, 68-72.

> The division of individuals into castes or into equivalent groups according to their nature and to the different rank of activities they exercise with regard to pure spirituality is found with the same traits in all higher forms of traditional civilizations, and it constitutes the essence of the primordial legislation and of the social order according to "justice."[585]

Each concrete individual belonged to one caste or another and was obligated to conform to it – this was his primary and sacred duty. Within his caste, the individual could observe his own particular nature and realize the spiritual order that had been prepared for him. In the "world of Tradition," an arrangement such as this was in no way characterized as violent, oppressive, or "unjust"; on the contrary, the individual harmoniously comprehended himself in the estate of his birth, and nothing about this birth was perceived as "accidental" or "blind," but rather as an expression of supreme law, unbeholden to any physical law.[586] Evola formulates this arrangement as follows: "It can be said therefore that birth does not determine nature, but that nature determines birth; more specifically, a person is endowed with a certain spirit by virtue of being born in a given caste, but at the same time one is born in a specific caste because one possesses, transcendentally, a given spirit."[587] Caste allows the individual to comprehend and remember his own will, which preceded his birth and in light of which his being-in-caste is a manifestation of cosmic harmony.

According to Evola, the "overcoming" of the caste system by the modern world of "equality" has led only to the desynchronization of individual social roles with the nature and calling that preexists the birth of the individual. A colossal number of existential crises result from this, as the individual, finding themselves in an uncharacteristic role

---

585 Evola, *Vosstanie*, 132 [*Revolt*, 89].

586 This principle is expressed in practically all traditional doctrines (as well as doctrines in close proximity to them). The most obvious example is the doctrine of karma found in Hinduism and Buddhism, as well as the Platonic and neo-Platonic doctrine of the soul.

587 Evola, *Vosstanie*, 135 [*Revolt*, 92].

on an unsuitable social tier, faces depression, emptiness, and disillusionment, which ends with deleterious consequences both for themselves and for those around them. As the Baron notes, the apparent "freedom" of modernity – that "illusion of a restless puppet"[588] – is absolutely incommensurable with the organic caste structure of the "world of Tradition," in which, from birth, the individual has been given the ability to learn of their own sacred "form" and its significance.

In *Revolt Against the Modern World*, Julius Evola postulates a normative political ideal: the "world of Tradition," which is organic, elegant, and saturated with immanent spirituality. This socio-political mode is oriented toward the transcendent and is essentially hierarchical; its key aspects are the following: a complex system of rituals, initiations, and the caste system that typifies all organic governments. The modern world, described by Evola as the existential antipode of the "world of Tradition," is oriented toward matter and is atomistic, vulgar, and bereft of authentic meaning, which is evinced by its substantial non-correspondence with traditional understandings of normality.

Conclusion

Having briefly surveyed the socio-political aspects to be found in René Guénon's and Julius Evola's key works, we can draw a few conclusions.

The Traditionalist worldview ontologically affirms an intimate connection between the material and spiritual worlds, whereby causality as such resides in the transcendent world, while the material (including its socio-political expressions) world represents the effects of spiritual causes. In rejecting the notion of progress that was essential to the philosophy of the Enlightenment, the classic figures of Traditionalism, drawing on traditional sources, laid the foundation for a doctrine of gradual degradation of both spiritual and material forms which bears directly on socio-political formations. The "hardening

---

588 Ibid., 138.

of the world" in Guénon's terms or the departure from the "world of Tradition" in favor of the "modern world" in Evola's leads to the chaotic perdition of social roles, the destruction of traditional institutions, and, therefore, to the formation of a mechanistic, totalitarian world void of any connection to traditional, spiritual foundations.

Traditionalism contrasts this skeptical view of the "soulless" modern world to the lucid, normative ideal of traditional normality, whose key aspects are: organically understood hierarchy expressed in a caste system, political teleology (the state and its institutions acting as a "bridge between worlds"), a clear delineation of social roles bound up with the existential destiny of "individuals" and their social "tier," and the allotment of exclusive importance to connection with the spiritual center, which is expressed in the supreme political role of "spiritual authority."

In connection with this, it is necessary to make note of two additional, significant aspects. First, the majority of the examples of "traditional normality" cited by Guénon and Evola are situated beyond historical time. In other words, the founders of Traditionalism appeal primarily to the models given in mythological and religious systems over acknowledged historical fact. The exemplary "glimmers" of Tradition in positive history (the world of antiquity, India, etc.) generally serve as evidence of the initial decay of traditional knowledge and of the first erosions of traditional socio-political institutions. Evola provides the methodological grounds for this approach which, while not problematic from the standpoint of Traditionalist doctrine as such, should nevertheless be borne in mind.

Second, the Traditionalist solution to the age-old problem of individualism and collectivism in political philosophy and social theory, i.e., the search for balance between the values of freedom and social consensus, is of great interest in this context. The Traditionalist worldview's treatment of the political might frighten some with its apparent "totalitarianism" and "unfreedom" which allegedly result from hierarchy and the caste system. However, to make such a determination would be to commit a profound error. In any discussion of such a social arrangement, one must take into consideration how the caste system, as an institution of the traditional world, was rooted in the spiritual nature of man and his existential inclination toward one or another sort of activity, and assignment to a particular caste was by no means always determined by one's birth into a particular social stratum. In the traditional view, observance of one's caste assignment led to a harmonious life for the individual, filled with meaning and free from any existential crises, such as those commonly provoked by the chaos into which our social roles have been flung. This harmonious being "in spirit" that was accessible to traditional man allowed the individual to lead a harmonious life in correspondence with his own nature in a world that was comprehensible to him, and within this world he was able to play a role that was essentially suited to him. We may consider this to be an expression of the highest type of authentic freedom – "freedom for," or the freedom of the master as opposed to the slave, who dreams of extricating himself from his falsely understood "oppression." This authentic freedom can only be achieved within the organicity of the traditional collective whole, which strips away the dichotomy of collective and individual that is false for the traditional world.

Proceeding from this exposition, the political dimension of Traditionalism is essentially idealistic, rooted as it is in the traditional, anthropological double nature of the individual as belonging both to the spiritual and material worlds, and it is also normatively elitist, which is to say that it emphasizes the necessity of hierarchy, inequality, and social stratification as intrinsic to organic societies. Moreover, the most important political aspect of Traditionalism is its idealistic teleology – the traditional government exists as a "bridge between worlds," connecting the supreme world of the spirit and the inferior world of matter, and drives its subjects toward the great and ultimate goal that is passage into another state of being. In this lofty normative model's emphasis on the ontological meaning of the political in the traditional world lies the ideal socio-political structure described by the classical Traditionalists.

Of course, the modern, "hardened" world can only be far removed from such an ideal, which makes any literal observance of the traditional model impossible. This existential fact was clearly understood by both Guénon and Evola, but this in no way prevented them from reconstructing the traditional, normative political ideal. At the same time, the reader must understand that attempts at practically reconstructing the traditional model within modernity, in which there are neither the spiritual, political, nor existential conditions for such, can lead to perilous distortions.

Nevertheless, the socio-political dimension of Traditionalism does not lose its relevance as a living model of "normality" which, when appealed to by certain individuals, can open up an existential palette that is far superior to the popular follies of our contemporary age. This practical aspect of Traditionalism will be further elaborated in our future contributions to *Passages: Studies in Traditionalism and Traditions*.

Translated by Charlie Smith and Jafe Arnold

EVOLA AND JUNG: FOR A REACTUALISATION OF TRADITION

Roberto Cecchetti

Making philosophy an experience, a praxis, means giving life to the unification of thought and feeling; in more esoteric terms, it means linking what is above to what is below, making knowledge effective, and filling the signifier with the signified. This is what actually distinguishes merely theorised initiation, which is, in a certain way, merely yearned for in a ceremonial sense, from effective initiation, which is so dear to the doctrine of Tradition. In psychic terms, according to a strain of depth psychology, this process would be none other than the correct work of integrating the opposites within the Self, that is to say, within the whole personality.[589] "Making the implicit explicit", "individuating oneself", "becoming what one is" are just some of the expressions which aim to reveal the secret of that staged process which James Hillman articulated as the psychic work of "soulmaking".[590] All

---

[589] According to Jung, the Self is none other than the totality of the personality, thought of as a sort of sphere, which comprises all the psychic dimensions, of both awareness and unawareness: consciousness, unconscious, preconscious, psychoid stages, symbols, archetypes, complexes. According to Jung, personality is divided, much like a *mandala*, into different opposite and complementary functions.

[590] "This book is about soul-making" — this is how Hillman's *Re-Visioning Psychology* begins — "The term *soul-making* comes from the Romantic poets. We find the idea in William Blake's *Vala*, but it was John Keats who clarified the phrase in a letter to his brother: 'Call the world if you please, 'The vale of Soul-making.' Then you will find out the use of the world...' From this perspective the human adventure is a wandering through the vale of the world for the sake of making soul. Our life is psychological, and the purpose of life is to make psyche of it, to find connections between life and soul." But what does Hillman mean with the term "soul?" "By *soul* I mean, first of all, a perspective rather than a substance, a viewpoint toward things rather than a thing itself. This perspective is reflective; it mediates events and makes differences between ourselves and everything that happens. Between us and events, between the doer and the deed, there is a reflective moment—and soul-making means differentiating this middle ground...In another attempt upon the idea of soul I suggested that the word refers to that unknown component which makes meaning possible, turns events into experiences, is communicated in love, and has a religious concern." J. Hillman, *Re-visione della psicologia* (Milan: Adelphi, 2019, 13-15 [James Hillman, *Re-Visioning Psychology* (New York: Harper & Row, 1975), ix-x].

of these attempts to put a secret inner work into words might appear as vague expressions to anyone who is not too familiar with the subtle process of the expansion of consciousness.

Julius Evola as well as Carl Gustav Jung were perfectly aware that art, philosophy, Hermeticism, and metaphysics risked becoming empty concepts if confined only to the academic dimension, a dimension in which such disciplines and fields of knowledge might no longer have any contact with the plane of individual reality. It is enough to cite the fifth chapter of the *Essays on Magical Idealism* to be aware of the practical perspective through which the philosophy of idealism is understood by Evola:

> What distinguishes magical idealism is its essentially practical character: its fundamental requirement is not to substitute one intellectual conception of the world for another, but to create a new "dimension" and a new depth in the life of the individual. Certainly, magical idealism does not fall into a strict opposition of theoretical and practical aspects; it already sees a degree of creative activity in theory and knowledge as such — and therefore only in what it can reveal itself to a reader —, but it holds that such a degree represents only a sketch, a beginning gesture towards a phase of deeper realisation, which is that of magic or practice properly called, in which the former has to continue and accomplish itself.[591]

The well-known process of the emptying of the symbol, the flight of the divine from the world, and the shift away from the original word have made the individual unable to approach practice, have detached him from the possibility of experience, and have condemned him to operate on an external plane in which the experiment is anything but the alchemical art, that is to say, anything but a transformative experience for the subject.

In our view, what makes the significant teachings of the aforesaid two masters of the foregone century similar to each other is to be found precisely in the fact that both of them opened up ways for us to understand and reactualise

---

[591] Julius Evola, *Saggi sull'idealismo magico* (Rome: Edizioni Mediterranee, 2006), 83.

the teachings of some of the most important Traditional disciplines.

In this sense, Jung is very clear and explicit, since it was precisely in his studies on alchemy that he cited Evola's discoveries and insights contained in the Italian's brilliant book dedicated to the study of Hermeticism.[592] It is precisely Jung, in a much-relevant passage contained in his text *Psychology and Alchemy*,[593] who summarises Evola's discoveries in this field, although certainly from a psychological perspective: "The alchemical *opus* deals in the main not just with chemical experiments as such, but with something resembling psychic processes expressed in pseudochemical language."[594] And in a footnote he quotes the Evolian text at length:

> Evola (*La tradizione ermetica*, pp. 28f.) says: "The spiritual constitution of man in the premodern cycles of culture was such that each physical perception had simultaneously a psychic component which 'animated' it adding a 'significance' to the bare image, and at the same time a special and potent emotional tone. Thus ancient physics was both a theology and a transcendental psychology, by reason of the illuminating flashes from metaphysical essences which penetrated through the matter of the bodily senses. Natural science was at once a spiritual science, and the many meanings of the symbols united the various aspects of a single knowledge."[595]

Evola, thanks to his will to restore vitality and relevance to the theoretical plain, paved the way for the Jungian discovery of the projective mechanisms of the psyche in alchemical language, which, through their outer symbolisations and imaginations which are otherwise difficult to understand, make explicit those psychic dynamics which Jung intended as universal. In Jung's eyes, the language and imagery of the Hermetic tradition

---

592 Julius Evola, *La tradizione ermetica* (Rome: Edizioni Mediterranee, 1996) [Julius Evola, *The Hermetic Tradition: Symbols and Teachings of the Royal Art*, trans. E.E. Rehmus (Rochester: Inner Traditions International, 1995)].

593 Carl Gustav Jung, *Opere XII, Psicologia e alchimia* (Turin: Bollati Boringhieri, 2006) [C.G. Jung, *The Collected Works of C.G. Jung, Volume 12: Psychology and Alchemy* (Princeton: Princeton University Press, 1968).

594 Jung, *Psychology and Alchemy*, 242.

595 Ibid.

became the ideal site for understanding the functioning of the psyche and unconscious complexes.

In the same way, another fundamental aspect which allows us to see a precise connection between Evola and Jung consists in their deep bond with idealism. Magical idealism as proposed by Evola, as an absolute idealism, may be compared to the way Jung thinks about the unconscious and therefore about the subject. If Evola explicitly dedicates himself to the study of idealism in the attempt to make it magical, that is to say, practical and effective, Jung expressed an underlying idealistic system which may be identified in some of his fundamental works, a system which, however, tends to remain more or less implicit within the various branches of his thought. Certainly, Jung did not want to trespass into the field of philosophy, and for this reason he always maintained that he did not consider himself a philosopher and he did not deal directly with philosophical questions, even though his works are inevitably affected by his vast cultural background which, in one way or another, always entails a certain philosophical substrate. Jung indeed defined himself as an empiricist, and by this appellation he meant that his starting point always had to remain the direct observation of the clinical cases with which he had to deal and from which he could derive a possible general theory of the psyche.

Comparing Jung and Evola is therefore certainly no easy endeavour, above all since Evola repeatedly condemned the psychological and psychoanalytical drift, which in his eyes was so pernicious that it could be considered an out-and-out component of modern neo-spiritualism, and as such was to be disregarded and rejected. Therefore, Evola, in his most Traditionalist phase, in which he decides to turn in an unequivocal and explicit way to the works of René Guénon as being closest to the purity of the most orthodox Tradition, banishes the psychological method (at least in the Freudian interpretation) from the possible paths for achieving some form of individual realisation. Freudianism has to be banished since it corrupts everything through the trap of the eroticisation of any dynamism of the psyche and the world: it would be a sort of reductionism that leads to a simplification of reality, whereby one would always end up seeing the same cause and the same root in any ambit of reality. In addition to this theoretical problem, there would be, above all and as Evola indeed believed, an effective risk for the subject who enters the maze of the psyche: the risk of getting lost within the unconscious without possibility of salvation. The same thing is affirmed, for instance, by the great knower and scholar of mysticism Marco Vannini,[596] who in the dimension of the soul, or, to put it in Jungian terms, the unconscious, finds the utmost risk for the development of the Spirit, which, from this outlook, is seen as the exact opposite of the soul, as the abode of the cognitive, speculative faculty — in a word, as the abode of the *Logos* and of Love in the Christian sense. Vannini claims that the soul, otherwise, would be like that sea which, however far one sails through it, never leads anywhere. The soul is therefore understood as a snare, as a place in which one gets lost, as the unconscious or subconscious from which one needs rather to free himself in order to reach the opposite polarity, the superconscious and the Spirit. Basically, there is the risk of finding oneself within that Luciferian-flavoured modern overturning of the symbol which is typical of the modernity of which Guénon spoke.

We are already approaching a series of problems that need to be made explicit if we want to clarify the important theme of the realisation of the personality, or of the individual. In fact, the pole star of both the world of Tradition and the psychological vision of things, in the sense of depth psychology, always remains the achievement of an authentic and total personality. However, upon a deeper look into the question, it should be noted that the so-called fulfilment of the personality ultimately does not mean anything more than the mastery over one's own individual destiny, and this is true both for Evola's

---

[596] See in particular Vannini Marco, *La morte dell'anima, dalla mistica alla psicologia* (Florence: Le Lettere, 2004).

magical idealism and for Jung in his *Symbols of Transformation*. It is interesting to note how the term "autarchy" often appears in the books of Erich Neumann, the great continuer of Jung's work, and how such an autarchy of the subject has to be attributed to the mastery over the unconscious as the place where the destiny of each individual is situated. It is, therefore, unequivocally a question of identifying an effective process that leads to the freedom of the subject. What might be the meaning of mastering one's own destiny if not effectively being free?

The first problem, therefore, seems to us to be that represented by Evola and Traditional thinkers' distrust towards the concept of the unconscious, a distrust originating from various factors: its libidinal-erotic component, its being the theatre of tragic dynamics which limit the freedom of conscience, its oceanic vastness, and its location, in topological terms, below.

On the other hand, the second problem seems to us to be more subtle yet no less relevant, and it is central for understanding one of the objectives of both Jung's and Evola's proposals: the relationship between Truth and language. We realise that such a vast theme cannot be tackled here, so we will limit ourselves to proposing an interpretive key to better understand what we mean by the term "reactualisation" and why it is precisely on the terrain of reactualisation that, in our opinion, our two protagonists meet.

As for the first reason of incompatibility, that relating to the unconscious, we can say that Evola is probably had a better understanding of Freud than Jung did, but, perhaps above all, he did not have any effective experience of the psychoanalytical practice, which he considered, as we have already said, to be a danger in all respects. Indeed Evola, clinching one of his articles about and against Jung, writes:

> But precisely for this reason, are not those theories, such as the one just mentioned, which hallucinatively focus on an innerly splintered humanity which deals with new "demons", instead of referring to the

natural animating and rectifying power that will always emanate from a superior human type, particularly deleterious?[597]

It is precisely here that one might wonder how to become that superior human type bespoken by Evola, but also: are we sure that mankind is not really split? According to Jung, there is no superior human type who has not had an experience of himself, and therefore of his own unconscious, and this, above all, is due to the fact that until one has come to terms with one's own unconscious, one is not free, let alone a superior man!

At this point, it is necessary to open a brief parenthesis about the development of the personality and the confrontation with the unconscious. Both Jung and Evola were indeed well aware of the work of a great jurist, a Swiss like Jung himself, who had laid the foundations for a psychological and archetypal reading of history and consciousness: Johann Jakob Bachofen. Bachofen, who was already old when Jung was still a boy, authored a well-known text, *Das Mutterrcht*[598] (1861), in which not only is a relationship established between the psyche and human institutions, and thus between the psyche and the dimensions of the political sphere for the first time since Plato, but in which the author also shows how the same fundamental categories of the juridical world are none other than the creations of a civilisation which evolved from a feminine-unconscious condition to a masculine-solar one. From this point of view, the confrontation with history and with the cultural expressions of nations becomes an out-and-out confrontation with the unconscious itself. Indeed, what is the beginning point from which the history of peoples unfolds? It is the phase in which consciousness is still subject to the power of the feminine as the unconscious element; for this reason, according to Bachofen, history, myth, and

---

[597] J. Evola, "*Lo svizzero Jung sta aggiornando Freud*", Roma (7 September 1950), reprinted in idem, *L'infezione psicanalista, scritti sulla psicanalisi 1930-1974* (Rome: Controcorrente, 2012), 104.

[598] J.J. Bachofen, *Das Mutterrecht (Il matriarcato)* (Turin: Giulio Einaudi Editore, 1988).

institutions show us none other than the strife of collective liberation from an original subjection to the unconscious. The goal is always the achievement of a community that rests on institutions of a solar type, that is to say institutions which are bearers of a patriarchal and masculine consciousness. The originating point is therefore the unconscious as the site of the feminine. It is for this reason that the confrontation with the unconscious is essential in our opinion, because confronting oneself with the past, with the foundations of the juridical sphere, with the development of institutions, with myth, is ultimately confronting oneself with the work of the collective unconscious that incessantly generates, from time to time, a given type of reality (we will return to this later, since it is already understandable how this manner of seeing things implies a clearly idealistic perspective). Evola, too, reminds us that the danger of the subjection of consciousness to the feminine is always present.

It was therefore a man of law who first approached myth and symbol, and the arcane world of the mothers, in an attempt to reach that pulsating core from which the manifestations of law spring. Thus, anticipating Freud, Bachofen provides us with an enlightening interpretation, characterised by a psychoanalytical flavour, of the vicissitude which remains at the centre of all other vicissitudes, that is, the myth of Oedipus, already seen and thought of as a psychic instance and at the same time as an expression of a phase in the development of the juridical sphere.

> The religious ideas that form the background to the figure of Oedipus as it emerges from the mythical tale are unequivocal. The swollen foot from which he takes his name qualifies him as the bearer of the natural, virilely fecundating force, whose telluric-Poseidonic conception often appears associated with the foot or the shoe, as is the case in Aeëtes' bronze-footed oxen, in the bull-footed Dionysus, in Mars Gradivus (from *gradior* [to advance, to walk], not from *cresco* [to grow, to swell]), in the shoe of Jason and Perseus, in the footprint left by Heracles, in the snake-like figure of Erythronius, and in still other images, such as that of the Onosceles-Empuses,

or in Charila, Tanaquil and Nitocris. The chariot that causes the swelling has a clear Neptunian meaning. For this reason, Hyginus says that Oedipus "excelled over all others", while Apollodorus says that he "distinguished himself by his strength over those of his age"; because of this, he is found on the seashore by Periboea, who had gone there to wash, and brought back to Laius. The name of the latter, in fact, like that of Laertes, derives from the root *la*, which designates the fecundating force and which, as for its meaning, is so suited to Oedipus that the legend was able to admit the detail according to which it was precisely thanks to the swollen foot that he was recognised as the son of Laius.[599]

Bachofen was the first to understand, at least in explicit terms, the feminine as an original place from which it is necessary to free oneself. In this sense, the masculine aspect is contained in potentiality within the unconscious, which is seen as female, and it is interesting to note how this idea was then taken up again by Jung and Neumann, who think that the unconscious contains within itself the tools that are needed to overcome itself. Oedipus is therefore the prototype of the hero who attempts to overcome the dangerous call of the feminine-unconscious.

> In the same passage, Oedipus is described by Hyginus as *impudens* [impudent, shameless], irrespective of the relationship with his mother. In this we may see an allusion to the fecundating force and to the pleasure of fertilising, in the acceptation as the most exuberant sexuality as represented by telluric life in the unruly matings which are typical of the stage of civilisation in the marshes; this is an aspect which gives the swollen foot, too, its most important meaning. In this stage of the natural force, as demonstrated by certain myths, the mother is understood as wife and, at the same time, daughter of the man who comes to her as a fecundator: according to their turn, each generation of men establishes a relationship with the maternal terrestrial matter with an attitude of fecundation. The son becomes husband and father; the same primogenial Woman, now fecundated by the forefather, in the future will mate with the nephew. Hence, the puzzle about Jocaste: *avia filiorum est, quae mater mariti* [grandmother to her sons is she who is mother to her husband]. According to this conception, Oedipus belongs to the ilk

---

[599] Ibid., 370-373.

> of the Σπαρτοί [the Sown Ones, that is, the Thebans], to the *genus dracónteum* [the ilk born from the teeth of the dragon]. Called to life by the male dragon, the Ladon of the depths of the seas, the Σπαρτοί [the Sown Ones] do not have a well distinguishable father, but only a mother, like the *spurii* [illegitimate] ones, whose name (from σπείρειν [to sow, to beget]) has the same meaning. From this state of things derives the possibility of patricide, given that the son ignores who his parent is. Oedipus' mother is Jocaste (meaningfully also called Epicaste), daughter of Menoeceus; the ancestry of the same Menoeceus, however, is traced back without doubt to the *dracónteum genus* of the Σπαρτοί [the Sown Ones]. We have to assume that, in the latter's progeny, the matrilineal right of descent is dominant, given that the maternal system emerges with extreme evidence. [...][600]

Hence, Bachofen tries to connect the tale of the myth, whose meaning is eminently psychic, to historical reality, in which he reads a progressive liberation from the realm of the feminine, that is to say from the unconscious. This is why Oedipus is seen as a figure who comes to establish a new era (in both psychic and historical terms).

> The fate of these (of the Sown Ones) is not at all dissimilar from that of the marsh plants which are born, grow and die without being mourned. Humanity has not yet risen above the condition of the lowest stage: that of telluric generation. A progress towards a higher level of existence is connected precisely with Oedipus. He represents one of those great figures whose sufferings and torments usher in a greater human civilisation; one of those figures who — although still anchored themselves to the ancient state of affairs from which they sprang — are the last great victims of this condition. But who, in this way, at the same time, become the establishers of a new era.[601]

In addition to the great ability to penetrate symbolic images, Bachofen introduces us to that representation of a psychic and historical development in stages which will be then taken up by Neumann.

---

600 Ibid.

601 Ibid.

If at first the sons are indistinct beings, devoid of a specific individual existence, and are simply children of nature, with the new era they acquire a true individuality under the patronage of the solar and male dimension. Eventually, the sons know an authentic birth.

> Together with the Sphinx, Jocaste's father, Menoeceus, the last representative of the *draconteum genus* [the ilk begotten by the dragon], also meets his end. The motif of falling off the walls, which recurs in many myths, always reveals the same connection with maternal tellurism, to whose sphere the walls belong, as they constitute a product of the Earth and, consequently, participate in the chthonic *sanctitas* [inviolability]. The simultaneous and common end of the Σπαρτοί [the Sown Ones] and the Sphinx shows that they both have an identical foundation, which now constitutes the background against which Oedipus stands out. In Laius' son, the masculine force reaches its own autonomous meaning alongside the feminine matter. In the name of Oedipus, virility acquires its dominant role. Furthermore, some aspects of his myth highlight his male lineage above all. The son grieves over the death of Paolibus, whom he assumes to be his father, and the state of his feet reveals Laius' paternity. With Oedipus, children begin to know the "authentic" birth.[602]

It was appropriate to quote these passages at length in order to show how the theme of historical development in correlation with psychic development is already found in Bachofen, an author studied by both Jung and Evola, and how this theme then finds its development in the researches of Jung himself and of Erich Neumann.[603] Indeed, one of Jung's capital works, *Symbols of Transformation*, deals precisely with the transformation of symbols understood as a product of the dynamics, that is to say, of energy, of the unconscious psyche. Myths, symbols, institutions, and the categories of politics are therefore understood as products of the unconscious, upon which it is necessary for consciousness to overcome itself

---

602 Ibid.

603 The reference text in which Erich Neumann tries to unify Bachofen's ideas with Jung's discoveries is Erich Neumann, *Storia delle origini della coscienza* (Rome: Astrolabio, 1978).

dialectically and reach higher levels of integration. In this sense, the confrontation with the unconscious is a necessary and unavoidable moment of a dialectical movement in which the negative is understood and assimilated. The problem pertaining to Truth and language leads us to a quick clarification of what we must understand by the term "reactualisation".

The discoveries concerning Hermeticism in general and alchemy in particular pushed Jung, and Evola before him, to conceive, within a renewed tension towards practical and effective experience, a truth which is no longer only an adaptation of thought to the thing, as in Scholasticism, or to a state of the world, but a truth which is ultimately a precise relationship between word and interiority. The reactualisation of Traditional mythical-symbolic elements means regaining possession of a word which is laden with meaning and through which it is possible to develop knowledge and a science of consciousness. The words of the alchemists are otherwise incomprehensible: the stone, the sacrifice, gold, and the metals appear at first glance as empty names.

How does this work translate into actual practice? How can the language of Tradition be made current again? It translates into a much more refined knowledge of our interiority, and into a possible sharing of the mythico-symbolic baggage of reference. Hence, after this work of adapting the word to a well-defined and experienced inner state, the word "sacrifice", the word "stone", and so on begin to have a true meaning, that is, they become anchored to our interiority — they finally mean something for us! Whereas before, it was thought, or rather it was profanely believed, that they meant something, although they were actually empty names. Once this level of real understanding has been reached, it is then possible to proceed working with the interior dimension, with the psyche, through symbols and their meanings, which are not vague and subjected to an indefinite hermeneutical and interpretative possibility, but are really very precise.

So, what does this precision concern? The precision of symbols and myths concerns something very specific: it concerns the process of the development of our consciousness. And this is because, at first, our consciousness is not already formed, it is not already free from its mergence with the darkness of the unconscious. Myth is precisely this: it is a narration of the unconscious which mysteriously contains in itself the keys for the unconscious to go beyond itself, the instructions to ensure that the consciousness frees and develops itself. This is why Neumann spoke about stages in the development of consciousness, stages which in some way derive from the older Bachofenian conception.

Having briefly addressed the issue of distrust towards the unconscious, and that of reactualisation through a different way of understanding the relationship between word and truth, we may now proceed to the last point of this work: the theme of idealism which links the Evolian horizon to Jung. In order to understand the idealistic aspect of Jungian theory, it is necessary to begin from the concept of *libido* as is exposed in the wake of the text *Symbols of Transformation*. *Libido* is no longer understood in an eminently erotic sense, as was the case in Freud; instead, Jung feels the need to broaden the concept of *libido* to the point that it coincides with an unconscious creative energy. According to Jung, the unconscious is in fact dynamic, that is to say, endowed with a force, with energy, yet it is also a kind of desiring and spontaneously creative will. If, according to idealism, and thus also for the radical idealism proposed by Evola in his magical phase, objective reality is the direct manifestation of the thought of the subject, who must overcome himself in a process of dialectical confrontation with the negative, then according to Jung it is in the unconscious, as man's hidden and directly unknowable volitional centre, that the production of reality originates. Jung tries to understand the ultimate mystery of magic: it is necessary to act on the unconscious to change reality, because the unrecognised unconscious desire is that determining force which we call destiny. Destiny is the unconscious, or better, the desire of the unconscious, unacknowledged. This is why so much attention is paid to the problem of the subject's freedom: the subject is dominated by fate, but fate is none other than a product of an unconscious which acts spontaneously and creates incessantly.

According to Jung, the unconscious also has its own end — an idea derived from Mircea Eliade's studies on alchemy, in which it was highlighted how nature itself would have as its purpose the transmutation of base metals into gold and therefore the realisation of an always unfinished creation[604] —, and this aim would be that of being reborn through the mother so as to then attain the goal of individuation. The Freudian risk of a real incest, which is well represented by the Oedipal tragedy, is replaced by a symbolic incest which represents the profound desire to be reborn through the mother. However, the road of regression towards the maternal is barred: we cannot return to the mother and be reborn. From this prohibition, from this barrier against the energy of the unconscious, the *libido*, the world of symbols and myths, is generated. This is why the mythico-symbolic world would represent the privileged access route for the unconscious, because in effect it would be a plane of reality created by the desiring *libido* itself. Jung explains that:

> The solar myth shows that the "incestuous" desire is based [...] on the singular idea of becoming a child again, of returning under the protection of the parents, of returning into the mother to be born again by her. Now, on the road that leads to this goal is incest, that is, the need to return in whatever way into the mother's body. One of the simplest ways would be for one to fecundate the mother and regenerate himself in an identical form. At this point, the hindrance represented by the forbidding of the incest may arise, which is why solar myths or myths of rebirth contrive all sorts of analogies of the mother in order to allow the libido to pour into new forms and thus effectively prevent it from regressing into a more or less concrete incest.[605]

---

604 See Mircea Eliade, *Arti del metallo e alchimia* (Turin: Bollati Boringhieri, 1980 [1956]) [Mircea Eliade, *The Forge and the Crucible: The Origins and Structures of Alchemy*, trans. Stephen Corrin (Chicago: University of Chicago Press, 1978)].

605 C.G. Jung, *Simboli della trasformazione* (Turin: Bollati Boringhieri, 1952), 224.

Incest therefore represents the will to generate spontaneously through the act of thought:

> The incest prohibition acts as an obstacle and makes the creative fantasy inventive; for instance, there are attempts to make the mother pregnant by means of fertility magic. The effect of the incest-taboo and of the attempts at canalization is to stimulate the creative imagination, which gradually opens up possible avenues for the self-realization of libido. In this way the libido becomes imperceptibly spiritualized. The power which "always desires evil" thus creates spiritual life. That is why the religions exalt this procedure into a system.[606]

In tragic representations, in certain works of art, in fairy tales, in poetic compositions, we can find the fundamental laws of our unconscious inscribed.

The dream of directing the unconscious is nothing else than the magical dream of producing a reality according to will. The work with the unconscious is never immediate, but always possible only through mediation. Thus, the individuative and finalistic process of the unconscious may be found in the alchemical work. Mircea Eliade, in the space of a few pages in which he takes into consideration Jungian intuitions on alchemy, writes:

> Such products of the unconscious, therefore, were neither anarchic nor gratuitous; they pursued a precise goal, individuation, which, for Jung, represents the supreme ideal of every human being [...] But if we bear in mind that the goal of the alchemist was the Elixir Vitae and the Philosopher's Stone, that is, the conquest of immortality and absolute freedom (possession of the Stone permitted, among other things, transmutation into gold and hence the freedom to change the world, to 'save' it), it becomes clear that the process of individuation, assumed by the unconscious without the 'permission' of the conscious, and mostly against its will, and which leads man towards his own centre, the Self-this process must be regarded as a pre figuration of the *opus alchymicum*, or more

---

606 Ibid. [C.G. Jung, *The Collected Works of C.G. Jung, Volume 5: Symbols of Transformation* (Princeton: Princeton University Press, 1976), 328].

accurately, an 'unconscious imitation', for the use of all beings, of an extremely difficult initiation process[...].[607]

Here, Eliade identifies the teleological character of the libidinal energy directed towards individuation and connects it to the soteriological aspect of the process of the Work which aims at the redemption not only of the spirit, but of matter as well, in that the alchemist's dream is to heal the world as a whole. The process, the *opus*, is none other than the rite, which in this sense constitutes a bridge to the unconscious energy.

Evola as well, in his *Theory of the Absolute Individual*,[608] will move towards the fulfilment of idealism on the level of praxis, tracing out with absolute logical-philosophical rigour the path which the I must complete in order to realise itself not as existence but as self-domain, that is to say, as freedom and value. Evola recalls the idealistic thesis according to which:

> All the determinations by which and with which the object is known — whatever order they refer to, including its relative possible "aseity", its dependence or independence from the I — are, and are certain, as particular determinants of consciousness, in the knot of which what is called reality is twisted without residue.[609]

According to the act of knowing, here the "objective" represents the sphere of determinateness while the sphere of the subject is defined by its being the act and principle of any object of experience. Within the pole of the I, we therefore have the stance of indeterminateness, of absolute freedom, of the feeling of the infinite.

In order to fully understand the multiple implications of Evola's speculations that develop out of his recovery of idealism, it is necessary to refer to the fundamental formula that Evola himself proposes to us as a synthesis of integral idealism. The three elements that constitute the triad of this formula already indicate a ternary procedure in the refusal

---

607 Eliade, *The Forge and the Crucible*, 223-224.

608 Julius Evola, *Teoria dell'individuo assoluto* (Rome: Edizioni Mediterranee, 1988).

609 Ibid., 31.

of any immediateness, which otherwise would threaten the work of synthesis operated by the dynamism of that element of the domain which characterises the I itself. X then indicates the object as "qualification of consciousness", A represents the assumption or mediation of such a qualification, and S represents "the power or infinity of the I". Hence, X is transcendentally implicated in A and A in turn is transcendentally implicated in S. This means precisely that the object X, as a qualification of consciousness, must be brought back within the sphere of the power of the I.

Under the profile of immediateness, and of experience according to determinateness, the duality that according to Evola represents the very task of the individual who aspires to this achievement in terms of absolute in-dividuality is instead perceived as a *conflict*, and the infiniteness of the I is felt as a never realised possibility. Actually, the perspective of integral idealism sees precisely in the determinateness of the object and in duality the possibility of that non-immediate task through which the I may come to determine itself as self-domain.

Autarchy, self-domain, and individuation effectively tend towards an individual completion — we could even say an initiatory completion — which may probably never be effectively concluded once and for all. The individual is destined to a tension towards fulfilment, in the awareness that the negative with which he necessarily has to deal as something other than himself is, according to Evola, ultimately nothing other than a product of his unknowledge, or, according to Jung, a product of the creative unconscious with its own energy. Considering the *non-I*, the negative, the pole of the object as *steresis*, that is, as privation or lack of subjective knowledge, or considering it as the product of the unconscious, is, in all respects, something very similar.

In conclusion, both Evola and Jung reveal to us the mysteries of Tradition and give us the keys to access the process of the realisation of our individuality, and it is for this reason that their Work is so valuable. Even in our times, by now so far removed from any possible connection with Tradition, it is thanks to the work of reactualising Traditional knowledge carried out by these great "knowers of secrets" that the path to self-domain, that is, the path to Freedom, is open for those who wish to engage with boldness and earnest diligence in the work of individuation.

Translated by U.X.A.

ABOUT THE AUTHORS

Alexander Dugin is a Russian philosopher, geopolitician, and the founding leader of the International Eurasian Movement. In the late Soviet Union, Dugin was a member of the underground Yuzhinsky Circle which introduced Traditionalist thought to Russia and translated and published the first Russian editions of René Guénon and Julius Evola. Formerly the head of the Department of Sociology of International Relations at Moscow State University, where he founded the Center for Conservative Studies, in 2011 Dugin oversaw the organization of the international Traditionalist conference "Against the Post-Modern World: Actual Problems of Traditionalism" and the journal *Traditsiia*. The author of more than 60 books translated into a dozen languages, Dugin's most recent publications include *Julius Evola: Political Traditionalism* (Academic Project, 2023) in Russian and *Templars of the Proletariat* (Arktos, 2023) in English.

Róbert Horváth (b. 1971) is a philosopher, scholar of religious studies, book and journal editor. He is one of the best known personalities of today's Hungarian "Traditional School". His main research areas are Śaivism, comparative theology, and environmental philosophy. He is a leading lecturer at the Last Exit Community Centre in Budapest.

Maxim Makovchik (b. 1987) is a philosopher, translator, teacher of Sanskrit, and researcher of tradition. He holds a Master's in Philosophy from the Saints Methodius and Cyril Institute of Theology at Belarusian State University.

Jonatán Gődény is a philosopher with a Master's degree. He is a frequent contributor to the Hungarian-language traditional journal *Magyar Hüperión*. His main fields of interest are Bon and Tibetan Buddhism, especially Dzogchen, on the latter of which he has translated Tenzin Wangyal's book into Hungarian.

About the Authors

Giovanni Sessa is the secretary of the Julius Evola Foundation. He has edited dozens of books and his writings have appeared in newspapers, journals, collective volumes, and conference proceedings. His recent books include *La meraviglia del nulla. Vita e filosofia di Andrea Emo* (2014), *Julius Evola e l'utopia della Tradizione* (2019), *L'eco della Germania segreta. "Si fa di nuovo primavera"* (2021), *Azzurre lontananze. Tradizione on the road* (2022), and *Icone del possibile. Giardino, bosco, montagna* (2023).

Troy Southgate is from Crystal Palace, South London, and has been an underground writer and activist for 35 years. He graduated in History and Theology at the University of Kent and holds a teaching certificate in English from Cambridge University. He was the founder of the National-Anarchist Movement (N-AM) and is the founding editor-in-chief of Black Front Press, where he has authored and edited more than 140 titles.

Gianfranco de Turris is a journalist, writer, and the President of the Julius Evola Foundation. A researcher in traditional thought and an acute cultural polemicist, de Turris was among the first in Italy to treat fantasy and science fiction literature, particularly Lovecraft and Tolkien, in mythical-symbolic terms. De Turris has been the editor and publisher of hundreds of volumes, including the collected works of Julius Evola published by Edizioni Mediterranee.

Giovanni Damiano teaches philosophy and history on the high school level and specializes in classical studies. He is a scholar of the works of Giorgio Locchi and Julius Evola, and he currently collaborates with the journals *Studi evoliani* and *Il Primato Nazionale*. Alongside his essays in collective volumes, his published books include *La filosofia della libertà in Julius Evola* (Edizioni di Ar, 1998), *Elogio delle differenze. Per una critica della globalizzazione* (Edizioni di Ar, 1999), *Per un'altra modernità Scritti su Evola* (Edizioni di Ar, 2013), and *Il pensiero dell'origine in Giorgio Locchi* (Altaforte, 2021).

About the Authors

Uligang Xanth Ansbrandt (a.k.a. Xantio Ansprandi) is a Lombard philosopher and mystic in the spirit of Perennial Traditionalism. His graduation thesis in Philosophy and Political Theology at the University of Bergamo has been published as *Eurasian Universism: Sinitic Orientations for Rethinking the Western Logos* (PRAV Publishing, 2022).

Jean-Pierre Laurant was born in 1935 in Paris and studied history at the Sorbonne University. He taught at a grammar school before entering the Sorbonne École Pratique des Hautes Études, where from 1976 to 2000 he specialized in 19th-20th-century esotericism. He is a member of the French National Centre for Scientific Research's Sociology of Religion laboratory. With Jean-Pierre Brach, he is a founding editor of the academic journal *Politica Hermetica*. He has contributed to some of the main dictionaries and encyclopedias on esotericism, such as the *Dictionary of Gnosis and Western Esotericism* (Leiden: Brill, 2005), and has authored and edited several books on the life and legacy of René Guénon.

Tamás Bencze (b. 1965) teaches translation theory, English, and Hungarian at the University of Debrecen in his hometown in Hungary. He studies Eastern and Western forms of Tradition and metaphysics. He has published a number of essays on and translations of Traditional authors in Hungarian Traditional periodicals. He has translated two of René Guénon's books into Hungarian.

Eduardo Zarelli is a teacher of philosophy, essayist, and publicist. He manages the publishing house Arianna editrice and collaborates with several journals. His published books include *Un mondo di differenze. Il localismo tra comunità e società* (2009) and *Idee per una vita ecologica. Ritornare alla natura per reincantare il mondo* (2012). His essays have been published in the collective volume *Architettura popolare e identità. La forma fisica delle culture locali* (2004) as well as in the G.R.E.C.E. Italia volumes *Il silenzio del cosmo. Ecologia ed* *ecologismi* (2021) and *Ordine multipolare. Geopolitica e cultura della crisi* (forthcoming).

Collin Cleary, Ph.D., is an independent scholar living in Sandpoint, Idaho. He is the author of *Summoning the Gods: Essays on Paganism in a God-Forsaken World*, *"What is a Rune?" And Other Essays*, and *Wagner's Ring and the Germanic Tradition* (all published by Counter-Currents). Cleary is one of the founders of *TYR: Myth-Culture-Tradition*, the first volume of which he co-edited. His essays have appeared in *TYR*, *Rûna*, and at Counter-Currents/*North American New Right*. A Master in the Rune-Gild, his work has been translated into Czech, Danish, French, Portuguese, Russian, and Swedish.

Askr Svarte (Evgeny Nechkasov) is a Russian Traditionalist philosopher, pagan in the Germanic-Scandinavian tradition, and the founding head of the Svarte Aske community and publishing house. He is the founding editor of the journal *Alföðr* (previously *Warha*) and the author of numerous works published in Russian and English, such as *Polemos: The Dawn of Pagan Traditionalism* (PRAV Publishing, 2020), *Polemos II: Pagan Perspectives* (PRAV Publishing, 2021), *Tradition and Future Shock: Visions of a Future that Isn't Ours* (PRAV Publishing, 2023), and *Gods in the Abyss: Essays on Heidegger, the Germanic Logos, and the Germanic Myth* (Arktos, 2020). He lives in Novosibirsk, Russia.

Charlie Smith is a translator and scholar of esoteric currents in Russian literature and thought. He holds a double BA in English and Russian from The Pennsylvania State University and is currently a PhD candidate at the University of Illinois Chicago, where he is writing his dissertation on the "Socialist-Surrealist" novelist Andrei Platonov. In addition, Smith specializes in the history and thought of the Yuzhinskii Circle, with a focus on the works of Yuri Mamleev.

About the Authors

Veleslav (Ilya Cherkasov) is a leading figure of the Slavic pagan movement in Russia and the author of dozens of books and lectures on Russian Native Faith and the Left-Hand Path.

Dmitry Moiseev holds a PhD in Philosophy from the National Research University – Higher School of Economics (HSE University) in Moscow, where he is a senior lecturer. He is a member of the Russian Philosophical Society and the Russian Society for the History and Philosophy of Science.

Roberto Cechetti is a practicing psychologist, philosophical analyst (Sabof), and lecturer in philosophy at the Erich Fromm School of Psychotherapy in Prato and Padova. He holds a Master's in Philosophy and attended the School Philo in Milan, where he became convinced that philosophy should be renewed as a life practice and healing tool. His main research interests include archetypes and symbolism, Jungian thought, Traditionalism, and the psychological roots of law. He has published a book on the thought of Carl Gustav Jung, *Il ritmo del desiderio. Da Jung alle pratiche filosofiche* (Mimesis edizioni, 2019) and an autobiographical text, *La metrica dell'apparenza* (Attucci editrice, 2017).

Uligang Xanth Ansbrandt (a.k.a. Uligango Xantio Ansprandi) is a Lombard philosopher and mystic in the spirit of Perennial Traditionalism. His graduation thesis in Philosophy and Political Theology at the University of Bergamo has been published, under the name Xantio Ansprandi, as *Eurasian Universism: Sinitic Orientations for Rethinking the Western Logos* (PRAV Publishing, 2022).

www.ingramcontent.com/pod-product-compliance
Lightning Source LLC
Chambersburg PA
CBHW070045080526
44586CB00013B/914